Nikolaus von Amsdorf

Champion of Martin Luther's Reformation

Robert Kolb

CONCORDIA PUBLISHING HOUSE • SAINT LOUIS

Concordia Publishing House

Founded in 1869 as the publishing arm of The Lutheran Church—Missouri Synod, Concordia Publishing House gives all glory to God for the blessing of 150 years of opportunities to provide resources that are faithful to the Holy Scriptures and the Lutheran Confessions.

Published by Concordia Publishing House
3558 S. Jefferson Avenue, St. Louis, MO 63118-3968
1-800-325-3040 • cph.org

Manufactured in the United States of America

1 2 3 4 5 6 7 8 9 10 28 27 26 25 24 23 22 21 20 19

Robert Kolb's book portrays the life, work, and theology of one of Luther's closest friends and a key member of the Wittenberg circle of reformers. Kolb's work highlights the way in which Amsdorf became a chief interpreter and defender of Luther's Reformation teaching, and consequently, how Amsdorf helped direct the transformation of the evangelical movement into the Lutheran Church. This book is a scholarly study in an accessible narrative style by one of the premier Reformation historians of our time.

—Rev. Dr. Gerhard Bode
Dean of Advanced Studies,
Associate Professor of Historical Theology,
Seminary Archivist,
Concordia Seminary, St. Louis, Missouri

After over forty years of Reformation and post-Reformation scholarship, Robert Kolb has returned with mature vigor and scholarly vitality to the subject of his dissertation: Nikolaus von Amsdorf. But this is no hagiography of Amsdorf. Kolb portrays this "knight of God," Wittenberg warrior, and "second Luther," with warts and all, simultaneously illuminating Amsdorf's polemical idiosyncrasies and pastoral and confessional passion. A champion for Luther's theology, Amsdorf was a persistent presence in early Lutheranism, especially among Gnesio-Lutherans, taking strong stands during significant controversies leading to the Formula of Concord. Several of these controversies are still smoldering in twenty-first century Lutheranism. Kolb's inimitable writing style is readily engaging, invitingly informative, and academically rigorous as he provides a wealth of historical information and perceptively personal and insightful theological detail on this respected elder bishop and theological companion of Luther. Kolb's work deserves assiduous attention and critical study, as Amsdorf's perspective on key theological issues continues to be relevant for contemporary Lutheran conversations.

—Rev. Dr. Timothy Maschke
Associate Pastor of Care Ministry,
St. Paul Lutheran Church, Grafton, Wisconsin
Professor Emeritus of Theology,
Concordia University Wisconsin, Mequon, Wisconsin

TABLE OF CONTENTS

ABBREVIATIONS

Bibliographical Notations

ET	English translation
s.d.	date not given (*sine dato*)
s.l.	place of publication not given (*sine loco*)

Manuscript Collections

Wf, Guelf.	Wolfenbüttel, Herzog August Bibliothek, Codex Guelferbytanus
Helmst.	Die Helmstedter Handschriften
Aug.	Die Augusteischen Handschriften
Extr.	Die Extravagantes Handschriften
Wr, ETLFB	Weimar; in 1971, the "Nationale Forschungs- und Gedenkstätten der klassischen deutschen Literatur, Goethe-Schiller Archiv" (of the former Thuringian Landesbibliothek, now the Thuringian Hauptstaatsarchiv Weimar), gathered with two other volumes of Amsdorf manuscripts in "Nachlass Nikolaus von Amsdorf."

Primary Source Collections

AS	*Nikolaus von Amsdorff, Ausgewählte Schriften*, ed. Otto Lerche (Gütersloh: Bertelsmann, 1938).
BC	*The Book of Concord*, ed. Robert Kolb and Timothy J. Wengert (Minneapolis: Fortress, 2000).
BSELK	*Die Bekenntnisschriften der Evangelisch-Lutherischen Kirche*, ed. Irene Dingel (Göttingen: Vandenhoeck & Ruprecht, 2014).
C&C	*Controversia et Confessio. Theologische Kontroversen 1548–1577/80. Kritische Auswahledition*, ed. Irene Dingel, 9 vols. (Göttingen: Vandenhoeck & Ruprecht, 2008–).
CR	*Corpus Reformatorum. Philippi Melanthonis Opera quae supersunt omnia*, ed. C. G. Bretschneider and H. E. Bindweil (Halle and Braunschweig: Schwetschke, 1834–1860).
Jäger, *Amsdorf*	*Nikolaus von Amsdorff, Ausgewählte Schriften der Jahre 1550 bis 1562 aus der ehemaligen Eisenacher Ministerialbibliothek*, ed. Hagen Jäger (Leipzig: Evangelische Verlagsanstalt, 2017).
LW	*Luther's Works* (Saint Louis/Philadelphia: Concordia/Fortress, 1958–1986).
MBW.R	*Melanchthons Briefwechsel. Register*, ed. Heinz Scheible (Stuttgart-Bad Cannstatt: Frommann-Holzboog, 1977–95).
MBW.T	*Melanchthons Briefwechsel. Texte*, eds. Heinz Scheible et al. (Stuttgart-Bad Cannstatt: Frommann-Holzboog, 1991–).
WA	*D. Martin Luthers Werke* (Weimar: Böhlau, 1883–1993).

Secondary Literature

Dingel, *Amsdorf*	*Nikolaus von Amsdorf (1483–1565) zwischen Reformation und Politik*, ed. Irene Dingel (Leipzig: Evangelische Verlagsanstalt, 2008).
Dingel and Wartenberg, *Politik*	*Politik und Bekenntnis. Die Reaktion auf das Interim von 1548*, eds. Irene Dingel and Günther Wartenberg (Leipzig: Evangelische Verlagsanstalt, 2006).
Gehrt, *Konfessionspolitik*	*Ernestinische Konfessionspolitik: Bekenntnisbildung, Herrschaftskonsolidierung und dynastische Identitätsstiftung vom Augsburger Interim 1548 bis zur Konkordienformel 1577* (Leipzig: Evangelische Verlagsanstalt, 2011).
VIEG	Veröffentlichungen des Instituts für Europäische Geschichte

Periodicals

ARG	*Archiv für Reformationsgeschichte*
ZKG	*Zeitschrift für Kirchengeschichte*

PREFACE

My friend Martin Treu at the Lutherhaus in Wittenberg once commented that he was looking forward to my "big Amsdorf book." I did not think at the time that another Amsdorf book would ever flow from my pen, and I still believe that. But for much of the past nearly half century since Bob DeGraaf published the first version of this volume, my revised dissertation on Nikolaus von Amsdorf, I have wished that I had done some things differently. Therefore, I was delighted and most grateful when Paul McCain of Concordia Publishing House approached me with the suggestion that Concordia republish my study. My own insights have grown since publication in 1978, and others have explored aspects of Amsdorf's life that had not fallen into my purview. Particularly fruitful was the encouragement given to Amsdorf research by the decision of Irene Dingel and Günther Wartenberg to make this friend of Luther the focal point of the Wittenberger Frühjahrstagung in 2007. In addition to the volume of essays that proceeded from that conference, a host of other secondary analyses have enriched the study of the Late Reformation in ways I could not have imagined in 1973. Most of them gained mention in my survey of the historical development of the Formula of Concord in the book composed with Charles Arand and James Nestingen, *The Lutheran Confessions: History and Theology of the Book of Concord* (Minneapolis: Fortress, 2012), from which I have taken a number of footnotes for this volume.

My Amsdorf book is not in the strictest or fullest sense a biography, although it does survey Amsdorf's life from his family background to his death. It concentrates, however, on the last eighteen years of his life and his participation in the debates that sorted out the legacy left by his Wittenberg colleagues, especially Martin Luther and Philip Melanchthon. It assesses his role in the debates of that period, which determined much of the agenda for Lutheran theology in the following centuries. The scholarly work of the past fifty years contributes to the analyses of Amsdorf's thought and the discussion of his role in shaping the Lutheran Reformation and the interpretation of Luther's legacy.

New manuscripts from Amsdorf's pen or contemporary copiers have also appeared in edited form since 1973. To a large extent, these newly uncovered sources have not been digested for incorporation into the volume because they seem to offer, at best, supplementary examples of the material that was at hand in 1968–1973, as my dissertation took shape. However, a more careful survey may produce new angles from which to assess Amsdorf's impact. One of the new collections of sources is a selection of manuscripts, edited by Hagen Jäger, in the former "Ministerialbibliothek" in Eisenach.[1] Hans-Peter Hasse has catalogued a collection of manuscripts and printed works in the Lutherhaus in Wittenberg (Stiftung Luthergedenkstätten in Sachsen-Anhalt).[2] Hartmut Kühne has provided a complete catalogue to the "Amsdorffiana" now held in the Thüringisches Hauptstaatsarchiv in Weimar. I encountered these documents in the Goethe-Schiller Archiv of the then "Nationale Forschungs- und Gedenkstätten der klassischen deutschen Literatur" of the former Thuringian Landesbibliothek in 1971. The five volumes in the collection at that time have been supplemented with two other volumes of material directly or indirectly related to Amsdorf under the designation "Nachlass Nikolaus von Amsdorf."[3] I have retained in this book the older cataloguing, referencing volumes 38–42 of the Goethe-Schiller Archiv catalogue, which are now volumes 1–5 of the "Nachlass."

Another great resource and impetus for further research about this time period is the nine-volume series *Controversia et Confessio. Theologische Kontroversen 1548–1577/80. Kritische Auswahledition*, edited by Irene Dingel, with the assistance of Henning Jürgens, Johannes Hund, Hans-Otto Schneider, Jan Martin Lies, and Kestutis Daugierdas (Göttingen: Vandenhoeck & Ruprecht, 2008–), which presents scholarly editions of works by Amsdorf and his contemporaries relating to the controversies of their time.

Another most helpful aid is Professor Dingel's edition of *Die Bekenntnisschriften der Evangelisch-Lutherischen Kirche* (Göttingen: Vandenhoeck & Ruprecht, 2014), with sections prepared by a team of scholars and diligently readied in final form by Irene Dingel, Marion Bechthold-Mayer, and Johannes Hund. The Formula of Concord is important in Amsdorf studies because its formulations on original sin, freedom of the will, justification, good works, and third use of the Law, as well as on election and adiaphora, assisted in resolving the debates in which

1 *Nikolaus von Amsdorff, Ausgewählte Schriften der Jahre 1550 bis 1562 aus der ehemaligen Eisenacher Ministerialbibliothek*, ed. Hagen Jäger (Leipzig: Evangelische Verlagsanstalt, 2017).

2 Hans-Peter Hasse, "Inhaltsverzeichnis des Manuskriptbandes MS 896 des Wittenberger Lutherhauses aus dem Nachlass von Nikolaus von Amsdorf," in Dingel, *Amsdorf*, 345–351.

3 Hartmut Kühne, "Die Weimarer Amsdorffiana-Handschriften—ein Inventar," in Dingel, *Amsdorf*, 353–372. Cf. the inventory of the collection in Ernst-Otto Reichert, *Amsdorf und Das Interim*, ed. Hans-Otto Schneider (Leipzig: Evangelische Verlagsanstalt, 2011), 11–21.

Amsdorf was involved. The two-volume work of Dingel and Bechthold-Mayer has finally provided the background materials for the Formula of Concord in useful form; the volume in which the stages of the Formula of Concord are gathered together and edited for the first time is particularly helpful (*Die Bekenntnisschriften der Evangelisch-Lutherischen Kirche. Quellen und Materialien Band 2: Die Konkordienformel*, [Göttingen: Vandenhoeck & Ruprecht, 2014]).

I must also express my appreciation to the publisher Koningklijke Brill NV; its rights and permissions department readily granted permission to republish this study with revisions. Brill had assumed control of the publishing firm of Bob DeGraaf at his death.

The original preface to the 1973 publication of my dissertation contained thanks to many others, particularly to my doctoral advisor, Robert M. Kingdon. Bob Kingdon became a friend through his careful guidance and cultivation of the historical skills of his students. After the completion of my dissertation, I had the privilege of working with him for twenty-five years on *The Sixteenth Century Journal*. His model as a practitioner of the calling and craft of the historian continues to shape my research and writing fifty years after I entered his seminar. My gratitude to the many others who helped the struggling graduate student of the late 1960s and early 1970s remains as strong today as in 1973, when I listed the whole host of them in the preface to the first edition of this study.

Nikolaus von Amsdorf was not the most intellectually gifted person among Luther's adherents and students; but he was a close friend of Luther, and his role in interpreting Luther's teaching and the Wittenberg way of reform carried Luther's insights into popular form and into the next generation. Though Amsdorf was only three weeks younger than Luther, he lived nearly two decades longer. The long-lasting influence of the Reformation was significantly shaped during those two decades of change and turmoil. Therefore, I hope this revised study aids readers in further understanding the construction of the Wittenberg legacy that lives on in many parts of the world even to our day.

Robert Kolb,
Concordia Seminary, Saint Louis

May 14, 2018
The four-hundred-fifty-third anniversary
of the death of Nikolaus von Amsdorf

Introduction

A SECOND LUTHER?

Luther once observed at table,

> Licentiate Amsdorf teaches purely and says what he thinks plainly, precisely, and candidly. When we were at the diet in Smalcald [in 1537, when the Smalcald Articles were subscribed], he said in a sermon, "This gospel belongs to the sick, the weak, the poor sinners, but there is not one of that kind of person here, for the great, the rich princes and lords, do not feel their sicknesses and weaknesses." That is the way he gets to the point in disputations, too. He is a theologian by nature.[1]

Johannes Brenz believed that Nikolaus von Amsdorf was Luther's natural and logical successor as leader of the Evangelical churches at the time of the reformer's death.[2] Friedrich Myconius, the reformer of Gotha and an intimate of the Wittenberg theologians, called Amsdorf "a man powerful in preaching and teaching."[3] Hieronymus Weller, a younger contemporary of Luther and Amsdorf, ascribed to Amsdorf the "highest authority" after Luther was gone, and he urged students of theology to study Amsdorf's works and recognize that he was "a second Luther."[4] It was even said that Luther bequeathed his spirit to Amsdorf.[5]

Yet, "natural theologian" or not, Amsdorf was not the man whom Luther's mantle fit. No one was able to wear it. Luther's followers recognized no single leader after the reformer's death. In Saxony, his disciples split into two parties, called "Philippists" and "Gnesio-Lutherans" by later scholars. They called each other "adiaphorists" and "Flacianists," while regarding themselves as "Evangelicals" or "Lutherans" or "adherents of the Augsburg Confession." However, Luther's close friend Amsdorf did continue to exercise a significant influence

1 WA TR 3:461, Nr. 3619.

2 CR 6:65.

3 Myconius, *Historia Reformationis, vom Jahr Christi 1517, bis 1542. . . .* , ed. Ernst Salomon Cyprian (Leipzig: Georg Weidmann, 1718), 48.

4 Hieronymus Weller, *Opera Omnia* 3 (Leipzig: Stock, 1702), 172.

5 Reported by Christian F. Paullini, *Historia Isenacensis* (Frankfurt/M: Bauer, 1698), 152.

on the Wittenberg Reformation after Luther's death. Amsdorf's ongoing influence arose not so much from the depth of his thought but from his decisiveness and determination, as well as the prestige he had won as Luther's friend and a crusader for Luther's cause.

Modern scholarship has paid Amsdorf less attention than he appears to deserve.[6] On the other hand, he seems to promise the modern student more than he delivers. As the only nobleman in Luther's inner circle, he promises a basis for interesting sociological comparisons, yet few traces of the impact of his noble background are found in his writings. Since he was the only close colleague who shared Luther's scholastic training and background, Amsdorf's thought invites important questions about the influence of the medieval doctors on Reformation theology. But his works do not answer these questions. His message was directed so exclusively toward lay readers and "simple pastors" that only a few hints of possible influence from his Scotist instructors appear in his tracts and manuscripts; even these are so general that their sources cannot be finally determined.[7] As one of the first Evangelicals to sit on a medieval bishop's throne, Amsdorf should offer a basis for evaluating the development of Evangelical institutional forms, but studies of his episcopal career show that he accomplished less as bishop than he had as Magdeburg's ecclesiastical superintendent or than he would in his very active retirement.[8] Finally, those who claim that Amsdorf became "the father of Lutheran orthodoxy" by scholasticizing Luther's message overestimate and misunderstand Amsdorf, a man who eschewed scholastic forms.[9] Still, Amsdorf's life deserves study because—particularly in the last two decades of his life, from 1547 to 1565—he occupied a singular position among sixteenth-century interpreters of Luther. After Luther's death, Amsdorf sparked and fueled a series of efforts to defend Luther's radical critique of late medieval religion. His efforts helped preserve and shape Luther's message for use in the Lutheran churches of early modern Europe.

The way of salvation has always been a central concern for Christians in every age. Luther's Reformation—though aided and supported by a host of religious, political, social, and economic factors—was born out of his own spiritual

6 Cf. as an exception *Nikolaus vón Amsdorf (1483–1565) zwischen Reformation und Politik*, ed. Irene Dingel (Leipzig: Evangelische Verlagsanstalt, 2008).

7 See below, pages 34–35 (note 58), 110, 111–112 (note 52).

8 Peter Brunner, *Nikolaus von Amsdorf als Bischof von Naumburg* (Gütersloh: Mohn, 1961), and Hans-Ulrich Delius, "Der Briefwechsel des Nikolaus von Amsdorf als Bischof von Naumburg-Zeitz (1542–1546)," Habilitationsschrift, Universität Leipzig, 1968.

9 Paul Charles Fischer, *Nikolaus D'Amsdorf, écrits et influence d'un controversiste Luterien du seizieme Siècle* (Strassburg: Silbermann, 1863), 49; and Hans Stille, *Nikolaus von Amsdorf, Sein Leben bis zu seiner Einweisung als Bischof in Naumburg (1483–1542)* (Zeulenroda: Sporn, 1937).

struggles to find the proper path to his Creator, to establish the right relationship with God. Luther's calling as a biblical exegete at the University of Wittenberg forced him into the study of Scripture. There he found insights that he applied successfully to his own spiritual trials. His religious experiences had been shaped initially by the popular religion of the time, by its dependence on ritual performance of sacred activities and pious practices for gaining and hanging onto God's grace. These views emphasized what the believer does for God. However, Luther discovered that the fundamental dynamic of the biblical faith is the action of the Creator, who takes the initiative to move toward his human creatures and to restore through his Son, Jesus Christ, and through his re-creative word of absolution the relationship broken by sin.

The religious forms and beliefs in places such as Luther's village were, in many ways, still dependent on the structure of the traditional religions that had existed long before the German-speaking tribes had been converted to Christianity. The traditional view Luther inherited—the route to heaven being dependent on a human being's efforts to reach God—was reinforced by Luther's semipelagian instructors, who relied heavily on the works of Gabriel Biel (ca. 1420–1495), a professor at Tübingen in the later years of his life. The University of Tübingen exercised significant influence on other universities, including the universities in Erfurt and Wittenberg, at that time.

Luther reacted against the system of earning salvation that his instructors had offered him, a system centered on "doing his best" to fulfill God's Law and produce good works. Against that system, Luther proclaimed a way of salvation centered in God's gracious intervention as Jesus Christ in human history. In the death and resurrection of Christ, Luther found that God had done everything necessary to save the sinner. Luther believed that God gives this salvation to those who receive the gift of faith in Christ. Against the legal structure of a moral system that enforces itself with rewards and punishments, Luther presented a relationship established by the freely given mercy of a gracious God through the gift of faith—which is trust in Christ.[10] He summarized that relationship in the concept of justification by grace alone through faith alone in Christ alone.

Luther saw himself as a prophet of God, presenting and defending the Gospel message concerning the relationship established by justifying faith. He believed that he was engaged in the same struggle that Augustine had waged against Pelagius and that Paul had fought against the Judaizers: the struggle of divine grace

10 Robert Kolb, *Martin Luther and the Enduring Word of God: The Wittenberg School and Its Scripture-Centered Proclamation* (Grand Rapids: Baker Academic, 2016), 1–10, 35–46.

against human works for salvation; the struggle of true faith in Christ in the worship of God against a false conception of faith and worship.[11] According to Luther, this false conception ignored a human being's radical and total inability to please God, and it obliterated the unfathomable mercy of God, which is the only way sinners are rescued from their alienation from their Creator.

Luther's insights supported him in his own spiritual crises and served the religious needs of many of his contemporaries in an effective pastoral fashion. But certain tensions inevitably arose among his followers as they tried to introduce his understanding of salvation and the Christian life more expansively to serve the religious needs of northern and eastern European cultures. The disciples of Luther came from different backgrounds and had varying concerns. Many had not experienced the same spiritual struggles as Luther, and from the societies in which they were living, all of them felt pressures to address other concerns beyond Luther's. Thus, already during Luther's lifetime and especially in the following generation, a struggle arose among Luther's disciples as they tried to refine a definition of his faith that could be used in a large part of German culture and in the neighboring cultures in the early modern period.

Alongside perennial concern for the doctrine of salvation, Christians have also always held the necessity of an understanding of the church: how believers relate to each other and how they relate as a group to the larger culture and its political authorities. The struggle to define the church's role and obligations in society became acute for Luther's followers after the Smalcald War of 1546–1547; clergy and princes confronted one another because the Lutheran princes were trying to extend their control over the churches in their lands, following the pattern of most early modern European rulers.

After Luther's death, problems in soteriology and ecclesiology led to the formation of the two parties within the Wittenberg movement, henceforth referred to as the Philippist party and the Gnesio-Lutheran party. Both parties wanted to preserve Luther's and Melanchthon's doctrine of justification through faith in Christ. However, although they focused their concerns through the same lens of the doctrine of justification, each party condemned the other for projecting false versions of related doctrines. Both parties wrestled with the tension between God's almighty nature and total responsibility for his creation, and human beings' total responsibility to be obedient to God. Luther and Melanchthon taught that both of these seemingly contradictory truths were biblical and

11 Robert Kolb, *Martin Luther as Prophet, Teacher, and Hero: Images of the Reformer, 1520–1620* (Grand Rapids: Baker Books, 1999), 30–32; Mark U. Edwards Jr., *Luther and the False Brethren* (Stanford: Stanford University Press, 1975), 112–126.

faithfully represented Scripture's teaching on the nature of God and the nature of mankind. But the difficulty of trying to work out this paradox in teaching and preaching as well as the differences in the groups' presuppositions and points of orientation led to the divisions after Luther's death.

Most Christian theologians have tried to divide the responsibility between Creator and creature, but most of the systems they have formulated fail to preserve the understanding that God's grace is totally responsible for the restoration of sinners to trust in God. However, Luther and Melanchthon did not lose that understanding. They insisted that both God and human beings are totally responsible within the defined spheres of responsibility. However, this challenge to human logic is complicated by the presence of sin and evil in the good creation of a holy God and even more so by the presence of sin and evil in the lives of God's baptized and sanctified people.

Luther steadfastly resisted the temptation to try to define a logical balance between an almighty God and dependent human creatures when assigning responsibility for sin. Luther was content to leave unresolved the mystery of how a creature can be totally dependent on God (since God is in charge of and active in all of his creation) and, at the same time, be held totally responsible for all of his actions before God. He refused to answer questions such as "How can evil exist if God is good and almighty?" and "Why are some saved and not others?" Such theodical questions (as they were later labeled) received no answer in Wittenberg. Instead, the Wittenberg reformers dealt with this tension by rightly distinguishing Law and Gospel. They believed the power of God is greater than the power of human creatures. They also insisted that only the Holy Spirit moves hearts and minds to trust in God and that only God's re-creative word of absolution gives sinners faith in Christ and an obedient life as God's children by faith in Christ. They affirmed that the proper understanding of God's creation of all that exists and his re-creation of sinners to be his children through the death and resurrection of Christ places total responsibility for all things upon God. Yet still they maintained that God's Law, which conveys his design for humanity, places total responsibility for trust in and obedience to God upon the human creature. And they affirmed that sinners and Satan are responsible for sin and evil.

The Gnesio-Lutheran party, often dubbed "Flacianists" in this period, tended to approach issues related to their faith from Luther's radically theocentric stance; as a result, they emphasized the total inadequacy of the human creature to establish his own relationship with God. Flacius's definition of original sin as the substance of the fallen sinner and Amsdorf's use of Luther's phrase "good works are detrimental to salvation" illustrate the radical positions Gnesio-Lutherans staked out in defense of the Wittenberg theologians' theocentric approach to theology.[12]

For several reasons, the Philippist party, on the other hand, was diverted from Luther's radical theocentric stance by a set of concerns that can be labeled anthropological—though certainly not anthropocentric. This party's members struggled with philosophical and practical problems related to the preaching of justification through faith; these problems were of a lesser—not primary—concern to the Gnesio-Lutherans. The Philippists reflected the Wittenberg theologians' concern for human responsibility in order to maintain the public moral order and an understanding of human active righteousness. They also were concerned about genuine, faith-filled Christian behavior, just as Luther had striven to cultivate obedient Christian living through preaching and catechesis. The Philippists wanted to scrutinize the psychological process of conversion and the activities of the believer's will so that candidates for pastoral ministry could apply both Law and Gospel to their hearers. They felt compelled to affirm strongly in the face of Roman Catholic criticism that the sinner is responsible for his own sin and that God is in no way responsible for sin and evil.[13]

The general theocentric emphasis of the Gnesio-Lutherans led them to assert and establish the church's independence from the prince, the secular government, even at great cost to themselves. In contrast, the Philippists'

---

12 See the later section "Good Works Are Detrimental to Salvation" (pp. 116–120). On the nature of these two groups, cf. Robert Kolb, "Dynamics of Party Conflict in the Saxon Late Reformation, Gnesio-Lutherans vs. Philippists," *The Journal of Modern History* 49 (1977): D1289–1305; reprinted in *Luther's Heirs Define His Legacy, Studies on Lutheran Confessionalization* (Aldershot: Variorum, 1996), I, and in *Calvinismus in den Auseinandersetzungen des frühen konfessionellen Zeitalters* (Göttingen: Vandenhoeck & Ruprecht, 2013), 151–167. The core concerns of the Gnesio-Lutherans remained the same during the period that led to the Formula of Concord (1577), despite several serious divisions among the group, including the controversy over Matthias Flacius's definition of original sin. However, those whom scholars label "Philippists" included two distinct groups, with some overlaps linking them. Over time, the Philippists' relatively "conservative" characteristics, reflecting more medieval customs and attitudes, gave way to a program centered on the Lord's Supper and the rejection of the true presence of Christ's body and blood in the Sacrament. Some, like Melanchthon's son-in-law, Caspar Peucer, accepted this change in the group's focus; others, like Georg Major and Johannes Pfeffinger, held to a view of Christ's presence in the Supper that was closer to Luther's and rejected the Philippists' positions labeled "Crypto-Calvinist" by Gnesio-Lutherans. That these later, younger "Philippists" (led by Peucer and Christoph Pezel) are better labeled "Crypto-Philippists" is evident in the "synergism" they continued to espouse—quite opposite of a "Calvinist" understanding of the freedom of the will and the doctrine of predestination. These "Crypto-Philippists" believed their view of Christ's presence in the Lord's Supper faithfully reflected Melanchthon's view, while the other Philippists believed Melanchthon's teaching on the subject had been much closer to Luther's.

13 See especially chapters 3 and 4 of this book.

anthropological emphasis often meant they sought to preserve the continuity between church and culture through compromise with the prince.[14]

Nikolaus von Amsdorf served as something of a grandfather figure for the Gnesio-Lutherans. His story illuminates the nature of the group and illustrates many of its characteristics; his later career also reveals a great deal about the group's background and origins. However, his roles in the Reformation were varied. As the dynamic superintendent of the churches of Magdeburg in the 1520s and 1530s, he fought against adherents of the pope in the streets and marketplace to gain the support of the common people; as a result, Amsdorf established Luther's message in a city later called the "chancellery of God" because of its role in defending Luther's approach to reform. Amsdorf reluctantly left Magdeburg in 1542 to become the beleaguered, frustrated Evangelical bishop of Naumburg-Zeitz. When he fled his episcopal palace in 1546 because imperial troops were threatening to advance into Saxony, Amsdorf claimed the epithet "exile of Christ"[15]—a title of honor for a man convinced that Christ's true Church would always remain a persecuted remnant. He retired to Magdeburg and then to Eisenach as an "exile of Christ"; but even in retirement he fought hard to prevent Luther's heirs from betraying their hard-won legacy. His contemporaries recognized the old bishop as a man who had "fought alongside Luther like a knight" and had maintained Luther's heritage steadfastly and faithfully after Luther's death,[16] as a brave man who was "constant in the confession of the truth."[17] Twice in the turbulent period following Luther's death, Amsdorf fired opening shots in tractarian battles that widened and deepened the personal and theological gulf between groups of Luther's Saxon followers. In other disputes between Philippists and Flacianists, Amsdorf doggedly defended his conception of Luther's message and rallied support for his views.

Amsdorf personified the personal, polemical tenor typical of the time period.[18] He was not a groundbreaking thinker. His theology betrayed no great

14 See especially chapter 2 of this book.

15 Irene Dingel, "Die Kultivierung des Exulantentums im Luthertum am Beispiel des Nikolaus von Amsdorf," in Dingel, *Amsdorf*, 153–175.

16 Christoph Irenaeus in the preface to the posthumously published *Testament vnd Letzter Wille* of Amsdorf (s.l., 1590), A3b.

17 Weller, *Opera*, 3:171.

18 Irene Dingel, "Zwischen Disputation und Polemik. 'Streitkultur' in den nachinterimistischen Kontroversen," in *Streitkultur und Öffentlichkeit im Konfessionellen Zeitalter*, eds. Henning P. Jürgens and Thomas Weller (Göttingen: Vandenhoeck & Ruprecht, 2013), 17–29; Dingel, "Pruning the Vines, Plowing Up the Vineyard: The Sixteenth-Century Culture of Controversy between Disputation and Polemic," in *The Reformation as Christianization. Essays on Scott Hendrix's Christianization Thesis*, eds. Anna Marie Johnson and John A. Maxfield (Tübingen: Mohr/Siebeck, 2012), 397–408; and Dingel, "Streitkultur und Kontroversschrifttum im späten 16. Jahrhundert. Versuch einer methodischen Standortbestimmung," in

flashes of originality. He recognized Luther as a prophet, and he tried simply to repeat Luther's message for a popular audience. Amsdorf's written defense of this heritage was largely polemical. Even in his own day, his reputation earned him a description as a "fierce enemy of all corruption and adulteration of true Lutheran, Evangelical truth. He could truly say with David, 'I hate them that hate you, O Lord, and loathe them that rise up against you' (Psalm 139:21)."[19] Therefore, the polemics of the written record of his thoughts do not give a complete picture of his theological abilities. It is possible Amsdorf's treatises seem mechanical in their presentation of the Evangelical message precisely because his genre was polemics. These polemics do not show how Amsdorf spoke God's Word when discharging his pastoral responsibilities. The Formula of Concord of 1577 also does not reflect the handful of peculiar emphases in Amsdorf's thought because those emphases were either rejected or ignored by the theologians who established the Formula as the official summary of Luther's thought for Lutherans.

Nonetheless, Amsdorf was a key figure in the process by which the Wittenberg Reformation transformed itself into the Lutheran Church and took its place in the early modern, western Christian ecclesiastical life.[20] Studying his life provides insights into these processes. He fought hard to maintain the radical integrity of the Wittenberg movement over against Rome. At a time when Amsdorf and others feared that the Roman Catholic emperor's might and the compromising spirit of other Evangelicals threatened to undermine if not eradicate Luther's infant movement, Amsdorf's voice rose above others in defense of the Wittenberg Reformation. When one group of Melanchthon's followers overemphasized their focus on human integrity and responsibility when codifying Luther's insights, Amsdorf's straightforward theocentric concept of Evangelical theology admonished Luther's disciples to teach salvation by grace alone through faith in Christ alone with radical simplicity.

People listened when the bishop spoke. He commanded a respect accorded to very few in the Evangelical camp once Luther was no longer its leader. Amsdorf's prestige was so great that his foes sometimes responded to Amsdorf's attacks

---

Kommunikation und Transfer im Christentum der Frühen Neuzeit, ed. Irene Dingel and Wolf Friedrich Schäufele (Mainz: von Zabern, 2007), 95–111. Also Peter F. Barton, *Um Luthers Erbe. Studien und Text zur Spätreformation, Tilemann Heshusius (1527–1559)* (Witten: Luther-Verlag, 1972), 7–15, provides a helpful discussion of the concept of "Late Reformation" and makes observations about the period's "personalism."

19 Cyriakus Spangenberg, *Adelspiegel* 2 (Smalcald: Schmück, 1594), 91b–93b.

20 On this transformation, see Irene Dingel, "Von der Wittenberger Reformation zum Luthertum. Konfessionelle Transformationen," in *Luther: Katholizität & Reform. Wurzeln – Wege – Wirkungen*, eds. Wolfgang Thönissen, Josef Freitag, and Augustinus Sander (Paderborn: Bonifatius; Leipzig: Evangelische Verlagsanstalt, 2016), 239–260.

by attacking his younger associates rather than directly challenging him. Sometimes his foes concluded that Amsdorf had not composed an attack that bore his signature in order to avoid openly contradicting him. Amsdorf's simple appeal to the common people was not the stuff from which great theological systems are created, but his ideas influenced the systems that others were constructing as they responded to the issues he raised. His personality and his position as Luther's friend and Magdeburg's superintendent projected his aging voice across the scene on which the Saxon Late Reformation developed, and his call for faithfulness to Luther aroused and encouraged others through the struggle to define the Lutheran confession. As a champion of Martin Luther's Reformation, as God's knight and Christ's exile, Nikolaus von Amsdorf, constant in his confession, served as one of the most important guideposts by which the development of the Lutheran Church in early modern Europe was set on its course.

1

STUDENT, PROFESSOR, SUPERINTENDENT, BISHOP

The Life and Times of Luther's Friend

WITTENBERG'S "PROFOUND MASTER AND KEEN DISPUTANT"

When Martin Luther arrived in Wittenberg in 1508 for his first semester of teaching, he met a young nobleman who was already giving lectures as a member of the university's arts faculty. Nikolaus von Amsdorf was his name. He was the grandson of Hieronymus, the chief secretary of the chancery of Saxon Elector Frederick II and later the administrator of Torgau. He was the son of Georg, a loyal courtier of Elector Frederick III ("the Wise").[1] Nikolaus came from a family of seven sons and two daughters. He left his family's estate near Torgau to study in Leipzig, where his father had also been a student. In 1502 when Frederick "the Wise" opened a new university in Wittenberg, Nikolaus went there to further his education. Amsdorf's maternal uncle, Johannes von Staupitz, played a key role in the organization of the new university. There Nikolaus advanced through the prescribed course of degrees for Master of Arts (1504) through Licentiate of Theology (1511), but he never proceeded to the doctorate.

Amsdorf's instructors taught philosophy according to the *via antiqua* ("old way"), and he followed in their footsteps when he became a young instructor, teaching Aristotle's logic as interpreted by the fourteenth-century thinker John Duns Scotus. Amsdorf's lectures competed with Andreas Bodenstein von Karlstadt's Thomist interpretation of the same subject at six o'clock each morning. In 1508, Amsdorf became a canon at the foundation located at the Castle Church in Wittenberg and seemed to have found his niche in life: a nobleman's son serving church and school. A contemporary described Amsdorf as a "profound master

1 Paul Brathe, "Das Geschlecht des Nikolaus von Amsdorf," *Archiv für Sippenforschung und alle Verwandten Gebiete* 21 (1944): 113–115.

of the liberal arts, a supporter of the Scotistic method, and a keen disputant, who in spite of his high birth did not hesitate to study the noble arts, which give luster to his noble blood."[2]

In 1508 when Luther and Amsdorf first met, neither had any idea that they would become close friends and would share the experiences of the Wittenberg movement for reform. For about eight years after they first encountered one another, the two men remained only acquaintances. At the time, Amsdorf belonged to a small sodality of professors aspiring to propagate a mild sort of educational reform often labeled "biblical humanism"; however, Amsdorf's work was still primarily shaped by the scholastic mold his instructors had passed along to him. The historical record provides no indication of Amsdorf's theological position during those years. Though labeled a "Scotist" in the Wittenberg curriculum, Amsdorf later said Thomas Aquinas had seduced him in his early years in Wittenberg. Like most of his contemporaries, Amsdorf's beliefs probably comprised an amalgam of ideas from several currents of thought. Any early influence that Amsdorf's uncle, Johannes von Staupitz—Luther's spiritual counselor in the Augustinian order—may have had on Amsdorf went unnoted in his later writings.

In September 1516, the heart of Luther's developing understanding of God's grace and human depravity was presented in a series of theses prepared for defense in disputation by Luther's student and colleague in the Wittenberg arts faculty, Bartholomäus Bernhardi von Feldkirchen. Amsdorf's reaction to these theses is the first indication that he was being converted to Luther's way of thinking. Amsdorf shared the theses with his friend Johann Lang, who was prior of the Augustinian cloister in Erfurt. Amsdorf's accompanying letter mentioned that Luther had given him a copy of Augustine. These records indicate Amsdorf responded warmly to the ideas his colleague was advancing.[3]

These ideas matured slowly in Luther's mind and also in Amsdorf's. In 1519, Amsdorf prepared for publication a statement of his faith at the urging of Luther and perhaps Christoph Scheurl of Nuremberg.[4] Amsdorf's first published

---

2 Johann Haussleiter, *Die Universität Wittenberg vor dem Eintritt Luthers nach der Schilderung des Mag. Andreas Meinhardi vom Jahre 1507* (Leipzig: Deichert, 1903), 47. Further information about Amsdorf's life can be found in Hans Stille, *Nikolaus von Amsdorf. Sein Leben bis zu seiner Einweisung als Bischof in Naumburg (1483–1542)* (Zeulenroda: Sporn, 1937). The university and the town of Wittenberg in this period are described in Heiner Lück, "Universität und Stadt Wittenberg zur Zeit des Nikolaus von Amsdorf. Ein Rekonstruktionsversuch möglicher Wahrnehmungen (1502–1524)," in Dingel, *Amsdorf*, 15–34, and Ulrich Köpf, "Nikolaus von Amsdorf an der Universität Wittenberg," in Dingel, *Amsdorf*, 35–55.

3 WA 1:142, 145–151; Luther's letters regarding these theses to Johann Lang and to Michael Dressel are found in WA Br 1:66, 57–58.

4 In addition to urging Amsdorf to put his ideas into print, Scheurl sent his thanks to Amsdorf and also the thanks of Scheurl's friend, Albrecht Dürer (*Christoph Scheurl's Briefbuch*, eds. F. von Soden and J. K. F.

tract, *A Christian Meditation How One Should Pray the Lord's Prayer, Drawn from the Sermons of Dr. Martin Luther of Wittenberg*,[5] introduced a pattern that would mark Amsdorf's ministry and way of thinking for the remaining forty-five years of his life. Simple in style and content and written in the vernacular, Amsdorf's first tract appealed to the common people and village priests; for the rest of his life, these groups of people were his primary audience and concern. He wrote the tract to propagate Luther's thinking. That continued to be the goal of his subsequent writing as well. He did not always draw the material in his tracts so directly from his friend as he did by paraphrasing and summarizing Luther in this first tract; but he did always use Luther's writings as the guideline for his own proclamation. Amsdorf's *Meditation* contained basic concepts of sin and grace that he would repeat again and again during his life. In that tract, he confessed that he was a wretched sinner with a nature poisoned by original sin inherited from his parents, and he acknowledged that even his good works were harmful if he put his trust in them for salvation.[6] For redemption from sin, Amsdorf turned to God, who had become "a criminal, a sinner, a fool" so that believers might become righteous. Luther himself later set forth his doctrine of justification in this way.[7] Amsdorf's first tract placed sole responsibility for human salvation in God's hands, a salvation which was effected through the substitutionary, atoning work of Christ. This simple understanding of the Christian Gospel would mark Amsdorf's theological writings from 1519 until the end of his life.

By 1519, Amsdorf's friendship with Luther had begun to pull him into a new kind of life, far different from his routine as an instructor of the liberal arts. In June 1519, he rode to Leipzig with Luther and Karlstadt and witnessed their debate with Johann Eck. Two years later, Amsdorf accompanied Luther to Worms; they were returning to Wittenberg together when Elector Frederick's men stopped the wagon and spirited Luther off to the Wartburg. Friends had informed Amsdorf of Frederick's plans to kidnap Luther and place him in protective custody; yet Amsdorf reportedly reacted so vehemently against the horsemen who interrupted their journey that Luther and Amsdorf's driver and

---

Knaake, 2 [Potsdam: Gropius, 1872], 82).

5 *Eyne christliche fur betrachtung So man wil bethen das heylige vater unser. Getzogen auss den predigtenn Doctoris Martini Luther zu wittemburg Von dem wirdigen Nicolao vonn Amssdorff Licenciaten in deutsch gebracht* (Leipzig: Wolffgang Stöckel, 1519, and in eight subsequent editions), WA 9:223–225.

6 Cf. chapter 3, pages 116–120.

7 For instance, in his Galatians commentary of 1535 and in his sermons on John's Gospel of 1528/1529, WA 40/1:433.26–434.20, LW 26:277; WA 40/1:437.18–438.13, LW 26:280; WA 28:353.28–355.27, LW 69:232–233; WA 28:391.27–392.19, LW 69:256.

traveling companion had no idea that Amsdorf was less concerned than they were about Luther's disappearance.

When Luther was taken to the Wartburg, Amsdorf returned to Wittenberg and worked with Philip Melanchthon to try to direct Luther's movement in his absence. The humanist prodigy Melanchthon and Amsdorf had quickly become friends when Melanchthon arrived in Wittenberg in 1518 to teach Greek at the university. With Luther, they had formed their own beer-drinking sodality, as Luther later fondly recalled.[8] Although Amsdorf's and Melanchthon's understandings of Luther's message later diverged at certain points, the memory of the time they shared together around beer steins never faded. While Melanchthon was alive, Amsdorf restrained himself from attacking his old friend in print with the same fierce polemic he used against some of Melanchthon's disciples, even though Amsdorf strongly objected to aspects of Melanchthon's interpretation of Luther. Likewise, when Melanchthon expressed strong objections to Amsdorf's stance on one subject or another after 1530, Melanchthon did so privately, or at least not in print.

During Luther's concealment in the Wartburg, Amsdorf and Melanchthon advised Elector Frederick on critical issues.[9] The two also shared the trials of those months in 1521 and 1522 when they had to temporarily assume Luther's leadership role. From one direction, they were pressed by the papal party, who wielded the threat of their excommunication, attached by Johann Eck to the bull *Decet Pontificem Romanum.* From the other direction, they were pressured by enthusiastic comrades such as Karlstadt and Luther's fellow Augustinian Gabriel Zwilling to support more wide-ranging reforms of ecclesiastical life in Wittenberg.[10] Luther did visit Wittenberg for a few days in December 1521 to check on the situation caused by the pace of reform Karlstadt and Zwilling were instigating. He stayed in Amsdorf's home, and with Melanchthon and a few other friends, they discussed how reform could best be promoted.[11] But at the end of December 1521, three self-styled "prophets" from Zwickau confronted Amsdorf and Melanchthon, claiming to have had heavenly visions. Amsdorf invited them into his home, where Melanchthon was also boarding, and the prophets thoroughly confused Luther's vicars.[12] Amsdorf and Melanchthon

8 WA 10/3:18.

9 CR 1:271–272, Nr. 94; MBW.T 1:236–237, Nr. 112.

10 Amy Nelson Burnett, *Karlstadt and the Origins of the Eucharistic Controversy: A Study in the Circulation of Ideas* (New York: Oxford University Press, 2011).

11 Irmgard Höss, *Georg Spalatin, 1484–1545. Ein Leben in der Zeit des Humanismus und der Reformation* (Weimar: Böhlau, 1989), 214.

12 In a letter dated to January 13, 1522, Luther counseled Amsdorf not to get upset over the three men from

must have been relieved in March 1522 when Luther decided to return to Wittenberg indefinitely.

Besides his work with Melanchthon, there were several ways Amsdorf specifically sought to fill the gaps during the time of Luther's absence. Amsdorf read Luther's notes on the Book of Hebrews to students who had come to Wittenberg seeking to hear the reformer himself. Amsdorf continued to conduct disputations for students.[13] He consulted with friends over questions of biblical interpretation, including with individuals as significant as Georg Spalatin, the private secretary of Frederick the Wise and the chief link between the electoral Saxon government and Luther's circle.[14] Amsdorf also wrote theses for disputation during this time.

One set of theses espoused the conviction that the Roman papacy was the Antichrist, a conviction Luther had been developing.[15] This was the first time Amsdorf publicly stated this idea, which became a standard theme in his writing for the rest of his life. The idea had not appeared in Amsdorf's simple meditation of 1519; rather, he became more convinced of this attribution as the hostility between Rome and Wittenberg intensified around 1520. In 1521 and 1522, the fierce and frustrating dispute Amsdorf and others waged against defenders of the Roman mass in Wittenberg strengthened Amsdorf's growing belief that the institution of the papacy fulfilled prophecies about the opponent of God named the Antichrist in Daniel, Paul's Epistles, and Revelation. In 1522, Amsdorf authored a preface and conclusion on this topic in an anonymous tract by Lazarus Spengler, the secretary of Nuremberg's city council and one of Luther's most prominent and dedicated lay disciples.[16] In that anonymous preface and

Zwickau who were claiming to have special revelations from God (WA Br 2:361.8–362.38; LW 48:364, Nr. 419). Luther told Amsdorf that he was writing the same day to Melanchthon with more detailed arguments against such "prophets," commenting on the nature of revelation and on the "prophets'" denial of infant Baptism. These letters indicate how closely Amsdorf and Melanchthon were working together; cf. Luther's letters to Amsdorf and Melanchthon addressing problems both men were facing in WA Br 2:422–423 and 424–427; LW 48:365–372, Nr. 449 and 450 (English: Nr. 112). Cf. Friedrich Christoph Ilgner, "Nikolaus von Amsdorf 'wider den rotten vnnd secten gaist,'" in, Dingel, *Amsdorf*, 252–255.

13 E.g., those on the mass, reprinted in Köpf, "Amsdorf," 52–53.

14 Höss, *Spalatin*, 222.

15 Printed in *Propositiones D. Mart. Luth. ab initio negocij Euangelici* (Wittenberg, 1538), N3a–N4a; reprinted in Köpf, "Amsdorf," 54–55. Cf. Scott H. Hendrix, *Luther and the Papacy. Stages in a Reformation Conflict* (Philadelphia: Fortress, 1981).

16 *Die haubtartickel durch welche gemeyne Christenheyt bysshere verfuret worden ist* (Wittenberg, 1522, and in two subsequent editions). Amsdorf's treatment of the pope as Antichrist departed from the model of medieval theologians and preachers in ways similar to Luther's; see Hans Preuss, *Die Vorstellungen vom Antichrist im späteren Mittelalter, bei Luther, und in der konfessionellen Polemik* (Leipzig: Hinrich, 1906), 83–181, and Ulrich Asendorf, *Eschatologie bei Luther* (Göttingen: Vandenhoeck & Ruprecht, 1967), 173–187. On Spengler, see Harold J. Grimm, *Lazarus Spengler, a Lay Leader of the Reformation* (Columbus: Ohio State University Press, 1978).

conclusion, Amsdorf labeled the papal system, rather than any individual pope, as the Antichrist because it suppressed the true worship of God and replaced it with hypocrisy and human fabrications. Amsdorf saw evidence of this in the papal prohibitions of the marriage of priests and the eating of meat on certain days. Amsdorf remained convinced until the end of his life that these prohibitions made the pope the devil's preacher, based on 1 Timothy 4:3. The critical events surrounding the Diet of Worms persuaded Amsdorf to believe the end time, when the Antichrist was to be unmasked, was at hand. The final assault of this enemy of God against the Gospel had begun, and Amsdorf perceived his entire ministry as taking place in the shadow of this eschatological struggle. The false church of might and glory was trying to destroy the true Church, the beleaguered remnant of God's people gathered around the Word of Christ. Amsdorf's ecclesiology, like his soteriology, took its final form in his Wittenberg years.

Another set of theses Amsdorf authored during the time Luther was hidden in the Wartburg addressed good works. Amsdorf believed a key weapon that the Antichrist used to divert attention from God's grace, as Amsdorf understood grace, was the papal emphasis on good works as a means of salvation. Amsdorf's position on this topic as set forth in 1522 in these propositions also remained essentially unchanged through the rest of his life, including through the controversies about good works in Magdeburg in the 1520s and through the discussions with those in the Wittenberg circle about good works and salvation in the last thirteen years of Amsdorf's life. Amsdorf's conviction echoed Luther's: Good works do not make a person good. Rather, a person becomes good by being reborn through the Holy Spirit; then that good person produces good works, just as a good tree produces good fruit. These echoes of Luther's teachings resounded in many of the pages of Amsdorf's tracts from 1522 through the 1560s.[17]

Even after Luther returned to Wittenberg, Amsdorf retained many leadership responsibilities in the Wittenberg reform movement. For example, when Katherine von Bora and her fellow nuns arrived in Wittenberg after escaping from the Cisterican cloister in Nimbschen on Easter Sunday 1523, Amsdorf sought to help find suitable husbands for these women who wanted to be part of the Wittenberg reform movement. As a reflection of Amsdorf's importance in that circle, Katherine von Bora, who eventually married Luther, suggested in early 1525 that she would prefer to marry either Luther or Amsdorf. In that

17 Johann Erhard Kapp, *Kleine Nachlese . . . nützlicher Urkunden* 2 (Leipzig: Braun, 1727): 553–554; reprinted in Köpf, "Amsdorf," 53–54. Amsdorf took his ideas and illustration from Luther, e.g., in his *On the Freedom of the Christian* of 1520, WA 7:61–62. Chapter 3 below deals with Amsdorf's later defense of this concept of good works that he was advancing already in the 1520s.

process, Amsdorf cared for the wellbeing of all of the women, not just of Luther's future wife.[18]

Amsdorf's years in Wittenberg were formative and determinative for the rest of his life in many ways. Not least among these was an experience that led to his departure from Wittenberg as well as revealed his view of the relationship between the secular government and the church. In early 1523, Elector Frederick's private secretary, Georg Spalatin, asked Amsdorf for his colleagues' opinions on the propriety of Frederick using force to defend his Saxon subjects against the reimposition of the papal religion by imperial troops. Luther, Melanchthon, Bugenhagen, and Amsdorf were asked to offer advice. Luther placed enough conditions on using force in this way that it was nearly impossible for the elector to raise the sword to defend the Reformation movement. Luther abhorred violence and desired public order and peace; therefore, he rejected the idea of using armed might to defend the Gospel. Melanchthon and Bugenhagen were more favorable than Luther to the idea of Frederick using force to defend the Gospel, but neither of them was willing to go as far as Amsdorf was.

Amsdorf agreed with Luther that the individual Christian suffers patiently for the faith and does not actively resist a secular government, even when being persecuted. But Amsdorf was convinced that the public office of a Christian prince compelled him to defend the Gospel. Therefore, the prince who is truly a Christian not only may but should use the sword on behalf of the Gospel, defending both his own subjects and others.[19] Amsdorf's view cannot fully be explained by the fact that, as a nobleman, he had been charged with public use of the sword to keep order and was more aware of threats to public peace and safety than others might have been, nor that his ideas merely reflect a nobleman's understanding of the aristocratic nature and constitution of the German empire at this point. He asserted the right of the Christian prince to intervene even in the lands of other rulers in reaction to the rising threat from the Roman party. Amsdorf did expect that one day God would judge and bring all things to a just end; but until Judgment Day, Amsdorf evidently believed that a Christian prince should defend God's elect from the Antichrist's agents, who were ready and eager to use the sword to suppress Amsdorf's understanding of the

18 Amsdorf prioritized helping settle all of the escaped nuns into homes. For example, he had attempted to link his aunt, the younger sister of Johannes von Staupitz and the prioress of the cloister, with Spalatin, but when the Nimbschen nuns arrived, Amsdorf assured Spalatin that should he prefer a younger woman, he should pick the most beautiful from among the escaped nuns to be his wife (Höss, *Spalatin*, 271).

19 The memoranda are printed in WA Br 12:35–45; cf. Eike Wolgast, *Die Wittenberger Theologie und die Politik der evangelischen Stände* (Gütersloh: Mohn, 1977), 101–108.

Gospel. No reaction from Frederick to any of these memoranda is extant, and in the course of events, Frederick had no recourse to this advice, since the imperial threat did not materialize at that time.

During 1523, however, Elector Frederick became rather irritated with Amsdorf's insistence that the electoral government permit the abolition of the mass in Wittenberg. Two confrontations with Frederick over that issue may have contributed to Amsdorf's departure from Wittenberg. In 1522, Amsdorf had also expressed a willingness to leave the university for parish life.[20] The fact that he had not pursued the doctorate degree may suggest his interest in academe was less intense than that of his colleagues.

In his twenty years at Wittenberg, Amsdorf had been transformed from a Scotist student and liberal arts instructor into an Evangelical reformer. Luther's insights and friendship directed Amsdorf's energies into new channels, and by 1524, Amsdorf was ready to depart from Wittenberg to serve Luther's cause and spread his ideas when the opportunity arose. His final eight years in Wittenberg had carved out for him his niche in history: standing with Luther, interpreting him for the people, and defending his understanding of the Gospel. Amsdorf spent the rest of his life doing just that.

MAGDEBURG'S PREACHER: WARNING AGAINST FALSE TEACHERS

Some fifty miles down the Elbe River from Wittenberg was the proud city of Magdeburg, glorying in its past all the way back to its founding by Emperor Otto I as a frontier town in 955. Being among the fifteen largest municipalities in the German-speaking lands and having nearly 20,000 residents, Magdeburg in Amsdorf's day looked confidently toward its future as a commercial and political power. According to imperial law, it was subject to the archbishop of Magdeburg. Albrecht of Hohenzollern occupied the archiepiscopal throne from 1513 to 1545. Under his administration, the city continued to engage in the see-saw battle it had been waging against its archiepiscopal overlords from at least the twelfth century. At the end of the fifteenth century, the then archbishop of Magdeburg, Ernst, brother of Frederick the Wise, had won back for the church from the civic leadership part of the control of the city that his predecessors had lost. So in the early sixteenth century, the civic leadership was struggling to

20 In a letter dated February 20, 1522, in Wilhelm Jannasch, *Reformationsgeschichte Lübecks vom Petersablass bis zum Augsburger Reichstag 1515–1530* (Lübeck: Schmidt-Römhild, 1958), 369–370; cf. also in Jannasch, 98–99.

regain the independence it claimed Emperor Otto I had awarded it. As a result of a guild revolt in the fourteenth century, the wealthy guildmasters were also part of the civic leadership, sharing power with the patricians of Magdeburg. Because the city had long chafed under clerical domination, its municipal policy and the Wittenberg Reformation found a coincidence of interest in the 1520s; the citizens of Magdeburg were only beginning to recognize this when Amsdorf accompanied Luther to Magdeburg in 1524.

Since 1521, the city council had been dealing with unrest stirred up by a series of Evangelical preachers. It had cracked down on a number of them, but in 1524, lower class agitation for reform broke out into riot when a young clothmaker was arrested for singing two of Luther's new German hymns and distributing copies of them. Formally the city council did nothing, but some of its members sent an invitation to Luther to visit Magdeburg and consult with them regarding possible measures to reform ecclesiastical life in the city. Luther, along with Amsdorf and a few others, arrived on June 24, 1524; they stayed for several days and conferred with civic leaders and preached to large numbers of the people. One measure Luther suggested was that Amsdorf could be called to the city; Amsdorf declined. He returned to Wittenberg, but by the end of July, he had changed his mind and was preparing to leave Wittenberg's university in answer to a call to become the pastor at Saint Ulrich's parish in Magdeburg. Delicate negotiations were required in this process because a Wittenberg professor leaving Frederick the Wise's electoral Saxony to become a pastor in a city under Archbishop Albrecht's jurisdiction could cause friction; Albrecht was a member of the Hohenzollern family, who were the rulers in the neighboring margravate of Brandenburg and the rivals of Frederick the Wise's family. Spalatin and Hieronymus Schurff, one of Amsdorf's colleagues on the faculty of law, conducted the negotiations and paved the way for Amsdorf to accept the call to Magdeburg.[21] The solution was that Frederick the Wise would give Amsdorf a leave of absence. This made clear that Amsdorf remained Frederick's subject and belonged to his university; therefore, the prince retained his claim on Amsdorf and could recall him to his service when he wished. On September 24, 1524, Amsdorf arrived in Magdeburg to assume the duties of pastor and superintendent of the city's churches.[22]

21 Höss, *Spalatin*, 256–260.

22 Hans-Otto Schneider, "Amsdorf als Statthalter Luthers in Magdeburg," in *Magdeburg und die Reformation, Teil 1, Eine Stadt folgt Martin Luther*, eds. Maren Ballerstedt, Gabriele Köster, and Cornelia Poenicke (Halle: Mitteldeutscher Verlag, 2016), 113–127. Cf. Stille, *Amsdorf*, 52–70.

Because of his status as a nobleman, Amsdorf was well suited to lead Magdeburg in the restrained and responsible ecclesiastical reform its civic leaders wanted. He was the equal of the noble cathedral canons, who represented the archbishop in the city, but he simultaneously commanded the kind of theological attention in electoral Saxony that only a close friend of Luther could, coming to Magdeburg at Luther's recommendation.

The opportunity to serve as a pastor in Magdeburg seems to have been attractive to Amsdorf for the reasons already mentioned: conflict with Frederick the Wise in 1523 and Amsdorf's interest in parish ministry instead of the university. Luther may have sensed that Amsdorf's skill in disputation and in the pulpit along with his stubborn conviction that the Reformation message was correct made him the right man for Magdeburg in 1524. Regardless, Luther suggested the right man, for Amsdorf fashioned Magdeburg into a bastion of Luther's movement that valiantly resisted the might of the emperor even after the Smalcald War two decades later.

The institutionalization of Lutheran reform had begun in Magdeburg even before Amsdorf arrived, and he continued to lead the city in that direction. Early in 1525, Magdeburg implemented the Wittenberg educational model at the Johannisschule under the leadership of Rector Caspar Cruciger. He and Amsdorf had become acquainted while Cruciger studied in Wittenberg. Together, they merged Magdeburg's parish and monastic schools. Cruciger's reforms of the city's educational system forged one of the first two secondary schools shaped by Luther's and Melanchthon's reforms and the principles of biblical humanism.[23] When Cruciger returned to Wittenberg in 1529, Georg Major, another student of Luther and Melanchthon, came to Magdeburg to head the school until 1536. Later, Major and Amsdorf came into conflict over the Leipzig "Interim,"[24] but the friendship that formed between them during their years in Magdeburg may have kept them from each other's throats during the initial stages of that later controversy.[25]

Difficulty beset Amsdorf at every hand during the first years of ministering in Magdeburg. In early 1525 during the Peasants' Revolt, Amsdorf attempted, at

---

23 Carsten Nahrendorf, *Humanismus in Magdeburg: das Altstädtische Gymnasium von seiner Gründung bis zur Zerstörung der Stadt (1524–1631)* (Berlin: de Gruyter, 2015), 60–66.

24 Quotation marks will be used with the word *Interim* when referring to the Leipzig "Interim." This was a pejorative term for the proposal Elector Moritz's government presented to the Saxon assembly of nobles and town representatives. The assembly rejected the proposal, but its critics published it, entitling it an "Interim" in order to associate it with Emperor Charles V's Augsburg Interim, a document for the reordering of church life and teaching in the interim until the Council of Trent.

25 Nahrendorf, *Humanismus*, 66–92. On the later dispute between Amsdorf and Major, see chapter 3.

some personal risk, to face down a mob that was sympathetic to local peasant revolutionaries. He failed to disperse the mob, but no serious violence erupted in the city during the Peasants' Revolt. There were also theological struggles. Amsdorf's efforts to introduce Luther's reforms were resisted by representatives of the old religious system and representatives of alternate ecclesiastical reforms. Many of Amsdorf's struggles with these opponents took place in verbal exchanges, but following Luther's example, Amsdorf also used the technology of print to assert his points in these confrontations. In Wittenberg, Amsdorf had learned not only the usefulness of the printed word but also how to cooperate with printers to attain his goals of establishing and defending reform. Amsdorf did work with two Magdeburg printers named Heinrich Öttinger and Hans Barth to publish his views; but he worked most closely with the printer Melchior Lotter. Amsdorf probably knew Lotter from Wittenberg. In 1529, Lotter transferred his operation to Magdeburg and served Amsdorf there for the following decades. Printers Hans Walther and Christian Rödinger came to Magdeburg from Nuremberg in 1530 and Wittenberg in 1539, respectively. Amsdorf worked with both to publish his message. After Rödinger later moved to Jena, Amsdorf's relationship with him still continued there.[26]

One conflict in which a verbal dispute became a battle in print began with an incident during a worship service. Amsdorf knew Dr. Wolfgang Cyclop from their years together as students in Wittenberg. Cyclop was a physician, who transferred from the University of Leipzig to Wittenberg in 1502 and who returned to Wittenberg's university, "the Leucorea," again in 1511 after briefly teaching in his native Zwickau.[27] Like Amsdorf, Cyclop was regarded as a "Scotist" by his contemporaries. Cyclop had actively promoted Luther's thought in Braunschweig-Lüneburg before coming to Magdeburg to practice medicine; but he had also turned to Ulrich Zwingli's interpretation of the Lord's Supper. Once when Amsdorf warned Cyclop from the pulpit to cease and desist from publicly denying the presence of Christ's body and blood in the Lord's Supper, Cyclop responded by laughing. Amsdorf and Cyclop then took up a debate about the Lord's Supper in print. Amsdorf's tactic in the debate was to claim a simple faith in Christ and plead a lack of learning in response to Cyclop's philosophical

---

26 Christoph Reske, *Die Buchdrucker des 16. und 17. Jahrhunderts im deutschen Sprachgebiet*, 2nd ed. (Wiesbaden: Harrassowitz, 2015), 628–629.

27 J. Klaus Kipf, "Cyclopius," in *Deutscher Humanismus 1480–1520 Verfasserlexikon* 1, ed. Franz Josef Worstbrock (Berlin: de Gruyter, 2008): 537–546; J. Klaus Kipf, "Wolfgang Cyclopius und die Einführung der Reformation in Magdeburg 1524–1526. Dargestellt anhand des Flugschriftenstreits mit Nikolaus von Amsdorf," in *Magdeburg und die Reformation*, 129–155.

arguments.[28] Throughout his life, Amsdorf would continue to strongly defend Luther's concept of the true presence of Christ's body and blood in the sacramental elements of bread and wine.

Another example of a conflict during Amsdorf's time in Magdeburg that began as a verbal dispute and then turned to printed arguments was Amsdorf's conflict with the Anabaptist Melchior Hoffman in 1527 and 1528. They sparred for several rounds, face-to-face and in print, about Hoffman's apocalyptic interpretations of Scripture and Amsdorf's treatment of Hoffman when he visited Magdeburg in 1527.[29]

The most serious attacks Amsdorf had to contend with in the 1520s, however, came from the Roman Catholic party in Magdeburg. Archbishop Albrecht exercised minimal control over the "old city," but in the "new city" and suburban Sudenburg, he enforced his edicts effectively. After the imperial diet at Nuremberg in 1524, Albrecht felt papal and imperial pressure to take sterner actions against Evangelicals in his lands. Therefore for both political and religious reasons, he brought Magdeburg's religious changes before the imperial court shortly after Amsdorf arrived to try to gain more control over the city through imperial backing. At the cathedral in the "new city" section of Magdeburg, Albrecht had allies who mounted formidable attacks against Amsdorf from the pulpit. Amsdorf took this threat from the cathedral canons seriously. For example, when two cathedral preachers, Boniface Bodenstein and Dr. Wolfgang Cubito, attacked Amsdorf in sermons on the festival of the Assumption of Mary, August 15, 1525, Amsdorf challenged them to a public disputation over the propositions that the mass is an abomination and that the festival of the bodily assumption of Mary into heaven is devilish and contrary to the Gospel. This invitation to a public disputation was declined, as were later challenges Amsdorf issued.[30] The canons preferred for Amsdorf to go with them to Cologne to place

---

28 *Vermanung Nicolai von Amssdorff an die von Magdeburg/ wider den rotten vnnd secten gaist D. Ciclops* (s.l., 1525, and in two subsequent editions), Cyclop replied in *Von dem Aller hochwirdigsten Nachtmahl Jesu Christi. Eynes durch Doctor Wolf Cyclop etc. Vorgenommen buchleins vorrede* . . . (Magdeburg, 1525), to which Amsdorf replied, *Auff Ciclops antwort replica* (Wittenberg, 1525). Cyclop wrote *Doctor Wolff Cyclops Antwort auff Nickel amssdorffs Replica* (s.l., 1526) and dropped from sight. Cf. Ilgner, "Amsdorf 'wider den rotten vnnd secten gaist,'" in Dingel, *Amsdorf*, 255–263, 274–279.

29 Against Hoffman, Amsdorf wrote *Ein vormanung an die von Magdeburg, das sie sich fur falschen Propheten zu huten wissen* (Magdeburg: Hans Bart, 1527); *Was Melchior Hoffman nicht ein wort auff Büchlein geantwortet hat* (s.l., 1528); and *Das Melchior Hoffman ein falscher Prophet vnd sein leer vom Ju[e]ngsten tag vnrecht, falsch vnd widder Gott ist* (s.l., 1528). During the controversy, Hoffman attacked Amsdorf in his *Das Niclas Amsdorff der Magdeburger Pastor ein lugenhafftiger falscher nasen geist sey offentlich bewiesen durch Melchior Hoffman*, facsimile in *Schriften des Vereins für Schleswig-Holsteiner Kirchengeschichte* 4 (Sonderheft, 1928); and in his *Dat Nicolaus Amsdorff der Meydeberger Pastor nicht weth wat he setten schriuen edder schwetzen schal* . . . (s.l., 1528). Cf. Ilgner, "Amsdorf 'wider den rotten vnnd secten gaist,'" in Dingel, *Amsdorf*, 264–268, 274–279.

30 The challenge was printed in a tract by two of Amsdorf's Magdeburg colleagues, Eberhard Weidensee

their disagreements before the archbishop there. Amsdorf responded in print, launching a three-year on-again, off-again public quarrel during which he outlined a series of plain, simple arguments against Roman Catholic doctrines, especially prayer to saints, the mass, the prohibition of clerical marriage, and works-righteousness.[31] His tone in these tracts is likely indicative of the many arguments he must have had in the streets or the marketplaces of Magdeburg with the canons and their dwindling number of supporters. Amsdorf's tracts were personal, informal, sharp, blunt, and without complex development of ideas.

The cathedral canons' counterattack led with the charge that the Evangelicals were forbidding good works. For that reason and other errors, they argued, the Evangelicals ought to be exterminated; yet the canons continued to decline opportunities to publicly debate the issues Amsdorf critiqued. Amsdorf called attention to evil works in the lives of the canons and carefully set forth his conviction regarding good works. He said good works proceed from God's grace at work in believers; this grace does not set aside the human will's activity but assists it.[32] Because the believer's good works are produced by the Holy Spirit, these works cannot be necessary for salvation. They are a consequence, not a cause, of justification, Amsdorf argued. His position on works reflected what he had taken from Luther, and it summarized his theses on good works composed in Wittenberg in 1522.

Some have suggested that Amsdorf's theological positions became increasingly arid and rigid after 1524. This interpretation argues Amsdorf's physical separation from Luther and Wittenberg in 1524 marked Amsdorf's departure from Luther's dynamic, lively faith into the straitjacket of orthodoxy.[33]

---

and Johann Fritzhans, *Wie Doctor Cubito/ Bonifacius/ vnd der sontags prediger yhm Thum zu Magdeburg/ Gottis wort lectern* (s.l., 1526).

31 Amsdorf's tracts from the period include *Widder die lugen prediger des hohen Thumbs zu Magdeburg* (Wittenberg, 1525); *Grund vnd vrsach auss der Cronicke Warumb Johannes Huss vnd Jeronimus von Prag verbrant seyn* (s.l., 1525); *Grundt vnd orsake worup Marquardus Schuldorp hefft syner suster dochtor thor ehe genamen* (s.l., 1526); *Dem Erwerdigen vnd Erbarn herrn Senior vnd dem gantzen Thum capitel zu Magdeburg meinen lieben feinden vnd verfolgern* (Magdeburg, 1528); *Vntterricht warumb die Thumprediger zu Magdeburg nicht disputirn wollen/ vnd doch von offentlich auff der Cantzel geeischet vnd gefordert haben* (s.l., 1528); *Den Thumbpredigern zu Magdeburg* (s.l., 1528); and *Auff erfordern der thumprediger zu Magdeburg erbeut sich zu disputirn auff den kunfftigen reichstag zu Regenspurg* (s.l., 1528?). Amsdorf's most extensive discussion of the issue of faith and works from this period is found in his *Das die werck nicht rechtfertigen—sondern der glaub allein/ Niclas Amsdorff, Widder die Thumprediger zu Magdeburg* (s.l., 1528), AS, 1–28.

32 In a set of theses composed at this time, printed under the title "Nicolai Amsdorfii Conclusiones," *Abhandlungen Alexander von Oettingen zum siebzigsten Geburtstag gewidmet* (Munich: Beck, 1898), 260.

33 E.g., Stille, *Amsdorf*, 57, 69. Otto Lerche, *Amsdorff und Melanchthon. Eine kirchengeschichtliche Studie* (Berlin: Lerche, 1937), 9, suggests that Amsdorf's departure from Wittenberg especially influenced his relationship with Melanchthon. It seems doubtful, however, that Amsdorf would have approved Melanchthon's expression of his views on good works and contingency even if they had remained together in

However, the records of Amsdorf's thought during this period are too sparse to provide conclusive evidence that his departure from Wittenberg had this effect. The sources that are extant suggest no grounds for seeing a transformation in Amsdorf's faith before and after his move to Magdeburg in 1524. On the key issue of good works, Amsdorf's popular tracts from the 1520s echo the theses he wrote for disputation while still a professor. Likewise, there is almost no difference in the tone and content of Amsdorf's writings on the papacy before and after 1524.

There are differences between Amsdorf and Luther's expressions of their faith. However, these differences are more accurately attributed to differences in Amsdorf and Luther's personalities and experiences, rather than a difference in concern for genuine faith versus doctrine. Amsdorf had not experienced God's wrath and grace to the degree Luther did. Nor did his writings convey the same dynamic warmth, power, and depth of many of Luther's tracts. Instead, Amsdorf's writing often is little more than a skeleton of Evangelical theology. His polemical public image did not reflect the richness of Luther's varied exposition of his faith. Yet, Amsdorf still genuinely expressed his faith at a level and in a manner he believed appropriate for reaching his intended readers, based on his deep conviction of Luther's teaching. It should be noted that Luther provided definitions of doctrine that were also more precise and careful than Amsdorf's. It is more enjoyable and more convincing to read Luther than Amsdorf on good works or the bound will, for example. But it is inaccurate to suggest authentic, living faith as well as doctrine were not significant concerns for both men.

Imperial and archiepiscopal prohibitions put an end to the public exchange of arguments between Amsdorf and the Roman party in Magdeburg in 1528. After that, Roman Catholic critics continued to fight against Amsdorf's reform but less publicly, while Amsdorf continued to deconstruct the population's medieval piety through his preaching. In the early 1530s, Amsdorf, having established the Evangelical church quite securely in Magdeburg's old city, looked beyond Magdeburg to comment on other problems of the growing Lutheran churches.

Amsdorf's work during his time in Magdeburg spread beyond the confines of that city. In Goslar, an imperial city southwest of Magdeburg at the edge of the Harz mountains, good works and their relationship to the justification of sinners had become key issues in the public argument over reform. As early as 1521, members of the lower class had agitated for Evangelical reform as part of their program for social change in the city. By 1528, a majority of the city's

---

Wittenberg; see below, chapters 3 and 4.

council members agreed Goslar's ecclesiastical life should be organized along Evangelical lines. The council requested that Amsdorf as the superintendent of Magdeburg come to and guide Goslar in implementing Evangelical reform. In the spring of 1528, Amsdorf spent six weeks providing that assistance in Goslar. After he returned to Magdeburg, a Roman Catholic theologian from Anhalt, Johann Mensing, launched an attack against the Goslar Evangelicals. Amsdorf came to Goslar's aid by publishing tracts against Mensing, reiterating his position on good works and repeatedly using the metaphor of a good tree that produces good fruit.[34]

Goslar's Lutheran party was under pressure from two directions, just as the Lutheran party in Magdeburg was. Two preachers who became popular in Goslar, Johann Grawert and Heinrich Knigge, the latter of whom was also one of Magdeburg's first Evangelical preachers in the early 1520s, were not satisfied with Goslar adopting a Lutheran theologian's position and urged more radical reform measures; they professed a Zwinglian understanding of the Lord's Supper. By January 1531, the council had asked Amsdorf to return to Goslar to restore order and to counter the Zwinglian tide. In Amsdorf's initial sermon, he preached on "the Word, sign, and Sacrament," reproducing much of Luther's argument against Zwingli.[35] Amsdorf also confronted Knigge and Grawert directly in a public disputation. With Amsdorf's assistance, the council was able to send the two preachers into exile. They still had influential followers in the city, so Amsdorf stayed on for some three months to consolidate the hold of the council and the Lutheran clergy in Goslar. During that period, Amsdorf composed an ecclesiastical ordinance for the Goslar church to specifically condemn Zwinglianism.[36]

Amsdorf was called upon to assist in other places near Magdeburg as well. He helped institute an Evangelical ecclesiastical ordinance for the church in the imperial city Einbeck in the 1530s. The church in Hannover consulted Amsdorf when writing a similar ordinance in 1534. He assisted with a limited visitation to

34 *Das der Pauler monich zu Dessa Johan Mensing ym glauben vnd vber den wercken ist vnsinnig/ tol vnd tho[e]richt worden* (s.l., 1528). Mensing addressed Amsdorf's views in his *Bescheidt Ob der Glaube alleyn on alle gute wercke dem menschen genug sey zur seligkeyt etc.* (Leipzig: Jacob Thanner, 1528). On the Reformation in Goslar, see Uvo Hölscher, *Die Geschichte der Reformation in Goslar* (Hannover/Leipzig: Hahn, 1902).

35 *Ein schöner Sermon/ von dem wort/ zeichen/ vnd Sacrament* (Wittenberg, 1531), and in seven other editions. Amsdorf followed up this attack with other tracts directed against the Goslar Sacramentarians, *Vrsach warumb die beide predicanten/ Er Johann Grawert vnd er Heinrich Knyge aus Goslar vertrieben sind* (Magdeburg, 1531), and *Das Johan Hussen lied vom Sacrament recht Christlich vnd aus dem Euangelio genomen sey/ an alle fromme Christen zu Braunswig* (Magdeburg: Michael Lotter, 1533).

36 "Kirchenordnung der Stadt Goslar," in *Die Evangelischen Kirchenordnung des 16. Jahrhunderts*, ed. Aemilius Ludwig Richter, reprint (Nieuwkoop: De Graaf, 1967), 1:154–157. Also *Die Evangelischen Kirchenordnung des 16. Jahrhunderts*, 7, 2, 2:184–185, provides an introduction to the several documents that were prepared for the regulation of church life at this time, pages 223–242.

churches in electoral Saxony in 1530. At the end of the 1530s, Amsdorf was also part of a team that visited the churches of ducal Saxony to try to establish the Reformation in the lands Duke Heinrich recently inherited from his brother, the arch-Roman Catholic, Duke George. For reasons not revealed, Heinrich's government did not see fit to call Amsdorf to the theological faculty of the University of Leipzig, now under Heinrich's jurisdiction, even though Amsdorf's former Wittenberg colleagues Philip Melanchthon and Justus Jonas had suggested it.[37] However, it was probably fortuitous that Amsdorf did not receive the appointment, since in such a role, he most certainly would have clashed with Heinrich's older son and successor, Moritz, during and after the Smalcald War.

An ongoing problem for the Lutheran churches continued to be the menace of violence against them. Emperor Charles V had threatened to enforce the Edict of Worms against Luther's followers in the spring of 1531. Circumstances outside his German empire prevented him from doing so; but the threat of military aggression coupled with continuing verbal attacks from papal supporters caused Amsdorf to concentrate a good deal of energy on the established church's response to the rebellious spirit of Wittenberg. Therefore, in the 1530s, Amsdorf issued a series of tracts against individual Roman Catholics and against the papal party in general, in an effort to win popular support for and rally the populace to the Wittenberg cause. One tract in 1533, a year before the election of Pope Paul III, was prompted by rumors that the papacy was going to call for a council. Amsdorf continued to express his suspicion of any papally-dominated council through other tracts in the mid-1530s, even when the threatened call for a council came in 1536. (As it turned out, the conditions when the council was set to meet in 1537 were unfavorable, and so its members did not assemble until 1545, in Trent.)[38] In a half dozen of these tracts, published in 1534 and 1535, Amsdorf specifically attacked abuses of papal power. Amsdorf criticized the pope's assumption of power over other Christians and his arrogation of political power to himself; Amsdorf's arguments were similar to (though less well developed than) those Melanchthon would express in the "Treatise on the Power and Primacy of the Pope" in 1537.[39] These tracts reveal Amsdorf's literary

37 Stille, *Amsdorf*, 131–133.

38 In the tracts listed in note 31 above and in his *Cogitationes Nicolae Amsdorfii, De Concilio Nvnqvam Fvtvrosi Per Papam Liceat* (s.l., 1533), and *Has Propositiones Defendet Nicolavs Amsdorfivs Magdebvrgae quando uolerint aduersarij* (s.l., s.d.).

39 E.g., *Eyn Gesprech zwischen eym Lutherischen vnd Papisten/ das der Römische hoff des Teuffels braut vnd das rechte Antichristlische reich sey/ vnd nicht die kirche Christi* (Magdeburg: Hans Walther, 1535); *Ein kurtzer auszog aus der Cronica Naucleri/ wie vntreulich vnd verreterlich die Bebste zu Rom mit den Romischen Keysern gehandelt haben* (Magdeburg, 1534, and two subsequent editions); *Warhafftige Historia vnd geschicht/ wie der Bapst ist der o[e]berste gewurden/ jnn der Christenheit. Aus bewerten Cronicken* (Magdeburg: Hans Walther, 1535);

imagination as he was able to create hypothetical dialogues between disputants to make his arguments concrete for readers and able to put to good use available historical works as material for his arguments.[40] Apparently Amsdorf's experiences in Magdeburg had solidified his conviction that papal interference in the political sphere and papal oppression in the spiritual realm had alienated many Germans. He believed if he could help the common people articulate these resentments, as the people of Magdeburg had done and effected Amsdorf's invitation to the city, he could prepare the way for other Evangelical preachers like himself to be effective in other communities.

Amsdorf also spoke out against papal oppression as part of an attack on Desiderius Erasmus in 1534. Amsdorf and Luther exchanged letters concerning Erasmus that year, and those letters were published. After that publication, Amsdorf also wrote a tract against Erasmus. He did not attack Erasmus for practicing humanist scholarship, nor was Amsdorf's tract filled with disparaging remarks about learning and reason (as his later tracts against Philippist foes would be). Instead, Amsdorf criticized Erasmus's continued obeisance to the Roman pope, saying Erasmus had fallen prisoner to the Roman Church instead of being captive to Christ.[41]

The threat to the Wittenberg teaching from those Luther labeled "Schwärmer," "ravers" continued to pose another ongoing problem for the Lutheran churches during Amsdorf's time in Magdeburg. Amsdorf lumped together Anabaptists and Zwinglians in a tract composed in 1535. The Anabaptist kingdom in Münster provoked his discussion of Baptism in that tract; but nevertheless, Amsdorf urged Evangelical princes not to think that they could remove the Münsterites' "ravings" by force of arms, as it was clear that several secular governments, including that of Philip of Hesse, were planning to do just that. In this case, Amsdorf assessed the practicalities of the situation and agreed with Luther's conviction about using violence on behalf of God's truth. He argued conversions could not be forced by military might because only

---

Eine kleine vnterricht auff die Co[e]lnische zedel mit yhren dreien schiffen (Magdeburg, 1535); *Vorkündigung des volkommen Ablas der Ro[e]mischen Bullen, So Bapst Paulus der dritt itzt im XXXV: jar hath lassen aussgehen* (s.l., 1535). Cf. Melanchthon's argumentation in his "Treatise," BSELK 796–837, BC 330–344.

40 In later controversies, he also tried his hand at the genre of satire, turning it against Philippist critics, who had subjected him and his associates to such satires. Cf. "Eine bis her ungedruckte satyrische Schrift aus dem 16. Jahrhundert (Nic. Von Amsdorfs Gespräch eines Raben mit einer Taube)," *Zeitschrift für die gesammte lutherische Theologie und Kirche* 25 (1864):78–86.

41 Contrary to the assertion of Stille, who needed instances of confrontation between Amsdorf and "humanism" for his interpretation (cf. his *Amsdorf*, 91–94), Amsdorf's critique of Erasmus was not based on Erasmus's "humanistic" characteristics but on ecclesiological issues; see *Epistolae Domini Nikolai Amsdorfii Et D. Martini Lvtheri, De Erasmo Roterodamo* (Wittenberg, 1533), and *Consilivm Et Ratio Epistolae De Erasmo, Ad Lvthervm Nicolai. Amsdorfii* (Magdeburg, 1533).

God's Word brings people to true faith. Fire and sword will only drive them further into error.

It was natural for Amsdorf to couple theses against both Anabaptists and Zwinglians together in this tract, for in his mind, his defense of the power of the Sacrament of Baptism was related to his defense of the true presence of Christ's body and blood in the Sacrament of the Lord's Supper. Amsdorf included Martin Bucer and his colleagues at Strassburg among those who denied the true presence of Christ's body and blood in the Lord's Supper. Amsdorf's suspicions of Bucer's efforts to find middle ground between Zürich and Wittenberg placed the Strassburg theologians also alongside the Münsterites in Amsdorf's mind.[42] In private correspondence, Bucer expressed indignation at Amsdorf's efforts to torpedo the Strassburg ministerium's attempts to reconcile the Wittenberg theologians with those working with Bucer in southern Germany. In early April 1535, he published a refutation in Latin of Amsdorf's theses that concerned his position.[43] Amsdorf's suspicions were not to be appeased, even by Luther, and Amsdorf refused to sign the Wittenberg Concord in 1536.[44]

During his years in Magdeburg, Amsdorf did spend the majority of his time serving and strengthening that city's church. However, his influence and leadership also extended beyond Magdeburg, through his visits to other cities and through his writing. When he sat down to write something for publication, he projected the embattled image that was imprinted on him in his early years in Magdeburg through the opposition from the Roman Catholic establishment and from those he believed were betraying the cause of reform. Threats from the Roman party and the princes allied with them menaced Luther's followers even when institutionalization brought some small measure of security to the Evangelical churches. Though Dr. Cyclop with his Zwinglian sympathies eventually vanished from Magdeburg, there were other threats from similar "ravers" in Goslar, Münster, and Strassburg that Amsdorf sought to fend off. Amsdorf recognized the enemies of the Gospel all around him, and he was convinced that their opposition to his proclamation of the Gospel was part of the final battle to be waged against God's Word at the end of time. He struck back in defense of

42 *Contra Zwinglianos & Anabaptistas themata* (s.l., s.d.); *Widder die Widder teuffer vnd Sacramentirer/ Etliche spru[e]che oder schlussrede* (Erfurt: Wolff Heinick, and Magdeburg: Hans Walther, 1535).

43 *Axiomata apologetica . . . de sacro eucharistiae mysterio et circa hoc Ecclesiarum Concordia, quibus respondet Thematis. N. Amßdorfij, Argentoratenses falso criminantibus* (Augsburg: Philipp Ulhart, 1535); see Thomas Wilhelmi, "Widerlegung der Thesen des Nikolaus von Amsdorf April 1535," in Martin Bucer, *Deutsche Schriften, Band 18. Nachträge 1541–1551 sowie Ergänzungen und Korrekturen*, eds. Sephen E. Buckwalter and Thomas Wilhelmi (Gütersloh: Gütersloher Verlagshaus, 2015), 671–672; edited text: 679–692.

44 On the Wittenberg Concord, see Gordon A. Jensen, *Wittenberg Concord. Creating Space for Dialogue* (Minneapolis: Fortress, 2018).

that Word against these attacks on the Gospel with earnestness and severity. His mature thought was born in the context of these struggles, and it found its way into the public forum in polemical tracts to respond to attacks on his proclamation of the Wittenberg message.

"THEOLOGIAN BY NATURE"?

In anticipation of the council that Pope Paul III called in 1536, Luther invited Amsdorf to come to Wittenberg in December 1536 to help formulate a doctrinal statement in the form of bullet points the Saxon government and other Evangelical rulers could use to talk with their theologians about a proper response to Roman Catholic arguments. This invitation demonstrated Luther's confidence in his friend Amsdorf, whom Luther later called a "theologian by nature." The document created during that gathering in Wittenberg—"the Smalcald Articles"—was Luther's own; but Amsdorf, Johann Agricola of Eisleben, Georg Spalatin, and members of the Wittenberg theological faculty likely provided some assistance since they had accepted Luther's invitation to meet with him concerning this task.

Amsdorf journeyed with Luther to Smalcald in January 1537 for the meeting of the Smalcald League. Amsdorf served on a key committee of theologians there and preached to the assembled princes and town council members. He subscribed to both Luther's "Smalcald Articles" and Melanchthon's "Treatise on the Power and Primacy of the Pope"—the two documents being reviewed by the Smalcald League.[45]

After 1537, Amsdorf joined the Wittenberg theologians in offering opinions on various issues to Johann Friedrich, who had succeeded his father, Johann, and his uncle, Frederick the Wise, in 1532 as the elector of Saxony.[46]

Amsdorf also sent an uninvited and unwelcome memorandum on bigamy to Landgrave Philip of Hesse in 1540. The landgrave had sought advice from Martin Bucer and Philip Melanchthon in his dilemma of being caught between love for his mistress, Margaret von der Saale, and his longstanding distaste for his wife, Christine of Saxony, daughter of Duke George. Luther had concurred with Bucer and Melanchthon that Philip of Hesse's bigamous marriage to Margaret was the best solution, even though that was contrary to imperial

45 BSELK 718–785, 796–837; BC 297–328, 330–344.

46 On Amsdorf's close relationship with Johann Friedrich the Elder, see Volker Leppin, "Nikolaus von Amsdorf und Johann Friedrich d. Ä.," in Dingel, *Amsdorf*, 103–115.

law. However, Luther counseled that the marriage be kept a secret lest it give offense. Amsdorf saw the matter differently. His memorandum to Philip of Hesse argued that if Philip could take another wife, his first wife ought to be allowed to find herself a fine young bachelor as her second husband by the same right. Amsdorf argued that all Christians are redeemed by Christ's blood and, therefore, have the same rights; in Christ, a man has no more right to remarry than his sister in the faith does.[47]

In early 1538, Amsdorf became tangentially involved in the first major public theological dispute among those in the Wittenberg movement. Johann Agricola was a student who joined Luther's movement in 1516. His experiences in the earliest stages of Luther's call for reform had impressed upon him the dangers of the medieval church's use of God's Law, closely connected with works-righteousness. Therefore, before Agricola left Wittenberg in 1525 to become the rector of the school and preacher in Eisleben, he began rejecting any use of the Law in the Christian life. Not long after Melanchthon was awarded the theological professorship that Agricola coveted in 1526, Agricola criticized Melanchthon for relying too much on the Law in his "Visitation Articles" for electoral Saxony. Luther was able to mediate between Agricola and Melanchthon and smooth the matter over in 1528.[48] However, when Agricola returned to Wittenberg in 1536, he reignited the wrath of its theological community by teaching that the divine Law plays no role in the Christian life and that the Gospel—not the Law—effects repentance and guides Christian living.

At first, Luther treated the matter as a semantic problem. But eventually he became convinced that Agricola was stubbornly perverting the message that Luther had taught. Agricola attributed to the Gospel functions that Luther had assigned to the Law, particularly accusation of sin that leads to repentance and also instruction in the proper Christian conduct for life. Agricola, on the other hand, claimed that Luther had abandoned his original position concerning the Law and that he, Agricola, was the one preserving that original concept. He did not grasp Luther's distinction of Law and Gospel and its critical importance for pastoral care and the assurance of the Gospel. In confrontations with his

47 William W. Rockwell, *Die Doppelehe des Landgrafen Philipp von Hessen* (Marburg: Elwert, 1904), 323–325.

48 Timothy J. Wengert, *Law and Gospel, Philip Melanchthon's Debate with John Agricola of Eisleben over Poenitentia* (Grand Rapids: Baker, 1997). On the opposition to Agricola's position expressed in the Saxon "Visitation Articles" of 1528, see *Der "Unterricht der Visitatoren" und die Durchsetzung der Reformation in Kursachsen*, eds. Joachim Bauer and Stefan Michel (Leipzig: Evangelische Verlagsanstalt, 2017), especially Volker Leppin, "Die Normierung der Frömmigkeit im 'Unterricht der Visitatoren,'" 167–194, Ernst Koch, "Die Bedeutung von Gesetz und Evangelium nach dem 'Unterricht der Visitatoren,'" 195–211, and Michael Beyer, "Hintergründe der Lehre vom 'freien Willen' und der 'christlichen Freiheit' im 'Unterricht der Visitatoren,'" 241–254.

colleagues in Wittenberg, Agricola backed down again and again, only to reassert his opinion as soon as the pressure subsided. His vacillations prolonged the discussion of the issues involved, and in 1540, he fled Wittenberg, even though the electoral government had forbidden him to leave the town. He became the court preacher for Elector Joachim II of Brandenburg and, because of that role, contributed to the mischief of the Augsburg Interim a decade later.[49]

In 1538, in the midst of the dispute between Agricola and Luther, Amsdorf spoke out against Agricola in an anonymous tract. Cast in dialogue form and entitled *Luther's Sepulture*, the tract actually dealt very little with the issue of Agricola's antinomian views. Instead, it condemned a certain student of Martin Luther for ambition and arrogance, which were doing more damage than the fire and sword of the Roman party.[50] The informal tone of the tract suggests its purpose was putting Luther's critic in his place, not providing a detailed analysis of theological arguments. The judgments of Agricola in the tract reflect an opinion Luther expressed early on in the dispute. Therefore, Amsdorf might have wanted to publish the tract in order to give wider circulation to Luther's view of the affair as Amsdorf heard it at Luther's table during a visit to Wittenberg.

Even though Amsdorf and Agricola did have some similar experiences, Amsdorf did not agree with Agricola's perversion of Luther's thought. Amsdorf and Agricola were attracted to Luther's message around the same time. Amsdorf was also uncomfortable with any ideas that suggested the Law motivates Christian living; rather he believed faith alone produces new obedience. Like Agricola, Amsdorf had developed a thorough horror of the kind of legalistic soteriology Luther was reacting against when he launched the Wittenberg call for reform. However, even though Amsdorf was later incorrectly called an antinomian, Amsdorf's view of the Law differed significantly from Agricola's. Amsdorf always

49 See also Joachim Rogge, *Johann Agricolas Lutherverständnis unter besonderer Berücksichtigung des Antinomismus* (Berlin: Evangelische Verlagsanstalt, 1960); Steffan Kjellgaard-Pedersen, *Gesetz, Evangelium und Busse: Theologiegeschichtliche Studien zum Verhältnis zwischen dem jungen Johann Agricola (Eisleben) und Martin Luther* (Leiden: Brill, 1983); Ernst Koch, "Johann Agricola neben Luther: Schülerschaft und theologische Eigenart," in *Lutheriana*, eds. Gerhard Hammer and Karl-Heinz zur Mühlen (Cologne: Böhlau, 1984), 131–150; Jeffrey G. Silcock, "Luther and the Third Use of the Law," Th.D. dissertation, Concordia Seminary, Saint Louis, 1993; Walter Sparn, "'Lex iam adest,' Luthers Rede vom Gesetz in den Antinomerdisputationen," in *Martin Luther – Biographie und Theologie*, eds. Dietrich Korsch and Volker Leppin (Tübingen: Mohr/Siebeck, 2010), 211–249.

50 *Sepvltvra Lvtheri* (s.l., 1538). Gustav Kawerau in "Die Flugschrift Sepultura Lutheri 1538," *Theologische Studien und Kritiken* 72 (1899): 281–293, argues convincingly that this tract ought to be attributed to Amsdorf instead of Justus Menius, identified as the author by Caspar Cruciger in 1538, CR 3:496. Amsdorf did claim to have written against Agricola in a memorandum composed in 1540, probably the memorandum he was invited by the Wittenberg faculty to sign along with Melanchthon, Jonas, and Bugenhagen, in Karl Eduard Förstemann, *Neues Urkundenbuch zur Geschichte der evangelischen Kirchen-Reformation* (Hamburg: Perthes, 1842), 325–327.

recognized that the Law has a role in the Christian's life, calling Christians to repentance, and he never assigned the Gospel a role in effecting repentance, as Agricola did. Amsdorf's tract against Agricola reveals the disgust Amsdorf had against those he regarded as traitors to Luther's cause. Such disgust also motivated Amsdorf's attacks on the Philippists a decade later.

Amsdorf also began to come into conflict with Melanchthon in the 1530s. Even though Melanchthon had boarded in Amsdorf's house and they had become friends at the beginning of Melanchthon's time in Wittenberg, the two did not always see eye-to-eye. Moreover, after Amsdorf moved to Magdeburg in 1524, he and Melanchthon developed different foci and accents in their expressions of Wittenberg thinking. Melanchthon was forced by his roles as university lecturer and ecclesiastical diplomat to consider the fundamental expressions of Luther's thought at deeper levels and in the face of new challenges. At the same time, Amsdorf's experiences in Magdeburg only confirmed his belief that the doctrine Luther had formulated against medieval Catholicism and the Roman papacy was the correct exposition of the Gospel of God's grace in Jesus Christ. The cathedral canons in Magdeburg confronted Amsdorf with essentially the same questions that Luther had faced at Leipzig and Worms. Amsdorf also could look to how Luther responded to the Zwickau prophets and Karlstadt with the Swiss in the mid 1520s for examples of how to counter those who devalued the forgiveness given in Word and Sacraments. Amsdorf's conversation partners were not equipped to respond to his expression of biblical teaching; as a result, they did not push him to develop his thinking any further.

Conversely, like Luther, Melanchthon continued to experiment with ways to best address, in the various situations he faced, the questions raised by the Wittenberg assertion of God's total responsibility for his world and humans' full responsibility to be what God intended. As a professor, he was called to cultivate the rhetorical skills and pastoral sensitivities of his students. As the ecclesiastical diplomat of the electoral Saxon government and the Smalcald League, he was charged with finding ways to preserve peace and gain toleration for the confession of the faith set forth in the Augsburg Confession.

The first evidence of a difference of opinion between Amsdorf and Melanchthon surfaced around the time of a minor controversy between Caspar Cruciger, Luther's and Melanchthon's colleague, and Conrad Cordatus, a pastor near Wittenberg who frequently took in lectures at the university. Cordatus accused Cruciger of denying the Gospel by teaching that contrition is a *conditio sine qua non* ("condition without which," a factor without which something cannot happen) for justification. Cruciger excused himself by referring to similar statements from Melanchthon. Cordatus, who had spent time in prison in Austria because he preached Luther's message, thought it improper to use anything but biblical terminology in describing salvation. He feared that Cruciger's expression vitiated Luther's emphasis on grace alone by suggesting that a person must perform the good work of contrition before he could be justified. However, Cruciger and Melanchthon were reacting against the confusion of Christian freedom with licentiousness they had discovered in Saxon villages during the visitation of 1527 and 1528. Even before the disagreement between Cruciger and Cordatus gained attention, Amsdorf wrote to Luther to express concerns about Melanchthon's understanding of good works. Rumors were circulating, Amsdorf warned, that Melanchthon was teaching "vehemently and without moderation"[51] that good works are necessary for eternal life. After battling the cathedral canons over similar language of good works being "necessary" for salvation, Amsdorf was disturbed by the possibility that Melanchthon was using such language. However, Melanchthon reached out to Amsdorf in a letter, expressing his sorrow that Amsdorf misunderstood Melanchthon's position and his hope that they might be able to reach an agreement.[52] The matter was laid to rest since Amsdorf apparently did not pursue the matter further, and Melanchthon even suggested that his friend from Magdeburg should be a mediator in the Cordatus and Cruciger affair.[53]

Melanchthon also found fault with Amsdorf at times during the 1530s. He was displeased with Amsdorf's attacks on Erasmus in 1534 and on the Wittenberg Concord in 1536. Melanchthon also was convinced Amsdorf was referring to him when Amsdorf warned Luther that he was nursing a viper at his breast. Yet still Melanchthon seems to have maintained a good opinion of Amsdorf through the 1530s. In 1538, Melanchthon included three sets of Amsdorf's propositions from earlier years in a collection of Wittenberg disputations, chiefly Luther's.[54] In 1539, Melanchthon recommended that Amsdorf assume responsibilities in the reform of ducal Saxony because Amsdorf was a "learned, experienced, and reasonable man;" Melanchthon also endorsed Amsdorf for a professorship in

51 WA Br 7:539–540, dated September 14, 1536. Luther mentioned Amsdorf's warning, CR 3:162, note * to Nr. 1466, with Amsdorf's letter also given.

52 MBW.T 7:269–270, Nr. 1805.

53 CR 3:180, Nr. 1480; MBW.T 262–264, Nr. 1802 (= WA Br 7:579–583); cf. CR 3:346; MBW.T 7:428, Nr. 1889. On the Cordatus controversy, see Martin Greschat, *Melanchthon neben Luther. Studien zur Gestalt der Rechtfertigungslehre zwischen 1528 und 1537* (Witten: Luther Verlag, 1965), 217–251, and Timothy J. Wengert, "Caspar Cruciger (1504–1548): The Case of the Disappearing Reformer," *Sixteenth Century Journal* 20: 417–441.

54 *Propositiones D. Mart. Luth. ab initio negocij Euangelici/ ab autore Tractatae/ usque in hunc diem* (Wittenberg: Johannes Lufft, 1538); Amsdorf's theses appear on leaves N1a–O6a.

Leipzig, even though Duke Heinrich did not give it to Amsdorf in the end.[55] Melanchthon praised Amsdorf as a "dialectician who knows how to conduct disputations over critical matters, better than others do."[56]

The second theological issue that set Amsdorf at odds with Melanchthon in the 1530s and 1540s was the latter's treatment of contingency in human actions in relation to the boundness of the will in its relationship to God. In his new edition of the *Loci communes* in 1535, Melanchthon hesitated and labored over the "large and difficult" questions of contingency and the cause of sin. Since God created all things good, Satan and the human creature must be the causes of sin, Melanchthon asserted. Also, God wants all people to be saved and shows no partiality (1 Timothy 2:4; Romans 2:11; Acts 10:34), so sinners must bear the responsibility for their sins. Therefore, the human situation is contingent, that is, not determined by God making sin necessary but by factors under human (and satanic) control. Scripture speaks of the ability of fallen sinners to perform works of civic righteousness, so some degree of freedom must be attributed even to the fallen human will, Melanchthon argued.[57]

Amsdorf did not understand why Melanchthon was concerned about the exercise of the will from any viewpoint other than the relationship between God and human beings in the justification of the sinner. Amsdorf did not work primarily in a lecture hall, and he had no need to determine how to present the full biblical message properly in that context, as Melanchthon did. Amsdorf believed Melanchthon was conceding too much to human ability and was thus detracting from God's honor. He could see nothing but a return to medieval doctrines of human contribution to salvation in Melanchthon's treatment of contingency. Augustine had battled Pelagius, Luther had battled Erasmus, and now Amsdorf feared Melanchthon was equivocating on the same issue. Interestingly, Amsdorf did not call into question Melanchthon's labeling the human will a material "*causa*" or factor in conversion or repentance; it seems Amsdorf understood Aristotelian philosophy well enough to know that material "causes" are the passive recipients of the action of the effective "*causa*." However, in two private memoranda, Amsdorf did note his strong disagreement with Melanchthon's treatment of contingency as a reversal of Luther's position in 1525 in *On Bound Choice* (*De servo arbitrio*).[58]

---

55 See p. 26 above.

56 Melanchthon praised Amsdorf, CR 3:713, Nr. 1814, and criticized him, CR 3:97, Nr. 1445 and 3:503, Nr. 1661; MBW.T 7:170, Nr. 1759; 8:70, Nr. 2009.

57 CR 21:273–274.

58 (1) "De contingentia. Disputatione prima pars," Dresden, Sächsische Landesbilbiothek. Msc. Dresd. A180, 725–770 (renumbered since Stille's use of the manuscript). Stille, *Amsdorf*, 97, dates the manuscript

Amsdorf's own position in these memoranda was based, in part, on Luther's argument that God's creatures are bound by the absolute necessity of divine decisions determining reality, an idea that Luther had abandoned in all subsequent writings after *On Bound Choice*.[59] Amsdorf's view of contingency was also based on Paul's analogy of a potter who uses his clay to make some vessels for destruction and others for mercy (Romans 9:21–23).

In striving to defend God's sole responsibility for the salvation of sinners, Amsdorf came close, by implication, to abolishing human guilt, replacing the idea that humans are guilty with the idea that they are appointed to be "vessels of wrath." In his memoranda on Melanchthon's treatment of contingency, Amsdorf wrote that God controls his creation completely, and what he wills takes place necessarily, unavoidably, and immutably. Using Luther's image of the sinner as a pack animal, Amsdorf contended God assigns some of his human creatures to be ridden by Satan and others to be ridden by Christ. Therefore, in reaction to Melanchthon's views, Amsdorf formulated a doctrine of double predestination—a logical defense for the sovereignty of God in the salvation process. Amsdorf also denied the universality of God's promise of salvation, limiting its validity only to those who believe in Christ. It is possible to see, then, that Amsdorf's beliefs foreshadowed the position on predestination subsequently developed by John Calvin and sharpened by some of his followers, including Theodore Beza.[60]

There were a number of factors that led Amsdorf to this view of election and predestination. He had not grasped the subtlety of Luther's application of the

---

to 1536 though without supporting evidence; it is likely that Amsdorf reacted quickly to the new edition of Melanchthon's *Loci*, published in 1535. (2) "Annotationes quibus indicator paucis que in locis communibus Philippi Melanchthonis displicent per N.A.," Wr, ETLFB 40:301–309. Stille, *Amsdorf*, 100–101, shows that this memorandum must rest on the 1541 edition of the *Loci*. Again, it is likely that the reaction was immediate. There is no justification for Lerche's dating the manuscript in Amsdorf's Eisenach years, i.e., after 1552; see Lerche, *Amsdorff und Melanchthon*, 9.

Duns Scotus, whose followers trained Amsdorf and whose positions Amsdorf conveyed in lecturing on Aristotle as a young liberal arts instructor, held to a strong doctrine of predestination, according to most of his modern interpreters; see Wolfhart Pannenberg, *Die Prädestinationslehre des Duns Skotus im Zusammenhang der scholastischen Lehrentwicklung* (Göttingen: Vandenhoeck & Ruprecht, 1954). Scotus and Amsdorf conceived of predestination as purely an act of divine will (Pannenberg, *Praedestinationslehre*, 40–43). Yet Amsdorf's doctrine of predestination differed from Scotus's in specific ways, even though Scotus's lectures presented his doctrine in greater detail than Amsdorf's relatively short critique did. Scotus made use of the distinction between *necessitas consequentiae* and *necessitas consequentis*, and Amsdorf rejected it in his memoranda (Pannenberg, *Prädestinationslehre*, 63). Amsdorf held to double predestination, and Scotus did not. While Amsdorf's views were influenced by his Scotist training, Amsdorf's view of predestination is imprecise and essentially attempts only to reproduce and defend Luther's views; see Robert Kolb, "Nikolaus von Amsdorf and Vessels of Wrath and Vessels of Mercy, a Lutheran Doctrine of Double Predestination," *Harvard Theological Review* 69 (1976): 325–343.

59 Robert Kolb, "Luther's *On Bound Choice* from Publication to the Formula of Concord," *Logia* 27.3 (2018): 23–25.

60 Richard Muller, *Calvin and the Decree: Christology and Predestination in Reformed Theology from Calvin to Perkins* (Durham: Labyrinth, 1986).

distinction of Law and Gospel to the doctrine of election. Instead, Amsdorf constructed a logical system; his was easier to defend and explain than Luther's, though it was more difficult to apply pastorally. Amsdorf was aware that there could be difficulties if his logical presentation of God's inscrutable will in the doctrine of salvation was preached as harshly as it had to be discussed among the learned. His solution asserted that believers should be directed only to God's will as it is revealed in Christ, not to speculate about anything else—just as Luther urged repeatedly in his lectures on Genesis.[61] That is what the common people needed to know. And the pastors needed to know that the human will contributes nothing to the process of salvation. Amsdorf was concerned about the pastoral difficulties of Melanchthon's view as well. Amsdorf wanted to prevent hearers and readers from falling back into a dependence on their own works or the efforts of their minds, as he had experienced in the lectures of his scholastic instructors and in the piety of his Magdeburg parishioners when he had arrived in the city. Also, some of the factors that influenced Melanchthon were irrelevant to Amsdorf. He cared little for Melanchthon's concern with the problems of how to move hearts and minds through proper use of communication skills; in contrast to Melanchthon, Amsdorf also had little contact with those in the Roman party who accused Luther of teaching Manichaean determinism. To Amsdorf, only the believer's relationship with God really mattered, so something like Melanchthon's affirmation that the human will can perform certain works of the Law without new birth by the Holy Spirit was inconsequential.

Some have suggested the differences between Amsdorf and Melanchthon on the topics of predestination and the human will and divine will reveal the contrast between a scholastic Wittenberg reformer (Amsdorf) and a humanist Wittenberg reformer (Melanchthon). But that distinction does not hold up when examined more closely. Amsdorf was reacting against what he recalled from his scholastic teachers when he condemned the notion that human beings contribute to their own salvation. And his simple argumentation in his treatises is less "Aristotelian" (scholastic) than Melanchthon's often detailed and extensive analyses. Scholastics of the nominalist stripe in the fifteenth century tended to have a more optimistic anthropology than some of their humanist colleagues.[62] Although Melanchthon's anthropology allegedly represents a "humanist" point

---

61 Robert Kolb, *Bound Choice, Election, and Wittenberg Theological Method From Martin Luther to the Formula of Concord* (Grand Rapids: Eerdmans, 2005), 35–48.

62 Heiko A. Oberman, "Some Notes on the Theology of Nominalism with Attention to its Relation to the Renaissance," *Harvard Theological Review* 53 (1960): 47–76. Lewis W. Spitz Jr. has shown that many "humanists" were rather pessimistic in their appraisal of the human creature; see "Man on This Isthmus," in *Luther for an Ecumenical Age*, ed. C. S. Meyer (Saint Louis: Concordia, 1967), 23–66.

of view, it is couched in Aristotelian language and concepts as was the teaching of the scholastics. Both Amsdorf and Melanchthon show elements of biblical humanism and its ways of thinking, such as their mutual deep concern for the humanist goal of teaching "purely," that is, teaching pure doctrine.[63] Melanchthon fits the humanist mold slightly better than Amsdorf, but Melanchthon also betrays more tendencies that can be labeled "scholastic" than Amsdorf, since Melanchthon frequently applied Aristotelian logic to the topics he was addressing. Rather than using the labels "scholastic" and "humanist," it is more appropriate to view both Amsdorf and Melanchthon as wrestling with the same theological tensions but emphasizing different elements in those tensions.

Much of the difference between these two disciples of Luther does not stem from significantly different training as much as from the significantly different realms in which their thinking, teaching, preaching, and writing occurred. Amsdorf engaged in debates in the vernacular and the public sphere, where death threats from the Roman party supported one side of the discussion. His skill in scholastic disputations prepared him well for this.[64] The assaults Amsdorf experienced in Magdeburg also caused his work to be more rhetorically charged than theologically sophisticated. Melanchthon was not afraid to speak harshly against his opponents,[65] but his exchanges took place with the theological leadership of the papal party in the German empire when Melanchthon represented the Saxon government and with the Smalcald League in a regular series of negotiations during the 1530s. Amsdorf addressed primarily merchants, artisans, and peasants—people who needed clear, simple explanations to be able to slowly digest Luther's Gospel and who struggled with falling back into spiritual self-confidence or despair because of medieval concepts of works-righteousness. Conversely, Melanchthon's theology was shaped by primarily academic and diplomatic contexts in which he had to respond to probing questions and thought experiments from students in lecture halls and accusations and philosophical

63 Opposing Stille's treatment of Amsdorf's and Melanchthon's differences and characteristics (e.g., *Amsdorf*, 33, 97, 100) is the analysis of Greschat, *Melanchthon neben Luther*, 133, 147, 155; Timothy J. Wengert, "Melanchthon and Luther / Luther and Melanchthon," *Lutherjahrbuch* 66 (1990), 55–88; and Irene Dingel, "Philipp Melanchthon, Freunde und Feinde," *Theologische Literaturzeitung* 135 (2010): 788–790. On the concept of pure or true teaching in the Middle Ages and the contemporary humanists' concern for "*doctrina pura*," cf. Philippe Büttgen et al., eds., *Vera Doctrina: zur Begriffsgeschichte der Lehre von Augustin bis Descartes* (Wiesbaden: Harrassowitz, 2009; note esp. Theodor Mahlmann, "*Doctrina* im Verständnis nachreformatorischer lutherischer Theologen," 199–264.

64 See Introduction, note 18, for bibliography on the transition from university disputation to public polemic in the Early Reformation.

65 Cf., for example, his reproof of the papal legate in Augsburg, Lorenzo Campeggio; Timothy J. Wengert, "The Day Melanchthon Got Mad: A Study in Lutheran Ecclesiology," *Lutheran Quarterly*, n.s., 6 (1991): 419–433.

arguments from Roman Catholic theologians in colloquies.

All who defended the old beliefs earned Amsdorf's swift and certain condemnation. Melanchthon strove to establish peace and harmony. This contrast may reflect differences in their personalities, but it certainly also arose out of their differing contexts. Melanchthon was not willing to sacrifice the heart of Luther's Gospel, but he raised his hackles against his conversation partners chiefly only when they had exhausted his patience.[66] This difference between Amsdorf's outspoken opposition to all things Roman and Melanchthon's more conciliatory stance toward certain elements of medieval practice and polity produced the third clash between Amsdorf and Melanchthon before Luther's death. The clash primarily concerned ecclesiology rather than soteriology, and it emerged at the Regensburg Colloquy in 1541. Amsdorf participated in much, though not all, of the proceedings surrounding the colloquy. He had missed the opening of the dialog initiated at Charles V's invitation in Hagenau; but he had participated in the sessions between Roman Catholics and Evangelicals at Worms in 1540, and he arrived in Regensburg for the diet and the colloquy held there in 1541. Melanchthon led the Evangelical negotiators in discussions with Gasparo Contarini and a number of German Roman Catholic theologians. The final document drawn up by the two sides displeased Melanchthon, but it roused fierce criticism from Amsdorf, who believed that Melanchthon had been spending his time in vain even trying to converse with the Roman Catholic party. Amsdorf denounced the final document for submitting to papal law rather than God's Word.[67] The document's emphasis on obedience to the church also particularly disturbed Amsdorf since he interpreted that as obedience to the Roman court. However, it must be noted that again Melanchthon and Amsdorf did not publicly exchange views on the colloquy.

Elector Johann Friedrich was attracted to Amsdorf's willingness to bluntly denounce positions that he found false. So in 1543, Johann Friedrich called upon Amsdorf to issue a critique of an ecclesiastical ordinance drawn up for Hermann von Wied, the archbishop elector of Cologne, who had decided to reform his lands along Evangelical lines. The authors of this ordinance were Martin Bucer and Philip Melanchthon. Amsdorf conceded that this "Book of Cologne" agreed

---

66 On Melanchthon's combining clear confession with attempts at reconciliation, see Ragnar Andersen, *Concordia Ecclesiae. An Inquiry into Tension and Coherence in Philipp Melanchthon's Theology and Efforts for Ecclesiastical Unity, Especially in 1527–1530* (Zürich: LIT-Verlag, n.d. [2016]), 181–323.

67 On the colloquy, see Suzanne Hequet, *The 1541 Colloquy at Regensburg: In Pursuit of Church Unity* (Saarbrücken: VDM Verlag Mueller, 2009). Melanchthon's memorandum on the Regensburg Book is printed in CR 4:413–431, Nr. 2278/2279; MBW.T 10:303–309, Nr. 2738; Cruciger's memorandum in CR 4:431–434. Lerche, *Amsdorf and Melanchthon*, viii, exaggerates the importance of Amsdorf's role at Regensburg when he states that Amsdorf torpedoed the colloquy.

with Luther's teaching; but he did criticize some parts of the "Book" for being obscure or insufficient. He had qualms about the statements on the true presence of Christ's body and blood in the elements of the Lord's Supper and on the possibility that grace can be lost by believers when they sin. His criticism ignored the fact that Luther upheld this possibility as he strove to make clear how to practice the proper distinction of Law and Gospel in the Smalcald Articles.[68] Amsdorf thought it unseemly that the "Book" did not mention Luther and that it did not attack the Anabaptists and the "ravers."[69] Melanchthon and other Evangelicals deplored Amsdorf's criticisms. However, even through all of this, Melanchthon continued to correspond with Amsdorf in a friendly fashion and to exercise responsibility for Amsdorf's nephews, Georg and Christoph, who were studying at Wittenberg under Melanchthon's care.[70] If the friendship between Amsdorf and Melanchthon was troubled by serious disagreement, it was not torn apart. Neither of them saw any need to bring their differences into the public arena, where cords of friendship are more easily cut by sharp differences because offense is more easily given and taken. Perhaps each of them felt that he had enough trouble without doing that.

By the time he composed his critique of the "Book of Cologne," Amsdorf's life had changed, though his theology had not. Shortly after Amsdorf returned to Magdeburg from Regensburg in 1541, the Roman Catholic bishop of Naumburg and Zeitz died. His lands lay between those of Elector Johann Friedrich and Johann Friedrich's cousin, Duke Moritz of Albertine or ducal Saxony. Johann Friedrich seized the opportunity to extend his control over the bishopric. The cathedral chapter elected a Saxon courtier, the Erasmian Julius Pflug, its new

68 BSELK 764–765, BC 318–319.

69 Amsdorf's criticism is pieced together from several reports, see CR 5:459, Nr. 3006; 5:461, Nr. 3008; 5:462, Nr. 3009; MBW.T 13:363, Nr. 3646; 13:372, Nr. 3652; 13:374, Nr. 3653; WA Br 10:614–618; Hans-Ulrich Delius, "Der Briefwechsel des Nikolaus von Amsdorf als Bischof von Naumburg-Zeitz (1542–1546)," Habiliationsschrift, University of Leipzig, 1968, Nrs. 435, 440.

70 Melanchthon criticized Amsdorf's attitude toward the "Book of Cologne" in letters to Gregor von Brück, Veit Dietrich, Joachim Camerarius, and Martin Bucer, in WA Br 10:6353; CR 5:459, Nr. 3006; 5:462, Nr. 3009; 5:473, Nr. 3021; MBW.T 13:363, Nr. 3646; 13:372, Nr. 3652; 13:374, Nr. 3653. The antipathy of others toward Amsdorf over this issue is found in letters in the *Briefwechsel der Brüder Ambrosius und Thomas Blaurer, 1509–1567*, ed. Traugott Schiess (Freiburg im Breisgau: Fehsenfeld, 1908–1912), vol. 1: Bucer, 289–329; Heinrich Bullinger, 283–284; Ambrosius Blaurer, 286–287, 296, 297, 304–305; Joachim Vadian, 295, 303. The friendly correspondence of the period between Melanchthon and Amsdorf is found in Otto Walz, "Epistolae Reformatoren," *ZKG* 2 (1878): 145, 149, 157–162; CR 5:324, Nr. 2875; 5:362–363, Nr. 2917; 5:798–799; 6:32–33, Nr. 3373; 6:73–73, Nr. 3409; 6:94–95, Nr. 3428; 6:149, Nr. 3475; 6:179–180, Nr. 3492; 6:181–182, Nr. 3495; 6:235, Nr. 4382; 6:239–240, Nr. 3565; MBW.T 13:111, Nr. 3471; 13:383–384, Nr. 3965; 15:140–141, Nr. 4810; 15:181, Nr. 4201; 15:287, Nr. 4274; 15:328, Nr. 4292; 15:337, Nr. 4300; 15:442, Nr. 4382; 15:450–451, Nr. 4391. Many of these letters concerned Amsdorf's nephews; on Amsdorf's attempts to win support and positions for his nephews, see Delius, "Briefwechsel," Nrs. 610, 618, 778, 788, 875.

bishop, but Johann Friedrich rode into Naumburg in January 1542 with Amsdorf at his side. Luther accompanied them, and he ordained Amsdorf as the bishop of Naumburg and Zeitz. Amsdorf would have preferred to remain in Magdeburg; but Johann Friedrich insisted he was the best man to reform the diocese of Naumburg and Zeitz, and Luther concurred. Other theologians favored Prince Georg of Anhalt for the position. But the elector felt closer to Amsdorf. Amsdorf's learning, piety, and celibate state also did commend him for the position.[71] He spent nearly five unhappy years in this episcopal office. He was beset by a hostile cathedral chapter and its allies among the nobles in the countryside, frustrated by an Evangelical pastorate in Naumburg that had enjoyed relative independence under the Roman bishop, threatened with legal action by the imperial courts, and often thwarted by the electoral administrator of the secular affairs of his bishopric, Melchior von Creutzen. Amsdorf had left Magdeburg with the greatest reluctance, and he often longed to return there, especially when he encountered a lack of support from the electoral government for plans for reform. Von Creutzen withheld funding that was badly needed for a visitation to the parishes in his diocese, and the funding was only received when Johann Friedrich finally loosened the purse strings in 1545.[72] However, it is interesting to note that among the books Bishop Amsdorf required each of his parishes to possess when the visitors inspected a congregation was Melanchthon's *Loci communes*, as well as the Bible, Luther's postils, Luther's catechisms, and the Smalcald Articles.[73] Apparently Amsdorf's reservations about Melanchthon's treatment of contingency in the *Loci* did not set aside Amsdorf's appreciation of the overall usefulness of the *Loci* for the parish pastor.

Only four years after he became bishop of Naumburg and Zeitz and in the midst of his mounting unhappiness and frustration with those episcopal duties, Amsdorf's life changed again when Luther died on February 18, 1546. Among the first three letters dispatched by Justus Jonas from Luther's death chamber in Eisleben was one to Amsdorf; the other two went to Elector Johann Friedrich and to Johannes Bugenhagen with the other Wittenberg colleagues. Amsdorf conveyed news of the loss to his former Magdeburg colleague, Georg Major, who was representing Saxony at the second Regensburg colloquy at the time. In the

71 Leppin, "Nikolaus von Amsdorf und Johann Friedrich d. Ä.," 111.

72 Cf. "Der Bischof Nicolaus zu Naumburg kündigt dem Zeitzischen Kapitel die vorzunehmende Kirchenvisitation an. 1545," *Archiv der sächsischen Geschichte* 2 (1785): 339–340.

73 *Die evangelischen Kirchenordnungen des 16. Jahrhunderts*, ed. Emil Sehling 1.2 (Leipzig: Reisland, 1902), 90–91. On Amsdorf's years as bishop of Naumburg-Zeitz, see Delius, "Briefwechsel," and Peter Brunner, *Nikolaus von Amsdorf als Bischof von Naumburg* (Gütersloh: Mohn, 1961). Delius's Habilitationsschrift is summarized in *Theologische Literaturzeitung* 96 (1971): 153–155.

exchange of mutual condolences that followed, Amsdorf's letters to Jonas and others show that Luther's death led Amsdorf to dwell on the impending punishment God would inflict on the impious and the chastening he would visit upon believers. Amsdorf informed Johann Friedrich that Luther's death signified the coming of God's wrath upon the ungrateful, who had only contempt for the Gospel; Amsdorf warned that Luther's death should call everyone to repentance and to prayer for the mitigation of divine wrath. Since the Smalcald War broke out later in 1546, Bishop Amsdorf's words proved to be rather prophetic about the years that were to come.[74]

A year before his death, Luther had written Amsdorf that both of them could expect death soon.[75] In fact, Amsdorf, only twenty days younger than Luther, survived his friend by nearly twenty more years. At the time of Luther's death, Amsdorf was almost at the end of his active career. During that career, he had secured the city of Magdeburg for the Lutheran faith and tried to lead the diocese of Naumburg in a similar way as its bishop. But the last eighteen years of his life, which he spent "retired" from any official position, would be even more significant than his career as an active reformer. As an elder statesman, his words commanded respect. His ideas were not always well developed. The written record of his thought suggests that he did not grasp the richness of Luther's proclamation of the Gospel as fully as many of Luther's students in the next generation did. Yet, because he defended his understanding of Luther's legacy, he became a symbol and model for many of Luther's younger pupils who opposed Melanchthon's stance after the Smalcald War. Amsdorf's support and encouragement helped that particular interpretation of Luther's message gain stature. That interpretation likely would have commanded attention and respect among Luther's followers even without Amsdorf's aid, and to be sure, he should not be called "the father of Lutheran orthodoxy"; but his role in the Late Reformation did significantly shape the subsequent Lutheran "Orthodox"

74 Jonas's letter to Amsdorf, insofar as it is extant, is printed in Christof Schubart, *Die Berichte über Luthers Tod und Begräbnis* (Weimar: Böhlau, 1917), 1–10; Amsdorf's letter to Major is on p. 17. Major's reply is printed in Gustav Kawerau, "Zwei Briefe aus den Tagen des Todes Luthers," *Theologische Studien und Kritiken* 70 (1907): 468–471. Amsdorf's letter to Jonas is found in *Der Briefwechsel des Justus Jonas*, ed. Gustav Kawerau, reprint (Hildesheim: Olms, 1964), 2:184, and his letter to Johann Friedrich in Karl Eduard Förstemann, *Denkmäle, dem D. Martin Luther von der Hochachtung und Liebe seiner Zeitgenossen errichtet* (Nordhausen: Förstemann, 1846), 129–130. Amsdorf also received a brief report of Luther's death with an expression of sadness from his nephew Georg, who was studying in Wittenberg at the time, Schubart, *Berichte*, 33. On the apocalyptic spirit of the time, see Robin Barnes, *Prophecy and Gnosis, Apocalypticism in the Wake of the Lutheran Reformation* (Stanford: Stanford University Press, 1988), and Volker Leppin, *Antichrist und Jüngster Tag. Das Profil apokalyptischer Flugschriftenpublizistik im deutschen Luthertum 1548–1618* (Gütersloh: Gütersloher Verlagshaus, 1999).

75 WA Br 11:132.

formulations of Luther's positions. Amsdorf's voice in the disputes of the 1540s through the 1560s echoed in many parts of the Formula of Concord, and the Formula set the agenda and shaped the terminology for much of seventeenth-century Lutheran theology.

Amsdorf's quarter century of service as a pastor with the responsibilities of superintendent and bishop had not changed his theological concerns from those developed through his earliest years with Luther in Wittenberg. Amsdorf continued to react vehemently against the legalistic works-righteousness he remembered learning as a child and as a university student. He was as determined as ever to affirm with Luther the sovereignty of God and the exclusivity of grace as expressed in the sacrifice and life-giving resurrection of Jesus Christ for the salvation of believers.

The polemical skills Amsdorf had developed during his active career prepared him well for the mission of his last eighteen years of life. The events of 1546, 1547, and 1548 were turning points for Amsdorf, convincing him more than ever that the last times had arrived. So he devoted the rest of his life to defending Luther's message against those who, he believed, were betraying the heart of Luther's theology. In the 1530s and early 1540s, Amsdorf had objected to Melanchthon's views on good works, the role of the human will in salvation, and the Evangelical Church's relationship to Rome. After 1547, Amsdorf decried even more harshly what he believed were similar views advanced by Melanchthon's disciples. He thought their teaching all too closely resembled elements of medieval theology, introducing what he believed to be papist belief and practice in Wittenberg itself. The affinities Amsdorf saw between these teachings and those of his scholastic professors in Leipzig and Wittenberg and the cathedral canons in Magdeburg who wanted to burn him at the stake led Amsdorf to aim his piercing, well-practiced polemic at his fellow members of the Wittenberg circle. It is Amsdorf's attempts to defend God's glory and Christian consciences in the years after Luther's death that comprise his most significant legacy. The events of those years, then, are the focus of the rest of this book.

2

AGAINST THE ADIAPHORISTS, WHO SUBMIT TO THE ROMAN ANTICHRIST

Amsdorf's Ecclesiology in the Controversies over the Interims

JUDGMENT ON THE HOUSEHOLD OF GOD

In 1521, Emperor Charles V outlawed Martin Luther and his followers throughout the German empire in what is commonly called "the Edict of Worms." Only circumstances beyond Charles's control kept him from carrying out this decree for a quarter century. By 1546, the situation in his far-flung empire had settled down enough so that Charles could finally move against those whom he perceived as not only rending the holy robe of Christ's vicar but also tugging at the imperial mantle. The emperor singled out the two most powerful Evangelical princes, Philip of Hesse and Johann Friedrich of Saxony, as rebellious subjects. In this way, he was able to give some members of the Smalcald League an excuse for not coming to their aid and, in the case of Duke Moritz of Saxony, even for actively taking part in the Habsburg military effort against these two princes. By singling out Landgrave Philip and Elector Johann Friedrich as violators of imperial law, Charles was trying to avoid the appearance of a crusade against the whole Evangelical faith, an offensive which might have incited the wavering Lutheran princes to unite with these two prominent leaders of the Smalcald League. The act of organizing that league was but one of the charges Charles brought against Johann Friedrich and Philip (though, in fact, Philip had been barred from the League by his colleagues because of his illegal bigamy). Johann Friedrich and Philip also had gone to war against Duke Heinrich of Braunschweig-Wolfenbüttel in 1542 and 1545, and Heinrich had been appealing to the emperor from one of Philip's jails ever since, requesting an imperial order for his release. Charges had been lodged against Johann Friedrich in the imperial court since 1542 also for his forcible seizure of the bishopric of Naumburg-Zeitz and his forcible seizure of the Stift ("foundation," a monastic-like institution of canons charged with saying masses for the dead) at Wurzen.[1]

Ill will between Johann Friedrich and his neighbor and cousin, who was also Philip of Hesse's nephew and son-in-law, Duke Moritz of Saxony, also worked to Johann Friedrich's and Philip's disadvantage. Johann Friedrich's use of force in Naumburg-Zeitz, Wurzen, and Braunschweig-Wolfenbüttel aggravated Moritz. He viewed these actions as incursions on the balance of power in the Saxon lands. Their great-grandfather, Frederick II, had divided his lands between his elder son, Ernst, and his younger son, Albert. Ernst's sons, Frederick the Wise and, after Frederick's death, his brother Johann, had received the title "elector" and significantly more territory than their uncle Albert. Because of this, Albert's eldest son, Duke George, nursed a bitter grudge against his "Ernestine" cousins; it was only exacerbated by George's sincere dedication to the old faith and the Roman obedience. However, George's brother who succeeded him, Heinrich, and his wife Katharina, duchess of Mecklenburg, introduced Luther's Reformation to the "Albertine" lands in 1539. Their son Moritz carried forward the reformation his parents began in their lands, in the area called Meissen in eastern Saxony. But in spite of their mutual Lutheran faith and his parents' high regard for Johann Friedrich, Moritz still developed an antipathy toward his electoral cousin that was akin to his uncle George's dislike of the electoral branch of the family.

Moritz was twenty years old in 1541 when he succeeded his father. He had been trained as a soldier and had volunteered for service in the Habsburg armies. He also became a friend of Charles V and his brother, King Ferdinand. At the Diet of Regensburg in 1546, Charles resolved to make use of this friendship as he drafted plans to act against Philip and Johann Friedrich. After a month of difficult negotiations, Moritz signed a treaty with the Habsburg brothers on June 19, 1546, pledging his loyalty and service to them. Moritz pressed them for guarantees that the Evangelical faith would be preserved, but Charles refused to incorporate such guarantees into the treaty. He did verbally promise that Moritz would not be required to renounce his faith.

Because the emperor had been preparing for war in other ways as well, such as signing a treaty with Pope Paul III on June 7 and garnering support and

1 The following events and developments are described on the basis of Franz Lau and Ernst Bizer, *A History of the Reformation in Germany to 1555*, trans. Brian A. Hardy (London: Black, 1969), 157–206; Georg Mentz, *Johann Friedrich der Grossmütige 1503–1554* 2 (Jena: Fischer, 1908): 313–562, 3 (1908): 1–112; and Hildegard Jung, *Kurfürst Moritz von Sachsen, Aufgabe und Hingabe* (Hagen: Jung, 1966), 57–96, 104–167.

declarations of neutrality from some Evangelical princes, Philip and Johann Friedrich decided to take the initiative, hoping to gain an advantage by striking first. They marched south toward Habsburg lands in July, initiating the military confrontation that Charles desired.

But because they were unable to agree on a common strategy, Philip and Johann Friedrich frittered away any advantage their initial moves may have won. Charles declared Johann Friedrich an outlaw on July 20 and in the next month ordered Moritz to enforce the imperial ban against his cousin. Between late October and Christmas, Moritz occupied most of electoral Saxony. At the end of December, Johann Friedrich abandoned the effort with Philip in the south to return to Saxony. Johann Friedrich advanced steadily, moving out of his own territory into Moritz's. But Moritz's ability to withstand a long siege at Leipzig, starting in January 1547, delayed Johann Friedrich's advance and thus prevented him from inflicting a decisive defeat upon the ducal Saxon forces. When spring came, Charles marched into Saxony with imperial and Spanish troops. The Habsburg army overtook and defeated the forces of Johann Friedrich and Philip at Mühlberg in Saxony on April 24, 1547. Both princes were taken prisoner. On May 19, 1547, Johann Friedrich was forced to sign the "Wittenberg Capitulation," surrendering his electoral title and lands. His sons retained some areas in Thuringia, but Wittenberg and much of the land he ruled were given to Moritz. Charles also gave the electoral title to Moritz as a reward for his service in the war.

During the Smalcald War, Bishop Nikolaus and the Wittenberg faculty gave Johann Friedrich their wholehearted support as he defended their faith. Amsdorf sold the episcopal jewels at his elector's request and raised other funds from the diocese for the war effort. Amsdorf also published his first tracts since coming to Zeitz, arguing that Johann Friedrich was not guilty of disobeying higher authorities but rather was merely defending his faith against the papal party. Amsdorf called Charles an enemy of Christ and refused to recognize him as a Christian emperor. He also warned of impending judgment on the household of God. The Germans were about to receive punishment for their failure to live according to God's Word as they had received it from Luther's proclamation of the Gospel.[2]

2 On Amsdorf's preparation for war, see Peter Brunner, *Nikolaus von Amsdorf als Bischof von Naumburg* (Gütersloh: Mohn, 1961), 148, and Hans-Ulrich Delius, "Der Briefwechsel des Nikolaus von Amsdorf als Bischof von Naumburg-Zeitz (1541–1546)," Habilitationsschrift, University of Leipzig, 1968. Amsdorf republished his *Ein kurtzer ausszog auss der Chronica Naucleri* at this time. (One printing appeared without location in 1545, and another was published by Heinrich Steiner in Augsburg.) He also issued *Bvllla des grossen Ablass welchen der Bapst Paulus der Dritte zu diesem Zuge vnd Ausreuttunge der Lutherischen Ketzereyen gegeben hat. Mit einner Vorrhede des Ehrwirdigen jnn Gott Herrn Niclaus Ammssdorff Bischoff zur Naumburgk etc.* (Erfurt: Wolfgang Stürmer, 1546), and *Ein Christlich gebet darin der Churfurst zu Sachssen etc. Seinne*

Amsdorf also vented his anger against Moritz; the threat of a ducal invasion of Amsdorf's bishopric jeopardized his retention of the office of bishop.[3] Indeed, soon after the outbreak of hostilities, Amsdorf joined Johann Friedrich's family in the fortress Grimmenstein at Gotha.

The imperial victory in the Smalcald War did cause Amsdorf's retirement from the bishopric of Naumburg-Zeitz. After the defeat at Mühlberg, he first moved to Weimar, the primary seat of the new government of Johann Friedrich's three sons, Johann Friedrich the Middler (age eighteen), Johann Wilhelm (sixteen), and Johann Friedrich the Younger (ten). Amsdorf advised not only the young lords, as Johann Friedrich's sons were called, but also Johann Friedrich himself, whose imperial death sentence had been commuted to life imprisonment. As he moved with the emperor's company and other members of his own court, including the court artist Lukas Cranach, Johann Friedrich received letters of consolation and encouragement from Amsdorf, especially commending Johann Friedrich's refusal to compromise his faith with the Roman party.[4] Amsdorf particularly lauded Johann Friedrich's steadfast rejection of the newly formulated imperial religious policy, popularly dubbed "the Augsburg Interim."[5] Amsdorf, along with others, promoted the idea that Johann Friedrich was a martyr for the Gospel.[6]

It was when Moritz's troops permitted the election of Julius Pflug to the bishopric of Naumburg-Zeitz that Amsdorf was officially forced into retirement from his post. Pflug was the courtier whom the cathedral chapter of Naumburg-Zeitz had elected for the position in 1541, but Johann Friedrich had prevented him from taking office by quickly making Amsdorf the bishop instead in this disputed territory. People still called Amsdorf "bishop" even after he was forced to give up his post. He also retained some of the functions of the office of supervisor for

---

vnschuldt: jtziges Kriegs: vor Gott vnd aller Welt offentlich bekent (s.l., 1546), a brief prayer with Amsdorf's polemical introduction.

3 In a manuscript, "Ein trost, warnung vnd vermanung wider des Gottlosen Hertzog Moritz. A. 1546," Wr, ETLFB 39:72a–79a, edited in Ernst-Otto Reichert, *Amsdorf und Das Interim*, ed. Hans-Otto Schneider (Leipzig: Evangelische Verlagsanstalt, 2011), 167–175. Cf. Christian Winter, "Nikolaus von Amsdorf und Moritz von Sachsen," in Dingel, *Amsdorf*, 177–195. Winter edited "Ein trost, warning vnd vermanung," as well as other writings of Amsdorf against Moritz in Dingel, *Amsdorf*, 197–215.

4 J. C. E. Schwarz, "Johann Friedrich's des Grossmüthigen Correspondenz mit Brück und Amsdorf vor dem Augsburger Reichstage 1547," *Zeitschrift des Vereins für Thüringische Geschichte und Altertumskunde* 1 (1854): 408–414.

5 Volker Leppin, "'. . . und das Ichs nicht fur gotlich sondern fur eine lauter teufels lehr halte und achte,' Die theologische Verarbeitung des Interims durch Johann Friedrich den Älteren," in Dingel und Wartenberg, *Politik*, 111–123.

6 Robert Kolb, "The Legal Case for Martyrdom, Basilius Monner on Johann Friedrich the Elder and the Smalcald War," in *Reformation und Recht. Festgabe für Gottfried Seebaß zum 65. Geburtstag*, eds. Irene Dingel, Volker Leppin and Christoph Strohm (Gütersloh: Kaiser/Gütersloher Verlagshaus, 2002), 145–160.

the churches in the ducal lands, including ordaining new pastors.[7] But certainly Amsdorf's life turned to a new chapter when he was no longer the official bishop of Naumburg-Zeitz in 1547. Personally, he had lost his official position within the structures of church and society. More importantly, though, in this new chapter of life, Amsdorf faced a new environment, one in which the very life and future of the Wittenberg reform was at stake and what he regarded as false interpretations of Luther's message were arising from within the Wittenberg circle.

THE WONDERFUL AND WINSOME INTERIM OF AUGSBURG

By the end of the Smalcald War, Charles's relationship with the papacy was deteriorating, but his grip on his German empire had never seemed firmer. So on September 1, 1547, Charles opened what was labeled as an "armored" diet, because of the presence of so many imperial and Spanish soldiers. At the diet, he appointed a commission under Sebastian von Heusenstamm, the elector-archbishop of Mainz, to draw up an interim solution for the religious problems of the German empire. The Council of Trent had gone into recess while the Smalcald War took place, so Charles's stated goal was to establish provisions for unity in the church until the Council of Trent could issue its final decisions and decrees. When the commission reached an impasse, three theologians were charged with composing a settlement: Michael Helding, suffragan bishop of Mainz; Julius Pflug, the newly installed bishop of Naumburg-Zeitz; and from the Evangelical side, Johann Agricola, who had celebrated Johann Friedrich's defeat in the Smalcald War as God's retribution for the harsh treatment Agricola had received from the elector in Wittenberg in 1540. These three theologians, with the aid of King Ferdinand's court preacher and two Spanish theologians in Charles's retinue, completed their work in early March 1548.[8]

7 Gehrt, *Konfessionspolitik*, 39–40, 61–65; Daniel Gehrt, "Der 'Erzbischof' von Thüringen? Nikolaus von Amsdorf und die Genese der ernestinischen Landeskirche nach dem Schmalkaldischen Krieg," in Dingel, *Amsdorf*, 217–236.

8 The text of the Interim is found in *Das Augsburger Interim von 1548, deutsch und lateinisch*, ed. Joachim Mehlhausen, (Neukirchen-Vluyn: Neukirchener Verlag, 1970). The controversy over the Augsburg Interim is documented in C&C, volume 1, with twenty-two publications edited with comment. On the Augsburg Interim, see Charles P. Arand et al., *The Lutheran Confessions, History and Theology of the Book of Concord* (Minneapolis: Fortress, 2012), 173–177; Irene Dingel, "Culture of Conflict in the Controversies Leading to the Formula of Concord (1548–1580)," in *Lutheran Ecclesiastical Culture, 1550–1675*, ed. Robert Kolb (Leiden: Brill, 2008), 18–34; Joachim Mehlhausen, "Der Streit um die Adiaphora," in *Bekenntnis und Einheit der Kirche. Studien zum Konkordienbuch*, eds. Martin Brecht and Reinhard Schwarz (Stuttgart: Calwer Verlag, 1980), 105–128; Horst Rabe, *Reichsbund und Interim. Die Verfassungs- und Religionspolitik Karls V. und der Reichstag von Augsburg 1547/1548* (Cologne/Vienna: Böhlau, 1971); Gustav Wolf, "Das Augsburger Interim," *Deutsche Zeitschrift für Geschichtswissenschaft* NF 2 (1897–1898): 39–88; Georg Beutel, *Über den Ursprung des*

In mid-April, the text of the Interim was published. Then on May 15, Charles published his "Declaration on Religion," an agenda for how the major elements of the Interim would be imposed on his Evangelical estates in practice. The settlement propagated by these two documents required Evangelicals to accept Roman dogma, though it did concede Communion in both kinds and the marriage of Evangelical priests who obtained special permission from their bishops. The Roman Catholic princes and bishops objected to the settlement being imposed on their lands. So the Augsburg Interim and the "Declaration on Religion" were decreed solely for the Evangelical estates of the empire.[9]

Charles began to execute his plan to exterminate the Lutheran movement, using his military force largely from his Spanish lands. He quickly enforced the Interim in Evangelical principalities and towns wherever possible, and his soldiers met with various degrees of compliance in different parts of the south German lands. Several hundred pastors were driven into exile from the duchy of Württemberg alone.[10] In the long run, the priests who filled their positions were too few and too unpopular to bring about much change in the local people's religious belief and practices, though there were a few exceptions like the city of Constance. However, none of that was immediately apparent. Instead, it appeared the Habsburgs could succeed in snuffing out the Evangelical churches.

Yet many of the Evangelicals chose to resist. Among the princes ordered to introduce the terms of the Interim were the dukes of Saxony, Johann Friedrich's sons. Some of their counselors urged them to comply, but they responded to the imperial order with a clear rejection.[11] Their clergy assembled to discuss it in Weimar July 26–28, 1548, and rejected compromise of any kind, following the example of Melanchthon, who let his sharp critique of the Interim's text escape

---

Augsburger Interims (Dresden: Paessler, 1888). Beutel traced the origin of the Augsburg Interim to a document drawn up by the Cologne theologian Johann Gropper in 1546. Reworked by Pflug, it was presented to the Augsburg Interim committee, where it was revised further. Agricola translated it into German.

9 On the dispute over Charles's original intentions for the Interim, see Lau and Bizer, *History*, 210–211, who agree with Leopold von Ranke, followed by Wolf, "Interim," 84–87, that Charles originally intended to enforce the Interim throughout the empire. According to Robert Stupperich, "Melanchthons Gedanken zur Kirchenpolitik des Herzogs Moritz von Sachsen (nach bisher unveröffentlichten Papiern aus den Jahren 1546/53)," *Reformatio und Confessio. Festschrift für D. Wilhelm Maurer*, eds. F. W. Kantzenbach and Gerhard Müller (Berlin: Lutherisches Verlagshaus, 1965), 89, Melanchthon agreed. Walther von Loewenich, "Das Interim von 1548," *Von Augustin zu Luther* (Witten: Luther Verlag, 1959), 394, agrees with the argument of Wilhelm Maurenbrecher that Charles had always intended the settlement for Evangelicals only; cf. Beutel *Über den Ursprung*, 107–116, for details of the argument. For his subjects still loyal to the pope, Charles issued in July 1548 his *Formula Reformationis per Caesarem Maiestatem Statibus Ecclesiasticis in Comitijs Augustanis ad deliberandum proposita* . . . (Augsburg, 1548).

10 Armin Kohnle, "Die Folgen des Interims am Beispiel Württembergs," in Dingel and Wartenberg, *Politik*, 83–96; Christian Peters, "Der Macht des Kaisers widerstehen. Die süddeutschen Theologen und das Augsburger Interim," in Dingel and Wartenberg, *Politik*, 65–81.

11 Gehrt, *Konfessionspolitik*, 42–44.

into print.[12] He had made the difficult decision to remain in Wittenberg and defend the integrity of its university even when that part of Johann Friedrich's territory fell to Moritz in Charles's mandate. Melanchthon could have followed the young lords to their corner of Saxony, but he feared Moritz would close the university in Wittenberg to eliminate competition with the older Saxon university in Leipzig. The duke did not and instead co-opted Melanchthon as an advisor. Moritz was walking a fine line between his subjects—in both his newly acquired lands and those he had inherited—and Charles. By adding Melanchthon to his group of counselors, he hoped to convince many of his subjects that his administration would ensure continuity with Luther's reform. It was while Melanchthon was serving in this capacity as Moritz's advisor that his condemnation of key elements in the Augsburg Interim escaped into print.

Amsdorf with others also published criticisms of the Interim. One of Amsdorf's letters to Johann Friedrich during this time commended him for rejecting the Interim, even while in captivity to the emperor. Amsdorf was also among the clergy members who assembled in Weimar in July 1548, working with Justus Menius, the superintendent of the churches in Gotha and Eisenach, and with Caspar Aquila, the superintendent of the churches in Saalfeld, to compose the ducal Saxon ministerium's confession of rejection.[13]

However, before Amsdorf published any criticism of the Interim under his own name, he wrote a critique that remained unpublished. That initial critique shows many of the same objections that Amsdorf put forward against the Interim in his later published critique. In his first critique, he did not criticize the initial articles of the Interim, which treated the human creature before and

---

12 Irene Dingel, "'Der rechten lehr zuwider.' Die Beurteilung des Interims in ausgewählten theologischen Reaktionen," in *Das Interim 1548/50, Herrschaftskrise und Glaubenskonflikt*, ed. Luise Schorn-Schütte (Gütersloh: Gütersloher Verlag, 2005), 292–311; see also Timothy J. Wengert, "'Not by Nature *Philoneikos*,' Philip Melanchthon's Initial Reactions to the Augsburg Interim," in Dingel and Wartenberg, *Politik*, 33–49; Günther Wartenberg, "Philipp Melanchthon und die sächsisch-albertinische Interimspolitik," *Lutherjahrbuch* 55 (1988): 60–82; Luther D. Peterson, "The Philippist Theologians and the Interims of 1548: Soteriological, Ecclesiastical, and Liturgical Compromises and Controversies within German Lutheranism," Ph.D. dissertation, University of Wisconsin-Madison, 1974, 113–214, 312–446; and Emil Sehling, *Die Kirchengesetzgebung unter Moritz von Sachsen 1544–1549 und von Georg von Anhalt* (Leipzig: Deichert, 1899).

13 The emperor's order is printed in August von Druffel, *Briefe und Akten zur Geschichte des sechszehnten Jahrhunderts*, 2 (Munich: Rieger, 1875), 136. The "Christian Declaration of the Preachers of the Young Lords . . . on the Interim" was not supposed to be printed, in order to avoid provoking imperial action against ducal Saxony, but it appeared within the year, *Der Prediger der Jungen Herrn Johans Friederichen Hertzogen zu Sachssen etc. So[e]nen Christlich Bedencken auff Das Interim* (Magdeburg, 1548), and was reprinted twice in the following year. Gustav L. Schmidt, *Justus Menius, der Reformator Thüringens* 2 (Gotha: Perthes, 1867), 42, credits Menius with sole authorship of the memorandum. Schmidt had apparently not seen Amsdorf's manuscript, "Aduersus Interimstas singulorum articulorum breuis confutatio Nicolai Amsdorfij iam exulis," Wr, ETLFB 40:263a–275a, edited by Reichert, *Amsdorf*, 184–196. On Amsdorf's role in the composition of this "Declaration," see Reichert, *Amsdorf*, 101–103.

after the fall into sin and Christ's redemption of sinners. In so doing, he failed to take issue with its statement about fallen sinners retaining a weak and damaged freedom of the will, able to perform virtuous acts even though in God's sight they are sinful creatures and their works are unacceptable. Amsdorf's deep-seated suspicion of ascribing any spiritual power to the human will outside grace did not rule out an appreciation of civil righteousness, and even in criticizing a document he found odious for several reasons, he did not condemn such a view—perhaps because he intended to strike a blow against the Interim without giving a detailed analysis.

Amsdorf's primary concern with the Interim was its treatment of salvation from sin, in accord with his typical prioritization of the theological matters of the relationship between God and human creatures versus the relationship between human creatures. The Interim reflected the influence of reform-minded followers of the papacy in Germany, but its dogmatic statements repeated the medieval doctrine that Amsdorf had rejected. It did not satisfy him or Melanchthon, or any other leading voice of the Wittenberg circle or other Evangelical camps, except Caspar Huberinus, a pastor in Augsburg and also nearby Öhringen.

Article four of the Interim taught that human love must be joined to the gift of Christ's merit in order to complete the justification of a sinner. Article eight of the Interim expressed similar ideas. Amsdorf saw in this doctrine the same stumbling block preventing true consolation of guilty consciences, and it resembled positions he had condemned alongside Luther in the earliest days of the Wittenberg movement. Amsdorf had battled precisely this concept of salvation in conversations and debates with the cathedral canons in the streets of Magdeburg. When a person must rely on some contribution of his own for assurance of salvation, Amsdorf warned, either false security and proud presumption arise in his heart or despair and doubt. Amsdorf commented that a believer can avoid either alternative only when he has confidence in God's mercy, when he recognizes that God saves through faith, and then when, as a result of that faith, he loves, serves, and fears God in response to divine mercy. Amsdorf spoke of that love as a fruit of faith, the result of faith in one who is already righteous. In this way, Amsdorf again recalled one of the earliest illustrations of good works he learned from Luther thirty years before.[14]

Amsdorf also objected to the Interim's ecclesiology. His hostility toward Rome led him to attack episcopal apostolic succession. Bishops loyal to Rome had persecuted the Gospel and had substituted human forms and external

14 Reichert, *Amsdorf*, 185–187.

ceremonies for true adoration of God. He had always believed the true Church of God was a persecuted remnant, for he and those in the Wittenberg movement had consistently seen that Satan is always attacking the true disciples of Christ in some way or other. The church of Rome was part of the great church of glory that always strives to eliminate the small, scorned true Church gathered around Christ's Word. Amsdorf additionally attacked the burdens of the papal decrees and canons that the Interim supported. In particular, he denied its affirmation that the church has power to issue authoritative interpretations of Scripture. He argued that Scripture is subject to no one, and it rules the Church, not vice versa. The ability to interpret Scripture is a gift from the Holy Spirit, not the prerogative of the current tenant of some office such as pope or bishop. Only the Antichrist arrogates and usurps the right to authoritatively interpret Scripture, Amsdorf wrote. Thus, Amsdorf rejected all claims that the bishop of Rome possessed particular power or position in terms similar to what Amsdorf had learned from Luther since 1520 and had argued repeatedly in Magdeburg.[15]

Amsdorf also critiqued the Interim's treatment of the Sacraments, reiterating his theological positions from earlier in his career. He declared that Christ instituted only two Sacraments: Baptism and the Lord's Supper. He affirmed that the sacramental bread and wine convey Christ's body and blood, and he rejected transubstantiation. He also rejected the sacrificial definition of the mass. He noted that the Interim did deny that the performance of the mass merits forgiveness of sins. But the Interimists were still bound to canons of the Roman Church that affirmed the idea, Amsdorf argued. He was convinced, then, that the Interim would not change the beliefs of faithful members of the Roman party on the issue of the sacrifice of the mass. Amsdorf, like several of his Saxon colleagues (e.g., Menius and Aquila) in their analyses of the Interim, attacked a number of other practices that reflected the medieval church's false use of ritual. These included invocation of the saints, masses for the dead, belief in purgatory, regulations for special celebrations and instructions for sacramental practice—all set forth in the final arguments of the Interim. Amsdorf and his colleagues regarded these as unacceptable reinstatements of papal abuses and tyranny and perversions of the Gospel itself.[16]

Amsdorf's influence lent weight to the tide of criticism that was growing in all parts of the Wittenberg circle. For instance, the pastors in Goslar, where

15 Reichert, *Amsdorf*, 187–190. On Amsdorf's ecclesiology, see Wolf-Friedrich Schäufele, "Kirche Christi und Teufelskirche. Verfall und Kontinuität der Kirche bei Nikolaus von Amsdorf," in Dingel, *Amsdorf*, 57–90.

16 Reichert, *Amsdorf*, 190–194.

Amsdorf had helped introduce Luther's Reformation twenty years earlier, called upon Amsdorf's authority as the standard by which the Augsburg Interim should be judged.[17] Even though Amsdorf's unpublished critique was presented article-by-article, neither it nor the Saxon preachers' memorandum based on it offered a detailed analysis of the Interim. Both overlooked some of the Interim's teachings. Amsdorf intended only to show his princes and others who received copies of his critique that the Interim could not be accepted and introduced without offending the will of God.

By the autumn of 1548, Charles's Spanish troops had withdrawn from Saxony. The young lords were able to hold control of their domains. Moritz faced such fierce popular discontent that he could not carry out his imperial master's will in his own lands, much less threaten Johann Friedrich's sons in their lands. Bishop Nikolaus might have courted martyrdom if the opportunity had presented itself; but instead, the political situation was such that it seemed there was no threat in insisting that the young lords stand firmly against any compromise with Amsdorf's longtime enemy, the papal party. Amsdorf urged them to stand firm, arguing that if their father refused to accept the Interim under duress in prison, his sons, free and safe in Saxony, could hardly do otherwise. However, it is hard to imagine Amsdorf was not well aware that renewed military aggression against adherents of Luther's message was possible.[18]

Such criticism as Amsdorf's was bound to reach the wider reading public in this age in which so much could be brought to the attention of larger audiences through print. As mentioned above, Melanchthon had professed no knowledge of plans to publish his critique of the Interim, but his criticism, more thorough than Amsdorf's, was published in Magdeburg in mid-July, heightening the emperor's enmity toward him.[19] In mid-summer, Erasmus Alber and Caspar Aquila, two exiles from the Wittenberg circle, fueled the fires of popular opposition with diatribes against the document that had deprived them of their pulpits,[20] and Amsdorf decided to toss on a published torch of his own.

---

17 Sehling 7, 2, 2:291.

18 Johann Friedrich's rejection of the Interim is printed in Gustav L. Schmidt, "Bekenntniss Johann Friedrichs des Grossmüthigen über das Interim," *Zeitschrift für die historische Theologie* 38 (1868): 431–444. Amsdorf wrote the young lords on November 4, 1548, that their time was the time of persecution prophesied by Daniel and Christ, in which one must either deny Christ and his Word or die. He urged them to remain faithful to Christ; Gustav L. Schmidt, "Drei Briefe Amsdorfs über das Interim, Aus dem Sächs. Ernest. Gesamtarchiv zu Weimar mitgeteilt," *Zeitschrift für die historische Theologie* 38 (1868): 469–471.

19 CR 6:924–942; MBW.R 5:297–298, Nr. 5182. The memorandum, signed by Bugenhagen, Cruciger, Major, Pfeffinger, and Melanchthon, was published under the title *Bedenken aufs Interim des Ehrwirdigen und Hochgelarten Herrn Philippi Melanthonis* (Magdeburg 1548); edited in C&C 1:40–75.

20 On Aquila, see Georg Biundo, "Aquila und das Interim," *Theologische Literaturzeitung* 74 (1949): 587–592. On Alber, see Waldemar Kawerau, "Erasmus Alberus in Magdeburg," *Geschichts-Blätter für Stadt und Land*

The critique Amsdorf published in 1548 against the Interim, entitled *Answer, Creed, and Confession on the Wonderful and Winsome Interim*, was addressed to his former parishioners in Magdeburg.[21] However, his moral authority as Luther's beloved comrade, strengthened by his new status as a living martyr or "exile of Christ,"[22] made his judgments also very influential among like-minded Evangelicals throughout the empire, even though Amsdorf did not hold an official position. As in his initial, unpublished reaction, Amsdorf did not analyze in detail the individual articles of the Interim in this published treatise, but he did raise the specter of returning Romanism, effectively convincing his readers to dig in and resist the papal and imperial forces, which could exert their military power again at any time, it seemed.

The principal fault of the Interim, Amsdorf told his friends in Magdeburg, was its article on the mass. Participation in the mass had been a pillar in the popular medieval understanding of religion. Inadequate catechesis of the German tribes at the time of their conversion meant that many of the religious structures from the traditional German religions were imported into their belief and practice of Christianity. One such traditional belief was that contact with the gods had to be established by human initiative, primarily through ritual forms and under the supervision of a hierarchy. This idea heavily influenced the theology of the mass in medieval Christianity, while Luther's realization that God takes the initiative in establishing and maintaining his relationship with his human creatures, through his Word, especially the promise of the Gospel of Jesus Christ, completely reversed the dependence on ritual action in the mass and other sacred activities in Lutheran teaching.[23] Because Amsdorf had grasped this massive shift in the perception of what it means to be Christian, he argued in his criticism of the Interim that the papacy had invented the doctrine of the sacrifice of the mass and had thus usurped God's authority. Christ instituted the Sacrament for the communion of the people, not as a sacrifice. Amsdorf also stoked the laypeople's hostility toward the Roman clerical system

---

Magdeburg 28 (1893): 19–29. Flacius and others followed in their train; see Oliver K. Olson, *Matthias Flacius and the Survival of Luther's Reform* 2nd ed. (Minneapolis: Lutheran Press, 2011), 84–111; Luka *Ilić*, *Theologian of Sin and Grace, The Process of Radicalization in the Theology of Matthias Flacius Illyricus* (VIEG 225; Göttingen: Vandenhoeck & Ruprecht, 2014), 75–97. See also Wilhelm Preger, *Matthias Flacius Illyricus* 2 (Erlangen: Bläsing, 1861), 541–550, for Flacius's titles against the Augsburg Interim.

21 *Antwort, Glaub, vnd Bekentnis auff das schöne vnd liebliche INTERIM* (Magdeburg: Michael Lotter, 1548), AS, 29–51, C&C 1:204–236. The treatise is dated August 1. On Amsdorf's overall reaction to the Augsburg Interim, see Armin Kohnle, "Nikolaus von Amsdorf und das Interim," in Dingel, *Amsdorf*, 135–151.

22 Irene Dingel, "Die Kultivierung des Exulantentums im Luthertum am Beispiel des Nikolaus von Amsdorf," in Dingel, *Amsdorf*, 153–175.

23 See Robert Kolb, *Martin Luther and the Enduring Word of God: The Wittenberg School and Its Scripture-Centered Proclamation* (Grand Rapids: Baker Academic, 2016), 46–65.

by denying any difference between priest and laity in the action of celebrating the Sacrament. He argued in a somewhat tortuous fashion that if, according to Roman theology, the layperson did not sacrifice the mass by participating in the ritual, then neither did the priest. Such an argument was more likely to impress the average person in Magdeburg who deeply trusted Amsdorf's judgment more than it would impress Julius Pflug, the new bishop of Naumburg, or even other Evangelical theologians.[24] Amsdorf's argumentation was usually stronger than the logic he employed in this case.

Amsdorf recognized that the Interim's concession of Communion in both kinds and marriage for priests could impress the laypeople, for these issues had been some of his own primary examples of papal tyranny in his earlier writing. However, Amsdorf reminded his readers that the tyranny that now so easily accepted these practices had not long before burned many believers in Christ who had supported these practices. Christ had always approved Communion in both kinds and clerical marriage, Amsdorf argued. Therefore, by claiming that they had the power to first eradicate and now permit these practices, the authors of the Interim demonstrated that they were not God's obedient servants but rather the devil's smithies.[25]

Amsdorf also warned against the "clever phrases" of the Interim. For example, the Interim's discussion of justification accentuated "faith"; however, that word, which sounded Evangelical, was not being used in the same way the Wittenberg reformers used it. The Interim meant that faith initiates justification and that love or works complete it, according to scholastic teaching. Amsdorf called upon all good Germans to reject this teaching. According to Amsdorf, that idea was the "opinion of Peter Maluenda," Charles's clerical counselor, who had assisted the committee in composing the Interim. Amsdorf clearly disapproved of such Roman Catholic Spanish theology, and he wanted his fellow German adherents of the Reformation to do so as well. His writings against the papacy had never blatantly appealed to German national feeling, but in his attack on the Interim, he was willing to casually allude to such a sentiment.[26]

In the 1530s, Amsdorf had appealed to 1 Timothy 4:1–3 to warn laypeople that Paul's words about deceitful spirits arising, teaching doctrines of demons, including forbidding marriage and commanding abstinence from foods, were being fulfilled in their time. In his public critique of the Interim, Amsdorf returned again to those ideas, this time decrying the Interim's rules on fasting.

---

24 AS, 32–38.

25 AS, 30–33.

26 AS, 38–42.

He stirred up old hostilities against the papacy by demonstrating the false basis of its claims of supremacy in the church and by showing how papal practice corresponded to the marks of the Antichrist in Scripture.

Amsdorf wrote in the critique of the Interim he directed to the citizens of Magdeburg that he heard the Antichrist knocking at the door of their city. He believed the Antichrist had already burst through the gates of Evangelical fortresses in the south, such as the duchy of Württemberg and some Evangelical towns like Nuremberg and Strassburg, which had reached compromise settlements with imperial forces. The final battle between God and Satan had begun, and in *Answer, Creed, and Confession*, Amsdorf called his former parishioners and others like them to battle against Satan's forces manifest in the Antichrist. Christ had come to bring not peace but a sword (Matthew 10:34) and had called upon his followers to abandon all else to follow him (Matthew 19:21). Christ warned against false prophets, which included the Roman see and court and their followers, according to Amsdorf. Believers should have nothing to do with them. The Empire's Evangelical governments had been commanded to substitute the Interim for the faith and practice of the Augsburg Confession. Persecution had come. Amsdorf wanted to fire up his people so that they would stand firm in the true faith that he had nourished in their midst.

Amsdorf believed that the emperor's forced imposition of the Interim would restore the common people's medieval misconceptions of the Christian message. Therefore he believed anything short of total opposition to the Interim would only confuse the common people about the break the Wittenberg reformers had made from Rome. If it was acceptable for Luther's followers to trade some of their beliefs and practices for peace and safety in the face of persecution by imperial forces, parishioners would certainly think more articles of the Evangelical faith could be bartered away. This uncompromising position, therefore, caused Amsdorf to privately disapprove of the suggestion by his Wittenberg colleagues, including Melanchthon, that some points of the Interim could be accepted even if many had to be rejected.[27] In the midst of what Amsdorf saw as the eschatological battle, his longtime friend Melanchthon was trying to avoid a fight. Although Amsdorf refrained from composing a public, printed attack on Melanchthon's position in the summer of 1548, Amsdorf believed that Luther's cause was at more risk if elements of the reform program were compromised rather than if imperial troops occupied Saxony; therefore, he rejected any acceptance of the Interim as dangerous.

---

27 "Antwort auff philippi Melanthonis bedengken auffs Interim," Wr, ETLFB 41:42a–45a; Reichert, *Amsdorf*, 181–183; cf. Melanchthon's positions, CR 6:930–932, 934, 939–940.

In the middle of all of this, however, Amsdorf's strident opposition to the Interim was embarrassing to the government of the young lords. They were pursuing a policy designed to avoid offense to the emperor as much as possible. Amsdorf's association with the young lords might have even endangered the imprisoned Johann Friedrich. By the end of 1548, Amsdorf had resolved to leave Weimar for Magdeburg, where he felt most at home.

CHIEF SECRETARY IN THE CHANCERY OF GOD

Magdeburg's municipal ambitions and its Evangelical faith had coincided nicely in the formulations of city policy during and after Amsdorf's superintendency. Amsdorf had done his work well; when the war clouds rolled in over north Germany in the late 1540s, the citizens of Magdeburg were firmly committed to the cause of Luther, as well as to their city's ambitions toward total self-governance. The city refused to pledge allegiance to Archbishop Albrecht's successor in 1545, Johann Albrecht of Brandenburg-Ansbach, who claimed his rights as governor of the city. At the same time, the municipal government strengthened the city's defenses by destroying a monastery and a church built against the city wall. Some weeks later, it increased pressure on the cathedral chapter, still secure in its enclave in the "new town." On June 1, 1546, the emperor issued an edict condemning these actions by the Magdeburg council. The council responded by summoning the cathedral chapter for a face-to-face confrontation about the relationship between the cathedral chapter and the municipal government. The canons fled; the council forbade the celebration of mass in the whole city, and it seized the cathedral chapter's treasures.

As a member of the Smalcald League, Magdeburg hosted a diet in February 1547 for League member governments in north German lands. When Johann Friedrich was defeated two months later, Magdeburg refused to come to an accommodation with the demands of its new imperial "protector," Moritz, and the emperor; on July 26, 1547, the city was placed under imperial ban, which suspended the city's rights of trade and supply. The ban also meant the city's holdings in the countryside could be plundered and seized by its enemies. If the municipal government persisted in defying the imperial ban, it risked military action. However, capitulating meant almost certain loss of the city's liberties and some likelihood of the Augsburg Interim being imposed on its citizens. The city council appealed to Elector Joachim II of Brandenburg and to Moritz, their neighboring princes who benefited most from the city's economic activities, to try to mitigate the ban and mediate a settlement with Charles. The city leadership insisted that it only wanted to defend its faith, not to offend the emperor. So the city did not capitulate, and it did offend the emperor. Charles instructed Moritz to reduce the city and end its opposition to his policies. As a result, from 1547 to 1551, Magdeburg merchants were subject to harassment as they traveled in the surrounding countryside, particularly in electoral Saxony and in Brandenburg. So when Amsdorf wrote his *Answer, Creed, and Confession on the Wonderful and Winsome Interim* addressing the Magdeburg citizenry, the threat of military force being used against the city was real; when he later returned there in 1548, he accepted the possibility of suffering persecution alongside his former parishioners and their neighbors. In early 1550, Moritz mounted a siege of Magdeburg which finally forced the city's accommodation in November 1551. The city's role in the Evangelical propaganda campaign against the emperor's and Moritz's religious policies, a campaign in which Amsdorf was a major contributor, as well as the city's general defiance of the emperor had provoked the emperor and Moritz too far.[28]

In 1792, nearly two hundred fifty years after these tensions, as German-speaking lands were being caught up in the throes of the initial invasion of French revolutionary forces, a theologically trained teacher and governmental official in Prussia named Heinrich Rathmann described Magdeburg's resistance to Charles V as defying imperial attempts to master the consciences and faith of the Germans. Magdeburg's defense of "freedom of conscience, freedom of religion, and the freedom of the citizenry" had demonstrated "what religious zeal, a love of freedom, and patriotism are able to accomplish when combined." He believed the example of the city lived on in the imagination of the populace even to his day.[29]

---

28 Friedrich Hülsse, *Die Stadt Magdeburg im Kampfe für den Protestantismus während der Jahre 1547–1551* (Halle: Verein für Reformationsgeschichte, 1892), 12–18; Olson *Flacius*, 147–210; Ilić, *Theologian*, 87–97. Thomas Kaufmann's assertion that the Wittenberg circle saw the events surrounding the siege of Magdeburg as "the end of the Reformation" misinterprets the evidence. The leaders of church and city in Magdeburg saw their efforts as the preservation of the Reformation and its continuation in completing the implementation of the Wittenberg reform program; cf. Kaufmann's *Das Ende der Reformation. Magdeburgs "Herrgotts Kanzlei" (1548–1551/2)* (Tübingen: Mohr/Siebeck, 2003), VII, 484. Those who signed the Magdeburg *Confession* insisted that "even though Luther is dead, he still lives, and the work that God has established through him—even if it appears in these days that it is almost snuffed out, it will remain to the Last Day and eternally, and it will be expanding into more lands and peoples . . . ," C&C 2:465. The Magdeburg remnant expected that God would revive the movement he had unleashed with Luther; cf. Nathan Rein, *The Chancery of God. Protestant Print, Polemic and Propaganda against the Empire, Magdeburg 1546–1551* (Aldershot: Ashgate, 2008), 232, who rightly argues: "The Reformation, in their [the Magdeburg theologians and their civic supporters] view had not failed. Rather, what had failed was a false and misleading version of the Reformation, one that depended more on controlling individuals and reinforcing lordly authority than on holding fast to the Gospel in preparation for the end times."

29 Quoted by Georg Schmidt, "Freiheit, Pluralität und Frieden. Überlegungen zur deutschen

THE ADIAPHORISTS ARE CHRIST'S ENEMIES

During his residence in Magdeburg, from 1548 to 1552, Amsdorf was not alone. His position coincided quite precisely with that of the members of the Wittenberg circle who were fleeing from the enforcement of the Augsburg Interim and were assembling in Magdeburg. Modern scholars designate his comrades-in-arms as "Gnesio-Lutherans." The Gnesio-Lutheran party and its opponent, the Philippist party (dubbed "the adiaphorists" by the Gnesio-Lutherans),[30] traced their roots to divergent interpretations of Luther's and Melanchthon's instruction from the 1530s. The two groups shaped their specific identities in the context of a conflict between Magdeburg and Wittenberg over a compromise Moritz put forward after the Augsburg Interim, as he tried to give the appearance of complying with the imperial mandate. In this way, Moritz's government hoped to appease the Habsburgs while also appeasing the nobles and towns in his lands who were faithful to Luther.

In 1547, Moritz found himself caught in a corner between his subjects—peasants, citizens of the towns, and noblemen, who largely were uncompromising supporters of the spirit of Luther's Reformation—and Moritz's Habsburg friends, who had not kept their word about his right to retain the Evangelical faith in his lands. Moritz tried to convince the Saxons that he was protecting them from the threat of Spanish troops, doing his best to preserve Saxon freedom and Luther's message, even while in fact the new elector was trying to stave off a Habsburg invasion by giving token compliance to Charles's religious program.

Charles had apparently shocked Moritz by imposing the Augsburg Interim only on his Evangelical subjects and by insisting that Moritz also bring his church into compliance with the Interim. To stave off revolt by nobles and towns in his lands, Moritz needed to maintain Luther's teaching in the electorate while also protecting his subjects from religious persecution from the imperial government. Some other Evangelical princes had capitulated to Charles and Rome. Joachim of Brandenburg had done so by political choice, and Ulrich of Württemberg at the point of a sword. The presence of Charles's military force and his Spanish soldiers in Saxony made Moritz step gently when he returned in the

Reformationsgeschichte," in *Faszinierende Frühneuzeit. Reich, Frieden, Kultur und Kommunikation, 1500–1800. Festschrift für Johannes Burkhardt zum 65. Geburtstag*, eds. Wolfgang E. J. Weber and Regina Dauser (Berlin: Akademie Verlag, 2008), 92–93.

30 It is important to note that in this period the term "Interimist" was almost always reserved for supporters of the Augsburg Interim, not for supporters of the Leipzig "Interim." Instead, those who supported the Leipzig "Interim" were labeled "adiaphorists" by their opponents.

summer of 1548; and he continued to do so even after the imperial troops had withdrawn from Saxony, convinced that they could easily return.[31]

In a series of memoranda, Moritz's theologians had counseled against accepting the emperor's new religious policy in the Augsburg Interim. They had conceded, however, that certain compromises concerning "adiaphora"—neutral practices neither commanded nor forbidden in Scripture—might be made in order to save Lutheran pulpits for Lutheran preachers. So in the middle of Moritz's conundrum following the Augsburg Interim, he formed a commission, including the Wittenberg theology professors on that commission, to draft a proposal of an official religious policy for the electoral Saxon territorial diet to ratify in December 1548. The proposal rested upon a fundamental principle laid out in article fifteen of the Augsburg Confession and its Apology: because the Christian faith is a matter of conveying and believing the teaching of Scripture rather than of ritual performance, sacred acts and religious activities that are not prescribed or forbidden by the Bible can be accepted or altered as best serves the church.[32]

The document emerged from a series of consultations by Moritz's special commission. In the commission's meetings between July and November in 1548, the new Roman Catholic bishops of Naumburg and Meissen were also called in by Moritz's lay and theological counselors as they tried to work out this new program for Saxon ecclesiastical life. The result, though, of their efforts was a proposal for Moritz's Leipzig diet that satisfied no one. So when the territorial diet met in December 1548, the nobles and towns of electoral Saxony at the territorial diet summarily rejected the Leipzig "Interim," and it did not gain the force of law in Saxony. But the debate over the document continued to rage for years afterward. The very effort to compromise placed the Gospel proclaimed by Luther in doubt, according to Amsdorf and his colleagues, so they sharply criticized the Leipzig Proposal and the spirit behind it. Those who helped formulate the document defended themselves, and the conflict grew ever more bitter.[33]

---

31 Jung, *Moritz*, 199–207; S. Issleib, "Moritz von Sachsen, 1547–1548," *Neues Archiv für sächsische Geschichte und Altertumskunde* 13 (1892): 197–219.

32 Charles P. Arand, "The Apology as a Backdrop for the Interim of 1548," in Dingel and Wartenberg, *Politik*, 211–227.

33 The text of the Leipzig Proposal is found in *Politische Korrespondenz des Herzogs und Kurfürsten Moritz von Sachsen*, eds. Johannes Herrmann and Günther Wartenberg, 4 (Berlin: Akademie Verlag, 1992), 254–260, and C&C 2:367–440 in the version edited by Flacius and Gallus. The stages through which the document went are found in CR 6:839–845, 853–857, 865–874, 888–890, 908–912, 924–942; MBW.T 5:266, Nr. 5110; 5:276–277, Nr. 5130; 5:282, Nr 5141; 5:293, Nr. 5170; 5:297–299, Nr. 5182; ET: *Sources and Contexts of the Book of Concord*, eds. Robert Kolb and James A. Nestingen (Minneapolis: Fortress, 2001), 184–196. The controversy over the Leipzig Proposal is documented in C&C 2, which contains eleven key documents from the controversy. The text of the Leipzig "Proposal" was published by the Magdeburg theologians before portions of it appeared in print from Moritz's government: *Der Theologen bedenken odder (wie es durch die ihren inn offentlichem Druck genannet wird) Beschluss des Landtages zu Leipztig . . . welches bedenken odder Beschluss*

In order to associate the Leipzig "Interim" with the Augsburg Interim, the Gnesio-Lutherans almost immediately dubbed the proposal "the Leipzig Interim," though scholars today call it "the Leipzig Proposal."[34] It did teach that divine grace is the cause of the justification of the sinner and that God's mercy, not human merit, saves sinners through forgiveness of sins based on faith in Christ's atoning work. It avoided the phrase "through faith alone," however, and it emphasized the role of good works, calling them "necessary for salvation." It stated that the human will does play a role in the reception of God's mercy, even though the believer receives that mercy through God's gracious working in him.[35] Without clear-cut affirmation of the exclusive role of grace and faith, the Leipzig "Proposal" or "Interim" invited Gnesio-Lutheran attacks, even though its authors tried to maintain Luther's understanding of grace and faith in salvation.

This issue was overshadowed at first, however, by the more obvious concessions on adiaphora found in the Leipzig "Interim." The document prescribed the rite of confirmation (holding out hope it could be transformed from a spectacle into an examination of faith), private confession before Communion, and extreme unction practiced "according to apostolic usage." These directives in themselves were not offensive to most of the document's critics; but their inclusion alongside Baptism and the Lord's Supper implied that this was a return to the seven sacraments of the Medieval Church. Much of the Latin rite of the Roman mass as well as traditional vestments, bells, and sacred vessels were also to be restored. If the Leipzig "Interim" was adopted, then, the worship service would once again appear much as it had in electoral Saxony before Luther. The Leipzig "Interim" also conceded the restoration of the canonical hours and services in memory of the dead; it reestablished many of the old festival celebrations, including Corpus Christi and Marian holidays. It forbade eating meat on

---

wir, so da wider geschrieben, das Leiptzigische Interim genennet haben (Magdeburg: Melchior Lotther, 1550). On the "adiaphoristic controversy," see Ernst Koch, "Der Ausbruch des adiaphoristischen Streits und seine Folgewirkungen," in Dingel and Wartenberg, *Politik*, 179–190; Joachim Mehlhausen, "Der Streit um die Adiaphora," in Brecht and Scharz, eds., *Bekenntnis und Einheit*, 105–128; Preger, *Flacius*, 1:108–204; and Hans Christoph von Hase, *Die Gestalt der Kirche Luthers. Der casus confessionis im Kampf des Matthias Flacius gegen das Interim von 1548* (Göttingen: Vandenhoeck & Ruprecht, 1940); Robert Kolb, *Confessing the Faith, Reformers Define the Church, 1530–1580* (Saint Louis: Concordia, 1991), 63–91; Oliver K. Olson, "Politics, Liturgics, and *Integritas Sacramenti*," in *Discord, Dialog, and Politics. Studies in the Lutheran Reformation's Formula of Concord*, eds. Lewis W. Spitz and Wenzel Lohff (Philadelphia: Fortress, 1977), 74–85. As mentioned above, it is important to distinguish the criticism of the Augsburg Interim from the controversy over adiaphora and the Leipzig Proposal; see Irene Dingel, "Culture of Conflict in the Controversies Leading to the Formula of Concord (1548–1580)," in *Lutheran Ecclesiastical Culture*, 1550–1675, ed. Robert Kolb (Leiden: Brill, 2008), 28–39. See also Günther Wartenberg, "Moritz von Sachsen," TRE 23:302–311, and the literature listed on pages 49 (note 12) and 52–53 (note 20) above.

34 Günther Wartenberg, "Das Augsburger Interim und die Leipziger Landtagsvorlage zum Interim," in Dingel and Wartenberg, *Politik*, 15–32.

35 CR 7:51–59, 61–64; MBW.R 5 311, Nr. 5210.

Fridays and Saturdays as a healthy dietary measure—not on biblical grounds but in accordance with the civil ordinances of the empire (meaning the Augsburg Interim). Concessions on ordination were the most difficult portions of the document to compose and the most challenging portions for which to win support from the members of the diet. The Leipzig "Interim" accepted the ordination of pastors by bishops obedient to Rome. Moritz's advisors were willing to recognize the bishops' right to ordain pastors if those bishops would abstain from persecuting the Gospel. Local Evangelical control over clergy was theoretically insured by a provision that candidates for ordination had to be presented to the bishop by the patron of the congregation, either the town council or a nobleman.[36]

The Leipzig Proposal was an eclectic document of theology not only because of the opposing pressures Moritz felt, but also because the theologians who helped forge the document came to the task with different sets of concerns. Prince Georg von Anhalt was the spiritual administrator of the bishopric of Merseburg from 1544 to 1550, where Moritz's brother August administered secular affairs—an arrangement similar to Amsdorf's at Naumburg. Von Anhalt had always supported conservative, cautious reform of liturgical and other ritual practices.[37] Johann Pfeffinger, Daniel Greser, Hieronymus Weller, and Anton Lauterbach, leaders of the churches in Leipzig, Dresden, Freiburg, and Pirna, had worked with Moritz for some years, and they had found him supportive of the Evangelical faith. The Wittenberg professors, on the other hand, were integrating themselves into a new government system with largely unfamiliar secular officials, and they had found protection and support under Moritz. What all these leaders had in common was a willingness to trust Moritz to protect their faith in the future.

Among the Wittenberg professors, Melanchthon had quickly become an advisor on whom Moritz could depend. Even though he had written in support of the princes of the Smalcald League before and during the war, he had criticized Johann Friedrich's conduct of the fighting. When the elector was defeated, Melanchthon was certainly sympathetic toward him; but Melanchthon's loyalties to his university in Wittenberg influenced him even more strongly. Because Moritz had supported instead of closed the Wittenberg university, Melanchthon

36 CR 7:215–221, 260–263; MBW.R 5:383, Nr. 5350; 5:400–401, Nr. 5387.

37 Sehling, *Kirchengesetzgebung*, esp. 21–84, and Franz Lau, "Georg III. von Anhalt (1507–1554), erster evangelischer 'Bischof' von Merseburg. Seine Theologie und seine Bedeutung für die Geschichte der Reformation in Deutschland," *Wissenschaftliche Zeitschrift der Karl Marx Universität Leipzig. Gesellschafts- und Sprachwissenschaftliche Reihe* 3 (1953/1954): 139–152.

served him loyally. Melanchthon also believed that the Lord of history had made Moritz his new secular lord. Moritz needed Melanchthon, believing an alliance with him would help convince the Saxon subjects that Moritz had not deserted Luther's cause. He offered Philip protection against Charles's threatened reprisal. Melanchthon also did not expect the current crisis to last long, since his astrological calculations suggested that Charles's death was imminent.[38] His long-held conviction that concessions in adiaphora might be made in order to promote peace and unity in the church certainly also played a role in his attitude toward the drafting of the Leipzig "Proposal."[39] In this matter, Melanchthon sought security and tranquility for his elector, his university, and his fellow Saxons. He did not share Amsdorf's view of the Saxon Lutherans' situation, nor Amsdorf's willingness to risk another imperial military occupation of Saxony. As a professor and counselor for the new elector of Saxony, Melanchthon was less free to espouse such radical views than an exiled bishop was in an outlawed city.

Melanchthon's colleagues in Wittenberg, among them Johannes Bugenhagen and Georg Major, followed his leadership in drafting and then supporting the Leipzig "Interim." The Magdeburg theologians as well as the leading clergy of Hamburg and other cities began to attack it as a compromise with the Antichrist soon after it was leaked to them. In one instance, Bugenhagen circulated a letter defending the Leipzig Proposal to King Christian III of Denmark in July 1549 and soon thereafter to several other princes. Nascent party lines within the Wittenberg circles had not cut off communication between its members on opposite sides of the divide. Thus, it is no surprise that Amsdorf obtained a copy of Bugenhagen's letter. Amsdorf wrote a response that remained unpublished in which he reproduced Bugenhagen's defense and then laid out critical arguments against it.[40]

Magdeburg had quickly become a center for anti-Interim agitation since few printing presses outside Magdeburg enjoyed the same freedom its printers did. When the electoral Saxon territorial diet refused to accept or ratify the Leipzig "Interim," the program remained theoretical on paper. Moritz's government

---

38 On Melanchthon's use of astrology and the place of astrology in Wittenberg instruction, see Claudia Brosseder, *Im Bann der Sterne: Caspar Peucer, Philipp Melanchthon, and andere Wittenberger Astrologen* (Berlin: Akademie-Verlag, 2004).

39 See the discussions in Stupperich, "Melanchthons Gedanken," 85–87; Jung, *Moritz*, 203–205; Hase, *Kampf*, 27; and Otto Vogt, "Melanchthon's und Bugenhagen's Stellung zum Interim und die Rechtfertigung des Letzteren in seinem Jonascomment," *Jahrbücher für protestantische Theologie* 3 (1887): 5–8; cf. also Martin Lohrmann, *Bugenhagen's Jonah: Biblical Interpretation as Public Theology* (Minneapolis: Lutheran University Press, 2012).

40 "Doctor Pomers brief an einen Fürsten mitt scholien, darinne ehr offentlichen bekennet, das man verbotten hat zu Wittembergk fleisch feil zu habenn, wies denn auch im Leipzigischen Interim stehet vnnd verwilliget ist. Daraus wirdt man wol sehen wer gelogen hat," Jäger, *Amsdorf*, 65–89.

introduced some of its provisions in some places. Wittenberg was not one of them but Torgau was; the deposition of pastors in Torgau who opposed Moritz's "Interim" gave Magdeburg "martyrs" to celebrate in this controversy.[41] Exiled pastors from locations in the south gathered in Magdeburg, and there were no restrictions on printers' subject matter. During these years, Amsdorf was a prominent leader among those criticizing the opponents of the Gnesio-Lutheran understanding of Luther's theology and the situation after the Smalcald War. Caspar Aquila told Duke Albrecht of Prussia that Magdeburg had assumed the role of the "chancery of God," and Amsdorf could be regarded as its chief secretary. Older exiles such as Caspar Aquila and Erasmus Alber were joined by some of Luther's last students, Nikolaus Gallus, Matthaeus Judex, and later Johannes Wigand and Matthias Flacius Illyricus. Flacius emerged as the leader of the critics of the Interim, although he did not leave his post as instructor of Hebrew in Wittenberg until nearly two years after Amsdorf and others had arrived.[42] Some of the exiled pastors and theologians received calls to local congregations. One such young pastor from Regensburg, Gallus, assumed the superintendency of the Magdeburg church. Others, like Flacius, found purpose in writing critiques of the developing German ecclesiastical scene. Flacius, Gallus, Amsdorf, and others in several towns in northern Germany carried out a print campaign against the Leipzig "Interim" for a decade.[43] In his writings, Flacius argued that a time of persecution calls Christians to confess their faith clearly and boldly. Such a time also requires rejecting concessions on adiaphora, like those proposed by the electoral Saxon theologians in their Leipzig "Interim." A secular government's mandate imposing these adiaphora on the church constituted a denial of Christian liberty and of the faith itself, Flacius argued. Such concessions comply with and grant concessions to the enemy of the faith in ways that confuse the faithful and obscure the heart of the biblical message.[44]

---

41 Issleib, "Moritz von Sachsen," 195–197; Sehling, *Kirchengesetzgebung*, 96–112. On the difficulties at Torgau, see Albert Chalybaeus, *Die Durchführung des Leipziger Interims* (Chemnitz: Oehme, 1905), 8–72. Amsdorf asserted that pastors in Colditz and Freiburg were also persecuted in the enforcement of Moritz's policies, *Das D. Pfeffinger seine missethat böslich leugnet* (Magdeburg: Ambrosius Kirchner, 1559), A2. Johannes Herrmann, "Augsburg—Leipzig—Passau. (Das Leipziger Interim nach Akten des Landeshauptarchivs Dresden, 1547-1552)." Dissertation, University of Leipzig, 1962, 160–161, confirms that pastors in other areas than Torgau were subject to legal and political pressures to bring them into compliance with electoral Saxon policy.

42 Preger, *Flacius*, 1:13–75; Mijo Mirkovic, *Matija Vlačić Ilirik* (Zagreb: Jugoslavenska akademijs znanosti i umjetnosti, 1960); Hase, *Die Gestalt der Kirche*, 34–46; Olson, *Flacius*, 147–210; Ilić, *Theologian*, 87-97; Irene Dingel, "Flacius als Schüler Luthers und Melanchthons," in *Vestigia pietatis, Studien zur Geschichte der Frömmigkeit in Thüringen und Sachsen. Festschrift für Ernst Koch*, eds. Gerhard Graf, Hans-Peter Hasse, et al. (Herbergen der Christenheit: Sonderband 4; Leipzig, 2000), 77–93.

43 Nine of these critiques are among the eleven documents edited in C&C vol. 2.

44 *Deren zu Magdeburgk so widder die Adiaphora geschrieben haben Jhres vorigen schreibens beschlus auff der*

Amsdorf's battle against this "Interim" began with private correspondence, in which he urged noncompliance with both "Interims."[45] Amsdorf's criticism, which spread rapidly by word of mouth among those in the Wittenberg circle, coupled with the public critiques by his friends, provoked Moritz's theologians to issue angry and harsh polemical rejoinders defending their prince's policies. Moritz could not afford to have his somewhat precarious hold on his new title and lands threatened by criticism from Magdeburg. Thus, his ecclesiastical establishment, including his advisors in Leipzig, especially Johann Pfeffinger and his university colleague Bernhard Ziegler, and the Wittenberg faculty, joined in that counter-criticism. In that still oral culture, the sermon served as a key means of propagating important messages to the public. Bugenhagen in Wittenberg and Ziegler in Leipzig used that forum to defend the new electoral Saxon religious policy, just as Magdeburg pulpits became venues for rejecting it. There were no secrets within the Wittenberg circle. That meant that Amsdorf received reports from friends in Wittenberg and Leipzig and knew what was being said and published about the Magdeburg theologians. Against these counterattacks from Wittenberg and Leipzig, Amsdorf directed ten tracts during 1549, 1550, and 1551.[46]

Relatively reserved in his initial criticism of the electoral Saxon stratagem, Amsdorf's tone became sharper as the months wore on and his old comrades persevered in what he viewed as compromising with the Antichrist. Initially, it seemed that Amsdorf was not eager to inject criticisms of individuals into the

---

Adiaphoristen beschuldigung vnnd lesterung die zeit jhrer belagerung vnd itzt zum teil neulich vnter diesen friedshandlungen wider sie ausgangen (Magdeburg, 1551), esp. A4a. This statement was signed by Flacius, Amsdorf, and Gallus. For other titles by Flacius supporting this position, cf. Hase, *Kampf*, 37; Preger, *Flacius*, 2:540–550.

45 Reichert, *Amsdorf*, 133–134, 241–245, treats and edits Amsdorf's epistolary reaction to a village conference at which an official of the counts of Mansfeld had tried to explain and win compliance with the Leipzig "Interim."

46 *Antwort auff der Wittenberger La[e]sterung: Quasi Magdeburgenses praedando velint defendere Evangelium* (Magdeburg, 1549); *Antwort auff Doct: Pommers scheltwort, so er auff der Cantzel aussgeschu[e]tt hat, am Sontag nach Vdalrici* (Magdeburg, 1549); *Auf die ku[e]nstliche Spottische vnd Bitterhonische ORATION So D. Ziegler zu Leiptzig am Oster Montag widder die bestendigen Lutherischen recitirt hat . . .* (Magdeburg: Michael Lotther, 1549); *Das Doctor Martinus kein Adiaphorist gewesen ist, vnd Das D. Pfeffinger vnd das buch on namen jhm, gewalt vnd vnrecht thut* (Magdeburg: Christian Rödinger, 1550); *Das nie no[e]ter ist wider den Ro[e]mischen Antichrist zu schreiben, vnnd predigen jtzundt zu dieser zeit do die Adiaphoristen mit gewalt in jhrenn schriften dringen, das man sich vnter den Bapst begeben, vnd jhn fu[e]r ein Bischoff vnd hirten der seelen widderumb erkennen vnnd annemen sol* (Magdeburg: Michael Lotther, 1551); *Das itzund die rechte zeit sey, Christum vnd sein Wort zu bekennen, vnd auff keine andere zu warten sey. Etliche Spru[e]che das man den Adiaphoristen nicht trawen noch gleuben sol* (Magdeburg, 1551); *Eine erinnerung an die Deudschen, das sie einfeltigen jhre Su[e]nde, so sie diese Fu[e]nff jar her gethan haben, erkennen vnd bekennen sollen, sich bekeren vnd bessern, Auff das sie selig, vnd mit dem hauffen nicht verdampt werden* (Magdeburg, 1551), AS, 51–61; *Ein kurtzer Brief an alle Christen, sonderlich an die gelerten* (Magdeburg: Michael Lotther, 1551); *Das Doctor Pomer vnd Doctor Maior mit jren Adiaphoristen ergernis vnnd zurtrennung angericht, Vnnd Derhalben sie vnd nicht wir zu Magdeburg vom Teuffel erwegt seint, wie sie vns schmehen vnd lestern* (Magdeburg, 1551); *Etliche Spru[e]che aus Doctoris Martini Lutheri schriften, Darinne er, als ein Adiaphorist sich mit dem Bapst hat vergleichen wollen* (Magdeburg, 1551). For an overview of the opposing Philippist position, see Peterson, "Philippist Theologians," 312–446.

controversy over the "Interim"; but it was inevitable that both sides would eventually attack those they believed to be propagating errors. Polemics can hardly ever be constrained to the issues under debate, and theologians are necessarily part of theology, especially when it is under dispute. That may be particularly true when theologians are also writing as agents of political forces. For the men bound to defend Moritz's political decisions in the theological and ecclesiastical realms, it became necessary to mount personal attacks against the Magdeburg theologians in order to discredit those who threatened the success of Moritz's plans. The Magdeburg theologians, Amsdorf chief among them, in turn consciously supported the Ernestine branch of the Wettin ruling family of Saxony, the sons of Johann Friedrich, in their claims to the political rights of the electoral title and the lands.[47] Many of the Magdeburg theologians felt betrayed by Melanchthon and those with him, since Amsdorf had opposed all associations with the papacy as anathema for some thirty years. Melanchthon also felt his friends in Magdeburg had betrayed him by failing to see the necessity of avoiding imperial-Spanish occupation of Saxony. He was also confused why his former colleagues in Magdeburg were not accepting this application of article fifteen of the Augsburg Confession and its Apology, while they believed it was not an application of article fifteen but rather a reversal of the fundamental position of the Reformation.

It is somewhat remarkable that the tone of the debate in 1549 did not immediately become bitter. It is also noteworthy that Amsdorf avoided entering the public lists against Melanchthon.[48] Instead Amsdorf concentrated on scolding and arguing with others in the electoral Saxon camp and criticizing their work. For his part, Melanchthon tried to not get involved in the exchange of tracts between Wittenberg and Magdeburg or its allies in Hamburg, even though Hamburg's ecclesiastical superintendent, Johann Aepinus, and its leading theological voice, Joachim Westphal, marshalled criticism against the Augsburg Interim, the Leipzig "Interim," and other aberrations coming from electoral Saxony in the 1550s.[49]

---

47 Robert Kolb, "Legal Case," 145–160.

48 Amsdorf composed a critique of Melanchthon's "Epistola scripta Ecclesiae Dei in urbe Francofurto ad ripas Meni," CR 7:321–326; MBW.R 5:412–413, Nr. 5409. Amsdorf's criticism remained in the manuscript, "Antwort auff das scriptum so sich anfehen In tanto Ecclesiarum mestitia etc vnd itzt hin vnd wider ausgebreitet wird wider die ihenigen so die meischnische Interim vnd alcoran nit wolln annemen. A. 1549," Wr, ETLFB 41:17a–27a; Reichert, *Amsdorf*, 231–240. Theodor Pressel, *Nicolaus von Amsdorf* (Elberfeld: Friedrichs, 1862), 161, believed the tract had been written against Julius Pflug. Otto Lerche, in *Amsdorff und Melanchthon, eine kirchengeschichtliche Studie* (Berlin: Lerche, 1937), 18, identified Melanchthon as the object of the memorandum's critique. This has been established in detail by Ernst-Otto Reichert, "In Tanta Ecclesiarum Mestitia . . . Eine Antwort Nikolaus von Amsdorffs an Philipp Melanchthon," *ZKG* 78 (1967): 253–270.

49 Roxane Wartenberg, "Städtische Theologen und das Interim, Johannes Äpinus in Hamburg," in Dingel

When Amsdorf analyzed what he perceived as the motivations behind the Leipzig "Interim," he was not sympathetic. He did not recognize any difference between his situation, as an exile in a city that had not yet felt the full weight of imperial wrath, and Melanchthon's and his colleagues' situation in service to a prince who was trying to stave off the threat of another imperial invasion. Amsdorf apparently also was not persuaded by Melanchthon's fear that the University of Wittenberg might be closed and that important anchor for Luther's message and mission might be lost. Amsdorf's appraisal of the reality of the imperial threat as well as the fragility of the university's future may not have differed greatly from Melanchthon's, but he believed compromise was a foolish and erroneous response to the situation.

Amsdorf scoffed at the adiaphorists' attempt to construct a reasonable compromise with the emperor and thus with the papal party. Their patched-together "Interim" could not satisfy Charles, he argued. Furthermore, the whole idea of compromise was the work of a spirit other than Christ's. Moritz's theologians did not come as black devils at midnight to condemn the Gospel openly, Amsdorf said, but rather as a snow-white devil who lured believers to deny Christ and his Word through silence and to submit to the Antichrist under the veneer of Christian discipline. The adiaphorists, therefore, were trying to serve two masters—Christ and Antichrist—Amsdorf believed.[50]

Amsdorf shared Flacius's position on the Leipzig "Interim." He detested the spirit and the letter of it at two levels. First, Amsdorf believed if the Leipzig "Interim" was introduced into parish life, it would indicate to the common people that medieval, papistic religion was being restored. The fact that its errors were being promoted by those who occupied chairs on Luther's own faculty made the matter worse. Worship in a congregation bound by this policy would have looked and sounded much like worship services had thirty years earlier. This apparent denial of the Reformation—even though, or perhaps because, it was expressed in externals—would have greater significance for the laypeople, the folks in the marketplace and the street, than all the words of explanation learned theologians could write or say to defend their concessions. The laypeople had long been Amsdorf's concern, and once again he became their advocate. Second, Amsdorf believed that even if the Leipzig "Interim" was not put into practice, its spirit indicated reliance on human diplomacy and deceit rather

and Wartenberg, *Politik*, 97–102; Irene Dingel, "Strukturen der Lutherrezeption am Beispiel einer Lutherzitatensammlung von Joachim Westphal," in *Kommunikationsstrukturen im europäischen Lutherum der Frühen Neuzeit*, ed. Wolfgang Sommer (Gütersloh: Gütersloher Verlagshaus, 2005), 32–50.

50 "Antwort auff Scriptum," Wr, ETLFB 41, 23a; Reichert, *Amsdorf*, 236–237; *Antwort auff Pommer*, A2b–A8b.

than on God. It betrayed a willingness to play fast and loose with God's Word in an effort to truckle to the pope. Amsdorf felt compelled to warn Saxon Lutherans that these maneuverings in the preparation of the proposal for the Leipzig diet were threats to their faith.

In addition to the Leipzig Proposal's soteriology as mentioned above, particularly the omission of the word "alone" from statements about "salvation by faith,"[51] Amsdorf objected with his Magdeburg colleagues also to the document's ecclesiology. The practical problems connected with the concessions of this "Interim" were legion. Particularly vexing were those that granted bishops obedient to the pope the right and power to ordain local pastors. At best, papist bishops ordaining Evangelical pastors would compromise the pastors in the eyes of their Evangelical parishioners.[52] The argument from Moritz's theologians that the external practices prescribed by Moritz's proposal could be accepted because they were adiaphora offended Amsdorf. Like Flacius, he observed that adiaphora cease to be neutral matters when they are prescribed, and he attacked the adiaphora the "Interim" chose to introduce. As with the Augsburg Interim, Amsdorf attacked the Leipzig "Interim's" prescriptions on fasting, calling them doctrines of the devil (based on 1 Timothy 4:1–3). He also charged that Moritz's "Interim" would restore the mass as a spectacle and thus exchange Christ's simple Communion service for an idolatrous, humanly-devised ceremony. Amsdorf was not criticizing the Leipzig "Interim" for restoring the Roman doctrine of the mass, since he acknowledged it was not doing that. However, he was accusing the "Interim" of restoring certain liturgical practices that would cause confusion. He viewed the worship service as the focus of the daily practice of the faith.[53] And he knew that for the Saxon congregants, the externals and appearances would speak a louder confession than doctrinal definitions. Therefore, to Amsdorf, the so-called matters of "adiaphora" were not inconsequential issues which could be conceded.

He upheld that, in theory, external ceremonies and ecclesiastical practice and customs were neutral matters that could be altered according to Christian freedom. They did not have to be uniform. He even insisted that the Magdeburg theologians did not object to practices just because they differed from their own. However, commanded uniformity contradicts the freedom Christians have in these matters. And though Christians may be free to make choices about ecclesiastical practice, that does not negate the importance of discernment and wisdom

51 *Das itzund*, A3b; *Das Dr. Martinus*, C1a–b.

52 *Das nie no[e]ter*, A4a–b.

53 *Auff Oration Zeiglers*, A2b–A3a.

to make these choices responsibly. Amsdorf believed the best ecclesiastical practices that could be chosen out of Christian freedom were those that were simple and Scriptural, since human pomp and ceremony are inimical to faith because they concentrate the worshiper's attention on their pageantry instead of the Word and God's grace in Christ.[54] This conviction reflected Luther's fundamental redefinition of the Christian faith as a matter of God's speaking to sinners rather than of human religious activities to please God. As a result, with Gallus and Flacius, Amsdorf did not at that time protest the use of certain vestments for reasons inherent to the vestments,[55] but rather because he feared that restoring what had been discarded with Luther's reforms implied to the common people that the reform movement had surrendered to Rome. He was willing to permit old customs to continue, but he steadfastly opposed any suggestion of compromise by returning to former usages, potentially casting a shadow over the Evangelical faith of parishioners.

Alongside his discussion of the prescriptions of the Saxons' "Interim," Amsdorf expressed his resentment of the Wittenberg theologians' arrogance toward those gathered in Magdeburg. Moritz's professors seemed to regard the Magdeburg theologians as irresponsible, intellectual riffraff and seditious rabble. Amsdorf's response to this was similar to what he had said to combat Anabaptists and Sacramentarians in his earliest days in Magdeburg. Christ had chosen simple fishermen to build his Church. God had called Luther rather than the *lumina mundi*, such as Cardinal Pietro Bembo, Erasmus, or the French reform-minded Guillaume Budé, to reform his church because Luther, like Paul, did not want to preach Christ to the wise or tailor his message to the wisdom of the learned of the world (1 Corinthians 1:26–29). Therefore, Amsdorf, too, would glory in his own simplicity and lack of learning. Amsdorf was even willing to go so far as to say the Church has always suffered most from the learned, who substituted philosophy for God's Word. Amsdorf asserted that pagan writings are a plague upon piety.[56] This observation is not found in Amsdorf's earlier writings, even against Erasmus. In fact, Andreas Karlstadt was placing similar blame

54 *Auff Oration Zeiglers*, A4a, B1b–B2a, D2a; *Ein kurtzer Brief*, A3b–A4a; "Antwort auff Scriptum," Wr, ETLFB 41:21b–22a; "Das die newen leiptzigischen Ceremonien nebern der reine[n] Lehr des Euangelij nicht künnen noch mögen angenom[m]en und gehalden werden," October 22, 1550, Jäger, *Amsdorf*, 22–61.

55 *Auff Oration Zeiglers*, A2a, B1a; *Das Dr. Martinus*, B4a; *Das Pomer und Maior*, A3b. As the "Chorrock" was being forced upon some pastors in electoral Saxony and some were being deposed because of their refusal to wear it, Amsdorf joined Flacius and Gallus in opposing the re-introduction of the garment (though, like Amsdorf, they did not object to its use if that usage was not associated with compromise by revival under pressure), *Antwort M. Nicolai Galli vnd M. Fla. Illyrici auff den brief etlicher Prediger in Meissen von der frage Ob sie lieber weichen den den Corrock anzihen sollen* (Magdeburg: Christian Rödinger, 1550); Amsdorf's subscription appears on B4a.

56 *Auff Oration Zieglers*, A4a, B4a; *Das Itzund*, B3a.

on learned discourse and those who practiced intellectual pursuits, including Luther, Melanchthon, and Amsdorf, in a way the Wittenberg reformers did not accept at the time Amsdorf moved to Magdeburg.[57] Amsdorf also had previously praised how intellectually gifted Luther was. One can only conjecture how some of the most intellectually gifted of Luther's and Melanchthon's students among Amsdorf's allies in Magdeburg reacted to his argument, for their response is not recorded.

Amsdorf also bitterly resented that Moritz's theologians accused those in Magdeburg of being schismatic. He did not deny that he believed true believers needed to separate from those supporting the Leipzig "Interim." He had said he would not recognize a pastor who had played the wolf against God's people through the "Interim" and who had served two masters, Christ and the Antichrist. He continued to counsel his friends not to receive Communion from the adiaphorists. He insisted that Moritz's theologians were those at fault for the schism, not the Evangelicals. The adiaphorists had joined themselves to the Roman Antichrist. and the angel of Revelation 18:4 commanded God's people to come away from Babylon—the Roman Church, according to Amsdorf—lest God's people take part in her sins and share her plagues.[58] Moritz's theologians had changed their confession and their practice. Like King Ahab, who accused Elijah of causing unrest for Israel by confessing the truth (1 Kings 18:17), the adiaphorists were accusing the true shepherds in God's Church of starting a fight when they were defending the sheep from the wolf.[59] Amsdorf repeatedly affirmed his concern for the unity of the Church and the Evangelical faithful, but for him that unity had to flow out of a common confession. The Leipzig "Interim" was not a clear common confession and instead sought to compromise in order to gain temporal security. Therefore, Amsdorf would battle against its program and spirit. Amsdorf was convinced that the document was part of the final attempt of the ungodly to root out Luther's Gospel. In his defense of Luther's Gospel against the adiaphorists, Amsdorf began to cite Luther as an authoritative interpreter of Scripture, implying also

---

57 Amy Nelson Burnett, *Karlstadt and the Origins of the Eucharistic controversy: A Study in the Circulation of Ideas*. (Oxford/New York: Oxford University Press, 2011), esp. 28–32.

58 Johann Walther, court musician for Johann Friedrich at Torgau until his imprisonment, served Moritz and August as musician in Dresden from 1548 to 1554. Walther sought Amsdorf's counsel on communing with adiaphorists; items in their correspondence are found in Wf, Guelf. Helmst. 83:499–500; 12.9 Aug., 451 (the same letter from 1550); Helmst. 82:503–594 (dated January 8, 1553). The correspondence is discussed by Karl Brinkel, "Zu Johann Walters Stellung als Hofkapellmeister in Dresden," *Jahrbuch für Liturgik und Hymnologie* 5 (1960): 135–143. Amsdorf's position is given in detail in a memorandum, "Ob ein Christ das Sacrament von den Adiaphoristenn empfahenn moge," Wf, Guelf. Helmst. 82:505–506; 8.6 Aug., 356–357.

59 *Das Pomer und Maior*, A1b–A3a, B2b, C2b; *Das Itzund*, A4a; *Deren zu Magdeburg*, A2a, B1b.

that the Magdeburg theologians' view was faithful to Luther's teaching while the adiaphorists' was not.[60] Rather than unite with the adiaphorists, Germany needed to repent, Amsdorf argued, for to her other sins she had added failure to recognize God's gracious visitation that brought the Gospel out of the dark into the light through Luther. As the eschaton approached, all believers must reject the compromises of this "Interim" and those who had created the schism it caused, Amsdorf urged.[61]

The controversy over the Leipzig "Interim" is but one example of the mixing of political and religious concerns that marks the whole course of the Reformation. Some of Moritz's enemies labeled him "the Judas of Meissen" (the traditional seat of the Albertines), accusing him of playing fast and loose with the Gospel, stealing the electoral title and lands from his cousin, Johann Friedrich, and forcing Johann Friedrich to suffer the martyrdom of imprisonment for Moritz's perfidy. Amsdorf gave him the accolade "Antiochus" for his role in the Smalcald War and his subsequent religious policy proposals.[62] For many in the Reformation, including Amsdorf, faith and friendship, religious confession and political considerations coincided. Amsdorf's response to the Leipzig Proposal from Moritz's government was motivated by his eschatological mindset, his concern for parishioners' perceptions, his devotion to Luther's legacy, and his loyalty to his friend, Elector Johann Friedrich. However, the ultimate reason Amsdorf was willing to go against his former colleagues and friends in Wittenberg in this crisis was that he was convinced the Wittenberg theologians were sounding and acting like the enemies he had fought for years. In the end, his conviction was so strong, no bond of human relationship would induce him to give up the precious Gospel he believed Luther had recovered and proclaimed.

Leading up to the siege of Magdeburg in 1550, the writings the Magdeburg city council issued with Amsdorf and his compatriots defending their resistance to the policies of Charles V reflect the severity of distrust that had developed between the Magdeburg theologians and their former colleagues who had become the "Interimists" and the "adiaphorists." The Magdeburg theologians portrayed the city and its people as loyal to the emperor. They averred that their

60 For an overview of the use of Luther's writings as a kind of secondary authority in this period, see Johannes Hund, "Autorität und Identität. Die Bedeutung Luthers in den nachinterimistischen Streitkreisen im Bereich der Wittenberger Reformation," in *Georg Rörer (1492–1557): Der Chronist der Wittenberger Reformation*, eds. Stefan Michel and Christian Speer (Leipzig: Evangelische Verlagsanstalt, 2012), 287–311. See also Irene Dingel, "Luther's Authority in the Late Reformation and Lutheran Orthodoxy," in *The Oxford Handbook to Martin Luther's Theology*, ed. Robert Kolb et al. (Oxford: Oxford University Press, 2014), 525–539.

61 *Antwort auff Pommer*, A2b; *Eine erinnerung*, A2a–B1b.

62 *Antwort auff Pommer*, A2b; *Auff Oration Ziegler*, A4b, cf. Kolb, "Legal Case."

resistance arose only out of concern for the preservation of their Evangelical faith and ancient municipal liberties.[63] During the siege of Magdeburg, Amsdorf wrote a document for the citizens of the city entitled *Consolation for Those in Magdeburg and for All Pious Christians* in which he reminded them that the siege was a test of faith, not punishment for rebellion, and that Christ calls his own to bear such crosses (Matthew 16:24). Amsdorf compared the German princes allied with Moritz to the Jews of old, who deserted God and suffered his wrath as a result. The visitation of God's wrath on Germany had just begun. He prophesied that things would be getting worse, and he wanted to encourage God's people to trust in God's presence and providence, even as God's wrath and judgment descended over the land.[64]

The city's pastors issued the most important apology of Magdeburg policy, the ministerium's *Confession, Instruction, and Admonition of the Pastors and Preachers of the Christian Churches of Magdeburg*, on April 13, 1550.[65] It was signed by

63 Texts of some of the tracts issued by the city, its ministerium, and individual pastors are given in Fredrich Hortleder, *Der Römischen Keyser . . . Handlungen vnd Rathschläge . . . Von Rechtmässigkeit, Anfang, Fort- vnd endlichen Ausgang dess Deutschen Krieges Keyser Carls des Fünfften* 2 (Frankfurt/M: Hoffmann, 1618), 805–913. Titles published in the city in this period are given in Kaufmann, *Ende*, 493–554, and Friedrich Hülsse, "Beiträge zur Geschichte der Buchdruckerkunst in Magdeburg," *Geschichts-Blätter für Stadt und Land Magdeburg* 17 (1880), 53–68, 150–181, 211–242, 358–397.

64 *Ein Trost an die zu Magdeburg Vnd an alle fromme Christen* (Magdeburg: Christian Rödinger, 1551), A2, A4a, B3a–B4a.

65 *Bekentnis Vnterricht vnd vermanung der Pfarrhern vnd Prediger der Christlichen Kirchen zu Magdeburgk, Anno 1550, Den 13. Aprilis* (Magdeburg, 1550), issued simultaneously in Latin, *Confessio et Apologia pastorum & reliquorum ministrorum Ecclesiae Magdeburgensis, Anno 1550, Idibus Aprilis* (Magdeburg, 1550); both German and Latin texts edited in C&C 2 442–629. In a note penned in the personal copy [now in the Herzog August Bibliothek in Wolfenbüttel 183.28 Theol. (1)] of Johannes Wigand, a friend of many concerned, who later succeeded Gallus as pastor of Saint Ulrich's church in Magdeburg, Nikolaus Gallus is identified as the author of the *Confession*. Cf. Robert von Friedeburg, *Self-Defence and Religious Strife in Early Modern Europe. England and Germany, 1530–1680* (Aldershot: Ashgate, 2002), 56–90, and on the wider context of developing Protestant resistance theory, Robert von Friedeburg, "Bausteine widerstandsrechtlicher Argumente in der frühen Neuzeit (1523–1668): Konfessionen, klassische Verfassungsvorbilder, Naturrecht, direkter Befehl Gottes, historische Rechte der Gemeinwesen," in *Konfessionalität und Jurisprudenz in der frühen Neuzeit*, eds. Christoph Strohm and Heinrich de Wall (Berlin: Duncker & Humblot, 2009), 115–166. See also David Whitford, *Tyranny and Resistance: the Magdeburg Confession and the Lutheran tradition* (Saint Louis: Concordia, 2001), and Rein, *The Chancery of God*. Despite the attention given the *Confession* by modern scholars because of its influence on broader European theories of resistance to higher authorities (see Robert M. Kingdon, "The First Expression of Theodore Beza's Political Ideas," *ARG* 46 [1955]: 88–100), the document attracted relatively little attention in its own time within the German-speaking lands, perhaps because princely forces did win the battle. Despite frequent criticism of and resistance to princely abuses of power in the subsequent two centuries among Lutherans, the *Confession* appears to have played little role in the development of the conviction among Lutheran pastors that they were obliged to call those with secular power to repentance for abuses of office, cf. Robert von Friedeburg, "Die lutherische Orthodoxie und die Debatte um das Widerstandsrecht," in *Religion Macht Politik. Hofgeistlichkeit im Europa der Frühen Neuzeit (1500–1800)*, ed. Matthias Meinhardt et al. (Wiesbaden: Harrassowitz, 2014), 307–322. Contemporary reports seldom mentioned it; see those by the city's secretary, Heinrich Merckel, and a Magdeburg citizen, Sebastian Besselmeyer, in Hortleder, *Handlungen*, 2:945–998, and by others, see *Die Chroniken der Deutschen Städte, Magdeburg* 2 (Leipzig: Hirzel, 1899), esp. 289–291, 136–137. One exception is Johann Sleidan. His *Commentariorum de Statu Religionis & Reipublicae*,

ten names. Gallus is most likely to have fashioned its arguments. Amsdorf's name was the first signed on the document, even though he probably did not have a primary role in its composition. He may have had a hand in the committee work leading to the approval of the document, though, and the ministerium's *Confession* certainly reflected the ideas he had held since Frederick the Wise first solicited his advice three decades earlier about using the sword to defend the Evangelical faith. Also, Magdeburg was Amsdorf's city, and he cared immensely about how their confession of faith affected their challenges and circumstances.

In the 1530s, the Wittenberg faculty had concurred with Amsdorf that God calls lesser magistrates to resist the tyranny of any higher magistrate who opposes the true worship of God.[66] The basic ideas in the Magdeburg *Confession* justifying the armed resistance of lesser magistrate to superiors—in this case, the German territorial princes to the emperor—had been shared by many who had known and studied under Luther and Melanchthon in the late 1530s and 1540s and had been shaped by the arguments of the jurists in the Smalcald League. The jurists argued that the constitution of the Empire permitted resistance to the emperor when he abandoned his pledges to the princes. Melanchthon and others also argued for a right to self-defense based on natural law. Luther left the matter of resistance to the jurists, but he did conclude, according to his concept of vocation, that rulers who abused the Gospel of Christ through their office and did not properly carry out their calling were deprived of their right to rule.[67] The exiled clergy who had gathered in Magdeburg believed that the imperial government was committing manifest injustice and abandoning its God-given vocation by suppressing the Gospel; therefore, the imperial government needed to be resisted.

The Magdeburg *Confession* could be considered the birth certificate of the ecclesiastical movement of the Gnesio-Lutheran party. Even though Amsdorf

Carolo Quinto Caesare, Libri XXVI (Strassburg: Theodosius Rihel, 1559), 677–678, discusses the city's theoretical defense of its position in relation to the emperor in 1550. However, he mentions the *Confession* of the ministerium of April 13 in only a few lines and devotes most of his discussion to the *Ausschreiben* issued March 24, 1550, by the city council (edited in C&C 2:630–641). That may indicate that Sleidan believed that the ministerium was doing no more than adopting the ideas laid down by the secular officials of the city. In all likelihood, the pastors exercised considerable influence over the members of the city council.

66 See chapter 1, p. 17 for Amsdorf's earlier opinion on the topic. The memorandum, dated December 6, 1536, is found in CR 3:128–131; MBW.T 7:292–296, Nr. 1818; and in *Das Widerstandsrecht als Problem der deutschen Protestanten, 1523–1546*, ed. Heinz Scheible (Gütersloh: Mohn, 1969), 89–92. Cf. W. D. J. Cargill Thompson, *The Political Thought of Martin Luther*, ed. Philip Broadhead (Sussex: Harvester, 1984), 91–103.

67 Cargill Thompson, *Political Thought*, 103–111, and Mark U. Edwards, *Luther's Last Battles. Politics and Polemics, 1531–46* (Ithaca: Cornell University Press, 1983), 20–37.

should not be considered the father or midwife of the document or the group, it is fitting that his name is at the head of the list of subscribers to the *Confession*. The movement reflected the concerns Amsdorf had felt more than a decade earlier when he suspected that his friend Philip Melanchthon was shifting his position on what Amsdorf considered certain basic elements of Luther's message. The group's initial leaders were Gallus and Flacius, students of Luther in a younger generation who had appreciated Melanchthon as preceptor and had adored him as an academic hero. For Amsdorf, Melanchthon was a treasured colleague and friend with whom he had led the Wittenberg movement thirty years earlier. Though their bonds with Melanchthon were different, they all bore a bitter sadness when they believed Melanchthon was betraying their common cause. Amsdorf's presence with these younger men from the Wittenberg circle lent encouragement and credibility to their confession of the faith and attempts to preserve the purity of Luther's teaching on the Gospel.

The goal of the Magdeburg *Confession* was to defend the decision of the city's secular authorities to submit to God's Word rather than to imperial decree. The *Confession* claimed to repeat only what is found in the prophetic and apostolic writings of Holy Scripture as it had been confessed at Augsburg in 1530 and had been taught by "the third Elijah," Martin Luther. Despite Luther's death, these confessors announced their determination to continue until the Last Day Luther's opposition to "the Babylonian captivity of the Antichrist," that is, the pope. It claimed also to only be a repetition of the Augsburg Confession.[68] Before arguing for the godliness and justice of resisting secular authorities who oppose and persecute the Gospel,[69] Gallus set forth seven articles summarizing the teaching of Scripture, Luther, and the Augsburg Confession, in order to assert the teaching of the Wittenberg preceptors as he and his Magdeburg colleagues understood it.

The first article of these seven in the Magdeburg *Confession* briefly affirmed the doctrine of the Trinity, the incarnation, and the life, death, and resurrection of Christ, slightly expanding the Augsburg Confession's first and third articles which paraphrase the Apostles' Creed.[70] The second article confessed "creation and sin," adding to the Augsburg Confession's second article discussion of original sin by briefly recounting the creation of all things and then asserting that the origin of sin is Adam and Eve's misuse of the gift of their free will by rejecting God. The result is that all subsequent human beings are born in sin, without

---

68 C&C 2:460–471. Latin and German versions of the *Confession* appear on opposite pages.

69 C&C 2:532–585.

70 C&C 2:474–475; cf. BSELK 92/93–94/95, 96/97–98/99; BC 36/37–38/39.

"true knowledge of God, without fear, faith, and love for God and the neighbor, full of self-love, error, presumption, disbelief, doubt, hostility toward God, which exhibit themselves in thoughts, lusts, words, and deeds against God and his holy commands"; these statements echoed and expanded upon Melanchthon's teaching in the Augsburg Confession's second article.[71]

The third article treated "the Law and good works," emphasizing the Law's accusation that convicts of sin. Here, Gallus distinguished the Law written on all hearts from the ceremonial and civil laws found in the Old Testament, which God had given only to one specific people, the Jews. Following the example Melanchthon set in the Augsburg Confession, the Magdeburg *Confession* condemned antinomians, the papal insistence on the role of human obedience in salvation, and those "who wish to force the Christian Church under the law of Moses in civil affairs," namely the Anabaptist groups.[72]

The fourth article on "the Gospel and justification" was the longest. It emphasized the ancient promise and delivery of salvation from sin through Christ's merit, which bestows "deliverance from sin, God's wrath, death, devil, and hell" and makes believers "righteous, children and heirs of eternal life and recipients of the Holy Spirit." It affirmed Luther's and Melanchthon's teaching that the imputation of Christ's perfect righteousness is the cause of the believer's righteousness, since Christ provided satisfaction for human sin. That righteousness and the new birth by the Word and Sacraments initiate the new life the Father gives as he "draws" people to himself (John 6:44). The new spiritual power to do good does not win or contribute to the believer's righteousness; the believer's righteousness consists solely of "the alien righteousness of the Son of God." Acknowledgement of sin and remorse over it are only produced by the Holy Spirit, who then bestows faith in Christ. It is that faith in Christ which makes believers righteous, bringing them forgiveness of sins and new life. After condemning nine errors taught by "papists and Interimists" about justification, this article rejected the adiaphorists' failure to clearly distinguish the gift of righteousness from God from the resulting practice of righteousness. The article also rejected the Leipzig "Interim's" omission of the word "alone" in the phrase "salvation by faith," the adiaphorists' affirmation of some power and freedom of the human will to call upon God, and the adiaphorists' compromise of Absolution by placing pastors under the jurisdiction of papal bishops.[73]

71 C&C 476–479; cf. BSELK 92/93–96/97, BC 36/37–38/39

72 C&C 2:480–487.

73 C&C 2:486–503.

Article five treated the Sacraments in general and then treated Baptism, the Lord's Supper, and Absolution specifically. In standard Wittenberg fashion and echoing Augustine, the Magdeburg *Confession* described three Sacraments as "visible words," affirming that they are fundamentally vehicles for conveying the promise of Christ's merits. The *Confession* rejected Anabaptists' views on Baptism, the ancient heresy of daily baptism by the "Hemerobaptists," and the "magical" view of Baptism that dismissed the importance of faith and instead added superstitious practices to the baptismal rite. Concerning the Lord's Supper, the Magdeburg *Confession* explicitly condemned the papal and Interimist views that the Lord's Supper works *ex opere operato*, the mass is a sacrifice, the cup should be withheld from the laity, and private masses can be celebrated. The papists' and Interimsts' errors on Absolution were also condemned, particularly the necessity of enumerating sins to receive forgiveness. The *Confession* also criticized the adiaphorists because the Leipzig "Interim" did not mention the role of faith in receiving Absolution. Just as individual Magdeburg theologians in their writing had been sensitive to the implications of the Leipzig "Interim," the Magdeburg *Confession* objected to how the Leipzig "Interim" discussed Confession and Absolution, Baptism, and the Lord's Supper alongside the other four practices that were considered sacraments in medieval theology. The *Confession* argued the Leipzig "Interim," therefore, gave the appearance that all seven were valid as sacraments and were being restored to the same level of importance in Christian practice—nothing other than an effort to compromise with the papacy.[74]

Article six of the Magdeburg *Confession* assigned the power of the Keys to the entire Church, as a visible assembly of those gathered around God's Word and Sacrament. Under normal conditions, the power of the Keys should be exercised by those who are ministers of the Church, but, in times when it is necessary, every member of the Church may exercise it. The Magdeburg *Confession* defined the power of the Keys in much the same way Melanchthon had in the Augsburg Confession: teaching God's Word, administering the Sacraments, forgiving or binding the sins of individuals or groups, calling ministers of the Church, reviewing and judging questions of religion, and preserving good order in the Church.[75] The ecclesiology of the papists was rejected as well as the Donatists' and Anabaptists' teaching that the Church only consists of those who practice holy lives .[76]

74 C&C 2:502–517.

75 C&C 2:518/519; cf. BSELK 194/195, BC 94.

76 C&C 2:516–524.

The final doctrinal article of the *Confession* treated the "walks of life" or "situations" of the political/societal sphere (*politia*) and of the family, with its economic responsibilities (*oeconomia*). God established marriage and civil government and made them ways of life in which godliness and holiness are to be practiced. The diminution of one or both by Anabaptists and papists was condemned in the Magdeburg *Confession*.[77]

In each of these seven articles, Amsdorf found the doctrine he had been teaching for thirty years. Whatever role Amsdorf might have had in advising Gallus and others about the wording of the Magdeburg *Confession*, the document expressed Amsdorf's theology more eloquently than he himself had; it became a new basis from which he expounded God's Word and Luther's teaching through the rest of his life.

Besides the writings involved with the Magdeburg siege, the publication of two different editions of Luther's writings in the 1540s and 1550s provides further evidence of the distrust that the Leipzig "Interim" introduced among those in the Wittenberg circle.[78] In 1539 at the instigation of Elector Johann Friedrich, a Wittenberg edition of Luther's Works began with members of the university staff as its editorial team. Moritz supported the project after he assumed control of Wittenberg. In 1548, the second German volume appeared, containing Luther's *That These Words of Christ, "This is My Body," Etc. Still Stand Firm against the Ravers.* In the volume, the editors omitted Luther's attack against Martin Bucer for his alteration of this treatise when Bucer reprinted it in Strassburg; the editors also omitted Luther's attack on Bucer for stating that Melanchthon denied the true presence of Christ's body and blood in the Sacrament. The editors also omitted Luther's admonition to guard against Sacramentarian sects.

Amsdorf was probably not aware that Luther had approved these omissions before his death. Instead, Amsdorf saw these alterations as one more instance of the Wittenberg theologians' betrayal of Luther's faith. Therefore in 1549, Amsdorf publicly criticized the work being done on the Wittenberg edition of Luther's Works. This touched off a controversy over the project. The young lords embarked on an edition of their own, the Jena edition, edited by Luther's amanuensis, Georg Rörer, who had been the editor of the Wittenberg edition until 1551.[79] Amsdorf conceived and directed the project with Rörer and the two court preachers in Weimar, Stolz and Aurifaber, and two Erfurt colleagues, pastor

---

77 C&C 2:524–529.

78 See page 70 (note 60) for sources on the use of Luther's writings in this period.

79 Johannes Schilling, "Auditor, scriba, Autor und Editor. Luthers Werke in Rörers Händen," in *Georg Rörer*, eds. Stefan Michel and Christian Speer, 171–179.

Andreas Poach and Luther's close friend Matthäus Ratzeberger, who was also the former electoral court physician.[80] The Jena edition was advertised as an antidote to the errors of the Wittenberg edition and as the Ernestine contribution to preserving Luther's legacy.

Melanchthon replied to Amsdorf's charges in his preface to the third volume of the Wittenberg edition in 1553.[81] Amsdorf responded in the preface to the first volume of the Jena edition, issued in 1555.[82] That same year, in order to counteract the harmful effect of Amsdorf's criticism of the Wittenberg edition, its managing editor, Christoph Walther, asserted that Amsdorf had not really written those criticisms that appeared with his name. Walther's tactic reflects just how much influence Amsdorf had among those in the Wittenberg circle. The two sides continued to exchange charges and critiques. The Jena edition won the battle for sales, as the Wittenberg edition's stockpile diminished more slowly.[83] The fact that the two groups at odds over the Leipzig "Interim" were willing to invest their resources in publishing competing sets of Luther's writings reflects just how much mistrust and ill will they developed for each other in a short time.

In 1555, the Religious Peace of Augsburg was signed, granting adherents of the Augsburg Confession a legal though inferior status in the Empire. It confirmed the softening of tensions inaugurated in 1552 by a truce in Passau after Elector Moritz had led an alliance of princes against the Habsburgs and defeated their forces. Moritz had fallen on the battlefield in the next year during a police action against the rebellious Albert Alcibiades of Brandenburg-Kulmbach. Amsdorf viewed Moritz's death as the overthrow of Satan with his Antichrist.[84] Therefore,

---

80 Gehrt, *Konfessionspolitik*, 68–73.

81 *Der Dritte Teil der Bu[e]cher des Ehrwirdigen Herrn Doctor Mart. Lutheri . . .* (Wittenberg: Hans Lufft, 1550).

82 *Der Erste Teil aller Bu[e]cher vnd Schrifften des thewren seligen Mans Doct: Mart: Lutheri vom XVII jar an bis auff das XXII VDMIAE* (Jena: Christian Rödinger, 1555), +4a.

83 *Das die zu Wittenberg im andern teil der bucher Doctoris Martini im buch das diese wort Christ (Das ist men Leib etc.) noch fest stehen mehr denn ein blat vier gantzer Paragraphos vorsetzlich aussgelassen haben wie folget* (Magdeburg, 1549). On the controversy, see Eike Wolgast, "Die Wittenberger Luther-Ausgabe. Zur Überlieferungsgeschichte der Werke Luthers im 16. Jahrhundert," *Archiv für Geschichte des Buchwesens*, 11, 1–2 (1970): 122–137; Wolgast, "Der Streit um die Werke Luthers im 16. Jahrhundert," *ARG* 59 (1968): 75–94; on the editions of Luther's Works, see Reinhold Jauernig, "Die Konkurrenz der Jenaer mit der Wittenberger Ausgabe von Martin Luthers Werke," *Lutherjahrbuch* 26 (1959): 75–94; Jauernig, "Zur Jenaer Lutherausgabe," *Theologische Literaturzeitung* 67 (1952): 747–762; Jauernig, "Zur Jenaer Lutherausgabe," *Wissenschaftliche Zeitschrift der Friedrich-Schiller-Universität Jena/Thüringen, Gesellschafts- und sprachwissenschaftliche Reihe* 4 (1954–1955): 267–277; Robert Kolb, *Martin Luther as Prophet, Teacher, and Hero. Images of the Reformer, 1520–1620* (Grand Rapids: Baker Books, 1999), 146–150.

84 Druffel, *Briefe*, 4:204; "Das der Rector zu Wittenberg In seiner Intimation vnd D. Pfeffinger in seiner predigt mit Ihrem anhang von H. Moritz die warheit geschriben, gepredigt, vnd gerühmet habenn," Wr, ETLFB 39:127–132; Reichert, *Amsdorf*, B, 259–265; "Wie christlich hertzog Moritz gestorben vnd wie billich ehr vnd sein bruder hertzog Augustus des löblichen Churfursten zu Sachssen seliger gedechtnis lande eingenommen vnd noch inne haben werden alle menschen aus folgenden bericht clerlich vernemen," Wr, ETLFB 41:389a–390a.

these developments should have rendered both the Augsburg Interim and the Leipzig "Interim" irrelevant.

However, the disputes they provoked and the issues they raised had made a definitive break within the Wittenberg circle. The Magdeburg theologians demanded that before reconciliation could take place, the theologians who had participated with Moritz had to repent for their weakness of faith that led them to make concessions to the papists in the face of the imperial threat in 1548. The theologians who had supported the Leipzig "Interim" continued to look upon the Magdeburg theologians as seditious schismatics and wrangling rebels, who had needlessly discredited efforts to fend off the emperor's suppression of Luther's Reformation.[85] Both sides felt betrayed. Melanchthon's students had expected their preceptor to boldly confess. Melanchthon had expected his students to sympathize with his attempts to preserve Lutheran pulpits for Lutheran preachers. Both sides felt the other had acted in bad faith. Mutual recriminations continued to deepen the divide.

When Johann Friedrich was defeated and taken prisoner at Mühlberg a little more than a year after Luther's death, Amsdorf believed that God's judgment was clearing the way for the Last Day. He was certain that the final eschatological battle had begun and that the enemies of the Gospel were making their final attempt to eradicate it. From a vantage point after the Religious Peace of Augsburg, it is difficult to appreciate the seriousness of the Evangelical situation in the years between 1548 and 1552. It is impossible now, nearly five centuries later, to grasp the genuine terror and concern many of Luther's followers felt and to appreciate the tentativeness and fragility of their situation. In 1548, Spanish troops were restoring papal doctrine and practices in Evangelical towns and lands in south Germany while many Evangelical princes and towns farther north were complying with the Habsburg religious program to various degrees.[86] Understandably, the Evangelicals feared for the future of their faith.

The duress of those circumstances and the severity of what was at stake did push Amsdorf and his colleagues in Magdeburg in a permanently polarized direction away from Melanchthon and his colleagues in Wittenberg and Leipzig. Even though Amsdorf and Melanchthon had a strong friendship, even such a friendship cracked under the pressure of needing to make concrete decisions

85 Robert Kolb, "Controversia perpetua. Die Fortsetzung des adiaphoristischen Streits nach dem Augsburger Religionsfrieden," in Dingel and Wartenberg, *Politik*, 191–209.

86 Roxane Berwinkel, *Weltliche Macht und geistlicher Anspruch. Die Hansestadt Stralsund im Konflikt um das Augsburger Interim* (Berlin: Akademie Verlag, 2008), and Rainer Postel, "Die Hansestädte und das Interim," in *Das Interim 1548/50. Herrschaftskrise und Glaubenskonflikt*, ed. Luise Schorn-Schütte (Gütersloh: Gütersloher Verlag, 2005), 192–204.

while facing the overwhelming threat of extinction that loomed over them. In 1556, Amsdorf wrote to Wolf Mülich, one of the courtiers of Johann Friedrich the Middler, "It is true that Philip is a valuable scholar, but Christ is much greater and higher than everything. Therefore, you cannot forsake Christ and his word for Melanchthon's sake. You must in such situations anger not only father and mother, emperor and king, but even leave behind your own body and life, to say nothing of your preceptor."[87]

In the instability after the Smalcald War, Amsdorf believed a stalwart and bold confession was the stance that needed to be taken. Melanchthon believed minimal concessions in order to retain as much of the status quo ante as possible was the appropriate stance. Others inside and outside the Wittenberg circle—including John Calvin in Geneva, Anton Corvinus in Braunschweig-Calenberg, Johann Aepinus and Joachim Westphal in Hamburg, and Johannes Brenz in Württemberg—shared with Melanchthon their negative opinions of the Leipzig "Proposal" and criticized his failure to make a bold stand against any compromise.[88] Even Melanchthon himself later admitted that his approach to the crisis over the Interims had been inadequate.[89] Yet the damage had been done. The Wittenberg reform circle had forever been divided.

GENERAL INSPECTOR AND ECCLESIASTICAL COUNSELOR

When Magdeburg came to a relatively amicable and lenient settlement with Elector Moritz to end the siege in November 1551, the city which had been Amsdorf's home for much of his adult life became an uncomfortable place for him. He was sympathetic to this compromise with the electoral Saxon government, for, he claimed, the city had been driven to the verge of starvation. Nonetheless, he felt compelled to retire from his city to the lands of Johann Friedrich. He wrote to his imprisoned elector and friend, Johann Friedrich the Elder,

> I cannot conceal from your princely grace that on November 9 Magdeburg swore allegiance to Moritz after a siege of a year and six weeks. The city was starved out and could not hold out any longer. It had been abandoned by everyone and had no hope of relief. Thus, it was forced to negotiate and

87 Cited by Gehrt, *Konfessionspolitik*, 83.

88 Calvin's letter is found in H. E. Bindseil, *Philippi Melanchthonis Epistolae* (Halle: Schwetschke, 1874), Nr. 311; Corvinus', Nr. 293 and 299; Brenz's, CR 7:290; that of Aepinus and his colleagues in Hamburg, CR 7:367–372. The Magdeburg theologians knew of opposition from those outside the empire; cf. the Magdeburg *Confession*, C&C 2:466, 11–16/467, 28–32.

89 CR 8:841; MBW.R 7: 478–479, Nr. 7945.

> has come to an agreement with Moritz, according to which it may maintain its religion, liberties, and the defensive walls around the city. . . . I cannot remain long under Moritz's rule. Fidelity and faith are disappearing from the earth.[90]

From prison, Johann Friedrich instructed his sons to make provisions for his old friend, though he warned them to keep Amsdorf at some distance from the court at Weimar. Amsdorf accepted the young lords' suggestion that he settle in Eisenach, where his widowed sister lived. He joined her household in April 1552. In 1554, a young Wittenberg student named Heinrich Hausen (1536–1587), who was also the son of a mayor of Eisenach, used the humanist skills that he had learned in Jena from 1551 to 1553 and had been strengthening in Wittenberg since 1554 to write an elegy on the birth of John the Baptist and dedicated it as a tribute with "never-ending respect" to Amsdorf, Eisenach's new resident and "a nobleman of outstanding erudition, piety, and virtue." In Heinrich's judgment, Amsdorf was indeed worthy of imitation. The fact that this treatise was published suggests Amsdorf's connections in the town were strong, since treatises of praise were rarely published at that time.[91]

The young lords appointed Amsdorf "ecclesiastical counselor and general inspector of the churches in ducal Saxony."[92] In this position—something of an unofficial bishop for Thuringia during the last thirteen years of his life—Amsdorf was more content and probably more influential than he had been as the titled bishop of Naumburg-Zeitz.

His relationships with Johann Friedrich's family remained close for a time. Amsdorf rode with the former elector in a triumphal parade when he returned as a martyr to his lands in September 1552 after more than five years in imperial custody.[93] The imprisonment had often been harsh and had sapped his strength. A year and a half after Amsdorf had composed a psalm of thanksgiving and praise for Johann Friedrich's return to ducal Saxony, he wrote a funeral

---

90 Druffel, *Briefe*, 1:796–798, Nr. 807. On the state of the city during the siege, see Stefanie Fabian, "*Ein feste Burg* wider den Kaiser – Alltag und Leben im belagerten Magdeburg," in *Magdeburg und die Reformation. Teil 1. Eine Stadt folgt Martin Luther*, ed. Maren Bailerstedt et al. (Halle: Mitteldeutscher Verlag, 2016), 403–423.

91 Heinrich Hausen, *In natalem Ioannis Baptistae elegia dedicata Reverendo Viro D. Nicolao Amsdorfio* (Wittenberg: Heirs of Georg Rhau, 1554), Alb.

92 Christian F. Paullini, *Historia Isenacensis* (Frankfurt/M: Bauer, 1698), 152. Amsdorf's protest against Magdeburg's surrender is recorded in his "Bedengken auff der fursten vbergebene Artikel. N. von Amsdorff, Exul," Wr, ETLFB 41:314a–321a, Reichert, *Amsdorf*, 246–253; cf. his discussion, 137–138. Cf. also an untitled manuscript, Wr, ETLFB 41:169a, Reichert, *Amsdorf*, 253, as well as Druffel, *Briefe*, 1:797. Johann Friedrich's instructions are found in Druffel, *Briefe*, 2:52–53. Cf. Gehrt, *Konfessionspolitik*, 39–40, 63–65, 74–75, 85–94, and Gehrt, "'Erzbischof.'"

93 Mentz, *Johann Friedrich*, 3:326–327.

sermon for his friend, age 51. Amsdorf had spent the final ten days of Johann Friedrich's life at his bedside. Amsdorf interpreted his friend's death on March 3, 1554, as a sign of God's grace, for God had spared the prince from the agonies Amsdorf foresaw coming upon the German people. In the funeral sermon, he urged Johann Friedrich's sons to repent and follow Christ's commands.[94] The honor granted to him in preaching at his friend's funeral again reflects Amsdorf's status in the Wittenberg reform movement since Luther himself had preached at the funerals of Johann Friedrich's uncle and father.

Amsdorf's exhortation of obedience and faithfulness to Johann Friedrich's sons in the sermon for their father's funeral was not aimed at particular sins with which the young lords had offended the bishop. Rather throughout his time in Eisenach, Amsdorf sought to encourage and remind Johann Friedrich's sons to continue to live as Christian rulers. The young lords had already learned to consult their ecclesiastical counselor on a number of problems. At their request, he had prepared a memorandum discouraging them from joining a league led by Moritz and other Evangelical princes against the Habsburgs. Though Amsdorf had not protested the formation or activities of the Smalcald League of Evangelical princes against the emperor, the aging bishop now regarded a league with Moritz as a sign and act of dependence on the temporal power of princes rather than on the protection of God. Meanwhile, Amsdorf continued to attack Moritz and his brother and successor, August, for their seizure of Johann Friedrich's lands and titles.[95]

Amsdorf reviewed ecclesiastical problems for the young lords as well. He passed judgment on books, and he affirmed the decision of the superintendent of Weimar to refuse Christian burial to a stable hand who died without any sign of religion. He participated in the examination of a Jewish woman who wanted to convert to the Christian faith. He served as liaison between pastors and the dukes. In 1553, he fashioned an ordination oath that included a pledge of faithfulness to "the holy Gospel, pure and simple, without any human additions, in accord with the Augsburg Confession and especially the Smalcald Articles."

94 *Wie sichs mit des Durchleuchtigsten Hochgebornen Fürsten vnd Herrn Herrn Johans Friderich des Eldern Christlichem abschied zugetragen hat. Sampt einer Leichpredigt vber dem Begrebnis zu Weimar Montag nach Letare gethan Anno 1554* (Jena, 1554), esp. A2b–B2a; cf. Gehrt, *Konfessionspolitik*, 74–81, and Siegfried Bräuer, "Nikolaus von Amsdorfs Schrift zum Tod Johann Friedrichs d. Ä.," in Dingel, *Amsdorf*, 117–133.

95 "Vom bundnis," Wr, ETLFB 41:279b–280b, an undated manuscript, fits best into the context of the deliberations by the young lords over the invitation from Moritz and other Evangelical princes to join the alliance against Charles V in 1552; see W. Wenck, "Kurfürst Moritz und die Ernestiner in den Jahren 1551 und 1552," *Forschungen zur Deutschen Geschichte* 12 (1872): 29. An example of Amsdorf's continuing reaction to Albertine Saxon propaganda against the young lords and their father is found in his "Antwort auff die leddern Müntz," Wr, ETLFB 41:367–369; Reichert, *Amsdorf*, 266–268.

With this pledge, Amsdorf with Johann Friedrich the Elder, in the short time he was out of captivity before his death, "set a milestone in the history of Protestant usage of confessional documents," anticipating the establishment of such documents as secondary norms for the public teaching of the Church.[96] He also helped organize the visitation of the churches of ducal Saxony in 1554.[97]

As unofficial bishop of ducal Saxony, Amsdorf also took part in the 1552 discussions of the ideas put forward by Andreas Osiander. Amsdorf's signature is first in the list of ducal theologians who issued a document entitled *Censure* against Osiander's doctrine, even though Amsdorf had not participated in the composition of the document.[98] Osiander had led the Lutheran movement in Nuremberg from 1522 until 1547 and played a prominent role in the development of the Evangelical faith in south Germany. Trained at Ingolstadt by Reuchlin and others, he incorporated elements of the neo-Platonic mysticism of the Cabbala into his theology, giving his thinking a decidedly different structure and content than that of other contemporary Lutherans. He and Amsdorf had participated in the Smalcald League's meeting in February 1537 where they subscribed to the

---

96 Gehrt, *Konfessionspolitik*, 61–65.

97 Julius Hartmann, *Erhard Schnepf, der Reformator in Schwaben, Nassau, Hessen und Thüringen* (Tübingen: Osiander, 1870), 102–105; "Bedenken Errn Nicolaus von Amssdorff wegen eines entleibten stalliungens welch der Superintends zu Weymar nicht begraben lassen wollen," dated April 26, 1547; Göttingen, Niedersächsische Staats- und Universitätsbibliothek, Codex MS. Jurid. 492, 31b–33a, in a copy from about 1608. A report on his interview of the Jewish convert is found in Wf, Guelf. Helmst. 878:114b–118b; cf. Hiram Kümper, "Das Glaubensverhör der Jüdin Rahel im Juni 1554 durch Nikolaus von Amsdorf als 'Modus et forma judaei convertendi'," *ARG* 99 (2008): 120–138, with an edited transcription of the document. An example of his intervention in behalf of a friend is his letter addressed to the young lords, dated October 28, 1554, suggesting financial assistance be given to Georg Rörer, Coburg, Bayrisches Staatsarchiv, 1554 x38, Jena, in LAA I, 28, b2 aa, Nr. 8, 18–19. On Amsdorf's role in the visitation of 1554, see chapter 3, pages 99–103.

98 *Censvrae der Fürstlichen Sechsischen Theologen zu Weymar vnd Koburg. Auf die Bekendtnis des Andreae Osiandri Von der Rechtfertigung des Glaubens* (Erfurt, 1552). Hartmann, *Schnepf*, 37–74, wished to excuse his subject, Schnepf, from responsibility for the document's harshly worded criticism of Osiander, so offensive to refined nineteenth century sensibilities, so he assigned authorship of the three critiques contained in the *Censurae* to Amsdorf, Viktorin Strigel, and Justus Menius. The case for authorship by Menius, Strigel, and Schnepf is cogently argued by Emanuel Hirsch, *Die Theologie des Andreas Osiander und ihre geschichtlichen Voraussetzungen* (Göttingen: Vandenhoeck & Ruprecht, 1919), 188–189. Cf. Timothy J. Wengert, *Defending Faith. Lutheran Responses to Andreas Osiander's Doctrine of Justification, 1551–1559* (Tübingen: Mohr/Siebeck, 2012), 95–97, 292, 369, 394–395. Osiander's works from this period are found in *Andreas Osiander d. Ä. Gesamtausgabe*, eds. Gerhard Müller and Gottfried Seebaß, vols. 8–10 (Gütersloh: Mohn, 1990, 1994, 1997). Osiander's works are listed in Gottfried Seebaß, *Bibliographica Osiandrica* (Nieuwkoop: De Graaf, 1971). On the early development of Osiander's theology, see Seebaß, *Das reformatorische Werk des Andreas Osiander* (Nuremberg: Verein für Bayerische Kirchengeschichte, 1967); on the controversy before and after Osiander's death, see Wengert, *Defending Faith*; Martin Stupperich, *Osiander in Preussen 1549–1552* (Berlin: de Gruyter, 1973), and Jörg Rainer Fligge, "Herzog Albrecht von Preussen und der Osiandrismus, (1522–1568)," dissertation, University of Bonn, 1972. The interpretation of Osiander's doctrine of justification of Hirsch, *Theologie*, ignores significant elements of Luther's understanding of justification, reflecting his following the interpretation of Luther set by Albrecht Ritschl and Karl Holl, and is effectively criticized by Stupperich, *Osiander*, and E. Roth, "Mörlin und seine Rechtfertigungslehre," *Jahrbuch der Gesellschaft für niedersächsischen Kirchengeschichte* 50 (1952): 59–81.

Smalcald Articles. Both preached at that meeting as well. Amsdorf later recalled that Osiander's sermon had raised serious questions about his theology but that his subscription to Luther's Articles had set aside suspicions and averted further confrontation.[99] Like Amsdorf, Osiander had opposed the Augsburg Interim and had even been forced from his pulpit in Nuremberg by the enforcement of the Interim there. When he was ousted from Nuremberg, Osiander's longtime friend Duke Albrecht of Prussia warmly welcomed him to his court at Königsberg and appointed him to a number of posts, including a university professorship. The infant university in Königsberg experienced faculty squabbling during its early years; but the eventual disputes that swirled around Osiander were more intense and bitter than anything the faculty had previously experienced.

The doctrinal issues which elicited responses to Osiander from theologians of Geneva, Magdeburg, Wittenberg, Königsberg, and other locations were soteriological. Osiander defined saving righteousness as the essential divine righteousness of Christ's divine nature; he said it is given to believers through faith, which brings Christ's divine nature to dwell in them. He rejected Luther's and Melanchthon's definition of saving righteousness as the imputation of Christ's death to sinners. Furthermore, Osiander separated redemption and atonement—the once-for-all event on Calvary—from justification. In fact, he paid little attention to the atoning work of Christ. On a number of specific points in the Wittenberg teaching on salvation, all those trained at Wittenberg criticized Osiander's teaching sharply. Gnesio-Lutherans, Philippists, Amsdorf, and Melanchthon all rejected Osiander's position as unfaithful to Holy Scripture and as a perversion of Luther's teaching. Amsdorf's writing against Osiander specifically rejected the Königsberg professor's separation of redemption and justification and of Christ's divine and human natures.[100] Amsdorf felt obliged in his own writing and in statements composed with other ducal counselors to periodically issue condemnations of Osiander's teachings. Amsdorf did not forget error and felt it was his duty to expose it.[101]

99 Reported in the edition of the Smalcald Articles issued by Amsdorf's colleagues, the court preachers Johann Stolz and Johann Aurifaber, *Artickel der Euangelischen Lere/ so da hetten sollen auffs Concilium vberantort warden/ wo es sein wu[e]rde . . . Gestellet auff dem Tage zu Schmalkalden. Anno. 1537 . . .* (s.l., 1552). In the editors' preface, dated March 27, 1552 (lf. B2b), they referenced Amsdorf's recollection, as recorded by Justus Menius in the *Censurae*.

100 *Auff Osianders Bekentnis ein Vnterricht vnd zeugnis Das die Gerechtigkeit der menschheit Christi darinnen sie entpfangen vnd geboren ist allen Gleubigen Su[e]ndern geschankt vnd zugerechent wird vnd fu[e]r jhr Person hie auff Erden nimmermehr Gerecht vnd Heilig werden* (Magdeburg, 1552), and his "Vnterricht vff Osianders opinion, Dornstag nach Jubilate 1553," (April 27), Wr, ETLFB 41:133a–136a. Cf. Wengert, *Defending Faith*, 41, 74, 378; cf. mention on pages 266 and 378 of others who cited Amsdorf against Osiander.

101 E.g., in a letter of June 12, 1554, commenting on a statement issued at a meeting of Evangelical governments at Naumburg which treated Osiandrism, Wf, Guelf. Helmst. 722:273a; in his *Offentliche Bekentnis*

Amsdorf did note when Moritz died that Satan with his Antichrist had been overthrown; yet Amsdorf believed the eschatological battle would not end until Christ returned in judgment. Therefore, Amsdorf did not wane in his battle the rest of his life against what he believed to be Satan's forces in the eschatological struggle. In 1558 and 1559 when Wittenberg faculty and students issued extensive defenses of the actions their teachers had taken in 1548 and 1549, Amsdorf prepared a critique of their arguments. In it, he repeated his old criticisms of the now deceased Moritz, his theologians, and his religious policy.[102] During Amsdorf's years in Eisenach, he again printed works against the Roman Church as well, repeating ideas he had been expressing since 1520. His critiques of the Council of Trent remained unpublished. His brief tracts that were published addressed in the vernacular popular concerns. His treatment of a problem that must have nagged at the back of many Evangelicals' minds in the 1550s is insightful: how could God permit the Roman papacy to survive if it really was the Antichrist? Amsdorf based his definition of the Church not on numbers but on submission to God's Word. Amsdorf continued to compare God's long-suffering of the German people in the 1550s and 1560s with God's tolerance of apostasy and idolatry among his Old Testament people in order to give them time to repent. This meant the visitation of God's judgment was soon going to break loose on all those who opposed his Word, Amsdorf continued to warn.[103]

Amsdorf was determined to defend the saving message of God's Word as he had learned it from Luther. As a result, the final thirteen years of Amsdorf's life

der reinen lere des Euangelij Vnd Confutatio der jtzigen Schwermer (Jena, 1559), B2b–B4b; and in "Warnung vnd vermanung das sich ein ider Christen für den schwirmen itziger Zceit hüte vnd beware," Wr, ETLFB, 41:139a–143a.

102 Against the Wittenberg theologians' *Ex Actis Synodicis Et Aliis Diligenter Et Fideliter Collecta Expositio Eorvm, Qvas Theologi Academiae VVitebergensis & harum Regionum alij . . . de libro Augustano, qui nominator Interim* (Wittenberg, 1559), Amsdorf composed "Vnterricht auff der Adiaphoristen zu wittenberg buch De actis synodis etc. Darinne sie sich weisbrennen vnd viel vrsachn aus der rethorica furwenden, das sie die mittel dienge billich gewilligt vnd nachgeben haben, Niclas von Amsdorff, 1559," Wr, ETLFB 39:4–21, dated September 1, 1559, with the Eisenach original in Jäger, *Amsdorf*, 93–113; cf. this manuscript, pages 26–41, for a rough draft of the memorandum. See also the German summary of the Wittenberg work in the edition of C&C 2:838–943.

103 Amsdorf's attacks on the papacy in the mid-1550s include *Ein gut newe Jar den grossen Herrn in dieser Welt geschanckt* (Jena, 1554); *Fu[e]nff fu[e]rnemliche vnd gewisse Zeichen aus go[e]ttlicher heiliger Schrifft, so kurtz vor dem Ju[e]ngsten tag geschehen sollen* (Jena, 1554); *Vnterricht vnd Vermanung auffs newe Jar so ich vor zweien jaren den grossen Herrn dieser Welt geschanckt habe* (Jena, 1555); *Das in der Schrifft ausdru[e]cklich verku[e]ndigt ist Das die Ro[e]mische Kirche vom Christlichen glauben abfallen Christum vnd sein Wort verleugnen vnd verdammen sol* (Jena, 1555), AS, 62–78. Again in 1562, Amsdorf published several attacks against the papacy: *Eine Predigt aus dem Comment des heiligen vnd trewen Dieners Christi Lutheri vber das fu[e]nfft Capitel Hosee gezogen von rechtschaffener vnd falscher Busse* (Jena: Donat Richtzenhan, 1562); *Ein Predigt aus den Schrifften Lutheri vber die Propheten gezogen. Das Deudscheland wie Israel Judea vnd Jersalem wird zusto[e]rt vnd verwu[e]stet werden vmb gleicher Su[e]nde willen* (Jena: Thomas Rebart, 1562); *Eine Vermanung vnd Gebet wider den Bapst vnd seinen Anhang* (Jena: Donat Richtzenhan, 1562).

were filled with controversy. Besides the Osiandrists and Romanists, Amsdorf returned from time to time during the last decade of his life to criticize the errors of the adiaphorists, yet unrepented, even when other disputes arose between Amsdorf's and Melanchthon's disciples. For Amsdorf, the adiaphorists' failure to repent confirmed that the spirit that produced the Leipzig "Interim" was also what led the Philippists down a path of error concerning the role of good works in salvation and the role of the human will in coming to faith. During his final years in Eisenach, these two soteriological issues became more and more prominent in Amsdorf's critiques of the Leipzig "Interim," replacing the ecclesiological problems with adiaphora that had been central to the Magdeburg theologians' critiques of the "Interim" in the late 1540s and early 1550s. In fact, these two soteriological issues became Amsdorf's chief concerns in his seventies and early eighties. His treatises during the controversies at the end of his life reflect how he dedicated these final years primarily to defending Luther's emphasis on salvation through faith alone, grace alone, and Christ alone.

3

A GOOD TREE PRODUCES GOOD FRUIT

Amsdorf's Soteriology in the Majoristic Controversy

GEORG MAJOR, BELOVED BROTHER

Georg Major had once regarded Nikolaus von Amsdorf as his "dear father and preceptor."[1] Amsdorf had once addressed Major as his "most beloved brother in Christ."[2] Their friendship may have begun as early as 1511 when Major arrived at age nine in Wittenberg to further his education. Their friendship certainly flourished while Major served as rector of the Magdeburg school from 1529 to 1537. In 1537, Major returned to Wittenberg and served as preacher in Wittenberg's Castle Church. Besides two brief superintendencies elsewhere, Major served as a professor of theology in Wittenberg from 1545 till the end of his life. Elector Johann Friedrich appointed him to the consistory that supervised ecclesiastical life in the electorate and sent him in Melanchthon's stead to the second colloquy of Regensburg in early 1546.[3]

As for many Saxons and nearly every member of the Wittenberg reform movement, the years 1546 and 1547 marked a watershed for Major. When he was in Regensburg at the imperial diet and he received Amsdorf's letter with the news of Luther's death,[4] Major returned to Wittenberg and plunged into defending Johann Friedrich's military action against Charles V.[5] The Spanish

1 *Auff des Ehrenwirdigen Herren Niclas von Ambsdorff schrifft so jtzundt neulich Mense Nouembri Anno 1551, wider Georgen Maior öffentlich in Druck ausgegangen. Antwort Georg: Major* (Wittenberg, 1552), A2a, edited in C&C 3:18–45.

2 In a letter written sometime in 1548, printed in Carl Eichhorn, "Amsdorfiana aus dem Codex chartacteus Nr. 43 der Dorpater Universitätsbibliothek," *ZKG* 22 (1901): 610.

3 Irene Dingel, "Die Rolle Georg Majors auf dem Regensburger Religionsgespräch von 1546," in *Georg Major (1502–1574): Ein Theologe der Wittenberger Reformation*, ed. Irene Dingel and Günther Wartenberg (Leipzig: Evangelische Verlagsanstalt, 2005), 189–206. This collection of essays contains treatments of various facets of Major's life.

4 Christof Schubart, *Die Berichte über Luthers Tod und Begräbnis* (Weimar: Böhlau, 1917), 17.

5 Major wrote an anonymous parody entitled *Ewiger: Göttlicher Allmechtiger Maiestat Declaration Wider Kaiser Carl König zu Hispanien. Vnd Bapst Paulum den dritten* (s.l., s.d.). Cf. Oskar Waldeck, "Die Publizistik des Schmalkladischen Krieges," *ARG* 7 (1909–1910): 35, 45.

advance into Saxony in late spring 1547 sent Major fleeing from Wittenberg to Magdeburg; but he returned and almost immediately was asked by Moritz in May 1547 to accept the superintendency of the church in Merseburg, an episcopal city where Moritz's brother, Duke August, was the secular coadjutor of the bishopric.[6] However, Merseburg received a Roman Catholic bishop as a result of the Smalcald War, and apparently this created a difficult situation for Major. Therefore, he returned to Wittenberg in February 1548 to teach. He assumed a different superintendency in late 1551, this time over the churches in the Mansfeld county. He experienced a year of conflict with the local clergy concerning the Leipzig "Interim" because their previous superintendent, Johann Spangenberg, a close friend of Luther and Melanchthon, had voiced sharp criticism of Moritz's religious policy before his death in 1550. The year climaxed when Albrecht, one of Mansfeld's counts, returned from the imperial imprisonment he had shared with Johann Friedrich since Mühlberg. Albrecht arrived in Mansfeld at Christmas in 1552 and dismissed Major from office without a hearing. Major's professorship in Wittenberg remained vacant, so he returned there and taught until his death in 1574.

The cordial relationship between Major and Amsdorf dissolved slowly through the controversies following the Smalcald War. Their friendly correspondence continued into early 1549, though their letters began to show the strain felt by friends caught on opposing sides of a feud such as what was developing within the Wittenberg circle.[7] Amsdorf and Major were each committed to the position of their own colleagues and political leaders—the city council of Magdeburg and the young lords of Ernestine Saxony on the one hand, and Duke Moritz on the other. It is surprising that with the strident enmity and violent condemnations passing between Magdeburg and Wittenberg, the two friends were not goaded into a public clash sooner.

Amsdorf at first refrained from publishing attacks against Major for his role in forging the Leipzig "Interim"; but because of the network among those in the Wittenberg circle, the Magdeburg members knew what was being said about them in Wittenberg and Leipzig, according to reports from their sympathizers there. Major provoked the public conflict with Amsdorf by publicly blaming the

6 In an effort to demarcate the secular responsibilities that had fallen to bishops in the Middle Ages from the spiritual aspects of that office, some Evangelical princes handed over the secular duties to lay administrators and thus freed the spiritual administrators, who bore the title "bishop," for pastoral leadership and care.

7 Correspondence between September 1546 and February 1549 exchanged by Amsdorf and Major is found in Otto Walz, "Epistolae Reformatoren," *ZKG* 2 (1878): 165–167, 170–173; and in Eichhorn, "Amsdorfiana," 22:610–611, 614–615, 618–620, 634, 636–639.

strife within Saxon Lutheranism on those in Magdeburg.[8] In late 1551, Amsdorf wrote a tract to refute that charge and similar accusations from another former colleague, Johannes Bugenhagen. Amsdorf argued many of the points he repeated throughout the Leipzig "Interim" controversy: he blamed Moritz's theologians for the strife in Saxon Lutheranism as a result of their compromise with the Antichrist, and he rejected the Leipzig "Interim" for omitting the word "alone" in the phrase "salvation by faith." He asked who was responsible for the phrase "good works are necessary for salvation." Such a statement implies that not only faith but also love makes human beings righteous, as the Augsburg Interim had also taught. That was not what Luther had taught. Amsdorf said that through his work on the Leipzig "Interim," Major had deserted the true Church for the papacy and had aided in persecuting the preachers of Torgau who lost their pastorates for refusing to accept the imposition of the surplice. Major was altering the belief they had fought to defend together in Magdeburg and for which they had suffered papal threats. Amsdorf concluded that his friend must have fallen from the faith.[9]

GOOD WORKS ARE NOT NECESSARY FOR SALVATION

An attack from someone as prestigious in the Wittenberg movement as Nikolaus von Amsdorf, Luther's friend and the exiled bishop, could not be ignored. And in fact, Major's tactic in response to being attacked by someone as important as Amsdorf only made the conflict worse. Major's *Answer*, published in early 1552,[10] reluctantly reproved his "friend and father" for trying to destroy him. In a standard Philippist ploy, Major shifted the blame for the strife in Saxony onto Matthias Flacius as a foreigner, a Slavic Croatian,[11] thus excusing Amsdorf for his mistake. He dismissed Flacius's beliefs because Flacius had not been called to any ecclesiastical office. He had surrendered his professorship in Wittenberg

8 E.g., in his *De origine et autoritate verbi Dei* (Wittenberg, 1550), A3b, A7a–b.

9 *Das Doctor Pomer vnd Doctor Maior mit iren Adiaphoristen eregernis vnnd zurtrennung angericht Vnnd den Kirchen Chrsti vnüberwintlichen schaden gethan haben. Derhalben sie vnd nicht wir zu Magdeburg/ von Teuffel erwegt seint/ wie sie vns schmehen vnd lestern* (s.l., 1551), esp. A2b–A3a, edited in C&C 2:752–777; cf. the Leipzig "Interim" text, CR 7:63.

10 Title in note 1 above. On the course of the controversy, cf. Matthias Richter, *Gesetz und Heil. Eine Untersuchung zur Vorgeschichte und zum Verlauf des sogenannten Zweiten Antinomistischen Streits* (Göttingen: Vandenhoeck & Ruprecht, 1996), 94–131, and Robert Kolb, "Georg Major as Controversialist, Polemics in the Late Reformation," *Church History* 45 (1975): 455–468.

11 On the continuing use of the mention of his Slavic origins, as well as other oft-repeated slurs against Flacius, see Robert Kolb, "Controversia perpetua. Die Fortsetzung des adiaphoristischen Streits nach dem Augsburger Religionsfrieden," in *Politik und Bekenntnis. Die Reaktion auf das Interim von 1548*, edited by Irene Dingel and Günther Wartenberg (Leipzig: Evangelische Verlagsanstalt, 2006), 191–209.

in protest against the Leipzig "Interim" and thus, according to Major, was not supposed to be speaking on theological matters (another standard Philippist critique of the Croatian). By shifting the blame away from himself for the controversy and offense within the Evangelical movement, Major tried to draw attention away from his own role in the composition of the Leipzig "Interim." His denial of complicity ignored his defense of its program as well as his attendance at certain key sessions where the text of the "Interim" was developed. His attempt to disassociate himself from the Leipzig "Interim" seems to suggest that he regarded his involvement as a mistake.

Major also rejected Amsdorf's appraisal of the nature of his involvement in the Leipzig "Interim." Major did acknowledge that he had taken part in some of the preparations. He denied that he had recognized the pope as the chief bishop of the church, or the mass and its ceremonies as true worship. Instead, he boasted that he had attacked the papacy itself rather than getting bogged down in criticizing trifles such as the wearing of surplices. All the while, Major sidestepped Amsdorf's basic criticism that the adiaphorists' whole project with the Leipzig "Interim" was wrong because ecclesiastical actions and worship practices speak louder than words, and thus, the document wrought confusion among the laity. It was, of course, also to Major's advantage to please Moritz by writing more against papal principles than against the specific issues prescribed in the Augsburg Interim.

Most significantly, though, Major countered Amsdorf's objection to the "Interim's" omission of the word "alone" (*sola*) in descriptions of saving faith and to the "Interim's" statement, "good works are necessary for salvation." In so doing, Major sparked what came to be called "the Majoristic controversy." After pointing out in his *Answer* of 1552 that he had often used the word *sola* (capitalizing it to show the importance of the word) with regard to saving faith in his recently published works, Major wrote:

> This I confess: I have previously taught and still teach, and want to teach my whole life, that good works are necessary for salvation, and I say openly and with clear and plain words, that no one will be saved through evil works and no one will be saved without good works, and I say further, whoever teaches otherwise, even an angel from heaven, is accursed. . . . Through evil works no one merits heaven but only hell. So it must follow that where there are no evil works, there must be good works. For a person must not be a stone or block of wood, which does neither evil nor good. But faith and the Holy Spirit and Christ,

> who dwells in us through faith, are active and powerful in us and drive us so that we live according to the Spirit, not according to the flesh, and produce all the fruits of the Spirit. . . . For it is impossible that a person has true faith and does not have at the same time all kinds of good works. The sun cannot exist without shining. So where Christ and the Holy Spirit dwell in a person, faith shines forth through good works.[12]

Major was convinced this teaching was simply what Luther had taught. Major believed good works could not merit or effect forgiveness of sins and eternal life, but he felt good works needed to be described as "necessary" in order to ensure that people would live good lives as a result of their faith. He intended the statement "good works are necessary for salvation" to mean God commanded his human creatures to perform good works, and thus, they are a necessary part of the saved life. Major was so convinced of this he asked a rhetorical question in his *Answer*: how could such an old teacher of the church as Amsdorf write that good works are not necessary for salvation? Major was convinced that Amsdorf's teaching was antinomian, and he refused to see how provocative his own question was.

In the charged atmosphere of the Saxon church at the time, little sparks could easily set off a grand explosion. Fear that the Gospel was going to be lost—whether through an imperial occupation of Saxony or through the compromising of electoral Saxon theologians—was the impetus for much of what was said, done, written, and believed by Luther's followers at that time. The exchanges between Major and Amsdorf were no exception.

Much of the disagreement between Amsdorf and Major hung on their differing definitions of key words, though their political circumstances continued to necessitate that they defend their respective positions—Moritz (in Major's case) and the Ernestine interests (in Amsdorf's case). Amsdorf associated the term "good works" with the late medieval framework of human deeds meriting God's favor. Major defined this term as the natural product of believing that God's word of absolution bestows righteousness upon sinners—as Major's Wittenberg instructors, including Amsdorf, had taught. Amsdorf understood the word "necessary" as "that which causes another thing to be"; Major used "necessary" to describe what naturally and, therefore, necessarily results from something—in this case, from faith. Amsdorf understood the German word "*Seligkeit*" in a restricted, theological sense: God's justifying act of rescuing sinners and restoring them to be his children. Major defined "*Seligkeit*" literally as "blessedness": the entire result of "*Erlösung*" (redemption), the entire result of God's

12 Major, *Antwort*, C1b–C2b.

gracious rescue and restoration of the righteousness of the sinner in his sight. That "blessedness" included the enjoyment of the God-designed life, filled with good works. Scholars have sometimes dismissed this controversy as "merely" semantic, but for the Wittenberg reformers, no theological battle could be "merely" semantic. Words constitute and convey reality when they come from the speaking God, according to Luther and Melanchthon; so their followers believed that it was necessary to select clear expressions in order to carry out the proper proclamation of God's message of salvation. In this case, a lack of clarity about the terms being used helped turn the theological and political tensions between Amsdorf and Major into a controversy.

Major had not participated in the debate between Conrad Cordatus and Caspar Cruciger in Wittenberg in 1536; he was teaching at Amsdorf's side in Magdeburg at the time. But from both Amsdorf and Melanchthon, Major had learned to be wary of antinomian excesses. Therefore, he shared his preceptors' concern that parishioners' behavior reflect the impact of the Gospel. The anthropological concern Melanchthon imparted to his students led Major to feel it was necessary to safeguard the Christian's moral life against misinterpretations of Christian liberty and the message of salvation through faith alone. Therefore, for Major, the phrase "good works are necessary for salvation" could counter nonchalance about Christian living and admonish Christians not to find security for their sins in a false conception of the Gospel. And that phrase in the Leipzig Proposal would also help convince Charles V that electoral Saxony was not defying the Augsburg Interim. Major did not understand how Amsdorf could take exception to such an obvious and fundamental teaching about the Christian life.

Amsdorf certainly did take exception. Amsdorf responded with a document entitled *Instruction on Major's Answer*, composed in Eisenach in 1552.[13] He declared that Major had set up a straw man by implying that Amsdorf taught that a Christian could live without good works and by implying that others were teaching that evil works could merit heaven. Major's writing had not stated either of those points directly, but Amsdorf wanted to meet every insinuation in order to convince his readers of Major's perfidy. It is difficult to know whether such tactics reflect genuine anger between two former colleagues and friends or whether such tactics simply reflect the habits of the medieval disputation.

---

13 *Ein kurtzer vnterricht auff D. Georgen Majors Antwort/ das er nit vnschu[e]ldig sey/ wie er sich tragice rhu[e]met. Das gute werck zur seligkeit nit von no[e]ten sind. Das gut werck zu eim Christlichen leben hie auff erden no[e]tig sind* ("Basel," 1552), edited in C&C 3:46–73. The designation of Basel as the place of printing is undoubtedly false. By this time Magdeburg was under Moritz's control, and printers there could not openly publish criticisms of his theologians. The type also seems to be that of Christian Rödinger.

However, Amsdorf did voice doubts about Major's good faith. He argued that not even the heathen doubt that people should perform good works. He also asserted that Major already knew that Amsdorf rejected every form of antinomianism. Therefore, the critical issue was whether Christians must perform works alongside faith to merit salvation. Major had declared that this was not the issue. Yet, to Amsdorf in the context of the early 1550s and the presence of the Leipzig "Interim," there was no other way to understand the phrase "good works are necessary for salvation." Amsdorf had always taught, as he did again in his *Instruction on Major's Answer*, that Christians fear and love God after their rebirth and that their lives are filled with good works. Those good works praise and give thanks to God; they confirm the believer's calling to the faith, mortify his old nature, and help his neighbor. The Christian is bound to perform such works as a child of God. But they cannot be considered necessary for salvation, the bishop argued.

Amsdorf had heard the very words "good works are necessary for salvation" many times before in his life. He reminded Major that the cathedral canons in Magdeburg had espoused that doctrine as they attempted to snuff out the infant Reformation movement that Major and Amsdorf had labored to establish there. Amsdorf also noted that two of Luther's papal archenemies, Johannes Cochlaeus and Georg Witzel, had used the same words as Major's proposition to convict Luther of heresy.[14]

Amsdorf also rejected any use of the proposition "good works are necessary for salvation" on behalf of the laypeople in the church. The phrase "good works" conveyed the connotation of human merit to the common mind, and Major's attempts to give it a new meaning would not alter that perception. Amsdorf was convinced the laypeople would easily be confused and led astray by the phrase "good works are necessary for salvation," no matter how hard Major tried to gloss it over and twist it out of its natural meaning that works earn salvation. Therefore, Amsdorf ignored Major's protests of not intending to imply that the believer must contribute good works to his own salvation.

In fact, Major's teaching on this issue derived from pastoral concern as much as Amsdorf's did. Major wanted to counter antinomianism at the parish level and maintain Christian discipline. He had witnessed problems with both during his

14 Cf. Johannes Cochlaeus's *Articuli CCCCC, Martini Luther, Ex sermonibus eius Sex & Triginta* (Cologne, 1525), and his *Ein no[e]tig und christlich bedencken auff des Luthers artickeln/ die man gemeynem concilio furtragen sol* (Leipzig, 1538), H2b–H3a; and Georg Witzel's *Antwort auff Martin Luthers letzt bekennete artickel/ unsere gantze religion und das concili belangend* (s.l., 1538), F1a, F3a–b. The latter two tracts are found in Hans Volz, ed., *Drei Schriften gegen Luthers Schmalkaldische Artikel von Cochlaeus, Witzel und Hoffmeister* (Münster: Aschendorff, 1932), 39–40, 85–88.

time as assessor of the consistory which Johann Friedrich the Elder established to address disciplinary cases in the congregations of electoral Saxony. Amsdorf shared those concerns, but he was moved much more powerfully by the danger that the laypeople might be led back to the medieval concept of human good works contributing to salvation. That concern was central to the Reformation movement when Amsdorf became a part of it. Therefore, he was convinced that anyone who did not also make that the primary concern, especially someone who was willing to compromise with the Roman party through a document like the Leipzig "Interim," was promoting Rome's understanding of the role of works in salvation. As in his conflict with Melanchthon in the 1530s, Amsdorf's theocentric approach to all theological questions clashed with Major's concern for how the Gospel motivates human responsibility.

Amsdorf was not the only reformer who associated Major's proposition with papal teaching. Though Amsdorf had already moved to Eisenach by the time he launched his *Instruction on Major's Answer* against Major, his colleagues in Magdeburg sprang to his aid, also countering Major's *Answer*. Flacius and Gallus responded with treatises attacking Major's proposition "good works are necessary for salvation" for many of the same reasons Amsdorf had. They agreed that Major's proposition could only be understood as it had always been—that good works merit salvation.[15] Flacius also prepared a single folio leaf response that contained a syllogism that made Major's conclusions seem absurd.[16]

Major had written his *Answer* from Eisleben, for shortly after Amsdorf's first attack on him, Major assumed his superintendency of the churches in Mansfeld county. The ministerium that he had come to supervise had opposed the Leipzig "Interim" from the beginning of the controversy over it, and its members harbored suspicions of their new superior. Before he left Eisleben at the end of 1552, Major worked on a defense of his understanding of salvation; he published it in early 1553 in the form of a sermon for the festival of Saint Paul's conversion. In it, he presented his understanding of justification, faith, and good works.[17]

---

15 Among other treatises, Flacius wrote *Wider den Evangelisten des heiligen Chorrocks D. Geitz Maior* ("Basel," 1552), edited in C&C 3:74–95, and Nikolaus Gallus issued *Auf des Hrn. D. Majors Verantwortung und Declaration . . . Antwort* Gallus ("Basel," 1552), edited in C&C 3:96–128; Otto Ritschl, *Dogmengeschichte des Protestantismus* 2 (Leipzig: Hinrich, 1912), 389–394, credits Gallus with the most insightful of the critiques of Major's position. Cf. Luka Ilić, *Theologian of Sin and Grace. The Process of Radicalization in the Theology of Matthias Flacius Illyricus* (VIEG 225; Göttingen: Vandenhoeck & Ruprecht, 2014), 97–105.

16 Flacius, *Ein kurtz Scartecklein Ill. Vber das lange Comment Maioris. Aus dem buch Maioris widder H. Amsdorff Anno 1552 ausgangen* (Magdeburg: Christian Rödinger, 1553).

17 *Ein Sermon von S. Pauli vnd all der Gottfu[e]rchtigen menschen bekerung zu Gott* . . . (s.l., 1553), edited in C&C 3:130–279.

This *Sermon* emphasized Major's belief in salvation by grace alone through faith alone, often capitalizing "alone" to accentuate his recognition of the importance of this word that excluded all works from justification. Major insisted that the only basis for salvation is the mercy seat of Christ. Faith must grasp no other object than Christ and must rely upon him alone as the only mediator between God and sinners. Major denied that good works can contribute to salvation; they do not prepare the way for grace, nor do they stand alongside faith in effecting salvation; they do not contribute to salvation as a consequence of faith. However, when discussing the new obedience of the believer, Major seemed to vitiate his defense of the exclusive roles of grace and faith in determining the relationship of God with his chosen people. The Christian experiences a new birth by faith, and the Holy Spirit fashions in him a new creature, created in Christ for the performance of good works (Ephesians 2:10). These good works—or the new obedience—that the Holy Spirit creates form the first part, the beginning, of the blessed life. Major believed that justification effects a state—salvation—in which the justified sinner lives as a reborn child of God. He referred to that life as *Seligkeit* in its broadest sense, meaning "blessedness." For Major, salvation resulted from and, thus, followed justification. Amsdorf regarded the two words as synonyms. Amsdorf used *Seligkeit* to mean "salvation" in the narrow theological sense—that which rescues and restores. Therefore, Amsdorf initially interpreted Major's statements that *Seligkeit* embraces good works to mean human deeds form an integral element of the action which rescues sinners from their sin and frees them from their guilt. This echoed the medieval scholastic formulation that faith had to be completed by acts of love in order to win salvation. Even when Amsdorf later recognized what Major was trying to say, he still felt Major's stubborn persistence in using unclear language must spring from a desire to undermine or soften Luther's rejection of any human contribution to salvation. This demonstrates that the context of the dispute over the Leipzig "Interim" framed Amsdorf's interpretation of everything the electoral Saxon theologians said in those days.

In this *Sermon*, Major tried to draw attention to his support of the basic Lutheran teaching that rejected any human contribution to the actual rescue and restoration of sinners. He even used Amsdorf's favorite illustration, learned from Luther, of faith producing good works in the life of a believer as a good tree produces good fruit. And he agreed with Amsdorf that first a believer must become a "good tree," being reborn and made righteous through faith. Major rejected Pelagianism by discrediting any work that is not performed in faith. He distinguished outer works (external compliance with God's commands) from inner works (truly godly virtues arising out of a true recognition of God in the heart). However, he wrote that faith was chief among these godly virtues, echoing part of the Leipzig "Interim." Amsdorf defined faith as the trust in Christ that is created by the power of God and that works in believers and defines their entire person. Major, on the other hand, at times reduced faith to a good work, even if he considered it the best good work.

Major tried to put his proposition "good works are necessary for salvation" in the proper light. However, the more he tried to explain his view, the more Amsdorf criticized Major's position. Major said his proposition meant good works are necessary for the reward God gives to believers when they reach heaven. He insisted that good works do not earn that reward, but he also did not clarify further the relationship between the heavenly reward and good works. Major asserted that though good works do not join with faith to effect salvation, good works are necessary to retain salvation; good works must be present to keep evil out of the believer's life and to free him from his flesh, his old nature. In Amsdorf's view, this came dangerously close to the reform-minded Catholics' teaching that the justified Christian is acceptable to God on the basis of works God's grace produces in the believer. However, Major believed retracting his words would encourage false security in sinners.

Major's long and detailed defense of his soteriology in the *Sermon* contained a handful of polemical statements. Major accused his opponents of breaking the Fourth Commandment when they attacked the electoral government, reviving the charge that the Magdeburg theologians were committing civil rebellion. Major also implied that Amsdorf had taught that repentance and the fruits of faith are not part of the Christian life. It was not Major's primary goal to provoke his antagonists, however. Instead, he strove to prove that he remained a loyal follower of Luther. He repeatedly rejected the doctrines that combined faith and works as the necessary ingredients of a believer's righteousness, including those found in the Augsburg Interim, and he repeatedly confessed that believers are saved by grace through faith alone. He was certain he had given sufficient explanation to justify his continued use of the phrase.

Amsdorf disagreed. He prepared a critique of what he called Major's "great Koran," though Amsdorf's manuscript was never printed.[18] Even the printers who knew Amsdorf well may not have wanted to publicize his "Preliminary Thoughts

18 "Ein Vorlauff auff Georg Maiors grosse buch von guthen wercken, Nicolaus von Amsdorff," Wf, Guelf. Helmst. 82:511–516. Cf. a much shorter polemical comment on Psalm 26, "Der xxvi psalm wider die Adiaphoristen kurtzlich erclert," Jäger, *Amsdorf*, 119–127.

on Georg Major's Big Book on Good Works" because of its strong language: it labeled Major's proposition as papist, heathen, devilish, and anti-Christian without effectively coming to terms with the issues Major's proposition raised. Amsdorf's printers were theologically astute enough to recognize that, for they were part of the Gnesio-Lutheran team.[19] The substance of what Amsdorf wrote in "Preliminary Thoughts" did nothing more than retrace the path his *Instruction* document had followed. Amsdorf was not persuaded by the recent development of a distinction between inner and outer works in Major's writing. That distinction had been designed to meet the earlier concern that Major's proposition would cause a dying person to not be sure if he had done enough good works to win salvation. Major had answered that the disposition of faith itself was a good work, an inner work, sufficient to assure the dying person that he was performing necessary good works. Amsdorf regarded this as still a matter of looking inward rather than to the cross of Christ.

The works against Major's *Sermon* by some of Amsdorf's Magdeburg colleagues were appearing in print at this time, however. Gallus and Flacius published treatises in 1553 and elicited supporting memoranda from the ministeria of Lübeck, Hamburg, and Lüneburg. These opinions, along with one issued by the Magdeburg clergy, were published with a preface by Flacius and Gallus, also in 1553.[20] In their requests for the memoranda from these ministeria, Flacius and Gallus described the controversy as a dispute between Major and "the revered Nikolaus von Amsdorf, the faithful and resolute servant of Christ, our father and most esteemed preceptor." They called their colleagues to join Luther in rejecting the papistic proposition which Major was reviving, entangling his readers in ambiguity and a meandering argument. The four ministeria treated Major's view in slightly different ways, but all agreed that it must be rejected. About the same time, the ministerium in Mansfeld, where Major had been the superintendent, also issued a rejection of Major's views.[21]

---

19 Amsdorf had a good working relationship with Christian Rödinger in Jena, who came from Magdeburg in 1553 to publish the Jena edition of Luther's Works at the invitation of Johann Friedrich the Elder. Thomas Rebart joined Rödinger as a printer in Jena in 1558. Donat Richtzenhan arrived the following year. Both served Amsdorf briefly. Cf. Christoph Reske, *Die Buchdrucker des 16. und 17. Jahrhunderts im deutschen Sprachgebiet* (Wiesbaden: Harrassowitz, 2015), 433–434.

20 *Auff die newe subtile verfelschung der Euangelij Christi/ in Doctor Maiors Comment . . . Erklerung vnd antwort Nicolai Galli* (s.l., 1553); *Eine kurtze Antwort II. Auff das lange Comment D. Ge. Von guten wercken* (s.l., s.d.); *Sententia Ministrorvm Christi in Ecclesia Lubecensi, Hamburgensi, Luneburgensi & Magdeburgensi, de corruptelis doctrinae iustificationis, quibus D. Georg. Maior adserit* (Magdeburg, 1553), reprinted in Conrad Schluesselburg, *Haereticorum Catalogus* 7 (Frankfurt/M: Saurius, 1597): 561–658.

21 *Bedencken das diese Proposition oder Lere nicht nütz not noch war sey vnnd one ergernis in der Kirchen nicht möge geleret werden. Das gute werck zur seligkeit nötig sind. Vnd vnmuglich sey one gute werck selig werden. Gestellet durch die Prediger zu Mansfelt Vnnd vnterschrieben von andern Predigern derselben Herrschafft* (Magdeburg: Michael Lotther, 1553), edited in C&C 3:280–314. A synod of the Mansfeld ministerium held in February 1554

From Eisenach, Amsdorf endorsed and welcomed these groups' support by publishing his own subscription to their critiques of Major's proposition.[22] Amsdorf's tone and treatment of his disagreement with Major remained unyielding in this publication in 1553. Amsdorf once more reported that Major's proposition could only be understood as teaching that good works earn salvation. In this tract, he acknowledged Major's distinction between inner and outer works, but he observed that because inner works result from rebirth, they cannot be necessary for it. He declared that God alone, not a believer's good works, preserves faith and salvation. Amsdorf would not waver, so long as Major insisted on upholding statements they both had risked their lives to oppose in Magdeburg.

Amsdorf's 1553 treatise, published less than two years after his original attack, was the last work he devoted to criticizing only Major in this controversy. But the controversy over the necessity of good works for salvation remained alive, and Major was forced to remain a participant, albeit an increasingly reluctant one. In 1555, Major complained to King Christian III of Denmark, the father-in-law of his prince, Elector August, that the controversy was a mistake, and Major denied ever having used the proposition "good works are necessary for salvation."[23] In later published works, Major amended his denial of the proposition by adding "in the sense in which it has been misunderstood"[24]; both forms of denial indicate Major's extreme distaste for the controversy he could not shake. He could neither abandon nor explain his proposition without sounding antinomian, and his foes perpetually distrusted his attempts to explain a position that they believed undercut the heart of Luther's and Melanchthon's teaching.

For a few years, Major ceased to be the focal point of the controversy, but his ideas (often labeled "Majorism" at the time) continued to cause conflict and strife for Amsdorf and many of his contemporaries.

---

also rejected Major's views, *Acta oder handlungen des Lo[e]blichen Synodi/ in der Stad zu Eisleben/ in der Graff vnd Herschafft Mansfelt/ den xiij. Febru. Des Jars/ 1554. versamlet/ wider etliche falsche Leren/ darinnen verdammet* (Eisleben: Jacob Berwalt, 1554), edited in C&C 3:354–389.

22 *Vnterschreibung des Herrn Niclas Amsdorffs der Sechsischen Kirchen Censurn vnd meinung/ wider Doctor Georg Maiors Antichristische lere von guten wercken als zur seligkeit no[e]tig* (Magdeburg, 1553).

23 In a letter dated October 4, printed in Andreas Schumacher, *Gelehrter Männer Briefe an die Könige in Dannemark, vom Jahr 1522 bis 1663* 2 (Copenhagen: Pelt, 1758), 197; cf. a similar letter dated April 1, 1558, Schumacher, *Briefe*, 2:224. For a fuller discussion of the context of Major's statement, see Kolb, "Georg Major as Controversialist."

24 *Repetitio: Widerholung vnd endliche Erklerung der Bekentnis D. Georgij Maioris. Von dem Artickel der Justification . . . vnd von Guten Werken* (Wittenberg: Lufft, 1558), B1a.

JUSTUS MENIUS HAS APOSTATIZED

Justus Menius left the Benedictine monastery in Fulda for the University of Erfurt in 1514. There he joined a circle of biblical humanists around Conrad Mutian and Crotus Rubeanus that had included Justus Jonas, Georg Spalatin, Johann Spangenberg, and other prominent followers of Luther. In 1519, Menius arrived at the University of Wittenberg and became a friend of Luther and Melanchthon and most likely of Amsdorf as well. Like many others in Wittenberg in the 1520s, Melanchthon's influence shaped Menius's expression of what he learned from Luther. Menius served as pastor in Thuringia through his career, as the ecclesiastical superintendent in Eisenach from 1529 to 1547, and as the ecclesiastical superintendent in Gotha from 1545 to 1556. There is no record that there was discord between Menius and Amsdorf when Amsdorf moved to Eisenach in 1552 and began exercising some of the powers Menius had been exercising in that part of Thuringia. Menius made important contributions to the Wittenberg reform program as a catechist, commentator, polemicist (especially against Anabaptists), and administrator. After the post-war division of Johann Friedrich's lands, Menius was one of several men closely associated with Melanchthon who served the young lords with Melanchthon's blessing. Menius also played a leading role in the ecclesiastical affairs of the new ducal Saxony, alongside Amsdorf, in the years immediately following the defeat at Mühlberg.

Thus it was natural for Johann Friedrich the Middler to include both Menius and Amsdorf in the task of visiting the churches in his lands soon after his father's death in 1554.[25] The dukes' court preacher, Johann Stolz, nominated Amsdorf as chief visitor and then appointed himself, Menius, and Erhard Schnepf, a professor in Jena, as Amsdorf's clerical assistants. They were accompanied by several secular counselors, with Christian von Brück at the head, the son of Gregor von Brück, the faithful chancellor to the Ernestine Saxon princes since the regime of Frederick the Wise. Johann, Luther's son who had become a lawyer, also served on the visitation team. The visitors were instructed to correct deficiencies in the doctrine, education, and moral conduct of the pastors and to improve their economic situation when congregations were providing inadequate support for their pastors. The visitors introduced a new ordination oath,

25 For the articles of visitation, see Emil Sehling, ed., *Die Evangelischen Kirchenordnungen des 16. Jahrhunderts* 1, 1 (Leipzig: Reisland, 1902), 222–228. The planning and conduct of the visitation is treated in Arno Heerdegen, *Geschichte der allgemeinen Kirchenvisitation in den ernestinschen Landen im Jahre 1554/1555* (Jena: Fischer, 1914), 18–63, 67–172, and in Rudolf Herrmann, "Die Generalvisitation in den ernestinischen Landen zur Zeit der Lehrstreitigkeiten des 16. Jahrhunderts (1554/55, 1562, 1569/70, 1573)," *Zeitschrift des Vereins für thüringische Geschichte und Altersthumskunde* 22 (30) (1915): 77–91, 94–109.

perhaps written by Amsdorf, in which a candidate pledged to teach the Gospel according to Luther's Smalcald Articles and to reject Zwinglian, Anabaptist, and "antichristian-Roman" teaching. The visitors tried to eliminate vestiges of papal practice, including impious, offensive images and Latin in litanies and collects. They attempted to move altars away from chancel walls, limited the use of special vestments, and imposed regulations on the ringing of church bells.[26] Johann Friedrich the Middler initiated the visitation in order to extend his control as prince over ecclesiastical life in his domains. The clerical visitors resented this; they also complained that von Brück, the dukes' chief secular advisor, practiced a tight-fisted economic policy in regard to the needs of the church.

However, theological disagreement created more of a disruption in the visitation than these other sources of discord. Near the end of their first visit, their inspection at Weimar, Amsdorf and Stolz demanded that the other visitors reject Majorism and root it out of ducal Saxony. They presented a number of books to their fellow visitors, asking that the contents be condemned for adiaphoristic and Majoristic errors. Menius refused. He did regard Major's proposition as suspect; but he was confident Major had not strayed from Wittenberg teaching, rather only from a proper formulation of what they all had learned as Luther's and Melanchthon's students. Menius said that he was uncertain about the content of the alleged adiaphoristic material and that he had never read Major's works. It seems highly unlikely that Menius, as one of ducal Saxony's most important ecclesiastical leaders, had not found time to study the exchange between Major, his own friend from Wittenberg, and Amsdorf, the most powerful clergyman in the area. It does seem likely, however, that Menius did not want to become embroiled in an acrimonious dispute with his colleagues. He argued that it was unwise to attack Wittenberg theologically and, thereby, disturb the political peace recently established by a treaty between ducal Saxony and electoral Saxony. He also pointed to Amsdorf's and Stolz's approval of Major's commentary on Philippians as proof that the controversy did not need to continue.[27]

There is no evidence that Amsdorf was trying to entrap Menius with the proposal to condemn Major. It is odd that Amsdorf had not proposed such a condemnation when he was working on the text of the visitation articles before the

---

26 For an account of the visitation, see Gehrt, *Konfessionspolitik*, 85–97.

27 The contemporary source of the narrative of much of his story is *Bericht Der bittern Warheit Ivsti Menii Auff die Vnerfindlichen aufflagen M. Flacij Illyric/i vnd des Herrn Niclas von Amsdorffs* (Wittenberg, 1558); see also Gehrt, *Konfessionspolitik*, 99–105; Richter, *Gesetz und Heil*, 132–169; Gustav L. Schmidt, *Justus Menius, der Reformator Thüringens* 2 vols. (Gotha: Perthes, 1867), esp 2:184–192; Heerdegen, *Geschichte*, 66–67; and Alvin H. Horst, "The Theology of Justus Menius," Th.D. dissertation, Concordia Seminary, Saint Louis, 1973, esp. 239–267. Menius referred to Major's *Enarratio epistolae Pavli, scriptae ad Philippenses* (Wittenberg: Hans Lufft, 1554).

team started their travels. Yet Stolz also had not found it necessary to address the problem in his formulation of the visitation articles. Amsdorf may have simply been unaware of other theologians' responses to Major. Little had been published about this debate, besides the work of Amsdorf's Magdeburg comrades who had jumped into the fray against Major. In fact, there is no documentary evidence of any printed or spoken public challenges to Amsdorf in ducal Saxony in the years prior to the visitation. Perhaps, then, Amsdorf was genuinely not expecting to encounter disagreement from any of his visitation team colleagues when he proposed a clear condemnation of Major's writings. This suggests that the controversy surrounding Major did start as a personal dispute between himself and Amsdorf.

Menius had, however, maintained friendships and contacts with the Wittenberg theologians during the controversies over the Leipzig "Interim." He also sent his sons to study in Wittenberg instead of Jena. Amsdorf's later criticism of Menius makes it clear that any hint of Menius's willingness to defend "the adiaphorists" quickly created an insurmountable divide between Menius and Amsdorf.[28] It is possible Amsdorf's response to Menius was so resolute because Amsdorf had long-simmering suspicions about Menius. On the other hand, it is not surprising Amsdorf was quick to condemn Major's proposition formally, since he was so intensely involved in the controversy against Major.

Menius composed one hundred ten theses on possible proper uses of Major's proposition.[29] In late November 1554, he requested ducal permission to leave the visitation team, pleading ill health. Amsdorf replied to Menius's propositions soon thereafter, after giving the other visitors his counter-propositions.[30] He rejected Menius's attempts to put positive constructions on Major's proposition; he maintained that the difference between the simple statement "good works are necessary for salvation" and Menius's understanding of the phrase, "good works are necessary for acquiring salvation" was not at all clear. Amsdorf rejected Menius's application of the phrase to the life of the reborn believer; he stated that the phrase simply destroys the need for Christ's work, for repentance,

28 Cf. his manuscript comment on Matthew 11:6 from late spring or summer 1558, "Ein Auslegung des spruchs Math. XI. Selig ist der sich an mir nicht ergert," Jäger, *Amsdorf*, 201–216.

29 The propositions are found in Wf, Guelf. 19.14 Aug. 4:207–213; see also Heerdegen, *Geschichte*, 66; Schmidt, *Menius*, 2:187–188.

30 Schmidt, *Menius*, 2:188, and Heerdegen, *Geschichte*, 66, assert that Amsdorf wrote first a set of one hundred ninety-five theses and then forty-six more on Christmas Day. Gottlieb Jacob Planck, *Geschichte der Entstehung . . . der Konkordienformel* (Leipzig: Crusius, 1796–1800), 4:519, mentions only one set of propositions, numbering one hundred seventy-eight, probably the set entitled "Propositiones Nicolai Amsdorffij contra Iusti Menij propositiones 25. Decemb 1554," Jäger, *Amsdorf*, 134–160; copies in Wr, ETLFB 40:311a–320a and in Wf, Guelf. Helmst. 82:684a–690a.

and for the Sacraments. Amsdorf affirmed once more that true faith always produces good works, and that the believer lives a new, Christian life. His remarks make clear that he viewed salvation as the dynamic action of God, not the state in which the justified sinner lives; he stated that salvation is simultaneous with, if not completely synonymous with, justification.

Amsdorf also rejected Menius's affirmation of the proposition "good works are necessary for salvation theoretically in the doctrine of the Law." In accord with the teaching of many Wittenberg students, but at odds with Luther's understanding that the only possible basis of the proper relationship between God and his human creatures lies in the grace of God, Menius contended that perfectly keeping God's commands would earn salvation (since such fulfillment of the Law would be the result of God's gracious regard for the creatures he made). Amsdorf insisted that the Law condemns and kills; everyone who lives by the works of the Law is under the curse.

This new formulation that Menius espoused would soon involve him in controversy with friends as well as foes. He did not reply to Amsdorf directly but instead contacted their colleague, Erhard Schnepf, the professor at Jena. Menius restated to Schnepf that he believed Major had intended to express a biblical truth in his proposition. He believed Major did not intend to say that good works are a condition for the reception of salvation, but he did concede that Major did not make his position as clear as was necessary. Schnepf met with Menius on January 2, 1555, and decided that, in spite of some suspect formulations in Menius's writings, his position was acceptable. Menius then met with his fellow members of the ducal Saxon visitation team while they were inspecting the church at Gotha. In that meeting, Menius still refused to condemn Major, arguing that Major's proposition was not "simply false but just ambiguous." Menius believed Major's proposition was true in hypothetical conditions: according to the doctrine of the Law, if a person could do all the good works God's Law required, that person would earn salvation.[31]

Johann Friedrich the Middler was upset by this dissension among his clergy and issued an order for Menius to abstain from any defense of Majorism. However, rumors were spreading through Saxony that Menius had deserted the Gospel, and he felt compelled to prepare an *Apology against the Untrue Slanders* for his own defense.[32] He sent it to Erfurt, outside ducal Saxony, for publication.

31 Schmidt, *Menius*, 2:188–191.

32 *Entschuldigung Justi Menii/ Auff die vnwarhafftige verleumbdung darinnen jm auffgeleget wird/ als solt er von der reinen Lere des Evangelij abgefallen sein* (Gotha, 1555), reprinted in Menius, *Bericht*, H1b-J1a. See Schmidt, *Menius*, 2:192–193.

The visitors learned of this and informed the ducal Saxon court. The court sent officials to confiscate copies of Menius's tract at the printer's shop. Johann Friedrich the Middler was not willing to let the affairs of his church get out of control. However, when he read Menius's tract, the prince found it inoffensive, and in the end, he permitted its release.

Amsdorf responded to Menius's *Apology against the Untrue Slanders* with a memorandum that argued the issue at stake was not how Major or Menius understood the words "good works are necessary for salvation" but rather how the common people would understand them, reflecting Amsdorf's abiding concern. He said that Menius's attempts to reinterpret Major's proposition made it mean the opposite of what the words seem to mean. Only clear concepts should be used in the church, so this proposition ought to be condemned to avoid misleading the laity.[33]

Menius recognized that Amsdorf's opposition to his stance posed a threat to him. On February 15, 1555, a ducal messenger delivered Menius a summons, stipulating that he appear before local ducal officials and commanding that he not leave the duchy. Menius left for Halle, outside the young lords' jurisdiction, the next day. He returned to Gotha on March 26 and wrote to Johann Friedrich the Middler to explain his action. His letter reasserted that he was firmly committed to Luther's teaching. But he also asked to be released from his office as superintendent of the church in Gotha if he was not going to be allowed to offer a public defense of himself against slander. Johann Friedrich's ambiguous reply postponed a final decision on the matter. So Menius continued in his office as Gotha's ecclesiastical superintendent.[34]

In early 1556, Menius published two books, *On Preparing for a Blessed Death* and *On Salvation*, in one volume.[35] Those topics could not be treated without commenting on good works. Menius's concern for virtuous action and for the righteous living of his parishioners was evident. He had been shaped by disputes with antinomian and libertine radicals early in his ministry as well as Luther's and Melanchthon's teachings about the human responsibility to obey God's commands. Menius declared that new obedience is necessary for salvation. To be saved, a believer must not only receive the Holy Spirit but must also let himself be ruled in faith by the Spirit. Menius repeatedly emphasized that

33 "Das Justus Menius von der reihnen lehr abgefallen sey durch seine eigene wort In seinen entschuldigung vberzeugt," Wf, Guelf. Helmst. 71a:119–120.

34 Menius, *Bericht*, J2a–K2a; see also Schmidt, *Menius*, 2:194–195, and August Beck, *Johann Friedrich der Mittlere* (Weimar: Böhlau, 1858), 2:288–289.

35 *Von der bereitung zum seligen Sterben* (Wittenberg, 1556); "Von der Seligkeit, Ein Predigt Justi Menij Vber das Evangelium Lucae X." begins on P3a.

salvation comes only through faith in Christ, and he rejected dependence on human works or merit for salvation as strongly as Amsdorf ever had. However, Menius also warned against teaching that good works are not at all necessary for salvation. Anyone who could keep God's Law perfectly, including the First Commandment to fear, love, and trust in God above all else, would win eternal life, he argued. He condemned antinomianism in words that aroused Amsdorf's suspicion. Whatever Menius may have meant, Amsdorf could and did interpret his words as an insinuation that Amsdorf had denied that Christians naturally perform good works, implying that Amsdorf regarded righteous living as an adiaphoron.

Amsdorf prepared an "Answer to the Tail or Final Portion of Justus Menius's Sermon on Salvation" in response to Menius's comments about those who viewed new obedience as an adiaphoron.[36] Amsdorf charged that the spirit of Johann Cochlaeus, one of Luther's harshest critics, and of Georg Witzel, an apostate who went back to Rome from the Wittenberg movement, permeated Menius's volume. Amsdorf deplored Menius's attempt to disturb the church of ducal Saxony. He rehearsed his oft-repeated objections to Major's proposition. His complaint reached the ducal court. The feud between Amsdorf and Menius had been going on for almost a year. Amsdorf's memorandum created another flare up when it reached the young lords in July. They immediately requested opinions from their leading theologians. Schnepf and two superintendents, Maximilian Mörlin and Johann Stössel, admitted that some of the statements in Menius's works were open to misinterpretation. Some among Schnepf's colleagues at the University of Jena and others in the Jena ministerium found nothing fundamentally objectionable in Menius's new books. The young lords decided to call their clergy to a synod at Eisenach in August.

GOOD WORKS ARE NOT NECESSARY FOR SALVATION, NOT EVEN THEORETICALLY IN THE DOCTRINE OF THE LAW

It is possible the young lords chose Eisenach as the site of the synod so that Bishop von Amsdorf would not have to travel. Age and infirmity were beginning

36 "Auf den Schwantz oder letzten anhang des Sermons von der Seligkeit Justi Menij Antwort. Niclas von Amsdorff, 1556," Wr, ETLFB 39:50a–55a (rough draft), 42:215–222 (copy in another hand, with corrections in Amsdorf's hand; this appears to have been prepared for the printer). According to Schmidt, *Menius*, 2:200–201, this document was printed. I have found no evidence beyond Schmidt's claim that it was.

to leave their marks on him. He played no decisive role during the deliberations, but he was present for them.

When Menius arrived on August 2, 1556, he hoped that the synod would finally settle the squabble in which he had become embroiled. Instead, the theologians would neither talk with him nor listen to him, according to his later, bitter statements about the synod. The written statements Menius had prepared were taken away from him until he was permitted to deliver them, on August 5. In these statements, he said the proposition "good works are necessary for salvation" was "ambiguous, equivocal, harmful, and dangerous." He continued to insist that he had not used the proposition "good works are necessary for salvation" without proper explanation in any of his written work or public statements. Any private use of the proposition among the ducal Saxon visitors had only been for the sake of disputation. He rejected the general use of the proposition. However, Menius maintained that the abstract or theoretical use of the proposition was proper in the doctrine of the Law. [37]

As evidence that this was not contrary to the Wittenberg teaching, Menius referenced the instructions Friedrich Myconius, Menius's predecessor in Gotha, had taken to England in 1538, representing the Smalcald League, in which the Wittenberg faculty was willing to accept the necessity of good works for salvation if the English insisted upon the proposition.[38] Menius also pointed out that the *Opinion* issued by the ministeria of Lübeck, Hamburg, Lüneburg, and Magdeburg against Major had stated that the doctrine of the Law does teach that good works are necessary for salvation. According to Menius's report of the proceedings, Amsdorf acted "like a vulgar sot," interrupting Menius's citation of the *Opinion* and exclaiming that Menius was an inveterate liar, that such a book had never been published in Magdeburg, and that if it had, they could chop off Amsdorf's own head—all of this even though Amsdorf had heartily endorsed the *Opinion*.[39] The text of the ministeria's *Opinion* does state, "It is the teaching of

37 Gehrt, *Konfessionspolitik*, 105–109, offers an overview of the synod; cf. the discussion of its results and impact in Richter, *Gesetz und Heil*, 132–169.

38 In 1536, commissioned by the governments of the Smalcald League, Melanchthon and others had formulated "Articles" which were to serve as the basis of negotiations with the government of Henry VIII of England and that were to pave the way for England's entry into the Smalcald League. In that text, which Myconius and his colleagues in the negotiating team that went to England in 1538 took with them, the three parts of the repentance that is necessary for salvation were summarized as "contrition, remorse; faith or the trust of the heart in God's mercy for Christ's sake, and new life or new obedience," Georg Mentz, ed., *Die Wittenberger Artikel von 1536. (Artickel der christlichen lahr, von welchen die legatten aus Engelland mit dem herrn doctor Martino gehandelt anno 1536* (Darmstadt: Wissenschaftliche Buchgesellschaft, 1968), 26/27 (25/26–46/47); cf. Irene Dingel, "Melanchthon's Paraphrases of the Augsburg Confession, 1534 and 1536, in the Service of the Smalcald League," in Dingel et al., *Philip Melanchthon. Theologian in Classroom, Confession, and Controversy* (Göttingen: Vandenhoeck & Ruprecht, 2012), 103–122.

39 Menius, *Bericht*, M2a–M3b. A copy of Menius's statement is found in Wf, Guelf. 64.11 Extr. 2°:174–177;

the Law that good works are necessary for salvation and that without them no one can be saved. That is the meaning of the Law. 'If you would enter life, keep the commandments' (Matt. 19:17), and 'do this, and you will live,' (Luke 10:28)." Menius did cite that text accurately.[40] However, no one took Amsdorf's invitation to inflict violent consequences on him for being wrong.

The other theologians at the synod did not react as vehemently as Amsdorf, but they did remain somewhat suspicious of Menius. They challenged his denial of ever having used the proposition in question. They also objected to the way Menius used the word "salvation" without distinguishing clearly enough between the believer's passive reception of grace and the believer's active obedience as a result of the indwelling of the Holy Spirit. Menius was applying Luther's and Melanchthon's fundamental distinction of passive and active righteousness, but Menius was placing them both within "salvation." The other theologians at the Eisenach synod rejected Menius's idea that the saving act of justification and the good works that result from that act could be equated. These theologians, like Amsdorf, wanted to distinguish clearly between the two kinds of righteousness, and between justification and good works. Two definitions of "*Seligkeit*" were still at work: one referring to God's act of delivering sinners and restoring their righteousness in his sight and the other referring to the state of being a justified believer, living in "blessedness," as *Seligkeit* can be translated literally. The theologians at the synod conceded that Major's proposition could have validity in the doctrine of the Law, but they also upheld that a theoretical use of the proposition is not applicable in the lives of Christians who live in the Gospel.[41]

In closed session, the theologians at the synod composed seven theses that they laid before Menius. All present subscribed, including Menius.[42] Six of the seven theses gave rise to no disagreement. The theses excluded Major's proposition from the doctrine of justification. Good works were defined as fruits of salvation, necessary for the Christian life but not for salvation. The fourth thesis asserted that faith maintains and preserves salvation; good works are not necessary for the retention of salvation. Theses five through seven defined justification and salvation in relation to each other; they stated that the errors of papal theologians concerning the necessity of good works for salvation were rejected.

Schmidt, *Menius*, 2:203–210. Menius cited *Sententia Ministrorvm* (note 20), C4a–b, Schlüsselburg, *Catalogus* 7:598.

40 *Sententia Ministrorvm*, C4b.

41 Their statement is copied in Wf, Guelf. 64.11 Extr. 2°:174–177; Schmidt, *Menius*, 2:210–216.

42 The text was printed in Flacius, *de voce & re Fidei . . . de iustitia christiana, sive Iustificatione & noua obedientia.* (Basel: Oporinus, 1563), 191–201; edited in C&C 4:29–44.

However, the first thesis of the seven caused disagreement among those gathered for the synod. It affirmed that the proposition "good works are necessary for salvation" may be tolerated in the doctrine of the Law from an abstract or theoretical point of view. The theologians distinguished the concrete use of the Law in the fallen world from a theoretical or abstract use of the Law in the ideal, perfect world God had created. They wrote,

> God's Law, comprehended in the Ten Commandments, is an eternal unchangeable rule or guiding principle, which demands perfect obedience from all reasoning creatures, angels, and human beings. Perfect obedience means sincere love toward God and other human beings, without any sin or evil lust. It promises temporal and eternal blessings to them who obey in this way. On the other hand, God's curse and wrath threaten temporal and eternal punishment to all angels and human beings who do not keep everything that is written in the book of the Law.[43]

However, though the theologians were willing to affirm that such a nuanced view of Major's proposition was true, the synod discouraged even such use of the proposition because it would confuse the common people and cause strife. Menius interpreted this thesis to mean his viewpoint had been justified, rather than censured. When he signed his name to the seven theses, his subscription also declared that he was innocent of all charges.

The first name among those who subscribed to the Eisenach synod's theses was "Nikolaus Amsdorf, Bishop." Menius reported, however, that Amsdorf protested the synod's conclusions and stormed out of the meeting in a rage after placing his name at the head of the list of eight ducal theologians who approved the synod's statement. As the aging bishop sat at home and thought over the synod, he continued to fume about its settlement. His dissatisfaction with the proceedings was fed by a warning the Evangelical ministerium in nearby Erfurt had sent to "the most worthy and most learned father in God, Nikolaus von Amsdorf, bishop of Naumburg" and the assembly at Eisenach. Though outside the jurisdiction of the young lords and nominally under the archbishop of Mainz, Erfurt's ministerium was led by Andreas Poach, one of Luther's younger students and confidants. Poach and his colleagues urged the Eisenach synod to reject any use of the concept of the necessity of good works for salvation. Poach

43 Copies of the text of the final settlement are found in Wf, Guelf. 64.11 Extr. 2°:181; Flacius, *de voce & re*, 191–205; and Schmidt, *Menius*, 2:222–237, where this quotation is found, 223–224.

ultimately opposed the synod's settlement because it had conceded the theoretical validity of Major's proposition in the doctrine of the Law.[44]

Amsdorf's fuming over the synod's resolution threatened to disrupt the ecclesiastical peace which Johann Friedrich the Middler had wrought in his lands, since other pastors might follow Amsdorf's lead and likewise become discontented with the Eisenach settlement. The duke sent two advisors to Eisenach to try to calm Amsdorf down. However, the work of these two advisors, Christian von Brück and Peter Bremen, was not very successful. After their visit, Amsdorf published a memorandum criticizing the Eisenach synod. In it, the bishop condemned certain terms that had been used in the synod's first thesis: *abstractum, concretum*, and *de idea*. Amsdorf contended that human wisdom had invented these obscure, confusing terms that could not be translated into the vernacular. They, therefore, benefitted no one and ought not be used. Amsdorf also rejected the content of the first thesis. No abstract Law exists in the world as it is, for the Law always teaches and commands works when it addresses real human hearers. Amsdorf did not expand on that simple statement, so further insight about why he rejected the theoretical viability of the concept is not clear. The impracticality of such speculation for daily pastoral practice probably generated Amsdorf's frustrations. Amsdorf may also have rejected the idea of an abstract Law that could theoretically grant righteousness because Amsdorf understood from Luther that the believer's righteousness is always a matter of God's gracious disposition. Luther held that it was not because Adam and Eve did good works that they were righteous in God's sight but because God regarded them as his children; their trust in God produced good works.

Amsdorf's criticism of the Eisenach synod in his memorandum also called into question the whole enterprise of colloquies. He described them as giving occasion for talking around issues with smooth words in order to compromise and deny the truth. From his viewpoint, Menius had used the synod to get off the hook.[45]

44 Several copies of the letter of the Erfurt ministerium are in Wf, Guelf., e.g. Helmst. 79:19–20; 64.11 Extr. 2°:167–168. This letter is dated July 30, 1556. It is likely that Viktorin Strigel, who presided at the Eisenach synod, sent Poach a report on the synod's conclusions, for he sent a report to their mutual friend in Wittenberg, Anton Otto, a pastor in Nordhausen, who held views similar to Poach's in the ensuing controversy (see Wf, Guelf. 64.11 Extr. 2°:123). Poach expressed his displeasure with the Eisenach synod's first article in a letter to Joachim Westphal in Hamburg, dated September 2, 1556, see D. H. W. Sillem, ed., *Briefsammlung des Hamburg Superintendent Joachim Westphal* (Hamburg: Gräfe & Sillem, 1903), 233–237. It contains a summary of the synod, which Poach states comes from Strigel's own hand. Poach also wrote a memorandum dated August 17, 1556, copied in Wf, Guelf. 64.11 Extr. 2°:123b–125b, which expressed similar ideas. On Poach and Otto on the role of the Law and good works, see Richter, *Gesetz und Heil*, 170–207, 251–291.

45 Amsdorf's memorandum is printed without date in Christian F. Paullini, *Historia Isenacensis*

Amsdorf's accusation that the Eisenach synod had let the truth slip away by prattling about the abstract stung the young lords. Amsdorf's charges were presented to Erhard Schnepf; Viktorin Strigel, Schnepf's colleague at the University of Jena; and Andreas Hügel, the superintendent in Jena. They rejected Amsdorf's charges and supported the first thesis from the synod's settlement. They requested ducal permission to publicly answer Amsdorf's memorandum, since manuscript copies of it were circulating widely. Apparently, this permission was not granted. For the next year, the controversy continued, but through private conversation, correspondence, and circulation of memoranda.

Amsdorf's objections to the Eisenach synod's first thesis prompted members of Johann Friedrich the Middler's ecclesiastical staff to lay the resolutions before Flacius and his colleague and friend in Magdeburg Johannes Wigand for a theological opinion from outside the dukedom. Their reply supported the concept of the theoretical necessity of good works for salvation within the doctrine of the Law.[46] This memorandum in late September 1556 provoked Amsdorf to exchange letters with them over the next nine months.

Amsdorf's willingness to dispute his friends in Magdeburg over this issue reveals how seriously he was disturbed by the first Eisenach thesis. He was willing to have an argument with his close friend Flacius about it—the same friend whom Amsdorf had recommended as a staff theologian to Johann Friedrich the Middler a few months earlier. The negotiations to appoint Flacius to Jena's theological faculty had already begun by the time of his disagreement with Amsdorf,[47] and since Flacius did assume that position in the midst of their disagreement, Amsdorf must not have vetoed his friend's appointment. And yet Amsdorf did not hesitate to criticize Flacius's ideas about the theoretical necessity of good works for salvation.

Amsdorf was so adamant about the error of the Eisenach synod's first thesis because it contradicted what Amsdorf believed about God's Law and its

(Frankfurt/M: Bauer, 1698), 171–172, and in Schmidt, *Menius*, 2:238–241. Amsdorf commented on the matter in correspondence in a letter to Johann Aurifaber, Johann Friedrich's court preacher, dated September 4, 1556, copies of which are found in Wf, Guelf. Helmst. 79:51, Nov. 863 4°:61b–62a; and in Menius, *Bericht*, O1a. The memorandum he sent with the letter is copied in Wf, Guelf. Helmst. 79:52, and Nov. 863 4°:79:60–61, printed in Menius, *Bericht*, O2a.

46 Under the title, "Von Nicolai Amstorfij Erinnerung bey dem Eisenacher Recess," a portion of the letter to Flacius and Wigand, perhaps written by their friend Johann Aurifaber, is found in Wf, Guelf. 64.11 Extr. 2°:191b–192a. Flacius's and Wigand's reply, "Sententia M. Iohan. VVigandi & Illyrici, de scripto Synodi Isenacensis, Anno Domini 1556," was printed in Flacius, *de voce & re Fidei*, 208–218. The memorandum is dated September 24, 1556.

47 Two of Amsdorf's letters to Flacius concerning the matter are found in Wf, Guelf. Helmst. 79:123, dated June 16, 1556, and Helmst. 79:124, dated June 29, 1556. Wilhelm Preger, *Matthias Flacius Illyricus* (Erlangen: Bläsing, 1859, 1861), 2:104–108, gives details on Flacius's call to Jena, as do Ilič, *Theologian*, 135–139; Olson, *Flacius*, 323–333.

functions. The Eisenach synod had viewed the Law as "an eternal, unchangeable rule or guiding principle." Flacius had learned from Melanchthon that this was true. His Gnesio-Lutheran comrades and his Philippist opponents for the most part agreed on this definition. Amsdorf shared Luther's view, which reflected Luther's Ockhamist training, which had led him to conclude that God gave the Law to his human creatures because of their transgressions, not for their justification (Galatians 3:19); God uses the Law as his tool to prepare sinners for the Gospel by pointing out their sins and instilling the fear of his wrath and curse in sinners. In Amsdorf's view, the Law could in no way be considered an instrument for salvation, contrary to the first Eisenach thesis. That was never its intended function, for that would make human performance the determining factor in the relationship of God with his human creatures. To what extent the Scotist principle that the Creator is in no way obligated to that which he creates was determining Amsdorf's thought and to what extent he was simply rejecting scholastic speculation about the abstract or the theoretical cannot be determined from his writings.[48]

Flacius and Wigand said, in disagreement with Amsdorf, that speculating about the theoretical necessity of good works for salvation in the doctrine of the Law was not idle. In their memorandum, they claimed that the Law of Moses demands good works for salvation. They believed the Law's purpose was broader than Amsdorf allowed. The Law reflected what the human creature was to be, according to the Creator's will; it defined what Adam and Eve were to do to preserve true, godly life. Flacius and Wigand maintained that the proposition "good works are necessary for salvation theoretically in the doctrine of the Law" was useful because it explained the origin of the conscience and helped people recognize God's unchangeable order, truth, and righteousness. Also, they believed it was impossible to understand or appreciate Christ's saving works without understanding that the Law demands good works for salvation.[49]

Amsdorf disagreed. For nine months, his letters to Flacius and Wigand protested their defense of the first Eisenach thesis.[50] Amsdorf did affirm with Flacius

48 Ritschl makes this suggestion, *Dogmengeschichte*, 3:404. Scotus regarded the Decalogue as God's positive Law for human creatures, Reinhold Seeberg, *Die Theologie des Johannes Duns Scotus, eine dogmengeschichtliche Untersuchung*, reprint (Aalen: Scientia, 1971), 488–491, and Étienne Gilson, *Jean Duns Scot, Introduction à ses Positions Fondamentales* (Paris: Vrin, 1952), 611–613. Amsdorf's understanding of the Law is also presented in an undated manuscript, "Propositiones de operibus Legis," Wr, ETLFB 40:331–333.

49 "Sententia Wigandi & Illyrici," 210–211, 213.

50 At least part of the correspondence between Amsdorf and Flacius on this matter is found in Wf, Guelf. Helmst. (1) 79:72, a letter from Amsdorf, dated October 10, 1556; the four leaves preceding this leaf have been removed from the volume after binding and may have been part of this letter or other related material; (2) 79:77a–80a, a letter from Amsdorf to Flacius, dated October 18, 1557; (3) 79:73b–76a, a letter from Flacius to Amsdorf, December 20, 1556; (4) 79:96b–97b, a letter from Amsdorf to an unidentified person,

that the Law demands perfect obedience from God's human creatures. Thus he recognized the validity of one of Flacius's prime concerns. However, in practice, in concrete circumstances, Amsdorf could only see one use for the Law: accusation and condemnation. He conceded that the Law reveals the standard by which sinners are judged because it does present the picture of what the human creature was before the fall. However, he could not agree with Flacius that this meant that obedience to the Law had ever established or could theoretically establish communion with God. Rather, the Law can only teach the impossibility of salvation through good works.[51]

Amsdorf's statements during this yearlong argument with his friends in Magdeburg do not reveal much about how he came to have such a polemical stance on these issues. It is possible his mind had become caught in the concrete by what triggered instinctual, emotional reactions. It does seem his strong disdain for any teaching that sounded like the adiaphorists' weaseling with words prevented him from engaging with or even precisely comprehending the nuances of Major's propositions, Menius's statements, and the arguments of Amsdorf's friends from Magdeburg. He continued to repeat that only God's gracious decision makes sinners acceptable to God. Even the perfect human being could be rejected by the Creator; the only way any person became acceptable to God was purely through God's grace, not because of perfect human obedience.[52]

---

dated the end of January in its heading and the end of February at its end (a copy); (5) 79:81a–83b, a letter from Amsdorf to Flacius and Wigand, April 22, probably 1557; (6) 79:83b–84b, a rough draft of Flacius's reply to Amsdorf, dated May 23, 1557; (7) 79:85a–88b, a letter from Amsdorf to Flacius, dated July 20, 1557. In addition, there are three memoranda from Amsdorf's hand on the subject:

(1) "Ad 18 argumenta Illyrici quibus conatur homo propositionem Maioris & Menij confirmare, opera bona in doctrina legis ad salute sunt necessaria. Responsio Nicolaj Amsdorfij," Wr, ETLFB 40:252–261, a reply to Flacius's "Quod Propositio, Obedientia legis perfecta, seu impletio legis est necessaria ad salutem, sit uera & modis omnibus in Ecclesia ferenda," Wf, Guelf. Helmst. 79:54b–64a. Flacius's memorandum is accompanied by three others: "Discrimen sententiae Saxonium aliorumque orthodoxum et Maioris ac Menej de operum necessitate ad salutem," 79:62a–67a; "Causae cur retinenda docendaque sit in Ecclesiae legalis sententia, Integra obedientia est necessaria ad salutem," 79:67a–68b; and "Iusticiam in hac vita per fidem imputatam a salute seu vita aeterna, plurimum differe, necessariaque esse in Ecclesia discernendam," 79:68b–71a.

(2) "Das die guten werck in doctrina legis nit von nöten seint, weder abstractiue noch concretius," Wr, ETLFB 39:134–140; AS, 98–105.

(3) "Wider den lughafftigen Teuffel der guthen werckenn wil zur Seligkeit notigt machen und damit Christi mertum und des glaubens aigenschafft unterdruckenn," Wf, Guelf. Helmst. 79:84a–96a.

The four items by Flacius are ascribed to Joachim Mörlin by Schlüsselburg, who printed them, *Catalogus*, 2:230–265. The fact that they appear in Flacius's hand in the Wolfenbüttel manuscripts is not absolute confirmation that they were originally written by him, but the fact that Amsdorf believed that the first of these four documents was written by Flacius seems to confirm his authorship.

51 See the three memoranda listed in note 50, particularly "Ad 18 argumenta Illyrici," passim.

52 Such a position could have arisen out of his Scotist background although we do not know enough about the specifics of central European Scotist teaching in the fifteenth and early sixteenth centuries to come to a solid judgment; cf. Werner Dettloff, *Die Lehre von der Acceptatio Divina bei Johannes Duns Scotus mit*

Furthermore, the human creature had lost the image of God through the fall and was incapable of performing truly good works. Christ was the only hope for the human creature because he had come to offer salvation through his own work of dying and rising. Amsdorf saw no use in fashioning fancy, hypothetical statements that did not apply to the reality of the sinful condition of the world. Major's effort to work out more of the details about the basis of human guilt and punishment through his propositions was not a worthwhile use of time, according to Amsdorf.

The other issue on which Amsdorf criticized Flacius and Wigand in the yearlong correspondence was agreeing with Menius's teachings on the relationship between justification and salvation. Amsdorf asserted that justification brings salvation and eternal life. He agreed it is true that salvation (literally "blessedness") will be perfected in heaven, but Christians do possess salvation from the time of their justification onward, albeit through faith and hope until heaven.[53] He wanted to uphold the teaching that God's gift of faith embraces all of God's saving action; Amsdorf quoted Luther to say that God's gift of faith gives all that is needed for the forgiveness wrought by Christ. Amsdorf argued that justification as the rescuing and saving gift must be distinguished from rebirth, the living out of the righteousness given in justification. He believed he was united with Luther and Melanchthon in refusing to isolate one part of God's giving from another, but he also insisted that justification needed to be distinguished from God's gift of power to live a godly life. Amsdorf's years of pastoral practice in Magdeburg had convinced him errors resulted when theology moved away from focusing on God, his gifts and his actions, to focusing on humans, their gifts and their actions.

Amsdorf was not afraid to use his polemical skills even against his friends. In his correspondence with Flacius in 1556 and 1557, Amsdorf suggested that perhaps Flacius's earlier attacks on Major's views had been insincere, in light of the position Flacius now was advancing. Eventually, Amsdorf told Flacius not to upset him any longer with letters if Flacius wanted to persist in his opinion. Flacius did want to persist in his opinion, but he also wanted to maintain his friendship with Amsdorf. He wrote in a nearly subservient tone as he sketched

---

besonderer Berücksichtigung der Rechtfertiungslehre (Werl/Westfallen: Colde, 1954), 84–87, 92; see also Dettloff's *Die Entwicklung der Akzeptations- und Verdienstlehre von Duns Scotus bis Luther, mit besonderer Berücksichtigung der Franziskanertheologen* (Münster: Aschendorf, 1963), 8–10, 93, 95–97, 200–202, 330–331, 334–336, which discusses the use of the principle, "nihil creatum formaliter est a deo acceptandum" and indicates that in general Scotus's insights on this subject were largely forgotten by the end of the fifteenth century, 362–365.

53 Wf, Guelf. Helmst. 79:78b, 94a–b.

his position carefully; he tried to be very tactful toward this crotchety old man whom Flacius could hardly afford to offend. He begged Amsdorf not to condemn him. He thanked his reverend father in the Lord for treating him with singular Christian kindness, and he asked for Amsdorf's guidance and correction. In spite of Flacius's efforts, Amsdorf was still not convinced that their positions were essentially the same.[54]

Common concerns shaped this dispute among friends. Flacius and Amsdorf had stood on the same side against Menius and others. But the settlement of the Eisenach synod also revealed a difference in their framework for thinking about human performance and its role in the relationship between Creator and creature. Flacius's posture toward Amsdorf in this dispute reveals the importance of Amsdorf's stature among his contemporaries. Flacius had shown himself in other circumstances to be unafraid of scorn or contempt from fellow theologians. He desired reconciliation with his foes, but always on his own terms. Yet in this dispute, he made special efforts to bridge the gap between Amsdorf and himself. Though he may have done so because he believed their differences were so small that they should not stand in the way of his and Amsdorf's common concerns, the tone of Flacius's letters to Amsdorf also suggests that he had a special fondness for Amsdorf as a spiritual father. Perhaps his eagerness to be reconciled with this spiritual father did spring from love for a man who was apparently more lovable in person than on paper. Whatever the reason, Amsdorf did claim a very important place in Flacius's mind.

THE BITTER TRUTH AND THE SWEET POISON OF LYING

Justus Menius did not share Flacius's regard for the bishop, though. From correspondence and conversations in Wittenberg while visiting Melanchthon at the end of September 1556, Menius realized how widespread and serious the rumors about his "Majorism" and "adiaphorism" had become. One of the young lords' court preachers, Johann Aurifaber, was speaking out against Menius at court as well. Menius became worried when the dukes sought opinions on the Eisenach synod's resolutions from Flacius, Wigand, and Joachim Mörlin, the ecclesiastical superintendent of the city of Braunschweig and brother of Johann Friedrich's trusted advisor, Maximilian Mörlin. Menius had thought that the

54 Wf, Guelf. Helmst. 79:73b–74a, 75b, 83b, 90a, 91b; cf. "Ad 18 argumenta Illyrici," Wr, ETLFB 40:275b, 258b, and "Das die guten Wergk," Wf, Guelf. Helmst. 79:39, 134.

synod had exonerated him once and for all, but now the dukes seemed to be wavering. At the end of November 1556, Menius left Gotha for electoral Saxony and refused to return unless the young lords offered certain guarantees. They were not ready to agree; so Menius accepted a call to Leipzig, where he died in 1558.[55] His last months were spent exchanging verbal attacks with theologians in ducal Saxony, especially Flacius, revealing a scurrility and rancor at least as intense as any exchange between the Wittenberg and the Magdeburg theologians.[56]

Menius avoided mentioning Amsdorf prominently in his first two tracts against Flacius, but they still provoked Amsdorf. Menius did sarcastically suggest in one tract that Flacius should be enthroned by an imperial diet in the middle of a marketplace with Amsdorf as one of the four high priests of the Flacius synagogue. (Menius assured readers, though, that he intended this suggestion to be ironical.)[57] But Menius's tracts irritated Amsdorf most by defending the Wittenberg and Leipzig faculties. Though the tracts were not addressed to him, Amsdorf composed a reply that attacked Menius for bowing down to the worldly wisdom of Wittenberg and Leipzig. Amsdorf did not deny that his friend Melanchthon was a highly learned man, but Amsdorf continued to believe his old friend ought to be reproved for letting Moritz's counselors talk him into supporting the Leipzig "Interim."[58] Amsdorf traced all of the controversy they had experienced in the 1550s to the Leipzig Proposal.

With Amsdorf's tract against Menius, Amsdorf won a mention in Menius's last word on the dispute, his *Report of the Bitter Truth on the Incomprehensible Accusations of Master Flacius Illyricus and Sir Nikolaus von Amsdorf.* It recited the story of Menius's support of ducal policy against the Augsburg Interim and told of his recent troubles. He repeated his earlier charges against Flacius in detail and also attacked Amsdorf.[59] Amsdorf's reply, "On the Sweet Poison of the Lying and the Bitter Anger, Envy, and Hatred of Justus Menius against the Thuringian

55 Menius, *Bericht*, P3b–Q2b; Schmidt, *Menius*, 2:245–252.

56 Against Menius's *Von der Seligkeit*, Flacius wrote *Von der einigkeit/ so für vnd wider die Adiaphora in vergangenen Jaren gestritten haben/ Christlicher einfe'tiger bericht* (s.l., 1556). The exchange continued with Menius's *Verantwortung Auff Matth. Flacij Illyrici gifftige vnd vnwarhafftige verleumbdung vnd lesterung* (s.l., 1557); Flacius's *Die alte vnd newe Lehr Justi Menij, jederman zur Warnung vnd jtzt zu einem verdrab* (s.l., s.d.), edited in C&C 3:390–406; Menius's *Kurtzer Beschaid Das seine Lare wie er für der zeit gefurt vnd noch füret nicht mit jr selbs streitig noch widerwertig sondern allenthalben einerley vnd der warheit des Euangelij gemes sey* (Wittenberg, 1557), edited in C&C 3:408–438; Flacius's *Apologia auff zwo vnchristliche Schrifften Justi Menij . . .* (Jena, 1558); and Menius's *Bericht*.

57 Menius, *Verantwortung*, F4a–b.

58 *Das Justus Menius sein Vocation vnd Kirche heimlich verlassen/ vnd von der reinen Lere des Euangelij abgefallen sey* (s.l., s.d.), esp. A2a–B4a.

59 See page 100 (note 27) above.

Ministers,"[60] remained unpublished, probably because Menius died about the time it was written. The *ad hominem* attack on Menius which it contained responded to Menius's accusations of a similar nature, that the bishop was a drunkard, had deserted Thuringia during the Interims controversies, and had wanted the dukes to execute Menius. Amsdorf met each charge, protesting particularly the ridiculousness of the last since he had not called for the execution of even the Anabaptists for religious reasons.

Menius's death ended his three-and-a-half-year feud with Amsdorf. The young lords had unwittingly set the two men on a collision course by calling them to serve together on the ducal Saxon visitation team in 1554. It is not surprising that Amsdorf wanted to use the visitation as an opportunity to prevent the implementation and use of Major's proposition with which he took issue. Menius had fought so long against radical antinomians that his disposition was to defend upright moral conduct against any suggestions of antinomianism; his friendship with the Wittenberg theologians also made him sympathetic toward those Amsdorf called "adiaphorists." The initial clash between Amsdorf and Menius stoked the old fires of the adiaphoristic controversy. The continuation of their disagreement also ignited new fires—controversies over the theoretical necessity of good works in the doctrine of the Law—even though their dispute failed to truly explore the issues at stake. The fact that they were on opposite sides of the Magdeburg-Wittenberg divide seems to have fueled their distrust of one another more than strictly personal grievances. They did exchange sharp words and mean-spirited accusations. Amsdorf's polemic against Menius may have become more spiteful than his writing against others, but if so, he was answering Menius in kind, as Menius's treatises in this dispute continued his reputation of having a poisonous pen, a reputation he earned in earlier engagements with other foes.[61] There were real differences between Amsdorf and Menius. They had different conceptions of God's Law, and their different experiences—Menius's with antinomian radicals and Amsdorf's with the cathedral preachers in Magdeburg—shaped their reactions to Major's proposition. Nonetheless, it is likely their discussions would have been much less bitter if the anger and frustration of the adiaphoristic controversy had not already infected their respective Philippist and Gnesio-Lutheran cohorts.

---

60 "Von der su[e]ssen gift der lu[e]gen vnd bittern Zcorn neid vnd has Justi Menij wider die Doringisch kirchn diener. N. Von Amsdorff," Jäger, *Amsdorf*, 163–174; copy in Wr, ETLFB 39:229–234.

61 On Menius's polemic against Anabaptists, cf. John S. Oyer, *Lutheran Reformers against Anabaptists: Luther, Melanchthon, and Menius and the Anabaptists of Central Germany* (The Hague: Nijhoff, 1964), 179–210.

GOOD WORKS ARE DETRIMENTAL TO SALVATION

By the time of Menius's death, a new, though small, controversy involving Amsdorf and Major's proposition "good works are necessary for salvation" had begun. This controversy was provoked by one of Amsdorf's attempts to counter Major's proposition. In a preface in 1557 for a publication of Luther's sermons on John 18–20,[62] Amsdorf stated that if Luther were still alive, he would condemn sects and "ravers" like the adiaphorists and Majorists. For Luther had taught, Amsdorf stated, that good works are not only not necessary to salvation but are even detrimental to salvation. He referred to Luther's 1535 commentary on Galatians as proof:

> Teaching and emphasizing works as necessary for salvation does more and greater harm than human reason can ever grasp or understand. For not only is the recognition of grace obscured through it, but Christ with all his benefits is thereby taken away and the whole Gospel . . . is perverted.[63]

Luther had used the formulation "good works are detrimental to salvation" on occasion since the 1510s; however, he used it less frequently as he grew older.[64] By saying "good works are detrimental to salvation," Amsdorf meant that trust in good works prevents the sinner from trusting in Jesus Christ as the only source of salvation. Anyone who read Amsdorf's comments on this proposition knew that was what he meant. But Amsdorf certainly laid himself open to criticism by such a statement, and those who had received Amsdorf's criticism in the past welcomed the opportunity to now call him to task. The response to Amsdorf's statement reopened the wound of disunity that Amsdorf thought was beginning to heal when the strife over the Eisenach synod's first thesis subsided.

The controversy smoldered; no one tried to fan it into a flame. Amsdorf defended his argument in a treatise, *That the Proposition "Good Works are Detrimental to Salvation" Is a Correct, True Christian Proposition, Taught and Preached by Saints*

62 This volume, *Das achtzehend vnd neunzehend Capitel vnd ein Stuck aus dem zwentzigsten S. Johannis von dem Leiden Sterben vnd Aufferstehung vnsers Herrn Jhesu Christi, Gepredigt vnd ausgelegt durch Doc. Mart. Luth. Anno M.D.XXVIII. vnd XXIX* (Jena, 1557), WA 28:765–767 (preface only), was one of several items from Luther's pen that Amsdorf brought to print during this period.

63 See Amsdorf's preface to the work, WA 28:766. The paraphrase is taken from Luther's 1535 commentary on Galatians, WA 40/1:112.16–21. Cf. Karl Thieme, "Die Schädlichkeit der guten Werke bei Luther," *Theologisches Literaturblatt* 29 (1908): 41–42.

64 Cf. Robert Kolb, "Good Works are Detrimental to Salvation, Amsdorf's Use of Luther's Words in Controversy," *Renaissance and Reformation/Renaissance et Réforme* 4 (O.S.16) (1980): 136–151.

Paul and Luther.[65] The only antagonist he named was a "Master Klügel," presumably a pun with the German word for "clever" and the name of the superintendent of Jena, Andreas Hügel.[66] Hügel had joined Viktorin Strigel in opposing Amsdorf's criticism of the Eisenach synod, and he later also supported Strigel against Amsdorf in the synergistic controversy. It is likely that Hügel not only sincerely objected to Amsdorf's proposition about good works undermining believers' faith but also that Hügel wanted to weaken Amsdorf's influence in ducal Saxony.

In his treatise *That the Proposition "Good Works are Detrimental to Salvation" Is a Correct, True Christian Proposition, Taught and Preached by Saints Paul and Luther*, Amsdorf based the proposition he espoused on two passages of Scripture: Galatians 3:10, in which Paul states that those who rely on the works of the Law are under a curse, and Philippians 3:7–9, in which Paul confesses that his righteousness under the Law has been a detriment (according to the Vulgate from which Amsdorf quoted). Amsdorf also confidently stated that this proposition reflected Luther's own view of works, since Amsdorf had heard and read Luther advance this position often while they were teaching together in Wittenberg. Amsdorf was not trying to start a controversy; he was simply trying to define and clarify his position on the question of how God saves people from sin. Amsdorf's treatise did affirm his belief in the necessity of good works as a result of faith, as the fruit of faith. But at the same time, Amsdorf was also convinced that his proposition on good works being detrimental for salvation was not confusing because to the common people, the term "good works" meant "works that merit salvation." Amsdorf affirmed again that God-pleasing actions in the Christian life are the work of the Holy Spirit in reborn believers, but faith maintains salvation. "When we commit sin," he said, "we do not lose salvation; we have already lost it through unbelief." Faith alone makes human works acceptable to God, since all human efforts are imperfect and please God only for Christ's sake. Outside of grace, no person and no work is good in God's sight; all is sin and thus condemned. [67]

Public attacks on Amsdorf's proposition in the following years were rare. The Wittenberg faculty decried the proposition for encouraging antinomianism, but

65 *Das die Propositio*. Amsdorf also developed his defense of his proposition in two extant manuscripts: (1) "Propositiones Nicolai Amsdorfij Contra nouas Maioristas," Wr, ETLFB 40:246a–251a; another copy 40:321a–326b; dated July 7, 1558; (2) "Widder die Maioristen so Georg Maiorem schützen vnd verteidigen," ibid., 39:80a–89a; another copy 39:58a–65b (possibly a rough draft of *Das die Propositio*).

66 A combination of Hügel and "klug," found in *Das die Propositio <Gute wreck sind zur Seligkeit schedlich> ein rechte ware Christliche Propositio sey/ durch die heiligen Paulum vnd Lutherum gelert vnd geprediget* (s.l., 1559), A4a, B2a–b, B3b, edited in C&C 3:468–487.

67 *Das die Propositio*, A3a–B2a, B3a–C1a; C&C 3:478–482, 484–487.

they blamed all "Flacianists" for it, even though it was an expression Amsdorf alone had recently used. Perhaps the fact that Luther had used the phrase discouraged a significant amount of criticism. Melanchthon severely but privately criticized Amsdorf's use of the expression. At the colloquy of Worms in 1557, Melanchthon did express his concern over its misleading implications in conversations with Evangelical theologians.[68] Only one Philippist tract—pseudonymous and published in 1562—devoted more than a few lines to Amsdorf's proposition. It called him an antinomian. However, it is likely that the true impetus for that tract was actually a tract Amsdorf wrote on a different topic in 1562, for the pseudonymous Philippist tract also disagreed with Amsdorf's renewed criticism of the Leipzig "Interim's" reintroduction of praying the seven canonical hours in the monastic regimen.[69] Even though many of Amsdorf's opponents in Evangelical Saxony in the late 1550s would have been tempted to put the worst construction on what he said, apparently his reputation spared him from severe public attack. While no one published a defense of Amsdorf's proposition during his lifetime, the Gnesio-Lutheran Johannes Wigand did defend Amsdorf's intentions in private correspondence.[70]

Though Amsdorf had no qualms about his proposition, since he was certain it expressed the teaching of Scripture as he had learned it from Luther, his opponents would have been somewhat justified in criticizing Amsdorf for it. It did muddy an already unclear dispute because it stated his views so extremely. Such muddying would have been even more frustrating because it came from a person who unyieldingly insisted that doctrinal definitions must be lucid and comprehendible or else they are useless.

After Amsdorf's death, some of the Gnesio-Lutherans began to express more openly their views that Amsdorf's proposition on the detrimental nature of good works for salvation should be rejected publicly. In 1567, Joachim Mörlin

68 Published attacks that allude to Amsdorf's proposition but simply identify it as Flacian include the defenses of Melanchthon published by Wittenberg theologians, *Scholasticorum Academiae Witebergensis . . . Epistolae Duae, Tertia, et Quarta* (Wittenberg, 1558), D1b–D2a, and *Ad Toties cum Fastidio et Nausea Repetitas Virulentissimas et falsissimas criminationes Flacij responsio . . . a Scholasticis Academiae Witebergensis* (Wittenberg 1559), G3a. Melanchthon's criticism of Amsdorf is found in memoranda to August of Saxony, CR 9:345, Nr. 6380; 9:405–408, Nr. 6425; MBW.R 8:142–143, Nr. 8398. Amsdorf replied to Wittenberg attacks in his "Auff der Wittenbergische rott briff so sie wider die Flatianer haben lassen aus gehen. Kurrze antwort. Niclaus von Amsdorff, 1560," Wr, ETLFB 39:244–258.

69 The tract appeared under the name of Christian Lauterwein of Seligenstadt entitled *Wieder Niclaus von Ambsdorffen vngegru[e]ndte schrifften darinne er gute wergk anzeucht/ Als seindt sie zur Seligkeit schedlich/ vnd die Horas Canonicas vngestu[e]mer weyse verwirfft* (s.l., 1562). Johann Pfeffinger may be the author of this attack on Amsdorf's proposition. Cf. Amsdorf's *Horas Canonicas Jn Klo[e]stern vnd Stifften singen/ Vnd gebotenen Adiaphora halten/ ist eben so wol Abgo[e]tterey/ Als die schentlichste Opffermesse* (Jena: Thomas Rebart, 1562).

70 Wigand's letter is cited in Christian August Salig, *Vollständige Historie der Augspurgischen Confession* (Halle: Renger, 1730–1733), 3:577.

left Braunschweig, where he had served as ecclesiastical superintendent for a decade, to assume leadership of the church in the dukedom of Prussia. As he left, he warned the Braunschweig ministerium against expressions he feared would lead to an undermining of the proper teaching on the Law of God and also against the dangers of a teaching on original sin that Flacius had put forward. Mörlin listed among the former the rejection of any form of the phrase "good works are necessary" by Frankfurt an der Oder professor Andreas Musculus, the rejection of the third use of the Law by Nordhausen pastor Anton Otto, and the phrase "good works are detrimental" when it is "stated in just these simple words and in general."[71] The same concern about Amsdorf's proposition was expressed in the *Corpus doctrinae* that Mörlin and his partner in the ecclesiastical leadership of Braunschweig, Martin Chemnitz, prepared for the church in Prussia in 1567.[72]

When Jakob Andreae published his *Six Christian Sermons on the Controversies Dividing the Adherents of the Augsburg Confession* in 1573, he echoed Amsdorf's concern that good works ought not be seen as a cause of deliverance from sin. However, Andreae affirmed that concern by saying that ignoring God's call to obedience through epicurean living is just as threatening as relying on good works for salvation. Andreae wrote the document for simple laypeople trying to find their way through the controversies.[73] The following year when he prepared the "Swabian Concord" with a more sophisticated theological treatment of the issues dividing the adherents of the Augsburg Confession, he labeled Amsdorf's proposition "offensive and harmful therefore in God's Church."[74] When David Chytraeus and Martin Chemnitz revised Andreae's "Concord" into the "Swabian-Saxon Concord," they did not dismiss as abruptly the idea that good

---

71 "Doctoris Joachimi Morlini letzte Unterredung mit dem Ehrwu[e]rdigen Ministerio zu Braunschweig/ vom Flacianismo," dated December 1, 1567, in Philipp Julius Rehtmeyer, *Historiae ecclesiasticae inclytae urbis Brunsvigae Pars III. Oder: Der beru[e]hmten Stadt Braunschweig Kirchen-Historie Dritter Theil* . . . (Braunschweig: Johann Georg Zillinger, 1710), 113.

72 *Repetitio corporis doctrinae ecclesiasticae Oder Widerholung der Summa vnd Inhalt der rechten/ allgemeinen Christlichen/ Kirchen Lehre wie dieselbige aus Gottes Wort/ in der Augspurgischen Confession/ Apologia/ vnd Schmalkaldischen Artickeln begriffen/ Vnd von Fu[e]rstlicher Durchleuchtigkeit zu Preussen etc. Auch allen derselbigen Getrewen Landtstenden vnd Vnterthanen/ Geistlichen vnd Weltlichen/ im Hertzogthumb Preussen/ Einhellig vnd bestendiglichen/ gewilliget vnd angenomen/ Ku[e]rtzlich zusammen verfasset* (Eisleben, 1567), I4a–K3a. Cf. Robert Kolb, "The Braunschweig Resolution: The *Corpus Doctrinae Prutenicum* of Joachim Mörlin and Martin Chemnitz as an Interpretation of Wittenberg Theology," in *Confessionalization in Europe, 1555–1700, Essays in Honor and Memory of Bodo Nischan*, eds. John M. Headley, Hans J. Hillerbrand, and Anthony J. Papalas (Aldershot, Hampshire: Ashgate, 2004), 67–89.

73 BSELK, *Quellen und Materialien Band 2: Die Konkordienformel*, ed. Irene Dingel (Göttingen: Vandenhoeck & Ruprecht, 2014), 42–43; ET: Robert Kolb, *Andreae and the Formula of Concord, Six Sermons on the Way to Lutheran Unity* (Saint Louis: Concordia Publishing House, 1977), 78–80.

74 BSELK, *Quellen und Materialien*, 2:102.

works are detrimental to salvation, but they did say that it is confusing to believers.[75] In the "Torgau Book" of 1576—a semi-final draft of what would become the "Solid Declaration" of the Formula of Concord in the following year—Andreae, Chytraeus, Chemnitz, and their fellow committee members affirmed that good works dare never be brought into the discussion of justification but that good works also should not be called "detrimental" without explanation.[76] Largely the same formulation was incorporated into the Solid Declaration in 1577.[77]

FROM CONCESSION THROUGH CONTINUING CONFRONTATION TO CONVERSATION

The direct pressure on and conflict with Georg Major had been diverted in the mid-1550s by the Gnesio-Lutherans' conflict with Menius. However, Amsdorf's and Flacius's attacks on Menius kept the disputes over Major's propositions alive. In 1555, Melanchthon himself suggested that, although it is important to emphasize the necessity of good works in the Christian life, the words "for salvation" in Major's proposition did imply that human merits play a role in obtaining salvation. He also stated that Major's proposition was not used in the churches of electoral Saxony.[78] The opinion of his former preceptor certainly must have been influential for Major as he reflected on his proposition.

A strong distaste for the controversy surrounding his proposition, especially as it continued in the Menius affair and in occasional attacks he received, prompted Major to issue a new *Confession on Justification* in 1558.[79] He asserted that it was necessary in order to respond to his antagonists' continuing slander. This *Confession* stated that Christ remains the beginning, middle, and end of justification and salvation and that it is necessary for believers to persevere in faith with incipient contrition and obedience and with the evidence of good works. Major also denied that he had used the proposition "good works are necessary

75 BSELK, *Quellen und Materialien*, 2:188–189.

76 BSELK, *Quellen und Materialien*, 2:414–415.

77 BSELK 1428–1431, BC 580–581.

78 CR 8:411–412, Nr. 5718; MBW.R 7:271–272, Nr. 7385, in a memorandum dated January 12, 1555. He continued to reject its use while insisting on the necessity of new obedience, e.g., in CR 9:405–408 (December 1557), 474–475 (March 4, 1558); MBW.R 8:199–201, Nr. 8543.

79 *Bekentnis D. Georgij Maioris von dem Artickel der Iustification . . . Vnd von guten wercken* (Wittenberg, 1558), in Latin: *Confessio De articvlo Ivstificationis* (Wittenberg, 1558), edited in C&C 3:440–467.

for believers for salvation" and promised never to use the proposition in the future. He interpreted and applied his proposition, in not so many words, to the Christian life as he still desired to safeguard the ethical norms of Saxon followers of Luther. His fear of antinomianism prevented him from completely rejecting the idea behind his original proposition, but his denial of the proposition indicates the depth of his revulsion against extended bitter squabbling. He tried to put the controversy behind him by claiming not only that he had been misunderstood but also that he had not really meant to advance the ideas for which he was being attacked. Indeed, it is likely he would not have used the proposition if the Leipzig Proposal had not used the expression.

At about the same time, Amsdorf composed an "Instruction on Good Works, that They are Not Necessary for Salvation but for a Christian Life."[80] This rather irenic treatise was never published. It attacked none of the Wittenberg theologians by name. Instead, it simply laid out what Amsdorf saw as the basic principles of his view of good works. The concept of good works being necessary for salvation is the basis of all human religions—Jewish, Turkish, pagan, or papist. Natural reason interpreting natural law creates such a concept of religion. However, God's Law shows people that they are sinners and that they need Christ. Christ fulfills the Law for believers and bestows salvation on them through faith. That faith produces good works naturally because it sanctifies the believer. Throughout the Christian's life, faith—not works—preserves his new obedience to God. This manuscript from 1558 is a strong attestation, though not the only evidence, that it is a misinterpretation of Amsdorf to suggest, as Nathan Rein has, that "for Amsdorf, any hint of a doctrine of sanctification, all disclaimers to the contrary notwithstanding, throws the individual believer back upon her own works and merits, and thus creates the harmful illusion that one can and should earn one's own salvation."[81]

Aside from strongly protesting the charges of antinomianism against himself, Amsdorf restrained his polemical tendencies in this positive position paper. However, Amsdorf was not ready to completely lay the issues to rest. He employed a number of cudgels against Majorism in 1558. In his published *Public Confession,* Amsdorf said Majorists and Menius refused to condemn the concept of the necessity of good works for salvation; therefore, they ought not

80 "Vnterricht von guten wergken wie sie nicht zur seligkeit sonder zu ein christlichem leben allen Christen nach erlangten seligkeit von noten seint. Niclas von Amsdorff. 1558," dated March 1, 1558, Wf, Guelf. Helmst. 71a:109a–118a.

81 Nathan Rein, *The Chancery of God. Protestant Print, Polemic and Propaganda against the Empire, Magdeburg 1546–1551* (Aldershot: Ashgate, 2008), 112.

be tolerated in the Saxon church.[82] Amsdorf's unpublished "Last Will and Testament" condemned "the spirit of Witzel, Menius, and the monks" for attacking him as an antinomian, for his preaching and catechetical instruction had always combatted antinomianism by stressing the necessity of the fruits of faith for a blessed, godly life.[83] In another unpublished document in 1558, "Against the New Majorists," Amsdorf acknowledged Major's decision to lay aside his proposition; but Amsdorf still found Major's response insufficient since he had not explicitly condemned the proposition's error.[84]

The controversy between Major and Amsdorf was drawing to a close, but still it was not quite over. Major published two series of sermons on the pericopes of the lectionary in 1562, and his postil on the Gospel Lessons aroused Amsdorf's ire once again.[85] In three manuscript memoranda, Amsdorf criticized Major for suggesting that a believer's works go with him before God's judgment throne.[86] Amsdorf believed Major was still trying to maintain that human works contribute to the believer's worthiness in God's sight. However, Amsdorf's remarks reveal how, at this stage, the dispute focused as much on how the controversy had been conducted as on the issues at stake in the controversy. The primary content of Amsdorf's memoranda was his critique of the Wittenberg attacks against himself and Flacius. Retreating from his earlier accusation against Major, Amsdorf insisted he had never accused Major of teaching that good works merit salvation—though Major claimed Amsdorf had accused him of this. Amsdorf claimed that he had always understood what Major wanted to say but

---

82 *Offentliche Bekenntnis der reinen lere des Euangelij Vnd Confutatio der jtzigen Schwerner* (Jena, 1558), D2a–D4a, AS, 92–96. On Amsdorf's published confession, see two essays in Dingel, *Amsdorf:* Robert Kolb, "'Bekentnis der reinen lere des Euangelij Vnd Confutatio der jtzigen Schwermer,' Nikolaus von Amsdorf und die Entfaltung einer neuen Bekenntnisform," 307–324, and Johannes Hund, "Amsdorfs Testament in seinen theologischen und historischen Zusammenhängen," 325–344.

83 "Warnung vnd vermanung das sich ein ider Christen für den schwirmen itziger Zceit hüte vnd beware," Wr, ETLFB 41:147–149; AS, 119–121.

84 "Contra novas Maioristas," Wr, ETLFB 40:250.

85 *Prima Pars Homeliarvm in Epistolas Dominicales* (Wittenberg, 1562), and *Prima Pars Homeliarvm in Evangelia Dominicalia et Dies Festos* (Wittenberg, 1562). He published a German translation of the preface, *Vorrede D. Georgij Maioris/ in die Aussglegunge der Sontags vnd Festen Euangelion . . .* (Wittenberg: Veit Creutzer, 1562), edited in C&C 3:488–519. On Major's postils, see Robert Kolb, "Georg Major as Preacher," in *Georg Major (1502–1574), ein Theologe der Wittenberger Reformation*, ed. Irene Dingel and Günther Wartenberg (Leipzig: Evangelische Verlagsanstalt, 2005), 93–121, and Timothy J. Wengert, "Georg Major (1502–1574). Defender of Wittenberg's Faith and Melanchthonian exegete," in *Melanchthon in seinen Schülern*, ed. Heinz Scheible (Wiesbaden: Harrassowitz, 1997), 129–156.

86 "Ein clein vnterricht auff die heidnisch vnd greüliche Postill Georg Maiors. Niclas von Amsdorff," Wr, ETLFB 39:260a–267b, perhaps incomplete, cf. Jäger, *Amsdorf*, 177–183; "Das Doctor Georg Maior in der vorrede vber seine new postill vns mit dreien lugen vnd einer grose Iniurien beschwert vnd vnrecht thut. Niclas von Amsdorff," Jäger, *Amsdorf*, 187–196, Wr, ETLFB 39:90a–99a, dated May 21, 1562, a more polished but incomplete copy of which is found on 39:100a–107b; "Wider Doct. Majorn," Wr, ETLFB 39:268a–275b.

that he had always felt Major's statements could only be interpreted as affirming that good works are meritorious. Amsdorf also considered Major's continued defense of his earlier statements to be a serious error in itself.

In some of these final memoranda in his dispute with Major, Amsdorf criticized Melanchthon more harshly than he ever had before. Amsdorf's early comrade-in-arms had died in 1560. It is unlikely that the reason Amsdorf refrained from publishing harsh public criticism of Melanchthon during Philip's lifetime was fear of how Melanchthon might reply. Instead, it seems Amsdorf and Melanchthon both restrained from criticizing one another with as much severity as they criticized other opponents because they had not forgotten their years of friendship and camaraderie in Wittenberg. Melanchthon's alleged criticism of Amsdorf at the colloquy of Worms in 1557 was insulting, but Amsdorf was not there to hear it, and it is possible that his friends did not tell the bishop what Melanchthon had said. Beyond that, Philip had criticized Amsdorf's proposition "good works are detrimental to salvation," but he had also celebrated Amsdorf's insistence on the necessity of the Christian's performance of good works.[87] Amsdorf's harsher criticism of Melanchthon likely came after his friend's death because Amsdorf knew words could no longer hurt Melanchthon personally. It seems that the preface to Major's Gospel sermons, where he praised Melanchthon and tried to use the Preceptor's prestige as a weapon against Amsdorf, provoked Amsdorf to speak out against Melanchthon while attacking Major.[88] It also seems Amsdorf attacked Melanchthon in the memoranda against Major because Major was attacking Flacius, who was Amsdorf's friend and also Melanchthon's fiercest critic.[89] The grievances that the bishop expressed focused on what Amsdorf regarded as Melanchthon's skillful and persistent suppression of Luther's teaching on the free will and on good works, and fostering of disunity and dissension in the Evangelical church by joining in forging the Leipzig "Interim." All in all, it probably was not Melanchthon's frustration with Amsdorf in the late 1550s that generated Amsdorf's attitude toward Melanchthon in the early 1560s. Rather, Amsdorf's feelings toward Melanchthon more likely arose directly out of Amsdorf's confrontation with Major.

---

87 The criticism is found in CR 9:365, 374, 405–408; MBW.R 8:142–143, Nr. 8398. Melanchthon cited Amsdorf's preface to the *Jhenische Hauspostill von D. Martin Luther* (Jena: Tobias Steinman, 1558), ()4a, in a letter to Georg Buchholzer, dated July 19, 1559, CR 9:843, Nr. 6785; MBW.R 8:365, Nr. 9003.

88 "Clein vnterricht," Wr, ETLFB 39:262a–b, and "Das Maior in der vorrede," Wr, ETLFB 39:98a, 91b.

89 On the Wittenberg attacks on Flacius at this time, see Robert Kolb, "Controversia perpetua. Die Fortsetzung des adiaphoristischen Streits nach dem Augsburger Religionsfrieden," in Dingel and Wartenberg, *Politik*, 191–209.

Like Melanchthon, Major had at one time shared a friendship with Amsdorf. Major realized that death was not far off for Amsdorf. Therefore, not long after manuscript copies of Amsdorf's memoranda began to circulate, in October 1563, Major wrote to his former superintendent to ask if he could visit Amsdorf when visiting a daughter in Eisenach.[90] The following summer Major and Amsdorf met for a brief and reportedly cordial conversation.[91] They did not talk about good works. Perhaps they both knew it would do no good to broach the subject. A decade of misunderstanding and recrimination had so entrenched their attitudes that one short conversation would not enable them to understand each another. Rather, it is remarkable that after so much bitter polemic the two men could meet and talk at all.

How did members of the Wittenberg movement end up in such a state of bitter division? The adiaphoristic controversy surrounding the Interims drove the wedge of suspicion between members of the Wittenberg circle. This suspicion fed misunderstanding as they shared public and private formulations of their ideas and concerns. Eventually patterns of misunderstanding, which were worsened by polemical tactics, hardened most of the members of the Wittenberg circle in their particular positions. Amsdorf is an instructive example through these controversies. Though the political-ecclesiastical conditions in Saxony in the 1550s certainly helped foster these controversies,[92] Amsdorf would have objected to Major's proposition under any political circumstances. The reason was that the issues raised by Major's proposition affected the heart of the Gospel, in Amsdorf's view, and anything that sounded like medieval theology or any other theological perversion that the Wittenberg reformers had denounced was a confusion and, therefore, loss of the insight and truth Luther had proclaimed. Though some of these concerns had surfaced earlier, such as those Amsdorf had raised in the 1530s when he supported Conrad Cordatus's criticism of similar statements by Melanchthon, the vitriol began to flow when one of their fellow reformers was willing to blatantly propagate a statement that Amsdorf believed was a contradiction of their mutual fundamental beliefs.

---

90 Major's letter, dated October 8, 1563, is printed by Walter Friedensburg, "Ein Brief Georg Majors an Nikolaus von Amsdorff, 1563," *ARG* 21 (1924): 254–255.

91 A report on their conversation is found in a letter from Cyriakus Spangenberg to Hartmann Beier, August 22, 1564, in Heinrich Rembe, *Der Briefwechsel des M. Cyriacus Spangenberg* 1 (Dresden: Naumann, 1887), 8. See Karl Brinkel, "Nikolaus von Amsdorf, als verjagter Bischof im Thüringer Land," in *Des Herren Name Steht Uns Bei, Luthers Freunde und Schüler in Thüringen*, eds. Karl Brinkel and Herbert von Hintzenstern 1 (Berlin: Evangelische Verlagsanstalt, 1961), 91.

92 Cf. Robert Kolb, "The Legal Case for Martyrdom, Basilius Monner on Johann Friedrich the Elder and the Smalcald War," in *Reformation und Recht. Festgabe für Gottfried Seebaß zum 65. Geburtstag*, ed. Irene Dingel, Volker Leppin, and Christoph Strohm (Gütersloh: Kaiser/Gütersloher Verlagshaus, 2002), 145–160.

Though there was much misunderstanding of intention and motivation in the controversy around Major's proposition, it was not merely an instance of intentional or unintentional failures to communicate clearly. It became a feud. Old friends felt betrayed by old friends. This prompted all involved to put the worst construction on their opponents' statements. Each person did have genuine pastoral concerns about the issues being discussed. However, the strength of conviction about the importance of these pastoral concerns—since they had all learned from Luther and Melanchthon that pastoral care was central to biblical proclamation—motivated them to each dig their heels in further with each criticism and statement. Friendships and loyalties changed, and the Wittenberg circle was eventually divided into two parties, especially at the leadership level.

The controversy between Amsdorf and Major and their colleagues was not a mere malicious logomachy. Those trained by Luther and Melanchthon had a common understanding of God's total responsibility for all in his creation—especially God's responsibility for the rescue of sinners from their sinfulness—and of the total human responsibility for obedience to God's Law. But unique experiences while applying that paradox to real life in the Church caused them each to lean in one direction of the paradox more than the other. Therefore, all the participants in the decade-long controversy over good works did have the same goal. They all aimed to bring to the common people the message of Christ's delivery of new life and righteousness to the children of God. However, the nuances each participant thought were important for that goal convinced others in the Wittenberg circle that the goal would be prevented rather than accomplished if such a position was established. This controversy was not a matter of mere logomachy for those involved because the delicate balance between preaching the Law and preaching the Gospel was at stake. The result of this controversy among Luther's followers in the 1550s was an irreversible redefinition of the Wittenberg Christian proclamation. One example of that proclamation was the fourth article of the Formula of Concord of 1577. In it, Amsdorf's revival of Luther's phrase, "good works are detrimental to salvation," was rejected; but, Amsdorf's teaching that good works are not necessary for salvation but are necessary for the Christian life was affirmed.[93]

93 BSELK, FC Ep, 1240/1241–1246/1247, FC SD, 1414/1415–1430/1431; BC, FC Ep 497–500, FC SD 574–581.

4

GOD THE POTTER AND HIS HUMAN LUMPS OF CLAY

Amsdorf's Soteriology in the Synergistic Controversy

CONFESSION AND CONFUTATION

The Religious Peace of Augsburg, confirmed by King Ferdinand in September 1555, gave princely and municipal adherents of the Augsburg Confession legal, though inferior, religious status in the German empire. It ushered in a new age in German ecclesiastical history and a new situation for the Evangelical churches. The Peace brought the Interims period to an end and marked the beginning of a period in which there was continuing pressure from the Roman Catholic party, which objected to the imperial peace and did not cease to call for military action against the Protestant princes. In such a climate, Evangelicals ever more urgently needed to settle the differences that divided them. Though no extant document reveals Amsdorf's reaction to the Peace of Augsburg, it seems the treaty meant very little to him. The Peace certainly did not signify a meaningful victory for Luther's followers, or even a reason to allay the battle. It is possible the urgency of the incentive for Evangelical unity did affect Amsdorf's approach to the discussions after 1555. However, in many ways, Amsdorf continued in the years following the Peace of Augsburg to do and say what he always had.

Amsdorf's standing within the church and his relationship with the Ernestine branch of the Wettin family made it possible—and even inevitable—for him to continue to play a prominent, though not decisive, role in ducal Saxony and beyond in the religious situation established by the Peace of Augsburg. Indeed, his reputation still commanded respect even outside the borders of Ernestine Saxony and drew him into a number of activities. For example, early in 1560, the Gnesio-Lutherans' bishop lent his weight to an appeal for a synod to consider the errors that were plaguing the churches of the Augsburg Confession since

Luther's death. The fifty-one subscribers proposed a distinctly Flacian solution, a synod of theologians, rather than a princely caucus, which their Philippist foes seemed to favor as the means for reconciliation. Amsdorf's name headed the list of subscribers.[1] His standing within the Wittenberg circle made him the figurehead for the like-minded gathered around Flacius and Gallus, even if others formulated their public statements. Another example took place in 1556. Amsdorf was asked to mediate a conflict between the counts and ecclesiastical superintendent Erasmus Sarcerius in the county of Mansfeld, an area dominated by those who supported a Gnesio-Lutheran agenda. Others also looked to Amsdorf for counsel and guidance.[2]

During this critical period, Duke Christoph of Württemberg established himself as a leader of Evangelical governments. In negotiations following the Truce of Passau of 1552, which set the foundation for the Peace of Augsburg three years later, Christoph played a prominent role when representatives of the governments and churches of several Evangelical estates, including electoral Saxony and Hesse, met in Naumburg in May 1554 to devise a plan for Evangelical action in negotiating the Religious Peace. Amsdorf condemned the doctrinal platform composed there because it failed to condemn Sacramentarians and papal abuses. Amsdorf was convinced that the times required a strong confession of the faith.[3] In the wake of the proclamation of the Religious Peace, Christoph actively pursued the cause of Evangelical unity. In January 1556, he and Elector Frederick II of the Palatinate sent a delegation to the court at Weimar to initiate a settlement of the internal disputes that plagued the churches that sought to follow both Luther and Melanchthon. The young lords received an inordinate amount of attention considering how much the power of their house had been reduced after the Smalcald War; however, they received this attention because their family had supported the Reformation and because their theologians were playing a prominent role in the disputes among Luther's followers.

The delegation sent by Duke Christoph of Württemberg and Elector Frederick of the Palatinate met with Amsdorf, the university professors Erhard Schnepf

---

1 *Supplicatorii Libelli Qvorvndam Christi Ministrorvm de Synodo Propter Controversias Gravissimas Congreganda* . . . (Oberursel, 1561), also published in German, *Demu[e]tige vnd notwendige Supplication Schrifften etlicher Theologen vnd Diener Jesu Christi/ eines Christlichen Synodi halben/ geschrieben an die Stende vnd Lerer/ so der Augspurgischen -Confession anhengig sind* . . . (s.l., 1561). It was drafted by Simon Musaeus and his colleagues at the University of Jena.

2 Daniel Gehrt, "Der 'Erzbischof' von Thüringen? Nikolaus von Amsdorf und die Genese der ernestinischen Landeskirche nach dem Schmalkaldischen Krieg," in Dingel, *Amsdorf*, 217–236, and Lothar Berndorff, "Nikolaus von Amsdorf als Argument. Zum Gebrauch protestantischer Schiedsautorität in Publizistik und Kirchenpolitik am Beispiel des Mansfelder Klerus," in Dingel, *Amsdorf*, 217–236.

3 In a letter to Johann Stolz, dated June 12, 1554, Wf, Guelf. Helmst. 772:273a–274a.

and Viktorin Strigel, and the court preachers Johann Stolz and Johann Aurifaber on January 12, 1556, in Weimar. Amsdorf and the ducal Saxons presented a hard line. They demanded that a series of errors be clearly condemned in a final settlement and that Evangelicals who had publicly promoted what the ducal Saxons regarded as errors offer public repentance before being recognized as brothers again. The ducal Saxons objected to the south German appeal for the adherents of the Augsburg Confession to adopt common liturgies and ritual because the ducal Saxons believed that would be contrary to evangelical freedom. They also counseled that Evangelicals should not participate in any colloquy called for by the papal party, such as what Emperor Ferdinand was currently planning. They argued such a colloquy would not be a free council and previous colloquies had not produced positive results. However, if the Evangelicals did enter into such discussions, the ducal Saxons stated that not only the Augsburg Confession but also Luther's Smalcald Articles should set the criteria to which the participants in the colloquy would be bound.

This Weimar meeting did not provide the settlement the Württemberg and Palatinate delegation had hoped for. The issues dividing the churches seeking to follow both Luther and Melanchthon were still creating a deadlock between the Gnesio-Lutherans and others in the Evangelical camp.[4]

Two months after that Weimar meeting, Amsdorf wrote a memorandum on efforts by princes committed to the Augsburg Confession to establish a united front among the Evangelical governments. Though Flacius and other Gnesio-Lutherans would propose a gathering of theologians only four years later and Amsdorf would then support the idea, Amsdorf opposed convening a synod of all Evangelicals at this time. Such a synod would include adiaphorists and Interimists from electoral Saxony who propagated errors about good works and free will, and representatives from south German churches who, according to Amsdorf, tolerated the errors of Caspar Schwenckfeld, whose reform program rejected the use of the external form of the Word (preaching, Scripture, and the Sacraments), and Andreas Osiander, whose doctrine of justification rejected Luther's understanding of God's pronouncement of forgiveness of sins. Amsdorf was also suspicious that a settlement imposed by the princes would lead the Evangelicals in the wrong direction, for the princes of this world pervert the

---

4 Gustav Wolf, *Zur Geschichte der deutschen Protestanten 1555–1559* (Berlin: Seehagen, 1888), 8–11; August Beck, *Johann Friedrich der Mittlere* (Weimar: Böhlau, 1858), 1:295–296. On the Gnesio-Lutheran demand for condemnation of errors and errorists, see Hans-Werner Gensichen, *We Condemn. How Luther and 16th Century Lutheranism Condemned False Doctrine*, trans. Herbert J. A. Bouman (Saint Louis: Concordia, 1967), 123–152.

Gospel. Amsdorf's condition for Evangelical unity was singular and simple: all Evangelicals should accept Luther's Smalcald Articles in every detail.[5]

Emperor Ferdinand wanted to continue what had begun with the Religious Peace of Augsburg by pushing ahead with his personal program for promoting religious unity in his empire. He summoned both Evangelicals and those faithful to Rome to a colloquy in Worms in August 1557. Johann Friedrich the Middler gave his representatives instructions to adhere strictly to Luther's teaching and to confess it forthrightly at the colloquy.[6] Amsdorf approved of those instructions and in a memorandum added his hope that the "Flacianists" (his allies) would not compromise at the colloquy—certainly not by making concessions in matters relating to God's Word.[7]

The ways disunity would hinder the Evangelicals from taking full advantage of the situation after the Peace of Augsburg became evident at the Worms colloquy. The Roman Catholic participants, less enthusiastic about their task than was the emperor who commanded their presence, shrewdly took advantage of the Evangelical disunity. Led by the Jesuit Peter Canisius, the Roman Catholic participants provoked the Gnesio-Lutheran representatives' sensitivities. The Roman Catholics raised the issues of Majorism and Osiandrism, and the ducal Saxon delegation—made up of Strigel, Schnepf, Johann Stössel, and the Jena lay counselor and law professor Basilius Monner, allied with the superintendents Erasmus Sarcerius of Mansfeld and Joachim Mörlin of Braunschweig—insisted that their fellow Evangelicals from electoral Saxony and Württemberg condemn both Majorism and Osiandrism. Melanchthon, the electoral Saxons, and Johannes Brenz and his Württemberg delegation refused to formally condemn Majorism and Osiandrism. The Gnesio-Lutherans withdrew from the colloquy as a result, and it soon collapsed. Amsdorf's friends suggested that Melanchthon had insulted their bishop during the colloquy. He did believe that Amsdorf had

---

5 "Auff das Pomirische vnd wittenbergische ansuchen etc ein kurtze antwort," dated March 2, 1556, Wr, ETLFB 41:355a–359b. Indeed, the theologians in Württemberg did take a more tolerant stance toward Osiander's views than did the Philippists and the Gnesio-Lutherans because of the close personal relationships that had developed between Osiander and Johannes Brenz in their work to introduce reform in southern German principalities; in fact, the Württemberg theologians did express some criticism of Osiander's formulations of the doctrine of justification; see Timothy J. Wengert, *Defending Faith. Lutheran Responses to Andreas Osiander's Doctrine of Justification, 1551–1559* (Tübingen: Mohr/Siebeck, 2012), 197–220.

6 Gehrt, *Konfessionspolitik*, 114–122.

7 Wolf, *Geschichte*, 316–326, reprints the ducal instructions and related documents, including Amsdorf's reaction. In the early 1520s, Amsdorf had rather quickly appropriated the Roman party's epithet "Lutheran" for himself and his friends. Similarly, in the 1550s, he did not hesitate to use the electoral Saxon epithet "Flacianist" for his comrades. Although the term later took on more specific meaning when the dispute between Flacius and other Gnesio-Lutherans over original sin arose, at this time it can be applied without confusion to the ducal Saxons and their allies—which is how the term was used by Philippists and also by Amsdorf.

been instrumental in developing the ducal Saxon delegation's hard line, and thus, Melanchthon implied Amsdorf was ultimately responsible for the colloquy's collapse.[8] Amsdorf had no regrets over its outcome, to be sure.

Others did. The failure of the Worms colloquy led to greater efforts to create a united front among the Evangelical estates. One such effort occurred in February 1558 when a number of Lutheran princes attending Ferdinand's coronation in Frankfurt am Main caucused to formulate and then issue a doctrinal statement called the "Frankfurt Recess." It was drafted though not finalized by Melanchthon. This statement sought to settle Lutheran differences, specifically those concerning justification (relating to Osiandrism), good works (relating to Majorism), the Lord's Supper, and adiaphora.[9] These princes sent a delegation to enlist the support of the ducal Saxon government, which had no representatives at the Frankfurt diet. Johann Friedrich the Middler turned to his theologians for an evaluation. Amsdorf again responded in a memorandum that expressed his disapproval of this attempt at Evangelical unity. He was dissatisfied with the treatment of each of the four issues in the Frankfurt Recess. It did not condemn, as Amsdorf believed it should have, a government's imposition of adiaphoristic practices on the church. Princes have no business making rules for the church, he wrote. Beyond that, Amsdorf was even suspicious of a church supported by a prince. The true Church is always a beleaguered remnant of God's people. Since the "Frankfurt Recess" seemed to be an effort to create an externally mighty "*Larvenkirche*" (masquerading church) in which God's Word and true faith would disappear, more than an effort to confess the apostolic faith, Amsdorf advised against accepting it.[10]

Amsdorf's fear that some Evangelicals were establishing a false church prompted him to prepare two confutations in 1558 against errors arising within

---

8 On the colloquy, see Wolf, *Geschichte*, 13–109, Beck, *Johann Friedrich*, 1:296–302, and Heinrich Heppe, *Geschichte des deutschen Protestantismus in den Jahren 1555–1581* (Marburg: Elwert, 1852), 2:173–197, Benno von Bundschuh, *Das Wormser Religionsgespräch von 1557, unter besonderer Berücksichtigung der kaiserlichen Religionspolitik* (Münster: Aschendorf, 1988), and Bjorn Slenczka, *Das Schisma der Augsburger Konfessionsverwandten von 1557: Protestantische Konfessionspolitik und Theologie im Zusammenhang des zweiten Wormser Religionsgesprächs* (Tübingen: Mohr/Siebeck, 2010). Documents on the colloquy are found in CR 9:199–354, 402–411, 451–461; MBW.R 8:99–147, 179, 195–198, Nr. 8299–8404, 8493, 8539–8540. Melanchthon's comments on Amsdorf are found in CR 9:274, Nr. 6342; 9:365, Nr. 6398; MBW.R 9:154, Nr. 8426; 9:115, Nr. 8332.

9 The text of the Frankfurt Recess is printed in CR 9:489–507; the meeting is treated Irene Dingel, "Melanchthon's Efforts for Unity between the Fronts: the Frankfurt Recess," in Dingel et al., *Philip Melanchthon. Theologian in Classroom, Confession, and Controversy* (Göttingen: Vandenhoeck & Ruprecht, 2012), 123–140, and in Gehrt, *Konfessionspolitik*, 125–129.

10 "Schrift wider das Interim und den Frankfurter Abschied," Wr, ETLFB 39:22a–25a, edited in Ernst-Otto Reichert, *Amsdorf und Das Interim*, ed. Hans-Otto Schneider (Leipzig: Evangelische Verlagsanstalt, 2011), 269–272. A similar memorandum, a copy, is in Wf, Guelf. Helmst. 81:36–44, incomplete.

the Evangelical camp. His *Public Confession of the Pure Doctrine of the Gospel and Confutation of Present Day Ravers* was published immediately; his "Last Will and Testament" did not appear in print until after his death.[11]

Both works began with Amsdorf's diagnoses of the times. Luther had prophesied that the Gospel would disappear after he died,[12] and Amsdorf asserted that Luther's prophecy was being fulfilled. The attractive, powerful church of the adiaphorists, created by human wisdom, was slandering and oppressing the small, scorned church that still held to the pure teaching of the Gospel. The church of the adiaphorists respected neither Luther nor God's Word, for they had composed the Leipzig "Interim," which exchanged the true Gospel for human laws, and then they had tried to lay the blame for the resulting disputes upon the true Church. These adiaphorists were adulterating the Gospel more than the papists ever had, Amsdorf charged. This time, Amsdorf faced a different foe than the Roman party in Magdeburg, but his description of the battle had not changed. In dealing with his opponents in electoral Saxony, Amsdorf believed that the small, persecuted church relying on God was ranged against the powerful church relying on the world's wisdom.

Amsdorf's *Public Confession* criticized the Evangelical negotiators at Worms in 1557 for failing to condemn Zwingli and Osiander, and for demeaning those who urged such condemnations. In *Public Confession*, Amsdorf listed "B. and the adiaphorists" as the villains at the colloquy. He also said "B." was the author of a preface in a book by Jakob Andreae. In "Last Will and Testament," Amsdorf directly stated Johannes Brenz's name, indicating that Brenz was the referent of "B." in *Public Confession*. Amsdorf was displeased with Brenz's attempts to mediate the Osiandrian dispute and with Brenz's preface to Andreae's book attempting to reconcile Lutheran and Zwinglian views of the Lord's Supper. This attack justified prior rumors that Amsdorf would publicly condemn Brenz.[13]

---

11 *Offentliche Bekentnis der reinen lere des Euangelij/ Vnd Confutatio der jtzigen Schwermer* (Jena, 1558), AS, 79–97, C&C 5:55–74; cf. the manuscript of this work in Amsdorf's hand, Wf, Guelf. Helmst. 71a:146–162, dated March 14, 1558. His "Warnung vnd vermanung das sich ein ider Christen für den schwernern itziger Zceit hüte vnd beware," Wr, ETLFB 41:137a–154b, AS, 106–107, is entitled "Mein testament darinne ich meinen schatz allen Christen bescheide," in an earlier draft, Wr, ETLFB 41:28a–41b. The former draft was later printed, *Testament vnd Letzter Wille Weiland dess Ehrwirdigen Edlen vnnd hochgelerten Herrn: Niclas von Ambsdorff der H. Schrifft Licentiaten. Darinne er seinen Schatz allen frommen Christen die es begern bescheidet*, ed. Christoph Irenaeus (s.l., 1590). Cf. Robert Kolb, "'Bekentnis der reinen lere des Euangelij Vnd Confutatio der jtzigen Schwermer,' Nikolaus von Amsdorf und die Entfaltung einer neuen Bekenntnisform," in Dingel, *Amsdorf*, 307–324, and Johannes Hund, "Amsdorfs Testament in seinen theologischen und historischen Zusammenhängen," in Dingel, *Amsdorf*, 325–344.

12 Cf. Robert Kolb, *Martin Luther as Prophet, Teacher, and Hero. Images of the Reformer, 1520–1620* (Grand Rapids: Baker Books, 1999), 178–183.

13 *Offentliche Bekentnis*, A3b; cf. Wf, Guelf. Helmst. 71a:147b. Brenz's high regard for Amsdorf (see introduction, note 2) had not prevented Amsdorf from becoming disturbed by what he regarded as Brenz's soft

Even though Amsdorf was conscious of Brenz's respect for him, Amsdorf could not abide any softening toward what he defined as erroneous, threatening the Gospel, and compromising God's Word.

Amsdorf's confutations of 1558 also condemned Majorism, Caspar Schwenckfeld's spiritualism, and Johann Pfeffinger's views on the freedom of the will. Although only the unpublished confutation has the word "Testament" in its title, Amsdorf viewed both confutations as his testament for his spiritual heirs. And the testament contained in both documents does reflect Amsdorf's public image and the pattern of his writing throughout his life. There is little positive exposition of biblical teaching in these writings; Amsdorf did not consider himself a teaching prophet. It seems he believed Luther had sufficiently performed that task for their generation. To the general reading public, Amsdorf was a student of the prophet Luther, a student who proclaimed an admonition and warning to remember the prophet's message. As a result, Amsdorf's testament was largely a series of critiques. It was not so much an endeavor to proclaim the Gospel as it was an endeavor to preserve the Gospel from perversion and adulteration. Therefore, once again he depicted the small, scorned band of Christ's faithful followers, gathered around his Word, while the arrows of error assail them from the mighty, false church. His enemies noted his polemical tone characteristically present in these confutations. Justus Jonas Jr., who was a jurist and diplomat for several princes, including August of Saxony, and who was also the renegade son of Amsdorf's friend, Justus Jonas the elder, commented on the "scandal-sheet" published by "the raving, muddled head of the uncouth ass, Amsdorf." Jonas correctly recognized that the bishop wrote for those Jonas called the common rabble, the poor, ignorant laypeople, and most preachers.[14] Amsdorf intentionally wrote for them because he believed that they, not the learned, followed Christ faithfully. As a result, Amsdorf did not write penetrating, thorough analyses of the Evangelical controversies. Instead, his final testament planted his typical simple blows against the corrupting

stand on Osiandrism. Christoph of Württemberg expressed concern to Landgrave Wilhelm of Hesse on December 7, 1555, over rumors of an impending attack upon Brenz, Christian Gotthold Neudecker, *Neue Beiträge zur Geschichte der Reformation* (Leipzig: Fleischer, 1841), 1:113–115; evidence of the rumor is also found in a letter from the young lords to Landgrave Philip of Hesse, December 15, 1555, Neudecker, *Beiträge*, 117–119. Amsdorf was highly critical of Andreae's *Kurtzer vnnd einfeltiger Bericht/ von des Herren Nachtmahl/ vnnd wie sich ein einfeltiger Christen die langwirige zwyspalt/ so sich darüber erheb/t schicken sol* (Pforzheim, 1557), in which Brenz wrote a preface. On Andreae's affirmation of Luther's understanding of the Lord's Supper in reaction to criticism like Amsdorf's, see Robert Kolb, "Jakob Andreae's Preaching in the Public Arena (Augsburg 1559)," *Lutheran Quarterly* 9 (2015): 10–32.

14 In a letter to Duke Albrecht of Prussia dated May 7, 1558, in Johannes Voigt, *Briefwechsel der berühmtesten Gelehrten des Zeitalters der Reformation mit Herzog Albrecht von Preussen* (Königsberg: Bornträger, 1841), 355–356.

thought currents within the Wittenberg circle.

A decade earlier, Amsdorf might have written a testament aimed primarily at papal and Sacramentarian foes. Instead, the changes in German religious life by 1558 directed Amsdorf's testament at the second generation of Luther's followers, exhorting them to be faithful and not compromise Luther's insights concerning the sovereign power of the God who saves sinners by giving them Christ's righteousness—by grace through faith in Christ alone.

WITHOUT CHRIST WE CAN DO NOTHING

One member of the second generation of Luther's followers that Amsdorf mentioned in his *Public Confession* was Johann Pfeffinger. Amsdorf believed that this Leipzig professor and pastor held a view of the human will's role in conversion that compromised God's sovereignty in the process of salvation. Pfeffinger had studied at Wittenberg in the mid-1520s. Imbued with a strong appreciation for the views of Melanchthon, his beloved preceptor, Pfeffinger left Wittenberg to serve as pastor in several Saxon villages. After the death of Duke George, he helped Duke Heinrich, Moritz's father, introduce the Reformation in the dukedom. George had not tolerated Pfeffinger in his dukedom, but Pfeffinger had preached across the border in electoral Saxony, not far from Leipzig, and many of the city's citizens had gone there to hear him. As a result, he had a following in Leipzig. In 1540, Duke Heinrich made Pfeffinger the superintendent in Leipzig. The University of Leipzig awarded him a doctorate in theology in 1543 and then called him to its theological faculty the following year. He was one of Moritz's leading clerical advisors from the time of the duke's accession in 1541 onward and taught at Leipzig until his death in 1573.[15] Therefore, his defense of the Leipzig "Interim" had upset Amsdorf,[16] who had become particularly sensitive to any deviation within Pfeffinger's public utterances away from what he considered the proper expression of Luther's teaching.

In 1550, a student at Leipzig criticized Pfeffinger's understanding of the free will, but no public dispute arose out of the incident.[17] However in 1555, Pfeffinger composed theses on the free will for a disputation at the university. These

15 Friedrich Seifert, "Johannes Pfeffinger, der erste lutherische Pastor zu St. Nicolai und Superintendent in Leipzig," *Beiträge zur Sächsischen Kirchengeschichte* 4 (1888): 33–162.

16 *Grüntlicher vnd Warhafftiger Bericht der vorigen vnd jetzigen/ fu[e]r vnd nach dem Kriege ergangen Handlungen/ von den Adiaphoris oder Mitteldingen . . .* (Leipzig: Valentin Bapst, 1550), edited in C&C 2:642–730.

17 Christian August Salig, *Vollständige Historie der Augspurgischen Confession* (Halle: Renger, 1730–1733), 1:648–649.

theses did not elicit a public critique from the Gnesio-Lutherans until Amsdorf published his *Public Confession* in 1558, though Nikolaus Gallus had by that time entered into an epistolary exchange with Melanchthon on the subject.[18]

Many of Pfeffinger's theses addressed concerns that had occupied Melanchthon's attention for at least two decades. These were the concerns that Amsdorf had critiqued in 1536 as being in conflict with Luther's position in *On Bound Choice*. Melanchthon, in his *Loci* in 1535, had tried to clarify what he believed were the following truths about human will: God should not be held responsible for the origin of evil and sin; the Wittenberg emphasis on grace alone should not be understood as deterministic; obedience to God's commands should not be evaded by some form of antinomianism. Because of these convictions, Melanchthon ascribed to the wills of Saul and David some element explaining their respective rejection and acceptance by God. To account for the difference between Saul and David, Melanchthon labeled the will in the act of conversion "a will that assents and does not resist," a will that has a "faculty of directing itself toward grace."[19] He insisted that the psychological processes of hearing and understanding were part of a human being's experience of conversion. When Melanchthon spoke and wrote in these terms, he nearly always also ascribed this activity of the will to the drawing power of the Holy Spirit. He was trying to explain within an Aristotelian framework the human experience of God's grace. Melanchthon strove to clarify his position by identifying the human will as the material factor (*causa* in Latin) upon which the effective or causative factor—the Holy Spirit—works through the instrumental factor, the Gospel.[20] Again, it is interesting to note the absence of objections from either Amsdorf or Luther to this use of the Aristotelian framework of causality. They understood the passive nature of Aristotle's *causa materialis*.[21]

---

18 Kolb, *Bound Choice, Election, and Wittenberg Theological Method: From Martin Luther to the Formula of Concord* (Grand Rapids: Eerdmans, 2005), 106–117.

19 See Melanchthon's *Loci communes*, CR 21:658–660, 664, and other references, CR 14:952, 23:435–436, 25:59–60, and the epistolary debate with Nikolaus Gallus, treated in Kolb, *Bound Choice*, 113–117.

20 CR 21:376, 658; cf, col. 1078. Melanchthon pointedly rejected the "Stoica und Manichaea deliria" of Luther and others in a letter to Elector August, March 9, 1559, CR 9:766; MBW.R 8:322–324, Nr. 8884; see also CR 8:736, Nr. 5968; 8:916, Nr. 6127; 9:565, Nr. 6543; 9:733, Nr. 6679; 9:783, Nr.6713; MBW.R 7:420, Nr. 7793; 7:517–518, Nr. 8042; 8:234, Nr. 8642; 8: 308, Nr. 8841; 8:329, Nr. 8886. Cf. Robert Kolb, "Melanchthon's Doctrinal Last Will and Testament: The *Responsiones ad articulos Bavaricae inquisitionis* as His Final Confession of Faith," in Dingel et al., *Philip Melanchthon*, 152–156.

21 Kolb, *Bound Choice*, 70–102. On Melanchthon's use of the three "*causae*" framework, see Timothy J. Wengert, "Philip Melanchthon and the Origins of the 'Three Causes' (1533–1535): An Examination of the Roots of the Controversy over the Freedom of the Will," in Dingel et al., *Melanchthon*, 183–208. On later use of Aristotle's *causae* in regard to conversion by Melanchthon and his students who became authors of the Formula of Concord, see Lowell C. Green, "The three causes of Conversion in Philipp Melanchthon, Martin Chemnitz, David Chytraeus, and the Formula of Concord," *Lutherjahrbuch* 47 (1980): 89–114.

Pfeffinger's theses in 1555 addressed five basic questions about the human will, devoting one section of theses to each question. In the first section, he stated that the human will has the freedom to maintain external discipline and perform moral works even though sin has weakened it. In the second section, he taught that the will does not have the freedom to surmount inborn human depravity, nor is the will able to overcome death. Christ's merit alone saves sinners by grace through faith; human nature itself cannot satisfy the Law of God through its own obedience. In the third section, he affirmed that the human will has no freedom in spiritual matters and cannot be moved to action in the spiritual realm without the aid of the Holy Spirit. In the fourth section, Pfeffinger sought to uphold the humanity of the sinner, even though the will is unable to effect spiritual change. In this section, he used Melanchthon's teaching on the three factors or *causae* of conversion: the Holy Spirit, the Word of God, and the human will. Pfeffinger stated that the human will does not resist the Holy Spirit but rather submits to the Spirit as it seeks aid from God. In the fifth section of his theses, Pfeffinger considered biblical passages relating to the topic, distinguishing those that relate to God's relationship with creation apart from Adam and those that deal specifically with the salvation of God's human creatures.[22]

Pfeffinger did want to preserve a Lutheran emphasis on the exclusive role of God's grace in the salvation of sinners. He insisted that nothing should detract from Christ's merit; it alone restores sinners to a right relationship with God. But Pfeffinger also wanted to present the whole picture of salvation, acknowledging the human aspects of conversion as well. The following excerpts illustrate Pfeffinger's struggle to emphasize the Holy Spirit's role in conversion while still acknowledging the psychological functions of mind and will.

> The mercy and merit of Christ are the cause of election, and the elect are drawn by God, but they are drawn through the Word and the Holy Spirit. No resistance can be rendered to the one who draws, and assent must be given to the promise of free remission of sins for the sake of the Son and reconciliation.[23]

---

22 Gustav Kawerau, "Pfeffinger," in *Realencyklopädie für protestantische Theologie und Kirche*, 3rd ed., ed. Albert Hauck (Leipzig: Hinrichs, 1896–1913), 19:231, states that Pfeffinger composed two sets of theses on the freedom of the will in 1555: "De libero arbitrio" and "De libertate voluntatis humanae quaestiones quinque." The edited text of the second is found in C&C 5:27–44. Cf. Luka Ilić, *Theologian of Sin and Grace. The Process of Radicalization in the Theology of Matthias Flacius Illyricus* (VIEG 225; Göttingen: Vandenhoeck & Ruprecht, 2014), 147–148; Wilhelm Preger, *Matthias Flacius Illyricus und seine Zeit* (Erlangen: Bläsing, 1859–1861), 2:114. Neither Otto Ritschl, *Dogmengeschichte des Protestantismus* (Leipzig: Hinrichs, 1912), 2:424, nor I have been able to locate the text of the former. The text of the latter was reprinted by Pfeffinger in his *Demonstratio Manifesti Mendacii, Sycophanticus germanice editus titulo Nicolai ad Amsdorf, Necessaria propter Veritatis assertionem & auersionem Scandali, & tuendam existimationem sincereae doctrinae* (Wittenberg, 1558), A4b–D1a.

23 Pfeffinger, *Demonstratio*, C2b, thesis 31.

> Human beings ought not resist the Holy Spirit but, as he moves our mind and heart, assent to him. For the Holy Spirit is received in this way by those who seek him, that is, those who do not spurn or reject him but who seek his aid with groaning, Acts 5 [perhaps 5:32, but with words also from Romans 8:26].[24]

Pfeffinger's presuppositions and concerns regarding the Creator and human creatures determined his propositions. He believed that the fall into sin did not completely destroy the human will that God created; therefore, the human will retained some powers to will and function after the fall, even while affirming that the "first sin" had wrought almost unimaginable damage to the will. He also was concerned that the human will should not be thought of as a stone or block of wood in the process of conversion, since it is not passive; God created it to act as a will, making decisions. Pfeffinger, therefore, stated that the human will struggles to receive and retain faith in Christ during conversion. Pfeffinger wanted to affirm the responsibility of the human creature for his own sin, so that God was not considered responsible for human sinfulness, rejecting a frequent, though false, accusation against Luther from Roman Catholic antagonists. Furthermore, Pfeffinger argued that God treats all people equally; he shows no partiality (Acts 10:34); he has promised all salvation in Jesus Christ, and it is his will that they come to a saving knowledge of the truth (1 Timothy 2:4). Since that was true, Pfeffinger suggested in the fourth section of his theses that the ultimate difference between the elect and the damned must lie in the level of resistance that they make to the drawing of the Holy Spirit.

Therefore, the difference between Saul and David, between Judas and Peter, and between the elect and the damned[25] was the response of their human will. The human will either resists God's advances, or does not resist them, embraces the Holy Spirit, and prays for his aid.

> Since the promise of grace is universal, and it is necessary for us to submit to the promise, it follows that some difference between those who are elect and those who are rejected ought to be assumed in our sin: clearly when we resist the promise, we are rejected, and on the other hand when we embrace the promise, we are accepted.[26]

24 Pfeffinger, *Demonstratio*, B2b–B3a, theses 11–12.

25 Pfeffinger, *Demonstratio*, B3b, thesis 17.

26 Pfeffinger, *Demonstratio*, C2a–b, thesis 30.

> God requires that we grasp the promise and assent [to it] and not resist or give ourselves up to doubt or despair.[27]
>
> We are, as Saint Paul says "in all seriousness," co-workers with God [1 Cor. 3:9], and this cooperation is supported and confirmed by the Holy Spirit.[28]

In interpreting the passage "many are called, but few are chosen" (Matthew 22:14), Pfeffinger asserted that while many are offered the promise of the Gospel, only the few who accept it, assent to it, and believe it are accepted by God.[29] In spite of Pfeffinger's desire to give God alone the credit for a believer's salvation, such statements about what distinguishes the elect from the damned asserted that the human will is the final determinant of whether the Holy Spirit enters a person's life.[30]

Melanchthon used more careful language than Pfeffinger when expressing his affirmation of the activity of the human will in conversion. But because of the intensity of the rivalry in the 1550s between the Philippists and the Gnesio-Lutherans, Melanchthon did not disown Pfeffinger's statements about the will, nor did he disavow Pfeffinger's statements, because Melanchthon was concerned that the Gnesio-Lutherans were dangerously close to advocating a deterministic position like that to which he objected in John Calvin's writings.[31] Melanchthon had distanced himself from Major's proposition on good works, but he was still deeply fearful of a determinism that deemphasized human responsibility so much that it compromised the demands of the Law.

Amsdorf did take issue with Pfeffinger's statements. The bishop was surprisingly slow to respond publicly, though before the end of 1555, he composed unpublished Latin theses criticizing Pfeffinger's positions.[32] He did address Pfeffinger's theses to some extent at the end of his 1558 *Public Confession*, but still Amsdorf's critique in that publication was not as extensive as one might expect from the seasoned polemist.[33] However, in 1559, he published a full-force polemic

27 Pfeffinger, *Demonstratio*, C3a, thesis 32.

28 Pfeffinger, *Demonstratio*, C4a, thesis 36.

29 Pfeffinger, *Demonstratio*, C1a, thesis 26.

30 Ritschl, *Dogmengeschichte*, 2:424, makes this point.

31 Timothy J. Wengert, "'We Will Feast Together in Heaven Forever': The Epistolary Friendship of John Calvin and Philip Melanchthon," in *Melanchthon in Europe, His Work and Influence beyond Wittenberg*, ed. Karin Maag (Grand Rapids: Baker, 1999), 26–33.

32 "Meditationes Nicolai Amsdorfij aduersus impian pfeffingeri disputationem, 1555," Wr, ETLFB 40:197a–213a, see esp. 197a–b, 209b. Another, somewhat altered but incomplete, draft of this critique, entitled "Contra Pfeffingerum scriptum," is found Wr, ETLFB 40:359a–373a.

33 Paul Tschackert, *Die Entstehung der lutherischen und der reformierten Kirchenlehre* (Göttingen: Vandenhoeck & Ruprecht, 1910), 522, states that Flacius launched a campaign against Pfeffinger's views at Jena in 1558, but he does not date his efforts precisely. A collection of Pfeffinger's disputations was republished under the title *In hoc Libello continentur utiles disputationes de praecipuis capitibus doctrinae Christianae* (Frankfurt/M:

against Pfeffinger: *That Dr. Pfeffinger Maliciously and Falsely Denies his Misdeed.* Also in 1559, Amsdorf composed but did not publish an imaginative account of the controversy in the form of a dialogue between a "Lutheran" and one who claimed that the will retains some ability to prepare itself to receive the Holy Spirit. The disputant who advocated for a significant role for the human will was labeled an "adiaphorist"—not a "synergist"—by Amsdorf.[34] Clearly Amsdorf's sense of betrayal over his colleagues' cooperation with Elector Moritz in the composition of the Leipzig "Interim" had not subsided; instead, he described anything else he perceived as denying the Gospel to be part of that same betrayal.

In his unpublished manuscript critiques, Amsdorf described Pfeffinger's theses as "papistic," expressing a doctrine of the freedom of the will like that taught by the "Ciceronian" theologians and the scholastic sophists of Rome.[35] Amsdorf described Pfeffinger's theses as the product of human reason; putting the worst construction on Pfeffinger's words, Amsdorf said that they affirmed that human powers grasp God's Word before the sinner receives the gift of the Holy Spirit. Amsdorf, therefore, believed Pfeffinger was denying the true condition of the human will after the fall into sin and was thus obviating the need for Christ's redemptive activity.

Neither Melanchthon nor Pfeffinger after him wanted to detract from the exclusive role of God's grace in human salvation. Like Luther and Amsdorf, they, too, sought to hold in tension strong positions on God's Law, demanding that human beings exercise their God-given responsibilities perfectly, and on God's Gospel, revealing that God is the Creator and re-creator who is fully responsible for all things. However, the proper distinction of Law and Gospel is difficult to accomplish and put into practice. As with so many of the controversies following Luther's death, the disagreement between Amsdorf and Pfeffinger stemmed from their prioritization of different concerns while trying to accomplish this goal. Amsdorf wanted to safeguard God's total responsibility for human salvation because the teaching of salvation by grace alone was fragile and could easily be corrupted. Pfeffinger and Melanchthon knew parishioners needed to hear both human responsibility and divine responsibility emphasized from the

Peter Braubach, 1558). Since the preface to this work is dated March 1, 1558, and Amsdorf's manuscript of the *Offentliche Bekentnis* is dated March 14, it seems less than likely that Amsdorf actually saw this new edition of Pfeffinger's theses. He might have heard rumors of its pending release.

34 "Ein gesprech vom freien willn zwischen eim Lutheraner vnd eim Adiaphoristen," revisions of a manuscript held in Wittenberg, in Jäger, *Amsdorf*, 223–245.

35 "Meditationes . . . aduersus impian pfeffingeri disputationem, 1555," Wr, ETLFB 40:197a–213a, see esp. 197a–b, 209b. The exact date of another set of theses by Amsdorf is unknown: "Nicolaij Amsdorfij disputatio contra Pfeffingeri sophiste lipsensis disputationem," Wr, ETLFB 40:289a–290b.

pulpit. Amsdorf had little interest in Pfeffinger's anthropological concerns. He marveled mockingly at Pfeffinger's insight that the human being is not a rock or stone. Amsdorf did not think it was theologically significant to note that human psychological functions did not cease with the fall. He thought it most important to emphasize that the will, though active and alive, is a depraved and corrupt captive of Satan, unable to assent to the promises of the Gospel without the Holy Spirit. The Spirit must make sinners willing and able to grasp God's promises and pray for his help. The Spirit must become the controlling agent in a person's life to enable him to be converted.[36] Amsdorf and Pfeffinger agreed that the will exercises freedom of choice in non-spiritual affairs and that the Holy Spirit must convert the sinner. But they disagreed on how to describe the will's assent to the Spirit's approach. Both began to rely more on their own primary concerns than on the proper distinction of Law and Gospel when thinking and writing on these issues.

Another reason that Amsdorf and Pfeffinger disagreed about the role of the human will in conversion is that Amsdorf disagreed with many of Pfeffinger's presuppositions. Amsdorf did not believe that the promise of grace had been extended to all people, contrary to Luther's view; Amsdorf applied 1 Timothy 2:4 to believers alone. He also asserted that God does treat people in different ways who are otherwise equals. Like a potter, God does what he pleases with the clay of humankind: he creates some as "vessels of wrath" and some as "vessels of mercy" (Isaiah 29:16; 45:9; Romans 9:20–29). Amsdorf had used the same argument against Melanchthon's view of contingency twenty years earlier. Interestingly, though, in critiquing Pfeffinger, Amsdorf did not advance as rigid a doctrine of double predestination as he had when previously critiquing Melanchthon's view of the human will. Amsdorf agreed with Pfeffinger that God is not the cause of sin; but Amsdorf did not explain how that could be true if his thesis on election was also true. Amsdorf asserted that sin originates in the human will, because the will has been corrupted through inherited sinfulness. God hates that sin and leaves the sons of wrath in the desires of their hearts. However, those who are saved owe their salvation to God's mercy alone, for he chose them without any merit in themselves. The only cause of the believer's election by God is divine mercy. Amsdorf was determined to defend Luther's position on this issue, and he repeated many of his friend's arguments concerning salvation and election. Yet it seems Amsdorf also felt the need to shore up his argument against the

---

36 "Meditationes aduersus pfeffingeri disputationem," Wr, ETLFB 40:197a–200a, 205a, 209a–210b.

participation of the human will in salvation by rejecting universal atonement.[37]

In the unpublished critique of Pfeffinger's theses, Amsdorf did not link errors in the theses on free will to Pfeffinger's participation in the composition of the Leipzig "Interim." However, Amsdorf did see a connection between Pfeffinger's theses on the free will and the Majoristic controversy about the necessity of good works for salvation. Amsdorf categorized both as "Ciceronian" and scholastic inventions and the same perversion of the Gospel.

Amsdorf's brief allusion to Pfeffinger within his *Public Confession* in 1558 initiated the public phase of what is usually called the Saxon Lutheran synergistic controversy. Amsdorf summarized Pfeffinger's position with the following citation from Pfeffinger's 1555 theses:

> The human being is able with his own natural powers to assent to the Word, to grasp the promise, and not to resist the Holy Spirit. Indeed, a person ought not resist the Holy Spirit, but as he moves our hearts and minds, should assent. For the Holy Spirit is received in this way by those who seek [him], that is, by those who do not spurn or reject him.

Amsdorf added, "That is what he said, if I remember correctly."[38] These words, the final sentence in the Latin paragraph, inserted into Amsdorf's German critique, would give Pfeffinger the basis for his dismissal of Amsdorf's attack. These few words of criticism in Amsdorf's rather brief critique of Pfeffinger in his *Public Confession* associated Pfeffinger's view with the opinions of Thomas Aquinas and Duns Scotus concerning the will assenting to the Holy Spirit's offer of the Gospel. Amsdorf also dismissed Pfeffinger's interpretation of Paul's statement "we are coworkers with God" in 1 Corinthians 3:9, without providing a reason for this dismissal.[39]

The synergistic controversy was certainly fueled by Amsdorf's critique of Pfeffinger, but Amsdorf was not the only member of the Wittenberg circle to

---

37 Wr, ETLFB 40:200a–204b, 209b; cf. "Disputatio contra Pfeffingeri disputationem," Wr, ETLFB 40:289a. For further details, see Robert Kolb, "Nikolaus von Amsdorf on Vessels of Wrath and Vessels of Mercy: a Lutheran's Doctrine of Double Predestination," *Harvard Theological Review* 69 (1976): 325–343.

38 *Offentliche Bekentnis*, D4b. Amsdorf later admitted that he had written the citation from memory since he did not have a copy of the disputation at hand when he composed the *Offentliche Bekentnis; cf. his Das D. Pfeffinger seine missethat bo[e]slich vnd felschlich leugnet/ vnd gewaltiglich vberzeugt wird/ das er die Kirchen Christi zusto[e]rt vnd zuru[e]ttet/ vnd die Schrifft verfelschet vnd verkert hab* (Magdeburg: Ambrosius Kirchner, 1559), B3b; the edited text found in C&C 5:177–180. In spite of that, he cited Pfeffinger's words very closely, altering word order in only three places and not altering the sense of the passage quoted; cf. Pfeffinger, *Demonstratio*, B2b–B3a. For an overview of the course of the synergistic controversy, see Friedhelm Gleiß, *Die Weimarer Disputation von 1560: Theologische Konsenssuche und Konfessionspolitik Johann Friedrichs des Mittleren* (Leipzig: Evangelische Verlagsanstalt, 2018), 163–187.

39 Amsdorf, *Offentliche Bekentnis*, D4b–E1b.

object to Pfeffinger's theses. Johann Stolz, one of the court preachers at Weimar, had prepared a set of counter-theses in 1556 but refrained from publishing them until soon after Amsdorf's *Public Confession* put the matter on the public agenda. Johann Aurifaber, Stolz's colleague at the court, published a preface to both Stolz's one hundred forty theses and Flacius's critique of Pfeffinger's opinions. All three assessments agreed that Pfeffinger had taught that human beings contribute to their own salvation with their own natural powers. Their critiques were more thorough and analytical than Amsdorf's in his unpublished manuscript; but they agreed with him on most points, and they expanded and grounded his arguments even more thoroughly. They affirmed that until sinners are reborn by the Holy Spirit's powers, they are Satan's captive and God's enemy. However, these other theologians who critiqued Pfeffinger differed from Amsdorf by not ascribing to God a role in the condemnation of the damned.[40]

Pfeffinger began to defend himself in print even before the appearance of Stolz's and Flacius's book. Only Amsdorf won mention in Pfeffinger's Latin *Exposition of the Obvious Lie with which the Scurrilous, Sycophant Booklet Tries to Defame Dr. Johann Pfeffinger* and in his German *Answer of Dr. Johann Pfeffinger to the Public Confession*.[41] Amsdorf's statements about Pfeffinger had been brief in *Public Confession*, so Pfeffinger might have overlooked them, if they had not come from someone as prominent as Amsdorf in the Wittenberg movement. Pfeffinger's *Exposition* reprinted his theses that had aroused the disagreement between himself and Amsdorf; but it avoided addressing the issues that Amsdorf had raised. Instead, Pfeffinger's *Exposition* advanced *ad hominem* arguments. Pfeffinger expressed his surprise that a man whom Luther regarded so highly could have changed and abandoned the teaching that Pfeffinger was certain was faithful to Luther. Pfeffinger also asked his readers how any sane person could deal with an attack that ended with the words, as Amsdorf's quotation of Pfeffinger had, "if I remember correctly." Pfeffinger did not say, however, whether Amsdorf had accurately cited him. Instead, he reprinted the complete text of the theses

40 *M. Ioannis Stolzii Concionatoris Aulici Ducum Saxoniae Refutatio propositionum Pfeffingeri de Libero arbitrio, cum Praefatione M. Ioannis Aurifabri. Matth: Fla: Illyrici de eadem controuersia* (Jena: Thomas Rebart, 1558); the edited text is found in C&C 5:85–103. Flacius also composed *Refutatio propositionum Pfeffingeri de libero arbitrio* (published in Stolz's *Refutatio*; the edited text is found in C&C 5:133–144) and *Bericht M. Fl. Ill./ von etlichen Artikeln der Christlichen Lehr/ vnd von seinem Leben/ vnd enlich auch von den Adiaphorischen Handlungen/ wider die falschen Geticht der Adiaphoristen* (Jena: Thomas Rebart, 1559), in which he dealt with Pfeffinger's position. All the subsequent controversies were placed in the context of the adiaphoristic controversy by both sides. Nikolaus Gallus joined the controversy with his *Quaestio de libero arbitrio* (Regensburg: Heinrich Geisler, 1559).

41 *Demonstratio*, see page 136 (note 22) above, and *Antwort: D. Johann Pfeffingers Pastoris der Kirchen zu Leiptzig: Auff die Offentliche Bekentnis der reinen Lare des Euangelij/ vnd Confutation der jtzigen Schwermerey Niclasen von Ambsdorff* (Wittenberg, 1558); the edited text found in C&C 5:153–173.

he had offered for disputation. Pfeffinger's conclusion claimed that he was only trying to follow the apostolic teaching on free will, and that he wanted only to say that the use of the will had not been completely destroyed in the fall. Though the will is corrupt, depraved, and unable to restore itself, nonetheless it is able in some way to respond to the Gospel by giving its assent. Like someone who turns toward rather than away from the light of the sun, so must the human creature cooperate with God when God's light shines upon that person's will.[42] These concluding remarks from Pfeffinger did nothing to reconcile Amsdorf to his position.

The *Answer* that Pfeffinger published was not much different from his *Exposition*, though it presented a bit more of an extended discussion of the issues than the *Exposition* had. Pfeffinger's *Answer* also blamed the dispute on Flacius, Gallus, Amsdorf, "and their mob," who were bent on falsifying Christian teaching and dividing the church. If the quotation Amsdorf had ascribed to Pfeffinger could be found in Pfeffinger's disputation, he promised that he would recant. But Pfeffinger did not. Instead, he repeated his earlier position. The Holy Spirit does not work with human beings as a sculptor works with a block of wood or stone, that is, without the person feeling, knowing, or understanding anything. He continued to insist that the ultimate reason some are saved and others are damned lies in their own reaction to the Holy Spirit. He did not believe that such a formulation implied that natural human powers contribute to salvation. Instead, he insisted he was doing no more than affirming the natural functions and personal responsibility of the one being converted.[43]

Amsdorf was not willing to let Pfeffinger sidestep the discussion so easily. In his *That Dr. Pfeffinger Maliciously and Falsely Denies his Misdeed*, Amsdorf complained that Pfeffinger was not meeting his criticisms but was, instead, only slandering his person.[44] Amsdorf threw back at Pfeffinger his accusation of deserting Luther and dividing the church. This Leipzig professor and his fellow adiaphorists were twisting God's Word to agree with reason and philosophy once more, Amsdorf said, just as they had in the Leipzig "Interim." Amsdorf said that Pfeffinger's affirmation of the exclusive role of God's grace in salvation was a contradiction to Pfeffinger's comments on the will's ability to assent to the Word. Amsdorf also charged that Pfeffinger was setting up a smoke screen by making a significant issue of human psychological functioning in conversion, even though no disagreement on that subject had arisen. Amsdorf's declaration of his own position

42 See *Demonstratio*, D2a–b.

43 *Antwort Pfeffingers*, C2a–D4a.

44 *Das D. Pfeffinger*, A2a–B3a, C4a–b, D3a–b.

was slightly different in this treatise than in his earlier writing. He emphasized that the Holy Spirit works only through the Gospel, and that the Gospel call is issued to all people. But God draws only the elect to himself, and he draws them only through Jesus Christ, through faith in Christ. Those who do not hear the Gospel of Christ cannot be saved.[45]

Pfeffinger's *Answer* and Amsdorf's *That Dr. Pfeffinger Maliciously and Falsely Denies his Misdeed* did not further the debate of the issues in view. Neither man went beyond his initial position. Neither developed a more penetrating critique of the other's position, nor did they attempt a reconciliation. And they did not publish subsequent works addressing these issues with one another. Amsdorf became distracted by events in ducal Saxony that led to a controversy over the free will among the faculty at Jena. Pfeffinger did not forget Amsdorf's critiques, but he did abandon the public debate. Pfeffinger did issue another defense later in 1559, but its harsh invective was directed only toward Flacius and concentrated on the questions of adiaphora proposed in the Leipzig "Interim." In a shorter section on the freedom of the will, Pfeffinger did not even mention Amsdorf's name.[46]

The lack of subsequently published works on this issue is not evidence that the differences between Pfeffinger's and Amsdorf's views had dissipated. Amsdorf was convinced Pfeffinger's statements on the will distracted from God's exclusive role in saving sinners and restoring them to life with him. Amsdorf regarded the proclamation of God's sovereignty and God's unconditioned mercy in Christ as the only task of the theologian. The theological questions that Pfeffinger was trying to answer relating to human responsibility and psychological processes hardly interested Amsdorf at all: the responsibility for the origin of sin; the rationale behind God's choice of the elect; the extent of damage wrought by the fall. If anything, Amsdorf viewed those questions and the answers Pfeffinger was proposing as part of the theology Amsdorf had rejected in the Reformation under Luther's influence.

The issue of the role of the human will in conversion became the "synergistic controversy" because Pfeffinger and Amsdorf were each motivated by their strong convictions and concerns. They both had pastoral concerns. Amsdorf feared that exploring and emphasizing human responsibility would lead back to a medieval emphasis on human contributions to the process of salvation.

45 *Das D. Pfeffinger*, C2a–D3b.

46 *Nochmals gru[e]ndlicher/ klarer/ warhafftiger Bericht vnd Bekentnis/ der bittern lautern Warheit/ reiner Lere/ vnstrefflichen Handlungen/ vnd vnuermeidliche notwendige Verantwortunge* (Wittenberg: Lorenz Schwenck, 1559), J1a–J4b; the edited text is found in C&C 5:221–265.

Pfeffinger feared that determinism would instill in Christians a lack of responsibility and a belief that God can be blamed as the origin of evil. Though both Pfeffinger and Amsdorf realized that they could not probe the depths of the mysteries of God, their dispute suggests they did not step back quickly enough from trying to probe those mysteries. The hostility created by the Leipzig "Interim" and the political changes in Saxony after the Smalcald War also helped poison the Wittenberg theologians' atmosphere enough to turn a disagreement into a controversy.

FRIENDS AND ANTAGONISTS

In 1548, Johann Friedrich the Middler reacted to his family's loss of the University of Wittenberg by establishing an "academy" in Jena for university-level education in his lands. In 1558, his academy gained official university status by an imperial grant. By that time, personality and theological differences related to the synergistic controversy had begun to cause clashes among the theologians on the new faculty. Even though Amsdorf was disagreeing with Flacius at the time about the abstract necessity of good works for salvation under the Law, Amsdorf still urged and petitioned the young lords to call Flacius to the theological faculty at Jena. Flacius had been working in Magdeburg, directing the composition of a history of the church, the *Magdeburg Centuries*.[47] In 1557, he left to join the university community in Jena and the ducal Saxon ecclesiastical establishment. Although Amsdorf was living some distance from Jena, his interest in the new ducal Saxon academy and university remained intense. He continued to significantly influence the institution throughout the 1550s. For example, Johann Friedrich that Middler commanded that Amsdorf receive reports on all theological disputations conducted at Jena.[48]

Flacius joined Erhard Schnepf and Viktorin Strigel on the university theological faculty. He also assumed duties as superintendent alongside Schnepf for the ecclesiastical life of the dukedom. Schnepf had become Jena's second theology professor in 1549 when the enforcement of the Augsburg Interim drove him from the University of Tübingen. He died in 1558, leaving two young men, Strigel and Flacius, without a moderating and mediating middle man in their company. Strigel had come to Jena at age 24 to teach philosophy and theology

47 Harald Bollbuck, *Wahrheitszeugnis, Gottes Auftrag und Zeitkritik: die Kirchengeschichte der Magdeburger Zenturien und ihre Arbeitstechniken* (Wiesbaden: Harrassowitz, 2014).

48 J. C. E. Schwarz, *Das Erste Jahrzehnd der Universität Jena* (Jena: Fromann, 1858), 60.

when the academy was established there in 1548. Melanchthon had recommended Strigel, and he had become the prodigy and rising star of the ducal Saxon ecclesiastical and intellectual scene. Flacius's arrival in Jena made Strigel fear he might lose his own prominence and dominance, since Flacius was four years his elder and his equal, if not his superior, in intellectual imagination. In fact, even before Flacius arrived in Jena, Strigel had publicly voiced his worry that Flacius might eventually play a role at the university. Strigel did support the Saxon dukes' Gnesio-Lutheran positions; however, the friendship he retained with his mentor Melanchthon fostered Strigel's antagonism toward Flacius, and he rebuffed Flacius's initial attempts to win his friendship. The fact that Flacius also received a higher salary than Strigel when joining the faculty did not help the situation.[49]

When the imperially-sponsored colloquy at Worms collapsed in September 1557, the ducal Saxon government sought to contribute to the goal of unity among the disputing Evangelical territories and towns. Johann Friedrich's advisors, including Flacius and Amsdorf, believed the most effective way to achieve reconciliation within the Wittenberg circle was to hold a convocation of theologians where detailed affirmations of biblical teaching could be formulated, along with explicit condemnations of false teachings and false teachers. The electoral Saxon officials and the theologians at Wittenberg and Leipzig—Melanchthon and his followers—preferred to place reconciliation efforts in the hands of princes, and they believed that general formulations of biblical teaching would suffice. They also advised setting aside controversy through "*amnistia*," ignoring and forgetting past differences, in sharp contrast to Flacius and his colleagues.[50]

Following the recommendation of their advisors, the ducal Saxon leadership commissioned a new confession and confutation of the errors that were dividing adherents of the Augsburg Confession so that unity among these adherents could eventually be achieved. Johann Friedrich asked Schnepf, Strigel, and Andreas Hügel, their good friend and the ecclesiastical superintendent of Jena, to compose the document in consultation with Flacius and Amsdorf. Twice,

---

49 Gehrt, *Konfessionspolitik*, 109–114. In addition to material on the university's early years in Schwarz, *Erste Jahrzehnd*, see also Julius Hartmann, *Erhard Schnepf, Der Reformator in Schwaben, Nassau, Hessen, und Thüringen* (Tübingen: Osiander, 1870). On Strigel, cf. Ernst Koch, "Viktorin Strigel (1524–1569). Von Jena nach Heidelberg," in *Melanchthon in seinen Schülern*, ed. Heinz Scheible (Wiesbaden: Harrassowitz), 391–404, and Robert Kolb, "Die theologische Pilgerschaft von Viktorin Strigel. Vom 'gnesiolutherischen' Hoftheologe zum, 'calvinistischen' Professor," in *Calvinismus in den Auseinandersetzungen des frühen konfessionellen Zeitalters*, eds. Herman J. Selderhuis, Martin Leiner, and Volker Leppin (Göttingen: Vandenhoeck & Ruprecht, 2013), 79–96.

50 Charles P. Arand et al., *The Lutheran Confessions, History and Theology of the Book of Concord* (Minneapolis: Fortress, 2012), 255–263.

Schnepf, Strigel, and Hügel politely declined the honor; finally, they explained to the dukes that they could not perform such a task if Flacius and Amsdorf were going to interfere. Johann Friedrich the Middler ordered them to proceed without Flacius and Amsdorf. Their "Confutation" arrived at the court in Weimar on Palm Sunday 1558, accompanied by a note that insisted Amsdorf and Flacius not be allowed to alter a word. Strigel's fear that his position as ranking theologian of ducal Saxony was threatened by Flacius's presence in Jena caused him to view himself as engaged in a battle for his power and position, and he knew where the lines had to be drawn. He and his friends in Jena and Wittenberg were working to undercut Flacius's newly-won position at the Ernestine court. And the *Book of Confutation* was another suitable context in which the rivals could test their strength.[51] However, the duke did permit Flacius and some of his followers to revise the "Confutation." Strigel, Schnepf, and Hügel could hardly recognize the document when Flacius's friends were finished with it. The ducal Saxon Gnesio-Lutherans, including Flacius, were also assisted by Joachim Mörlin, superintendent of Braunschweig city, and Erasmus Sarcerius, superintendent of Mansfeld county, in making revisions. Mörlin and Sarcerius had supported the ducal Saxon demands to condemn false teachers and teachings at the colloquy of Worms in 1557. The revision of the "Confutation" was not only an insult to Strigel and Hügel; they found its contents objectionable at several points.[52]

This revised "Confutation" reviewed and rebutted the errors of Servetus, Schwenckfeld, the antinomians, the Anabaptists, the Sacramentarians, Osiander, Stancarus, Major, and the adiaphorists, as well as errors concerning the free will.[53] It followed the form of Amsdorf's *Public Confession*, but it was far more detailed and analytical than that popular work's analysis.

---

51 Ilić, *Theologian*, 144–147.

52 According to the author of "Brevis narratio de controversia inter Flacium etc. et Victorin. Strigelium et Hugelum," the authorship of the revised *Book of Confutation* is assigned to Maximilian Mörlin, superintendent in Coburg, Johann Stössel, superintendent in Heldburg, and Simon Musaeus, new professor at Jena, with further revisions by Johann Aurifaber, court preacher in Weimar, Flacius, and the two from outside ducal Saxony, Joachim Mörlin and Erasmus Sarcerius (Wf, Guelf. Helmst. 64.2:244; cf. Beck, *Johann Friedrich*, 1:309, and Hartmann, *Schnepf*, 117–122. Cf. Gehrt, *Konfessionspolitik*, 129–165, and Gleiß, *Weimarer Disputation*, 44–56).

53 *Illvstrissimi Principis Ac Domini, Domini Iohannis Friderici Secvndi, Dvcis Saxoniae . . . solida & ex verbo Dei sumpta Confutatio & condemnatio praecipuarum Corruptelarum, Sectarum & errorum, hoc tempore ad instaurationem & propagationem Regni Antichristi Rom. Pontificis aliarumque fanaticarum opinionum . . . contra ueram sacrae Scripturae, Confessionis Augustanae & Schmalkaldicorum Articulorum Religionem . . .* (Jena: Thomas Rebart, 1559); *Des Durchleuchtigen Hochgebornen Fu[e]rsten vnd Herren/ Herren Johans Friderichen des Mittlern/ Herzogen zu Sachssen . . . in Gottes wort/ Prophetischer vnd Apostolischer Schrifft/ gegru[e]ndete wort Confutationes/ Widerlegungen vnd verdammung etlicher einheit her/ zu wider demselben Gottes wort/ vnd heiliger Schrifft/ auch der Augspurgischen Confession Apologien/ vnd den Schmalkaldischen Artickeln/ Aber zu fu[e]rderung vnd wider anrichtung des Antichristischen Bapstums eingeschlichen/ vnd eingerissenen Corruptelen/ Secten vnd Irrthumen . . .* (Jena: Thomas Rebart, 1559; the edited texts of both Latin and German "Books" are found in C&C 5:308–501).

The events of 1558, including the outcome of the *Book of Confutation*, demonstrated that Flacius's influence at court—presumably strengthened by Amsdorf's support—was not only rising but was already unrivaled. The final text of the *Book of Confutation* reflected his views. He prevailed against Strigel and Hügel when a synod was called to Weimar to address the original three authors' objections to the revised *Book of Confutation*. Flacius's friend, Simon Musaeus, was chosen as Schnepf's replacement when Schnepf died on November 1, 1558. Flacius and his comrades persuaded Johann Friedrich the Middler to publish their *Book of Confutation* as an official confession for ducal Saxony, requiring all pastors and teachers, including university professors, to subscribe to it.[54] Only two of the approximately five hundred parish pastors in ducal Saxony protested, one on grounds of tone and method rather than content.[55]

Strigel could not comply with Johann Friedrich's edict that granted Flacius's request on January 24, 1559. In a letter dated February 4, Strigel informed the dukes of his four basic objections to the *Book of Confutation*. He rejected the *Book*'s position on the free will. He also rejected its condemnation of a broader definition of the Gospel to include the call to repentance as well as forgiveness of sins; Strigel believed that Flacius was wrong in limiting the meaning of "Gospel" to only God's grace in Christ. Strigel also contended that alongside its condemnation of the proposition, "good works are necessary for salvation," the *Book* should mention that Major had withdrawn his proposition. Strigel argued that the *Book* attributed more evils to the Wittenberg theologians than those of which they were actually guilty.[56]

Strigel's objections to the *Book of Confutation* undoubtedly were sincere, even if his loyalty to Melanchthon, his dislike of Flacius, and his resentment of Flacius's new dominance in ducal Saxony also contributed to Strigel's resistance toward the *Book of Confutation*.

Johann Friedrich the Middler was a respectable lay theologian who could read the Scriptures in their original languages. He also had many of the same goals and intentions as other princes in that time period. In the aftermath of the Peace of Augsburg, he wanted to consolidate his hold over his lands and his church. Therefore, quibbling, independent-minded theologians did not help toward that goal and annoyed him. So Strigel's obstinacy invited discipline.

54 Gehrt, *Konfessionspolitik*, 129–137.

55 Gehrt, *Konfessionspolitik*, 155–156.

56 Beck, *Johann Friedrich*, 311–312; on the developing situation in ducal Saxony, see also Gehrt, *Konfessionspolitik*, 144–165, Preger, *Flacius*, 2:116–126, Ilić, *Theologian*, 144–147, and Albert Pommerien, *Viktorin Strigels Lehre von dem Peccatum originis* (Hannover: Stephanusstift, 1917), 5.

The duke asked Amsdorf, Musaeus, and Johann Stössel, the superintendent in Heldburg, how he should deal with Strigel and his supporters. They suspected that their "dearest friends and brothers, for the time being our antagonists," in this case were acting out of ambition and envy, for Strigel had previously demonstrated his faithfulness to the Gnesio-Lutheran cause by denouncing the adiaphoristic Leipzig "Interim" and supporting the confutation of errors throughout the previous decade. The duke must make one of two bad choices, they decided. He could either let the squabbling continue to divide and confuse his lands, or he must dismiss Strigel and Hügel if they continued to refuse to subscribe to the *Book of Confutation*. Amsdorf, Musaeus, and Stössel suggested that the dukes give Strigel and Hügel a bit more time to consider the matter—albeit while in "custody."[57] Their position on the *Book of Confutation* aligned them with the "adiaphorists," according to Amsdorf and his colleagues; and that was enough to place them under suspicion.

It is not clear who devised the procedure that Johann Friedrich the Middler used to give Strigel and Hügel the time and place to consider the matter.[58] However, the proceedings that occurred are well documented. On Good Friday, March 24, 1559, one hundred foot soldiers and fifty or sixty horsemen, "among whom was not a single noble," interdicted the road that led from Weimar to Jena, so that no one could alert Jena to their presence. The next day, Easter Eve, the troops rode into Jena, battered down Strigel's door with axes, hauled him out of bed amidst exchanged insults and the screams of his wife, and carried him to the fortress Leuchtenberg, where Hügel was also interned.[59] There, and later at the fortress Grimmenstein, the two were given time to reconsider their rejection of the *Book of Confutation*, while the dukes also sent theologians to help persuade them to subscribe. During Strigel and Hügel's internment, Amsdorf reviewed their written arguments and also visited them. He, too, failed to win

57 "Antwort auff das ander theil der instruction welcher gestalt zu procediren sey da obgemelte D. Victorinus vnd der Pfarrherr von jena auf ihrer meinunge trotzig vndt halsstarrig berufen werdenn," Wf, Guelf. 12.8 Aug. Fol., 264a–268a, a copy of the original.

58 Preger, *Flacius*, 2:123, claims that Flacius and Musaeus had no part in the arrest of Strigel. J. C. E. Schwarz, in his article on Amsdorf in the *Realencyklopädie für protestantische Theologie und Kirche*, 3rd ed., ed. Albert Hauck, 1:202, states that Amsdorf appears to have counseled such a course. His conclusion seems warranted on the basis of the "Antwort auff das ander theil," Wf, Guelf. 12.8 Aug. Fol., 268a, in which Amsdorf, Musaeus, and Stössel suggested that Strigel and Hügel be given time to consider the matter and that the ducal government could use ἐρυμίαν for such consideration. This word could be derived from the Greek verb ἐρύκω, "to restrain, curb, keep in, detain," or more likely could be an alternate misspelling of ἐριμία, "fortification" or "castle." Gehrt, *Konfessionspolitik*, 156–159 provides an overview of these developments.

59 What the reports of the incident by Justus Jonas the younger may lack in accuracy, they make up for in colorful detail; see his two letters to Duke Albrecht of Prussia, April 23 and May 4, 1559, in Voigt, *Briefwechsel*, 569–584; see also Beck, *Johann Friedrich*, 1:312–313.

their compliance, just as the other theologians had.[60]

In a memorandum on Strigel and Hügel's objections to the *Book* prepared for Johann Friedrich the Middler, Amsdorf argued that the Law alone works repentance because it condemns sin. To define the Gospel in such a way that it embraces repentance as well as forgiveness vitiates the proclamation of salvation by grace through faith in Christ alone. Amsdorf also labeled Strigel's comments about free will as double talk. Although the arguments Amsdorf leveled against Strigel's description of free will sounded much like those Amsdorf used against Pfeffinger, Amsdorf still considered Strigel his "friend" and did not associate him with the synergistic professor in Leipzig. Amsdorf advised that Strigel needed to love the truth more than he loved his adiaphoristic friends and that Strigel ought to follow Christ's call to leave rulers, parents, and certainly the wise of this world for the Gospel's sake (Luke 14:18–21).[61]

Even though neither Amsdorf nor any other ducal advisor could sway Strigel and Hügel as prisoners, Johann Friedrich the Middler gave in to diplomatic pressure from other Evangelical princes and Emperor Maximilian and released the theological prisoners on September 5, 1559. However, Strigel remained under house arrest and then city arrest for almost four years.

And the theological differences that had set Strigel and Hügel at odds with the subscribers to the *Book of Confutation* still needed to be resolved. Strigel wanted a general synod of all Evangelical churches to meet, but Flacius favored a different setting in this instance. He sought and won the court's approval for a public disputation between himself and Strigel. Strigel agreed to participate in a disputation with Flacius. Simon Musaeus and Balthasar Winter, Hügel's successor as superintendent in Jena, helped Flacius formulate theses on the free will, definitions of Law and Gospel, Majorism, adiaphorism, and academic privileges (such as the right to explore use of Aristotelian terminology, a right which Strigel had invoked). The disputation began in Weimar on August 2, 1560.[62]

60 Documents relating to the confinement are found in Wf, Guelf. Helmst. 64.2: "Die Erste Victorini auss Leuchtenburg antworth," 90a–91b, "Des pfarhers Erste Antwort auss Leuchtenburgk, auf des Ehrwirdigen Achtbarn vnd Hochgelehrtenn D. Christian Bruck Sechsischen Cantylers gestriges Furbringen vnterthenige Antwort," 91b–94a, "Die ander Antworth Hugels auss Leuchtenburgk," 94a–97b, "Victorini Ander Antworth auss Leuchtenburgk," 97b–100a. Amsdorf's critique follows: "Ambsdorfij bedencken vber die zwo antwort der zweijen auss Leuchtenburgk," 101b–107a. Pommerien states, *Strigel*, 11, that Amsdorf took part in a colloquy with Strigel and Hügel in Gotha, near the fortress Grimmenstein, along with Flacius, Musaeus, Stössel, and others.

61 "Ambsdorfij bedencken," Wf, Guelf. Helmst. 64.2:103a–107b.

62 Detailed protocol reports on the disputation are found in Flacius's *Dispvtatio de originali peccato et libero arbitrio, inter Matthiam Flacivm Illyricvm & Victorinum Strigelium* (Eisleben, 1563); the edited text is found in C&C 5:539–551. On the structure of the disputation and its course, see Gleiß, *Die Weimarer Disputation*, 92–162, 188–247. Gehrt, *Konfessionspolitik*, 184–186, and Hans Kropatscheck, "Das Problem theologischer Anthropologie auf dem Weimarer Gespräch von 1560 zwischen Matthias Flacius Illyricus und Viktorin

Johann Friedrich the Middler had invited Amsdorf, but no record indicates that he actually attended.[63] Central to the discussion was the fundamental relationship between God's power and the power of the human will after the fall into sin.

Johann Friedrich the Middler suffered a tragic loss after the thirteenth session of the disputation: his infant son, the eldest child and heir apparent, died. In the face of this tragedy, the disputation was adjourned as the court turned to making funeral arrangements. The disputation was never reconvened. The disputation would haunt both Flacius and Strigel until their deaths. By the time of the disputation's adjournment, a serious difference of expression and understanding of Christian anthropology had surfaced between Flacius and Strigel. Flacius wanted to define what it means to be human by using Scriptural language only. Strigel thought it was beneficial to use Aristotelian modes of analysis so that there could be a structure for understanding and presenting biblical anthropology. This point of impasse caused the disputation to be bogged down in questions of conversion and original sin.

Both men agreed that God's grace is alone responsible for the conversion of the sinner, but Strigel wanted to further specify that the human will is a concurring factor (*causa*) along with the Holy Spirit and God's Word. The will, according to Strigel, is subordinate to the aid God gives; therefore, the will is the formal factor in conversion (differentiated from Melanchthon's view, which had designated the human will as the material factor), the Spirit is the efficient factor, and the Word is the instrumental factor. Strigel also was defining conversion as an action that continues throughout the Christian life, equating *conversio* with ongoing repentance as well as initial conversion. This definition was common, and all the Wittenberg theologians had at times used *conversio* with that sense. Thus, Strigel agreed with Flacius in denying that the sinner cooperates in his initial conversion. But Strigel also insisted that the converted will cooperates in the continuing process of *conversio*, as the sanctified believer daily turns from sin to God. For Strigel, the human will is a neutral, unbound psychological force. Strigel spoke from a philosophical and psychological view to maintain that the fallen will still retains its "*modus agendi*"—its ability to make decisions—even despite its sinfulness. The fall had not changed the essence of the human creature; he described original sin as an accident—in the Aristotelian sense of the word—that adheres to the human essence or substance that God created. For

---

Strigel," licentiate dissertation, University of Göttingen, 1943, esp. 39–103. See also Pommerien, *Strigel*, 7, 12–17, and Beck, *Johann Friedrich*, 1:319.

63 Gleiß, *Die Weimarer Disputation*, 110–111.

Flacius, the extent of what needed to be said about the human will was that after the fall, it is actively in opposition to its Creator.

Though he used Aristotelian tools of logic for many purposes, Flacius had no interest in this sort of philosophical anthropology. In the disputation with Strigel, Flacius maintained that the human creature lost the image of God in the fall. Now the human creature conforms to the image of Satan, which provides the pattern for sinful living. In Strigel's Aristotelian terms, Flacius stated that the human being *is* changed in his substance by sin; and therefore sin is not an Aristotelian accident, an external characteristic that does not define the person in his essence. In fact, Flacius was so convinced that human existence had become fully enveloped in revolt against God, he went so far as to say that original sin had become the substance of the sinner. Though the Gnesio-Lutherans appreciated Flacius's desire to use only Scriptural language, his idea that original sin had become the substance of the sinner would eventually alienate him from many of the Gnesio-Lutherans when his own views became the subject of a controversy between 1567 and his death in 1575 and even through the end of the century.[64]

Amsdorf did not attend the Weimar disputation. Perhaps he was not fully aware of the content of the disputation because it was limited to the semiprivate discussion at court. Still, it is hard to imagine that Amsdorf's friends did not inform him of the proceedings.[65] Despite indications that he disagreed with Strigel's position on original sin, Amsdorf did not denounce him publicly. In 1562, Amsdorf indicated that he agreed with Flacius's position. In a letter to Johann Friedrich's lay counselor, Basilius Monner, Amsdorf reflected his own struggle to find the proper language to describe original sin. First, he tried calling it a strong accident. A few sentences later, he defined original sin as substance, despite

64 Ilić, *Theologian*, 188–195, 204–213. On the condemnation of Flacius's teaching in the Formula of Concord, cf. Robert C. Schultz, "Original Sin: Accident or Substance: The Paradoxical Significance of FC I, 53-62 in Historical Context," in Lewis W. Spitz and Wenzel Lohff, eds., *Discord, Dialog, and Concord. Studies in the Lutheran Reformation's Formula of Concord*, (Philadelphia: Fortress, 1977), 38–57; Walter Sparn, "Substanz oder Subjekt? Die Kontroverse um die anthropologischen Allegmeinbegriffe im Artikel von der Erbsünde (Artikel I)," in Lewis W. Spitz and Wenzel Lohff, eds., *Widerspruch, Dialog und Einigung, Studien zur Konkordienformel der Lutherischen Reformation* (Stuttgart: Calwer Verlag, 1977), 107–135; and Sparn, "Begründung und Verwirklichung, Zur anthropologischen Thematik der lutherischen Bekenntnisse," in Martin Brecht and Reinhard Schwarz, *Bekenntnis und Einheit. Studien zum Konkordienbuch* (Stuttgart: Calwer Verlag, 1980), 129–153. On the continuing defense of Flacius's doctrine of original sin, see Irene Dingel, *Concordia controversa, Die öffentlichen Diskussionen um das lutherische Konkordienwerk am Ende des 16. Jahrhunderts* (Gütersloh: Gütersloher Verlagshaus, 1996), 467–541. On the continuing resistance to Flacius's condemnation by laity, see Robert J. Christman, *Doctrinal Controversy and Lay Religiosity in Late Reformation Germany: The Case of Mansfeld* (Leiden: Brill, 2012).

65 Amsdorf's letter to Bartholomaeus Rosinus suggesting that this is true, dated May 13, 1562, is printed in Christian F. Paullini, *Historia Isenacensis* (Frankfurt/M: Bauer, 1698), 187–188.

some apparent reservation. He stated this, however, for the same reason that Flacius had: he wanted to affirm as strongly as possible the sinner's utter impotence before God and his total dependence on God's saving action in Christ. To the essence or substance of a human being belong not only reason and will, but also reasoning and willing properly and correctly; and sin has eliminated that possibility in human beings. Since inherited righteousness is the substance or essence of the righteous person, Amsdorf argued, original sin and unrighteousness must be the substance and essence of the sinner. They cannot be removed apart from rebirth through the Holy Spirit. For if rebirth is not a transformation of the human substance, Amsdorf stated, then any person could free himself from accidental unrighteousness without the Holy Spirit's power in rebirth.[66]

Strigel's performance at the Weimar disputation impressed Johann Friedrich the Middler. His lay counselors, who found Strigel much more tractable than Flacius on the issue of princely control of the church, urged that Strigel be permitted to teach again. The duke agreed. In the weeks after the Weimar disputation, Strigel and Hügel organized their supporters in Jena and in Weimar for an active campaign against Flacius's party. The campaign continued from late 1560 into 1561, and Strigel and Hügel slowly regained the dominance over ducal thinking and planning that they had once possessed.[67] For the first time, Amsdorf offered significant opposition to the son of his friend Johann Friedrich the Elder, for Amsdorf was not willing to abandon those he considered his own spiritual sons, Flacius, Musaeus, Aurifaber, and their comrades. Yet even Amsdorf conceded that Flacius's tendency toward fomenting conflict had helped bring on the crisis at the university.[68]

Amsdorf's age and infirmities had begun to limit his influence in ducal Saxony. Nonetheless, he did not stop trying to use the influence he still had to aid his comrades as the controversy over the human will continued to become worse. In the maneuvering against those associated with Flacius, the new superintendent in Jena, Balthasar Winter, got in trouble with Johann Friedrich the Middler for barring from the Lord's Supper two members of the law faculty. Winter had refused to give Matthias Wesenbeck the Sacrament because he rejected a request to comment on the *Book of Confutation* when Winter examined his suitability as a baptismal sponsor. Winter had barred Christoph Dürfeld from the Lord's Supper for stating that Seneca taught theology

66 This letter is printed in *Christliche Bekentnus M. Matth. Flacij Illyrici Von der Erbsund*... (1571), Y3a–Y4b and is there dated November 6, 1562; Paullini printed it, *Historia*, 195, dated October 6, 1562.

67 Gehrt, *Konfessionspolitik*, 186–194.

68 Gleiß, *Die Weimarer Disputation*, 149.

as well as Scripture does. Upon hearing of Winter's actions, Flacius feared that such a confrontation with the law faculty might alienate Johann Friedrich the Middler. Flacius urged Winter to keep the duke and his court fully informed of the situation, in the hope that if the duke understood the issues, he would continue to support Winter and Flacius's party. However, Flacius's fears materialized instead. The duke's lay counselors who were sympathetic to Strigel, along with two ecclesiastical superintendents and former associates of Flacius, Maximilian Mörlin and Johann Stössel, quickly moved to deal a blow to Flacius and his supporters, who still included nearly all the ducal Saxon clergy at the time. Winter was removed from office in October 1560. However, his replacement, Johann Cuno, continued to admonish the same members of the law faculty that Winter had been disciplining. So a month later, Johann Friedrich the Middler ousted Cuno as well. Stössel then assumed the office. Winter died soon after his dismissal. Though he had been ill for some time, his death occurred close enough to the time of his dismissal that he was held up as a martyr for the Flacian party.[69]

Though Amsdorf had apparently questioned Winter's actions in dealing with Wesenbeck, he vehemently opposed the duke's interference in ecclesiastical affairs when he removed Winter from his office. Amsdorf fired off a memorandum to the court, arguing that no emperor or king, much less "drunken and godless counselors," can command pastors to dispense Absolution and distribute the Sacrament to the unworthy. When princes wanted to help the true church, Amsdorf welcomed their aid. But he would not tolerate a prince's usurpation of God's own power.[70]

That was also the reason the bishop opposed Johann Friedrich the Middler's subsequent attempt to consolidate his power over the church with a reconstructed consistory. The consistory, which would include a majority of secular counselors alongside theologians, would have veto power and sole authority to excommunicate in the duke's lands. Since Johann Friedrich the Elder had organized the Saxon consistory in the late 1530s, it had consisted of both theologians and secular counselors, but it had not given veto power to the latter. The duke stated, with reference to recent events in Jena, that he would not abide his theologians introducing a Spanish inquisition in his domains. He had already—in August 1560—suspended the right of superintendents to excommunicate without ducal approval. In November 1560, his plan for a consistory was

69 Details on the situation are related in Gehrt, *Konfessionspolitik*, 165–176; Beck, *Johann Friedrich*, 1:322–323; Preger, *Flacius*, 2:135–142; and Salig, *Historie*, 3:575–585, 627–646.

70 Beck, *Johann Friedrich*, 1:325; Preger, *Flacius*, 2:135–142.

completed. He published it in July 1561, despite his theologians' protests. The consistory was to meet four times each year under the duke's presidency. Four theologians—Mörlin, Stössel, and two other superintendents, Caspar Molitor and Bartholomaeus Rosinus—would serve on the consistory with four secular counselors, including Chancellor Christian von Brück.[71]

Amsdorf strenuously disapproved. He insisted on the independence of the church in its sphere of responsibility and competence. Christ gave the Church and its teachers the right to formulate its decisions. He did not give the prince the right to impose his decrees on the church without its consent. Local pastors had no such right, much less the prince. The consistory process violated the Scriptural process laid down in Matthew 18 for dealing with public sinners. Furthermore, Amsdorf feared that no one would confide in a pastor who functioned as an arm of the prince, a policeman. Pastors would let the exercise of Christian discipline fall into disuse to avoid the difficult trip to Weimar required for obtaining a decree of excommunication.[72] The bishop resisted those in the pastoral office having any role in what is labeled today "social disciplining"—a task that belongs to secular officials. Preaching the will of God for human life sufficed for cultivating proper behavior, and the preacher had no place in the governing structures of the dukedom. For Amsdorf, as for Luther, *politia* and *ecclesia* had distinct tasks, even when they sometimes had similar purposes and goals. However, Johann Friedrich was no longer listening to his bishop. Instead, he had become bent on incorporating his church into his governmental structure. He inaugurated the restructured consistory. Those like Amsdorf who believed that the Church belonged to Christ, not the prince, lost the battle for ecclesiastical liberty. Even so, these Gnesio-Lutherans had established a tradition of clerical critique of secular authority that did not die out.[73]

In early 1561, the duke intensified his efforts to clip Flacius's wings. The duke forbade his theologians at Jena to publish without court approval and restricted their public preaching. The theologians' protracted negotiations and vehement protests won them nothing. Johann Aurifaber was dismissed from being a court

71 *Ordenung vnd summarischer Process des Fürstlichen Sechsischen Consistorij, Auffgerichtet in dem jar 1561* (Jena, 1561); see Gehrt, *Konfessionspolitik*, 196–201; Beck, *Johann Friedrich*, 1:327–333; Preger, *Flacius*, 2:157–165; Salig, *Historie*, 3:633–635.

72 "Articuli de clauibus Ecclesiae et iuribus pastorum contra Consistor. Jenense," Wr, ETLFB 40:347a–348a; see also a brief excerpt from a letter on the consistory to Rosinus, dated August 7, 1561, in *Fortgesetzte Sammlung von alten und neuen theologischen Sachen* (1722), 29–30, and a letter to Johann Friedrich the Middler, dated September 16, 1561, in Rudolf Ehwald, "Beschreibung der Handschriften und Inkunabulen der Herzogl. Gymnasialbibliothek zu Gotha nebst vier Briefe von Eobanus Hessus, Melanchthon, und Niclas von Amsdorff," in *Programm des Gymnasiums Ernestinum zu Gotha* (Gotha: Engelhard-Reyher, 1893), 18–20.

73 See chapter 2, page 71 (note 65).

preacher because he could not satisfactorily support his allegations that false doctrine was being taught in ducal Saxony. The difficulty of Flacius's supporters receiving official permission for new calls led Simon Musaeus to leave Jena to negotiate a call for himself as superintendent in Bremen, without ducal permission. There was also trouble in 1561 for the two new members of the Jena theological faculty—Johannes Wigand and Matthaeus Judex—who had previously been Flacius's co-workers on the *Magdeburg Centuries* and had received calls to Jena only in 1560. In October 1561, Judex was removed from his office as professor for publishing a book on the papacy without official approval. In response, he published a sharp criticism of princely censoring of theologians' works.[74] In November, a ducal commission began to review charges against Flacius and Wigand. That commission dismissed them both on December 10, 1561, a favorite time of year for sending dissidents into exile. Flacius and Wigand appealed to the duke without avail. He had turned against them.[75] Johann Friedrich the Middler also ignored Amsdorf's defense of the Jena theologians and his protest of the defaming of Flacius in official circles. Amsdorf wrote letters to those outside ducal Saxony attempting to counter accusations against Flacius.[76]

Over the course of only a few years, Amsdorf and Flacius had fallen from positions of privilege in the young lords' government to the status of outcasts, removed from positions of leadership and ignored and censured. Amsdorf had exerted significant effort to bring Flacius to the University of Jena and promote his authority there. When Flacius arrived in 1557, Johann Friedrich the Middler had supported him and Amsdorf's allies in Jena. Flacius's rapid rise to prominence in ducal Saxon ecclesiastical life reflects not only his own intellectual talent but also Amsdorf's position of influence in the ducal lords' court. Nonetheless, Flacius's rival Viktorin Strigel succeeded in winning the broader support of the ducal Saxon government, particularly that of the duke, Johann Friedrich the Middler, in part because of the way in which Flacius and his colleagues exercised their power.

The entanglement of theological, personal, and political concerns was far

74 Judex, *Der Ewigen/ Allmechtigen G[o]ttlichenn Mayest. Mandat/ vnd ernstlicher befelch/ wes sich ein yeder Christ/ nach seinem beruff/ vnnd stande/ gegen dem offenbarten Antichrist/ das gantze Babstumb/ halten solle/ widerheolt vnd erklert* (s.l., 1561); cf. Gehrt, *Konfessionspolitik*, 195–196. Judex published his critique of princely censorship, *De typographiae Inventione, et de praelorum legitima inspectione, libellus brevis et utilis* (Copenhagen: Johannes Zimmermann, 1566); cf. Robert Kolb, "Matthaeus Judex's Condemnation of Princely Censorship of Theologians' Publications," *Church History* 50 (1981): 401–414.

75 Gehrt, *Konfessionspolitik*, 201–212.

76 Details of the fall of the Flacian party are given by Salig, *Historie*, 3:845–875; Beck, *Johann Friedrich*, 370–381; Preger, *Flacius*, 2:157–180. Amsdorf appealed particularly to Basilius Monner, a ducal counselor long friendly to the Gnesio-Lutherans, in letters of June 17, 1561, copied in Wf, Guelf. 64.62 Extr. 2°:121a–122a, and of November 6, 1562, printed in Flacius's *Christliche Bekentnus*, Y3a–Y4b.

from over in Saxony. Johann Friedrich the Middler could not brook opposition to his desire to consolidate princely control of the church, a desire that was common among early modern European rulers. The Gnesio-Lutherans eventually regained leadership in Ernestine Saxony after Johann Friedrich the Middler overplayed his hand by supporting a rebel noble, Wilhelm von Grumbach, and ended up in imperial prison in 1567. His brother and successor as the sole ruler of the dukedom, Johann Wilhelm, who had supported the Flacian party, ignored diplomatic pressure to exclude Gnesio-Lutherans from his university. The pressure did recede somewhat, though, since Flacius himself was not involved when his colleagues, led by Wigand, returned to Jena and Weimar in 1568.

AGAINST VIKTORIN'S SYNERGISM: NO COOPERATION OR *MODUS AGENDI*

When Johann Friedrich the Middler purged the Jena faculty in the 1560s, he solved the problem of opposition to his consistory, but he did not thereby resolve the theological issues regarding the freedom of the will. Strigel remained under house arrest, refusing to subscribe to the *Book of Confutation*. Johann Friedrich the Middler asked the dukes of Mecklenburg and Duke Christoph of Württemberg, the most prominent Evangelical prince in the empire, to assist him in reaching a settlement. David Chytraeus, the representative for the dukes of Mecklenburg, could not travel because of illness and instead sent a memorandum in reaction to Strigel's position. The memorandum has been lost, but reactions to it by a number of those whom the ducal Saxon government consulted, among them Amsdorf, are extant, though they do not reveal precisely what Chytraeus's position was. In early May 1562, Christoph Binder and Jakob Andreae, the arbitrators whom Duke Christoph sent, traveled to Weimar. Strigel overcame their doubts about his position on the free will. During a week of conferences, Strigel and the Württemberg theologians formulated an agreement, popularly called the "Declaration of Viktorin."[77] However, within a year, the Württemberg theologians would challenge subsequent statements by Strigel, feeling that they had been duped by his ready agreement with them in Weimar, and Strigel's response

77 The text of the "Declaratio Victorini" is edited and analyzed in Daniel Gehrt, "Strategien zur Konsensbildung im innerlutherischen Streit um die Willensfreiheit. Edition der Declaratio Victorini und der ernestinischen Visitationsinstruction von 1562," *Zeitschrift für Thüringische Geschichte* 63 (2009): 143–190; cf. Gehrt, *Konfessionspolitik*, 216–246. See also Gleiß, *Die Weimarer Disputation*, 251–262. The edition of Conrad Schlüsselburg, *Haereticorum Catologus* (Frankfurt/M: Saurius, 1597–1599), 5:88–91, is accompanied by the Württemberg censures of Strigel sent to Johann Friedrich the Middler on July 10, 1563, 5:452–459, and Strigel's reply, 5:462–465.

to justify his later position did not satisfy them.[78]

The "Declaration" that Strigel and the Württemberg theologians created was intended to become the new definition of what pastors and teachers were to preach and teach in ducal Saxony. It first affirmed that God alone effects salvation. The first sin so weakened Adam in mind, will, and heart that all his heirs have no power to bring themselves back to God. Second, the "Declaration" stated that human beings possess a *modus agendi*, a capacity or aptitude that makes people capable of receiving God's Word and the Sacraments. Before a sinner can believe, the Holy Spirit must restore to this *modus agendi* freedom of choice, the *liberum arbitrium*, which is the substance of the human mind and will. Andreae and Binder agreed to this statement because they believed Strigel was affirming only the psychological functioning of the human mind and will during the conversion process. However, the clergy of ducal Saxony saw more lurking behind Strigel's words and reacted quickly and strongly to the "Declaration."[79]

Amsdorf was among those who protested the "Declaration of Viktorin." Before he read the "Declaration," it seems he still hoped he might reconcile with his "friends turned antagonists." He wrote to Rosinus in Jena not long before reading the "Declaration" in early 1562, and Amsdorf's comments about Strigel suggest, surprisingly, that he bore Strigel no animosity, even though Strigel had a role in exiling Flacius and Amsdorf's other friends. The bishop told Rosinus that he saw no reason why Strigel should not be allowed to return to teaching, since he had not been excommunicated. If Strigel did teach false doctrine, his errors were not public matters but matters to be debated within the university. Amsdorf was concerned that unnecessary public controversy be stilled.[80]

Two weeks later, Amsdorf sent Rosinus another letter. Now he had read the "Declaration," and his attitude had changed because of what he considered its lack of clarity on the human role in conversion. The first article of the "Declaration," affirming the human creature's complete dependence on God's grace, pleased Amsdorf. But he objected to the section on the *modus agendi*. He interpreted the term theologically rather than psychologically, and so he was convinced that any *modus agendi* meant "the power, means, and way in which a

78 Gehrt, *Konfessionspolitik*, 217–218.

79 The protestors' story is told in *Warhafftiger vnnd Gru[e]ntlicher Summarien Bericht Etlicher Predicanten Wie vnd Worumb sie in LXII. Vnd LXIII. Jahre in Thu[e]ringen seind jres Ampts entsetzt vnd zum theil verjagt worden. Dorinnen auch von M. Sto[e]ssels Schlussreden den 10. Augusti des 1563. Jares zu Jena disputirt etwas gesagt wirdt* (s.l., 1564). From outside ducal Saxony came comments such as those by Tilemann Hesshus, *Analysis declarationis Victorini* (Magdeburg, 1562), and by the preachers of Mansfeld, *Sententia ministrorvm verbi divini in comitatv Mansfeldensi. De formvla declarationis Vict. Strigelij in qvaestione de libero hominis arbitrio* (s.l., 1562); the edited text is found in C&C 5:645–656.

80 Paullini, *Historia*, 187–188.

person can do something himself, alongside God's working, or that he is fitted to work in such a way for himself." Amsdorf agreed that people have psychological capabilities that differentiate them from animals, and thus, humans are different from logs or lumps of clay. But concerning effecting salvation, Amsdorf insisted that the human creature does not act any more than does a log or a lump of clay. For God holds all creatures in his hand and governs them all with his Word. Amsdorf's convictions regarding God's providence and God's election of his righteous people determined Amsdorf's judgment of the "Declaration."[81]

The duke requested that Amsdorf evaluate the "Declaration," and the bishop sent the court a memorandum with his objections. He accused the Württemberg theologians of simply trying to pacify Strigel. He also repeated his conviction, expressed in his *Public Confession*, that Andreae had shown Sacramentarian tendencies.[82] Amsdorf linked his own position on the free will to Luther and Strigel's to Melanchthon.

Amsdorf also wrote other memoranda and correspondences to court officials and friends, informing them of his opinion of the "Declaration."[83] It is worth noting that Amsdorf did not refer to the Leipzig "Interim" in his critiques of Strigel's position. Perhaps this was because Amsdorf knew clearly that Strigel had strongly represented the ducal Saxon position against Moritz's government in the 1550s. It was difficult to accuse Strigel of participating in the Leipzig "Interim" when there was clear evidence that he had consistently opposed the "Interim." However, Amsdorf's later criticism would eventually categorize Strigel as an adiaphorist.

The "Declaration" had been written to settle the disputes within ducal Saxony, but it could not fulfill that purpose if the clergy of the dukedom did not support it. At Duke Christoph's suggestion, Johann Friedrich launched a visitation of

81 Paullini, *Historia*, 191–192, in a letter dated May 29, 1562, accompanied by a note dated June 3, 1562.

82 Andreae himself had recognized his need to affirm his commitment to Luther's understanding of justification and the Lord's Supper and did so in two sermons preached at the Diet of Augsburg in 1559; see pages 132–133 (note 13) above.

83 The memorandum for Johann Friedrich is printed in Beck, *Johann Friedrich*, 2:261–263. Amsdorf also recorded his criticisms in a series of memoranda, including "Antwort auff die vier spru[e]ch da mit die theologie den modum agenda hominis beweisen vnd beweren willen," Wr, ETLFB 39:219–227, copy in Eisenach, Jäger, *Amsdorf*, 253–265; "Das Victorini declaratio ein lauter traum vnd ein menschn gedicht ist der nimant mit gutem gewissen sich vnter schreiben kan," Wr, ETLFB 39:199a–297b: "Nicolai Ambsdorfij Judicium von des ketzers Strigelij Declaration," Wf, Guelf. 12.8 Aug. Fol., 160; and "Sententia Nicolai Ambsdorfij, de declaratione Victorini, Anno 62. 24. Iunij," Schlüsselburg, *Catalogus*, 5:546–550. The letters Amsdorf wrote against Strigel include one to ducal counselor Peter Bremen, dated August 7, 1562, printed in Flacius's *Erzelung, Wie der Hochwichtig vnnd langwirige Religionstreit worden sey* (Regensburg: Heinrich Geisler, 1563), G2b–G3a (the edited text is found in C&C 5:671–714), and three to Nikolaus Gallus from 1562 and 1563, Munich, Staats- und Universitätsbibliothek, Cod. Germanicus 1318:159, 222–223, 231–232, all copies.

his churches in July 1562 to procure subscriptions to the "Declaration." Maxmilian Mörlin and Stössel joined Chancellor von Brück and three other secular counselors on the visitation team.[84] They met first with pastors from the Jena area on July 10. Seventy of the eighty-eight clergy gathered there rejected the "Declaration"; so Stössel wrote a "Superdeclaration," in which he tried to meet the demands of the pastors.[85] This document stated that the ruined human will has no power to cooperate in conversion; conversion is effected by God's grace alone. The "Superdeclaration" defined the *modus agendi* as the physical ability to hear God's Word (called "the external hearing") and a passive potential or aptitude for hearing. At that time, Stössel also devised a formula for subscription to the "Declaration" and the "Superdeclaration" in which the subscriber repudiated synergism and ascribed full responsibility to God alone for the salvation of sinners. This formula also defined the *modus agendi* as "the external means of the ministry of the Word," that is, the use of human language expressing the Gospel as the Holy Spirit's instrument for creating and sustaining faith.[86] With these clarifications and specifications, many subscribed; some did not. Among the latter group was Alexius Bresnicer, superintendent of Altenburg. He objected more to princely encroachment on ecclesiastical affairs than to the text of the "Superdeclaration." The ducal government somewhat arbitrarily offered various deals to the pastors who held out. Eventually the duke stipulated that those who refused to comply in one form or another would be deprived of their office.

A similar confrontation between the clergy and the visitation team was repeated in Weimar, Gotha, and another meeting between the visitors and the Jena clergy. In Eisenach, Amsdorf was permitted to compose his own subscription:

> Since the declaration of the visitors [the "Superdeclaration"] publicly attests that the human creature is completely passive in his conversion and that the *modus agendi* is not a human *modus agendi* but God's, who deals with people through the ministry of the Word as an instrument, then I consent and subscribe to the declaration of the visitors, and to nothing else.[87]

---

84 The visitation is discussed by Beck, *Johann Friedrich*, 1:384–390; Salig, *Historie*, 3:891–900; and Rudolf Herrmann, "Die Generalvisitationen in den Ernestinischen Landen zur Zeit der Lehrstreitigkeiten des 16. Jahrhunderts (1554/55, 1562, 1569–70, 1573), "*Zeitschrift des Vereins für thüringische Geschichte und Altertumskunde* 22 (30) (1915): 111–119.

85 The text of Stössel's "*Superdeclaratio*" is found in Paullini, *Historia*, 192–194, and in Gehrt, "Strategien."

86 This text is found in the *Summarien Bericht*, K3b.

87 Paullini, *Historia*, 188; Gehrt, *Konfessionspolitik*, 222–236. Amsdorf wrote a set of theses in reply to Stössel; cf. *Summarien Bericht*, M1a–M4a. They are perhaps his best critique of Strigel's position.

Amsdorf subscribed because he was too old to fight and too infirm to flee. However, he still continued to criticize the "Declaration," the "Superdeclaration," and the work of the duke's visitation team. His criticism was tolerated because he was the bishop.

His criticisms of the visitation team's work were largely ignored at court. In a memorandum, he severely criticized the visitors' mission and method. He compared them to the Arians who had persecuted pious bishops with their overlord's cooperation. Civil criminals were not punished as severely as the pastors exiled by the visitors had been, Amsdorf complained; he also claimed that the exiled pastors were being unjustly slandered and maltreated. His ecclesiology defining Christ's true Church as the persecuted remnant appeared also in this memorandum: the true prophets of the Lord had been treated in this manner throughout history. Because true prophets were persecuted, the Gospel had left the Orient for Rome and had later left Rome for Germany. Amsdorf prophesied that it would also leave Germany before long. He also accused the visitation of forcing pastors into hypocrisy and being simply an attempt to humor the duke and serve his whim.[88]

During the winter of 1562–1563, more than thirty pastors who rejected any form of subscription to the "Declaration" or "Superdeclaration" were sent into exile. Strigel also secretly left Jena in early October 1562 to accept a position at the University of Leipzig. Four years later, the dean of the theological faculty, Johann Pfeffinger, suspended Strigel's right to continue teaching in Leipzig because Strigel held that Christ is spiritually present in the Lord's Supper and avoided affirming the sacramental presence of Christ's body and blood with the elements. So Strigel moved to Heidelberg and taught ethics there until his death in 1569.[89]

However, Strigel's "Declaration" retained its confessional status in ducal Saxony even after Strigel left, and Amsdorf continued to object to it.[90] At this

88 Amsdorf wrote to Johann Friedrich the Middler in a letter, dated January 1, 1563, printed in *Die Männer der Reformation* (Hildburghausen: Bibliographische Institut, 1859), 33, and he voiced similar protests in a letter to Rosinus, dated November 30, 1562, copy in Wr, ETLFB 42:70a–71b, printed in part in Paullini, *Historia*, 192. He also prepared the following memoranda critical of the visitors: "Vrsachen worvmb sich nimant Victorini declaration mit gutem gewissen vnter schreiben kan noch sal," Wr, ETLFB 39:142a–149a, and in an Eisenach copy, Jäger, *Amsdorf*, 268–277; "Wider die weimarschen Visitatoren," Wr, ETLFB 39:160a–165b," apparently interrupted and continued, Wr, ETLFB 39:176a–181b, dated April 23, 1563; "Das der Visitatores erclerung nimant mit gutem gewissen annemen kan, Niclas von Amsdorff," Wr, ETLFB 39:166a–175a.

89 On Strigel, see page 146 (note 49) above.

90 E.g., in his *Wider die Synergia Victorini. Nemlich Das der Mensch in seiner Bekerung/ kein Synergiam noch modum agendi/ habe noch haben kann/ das ist/ allerding nichts mit wircke in seiner Bekerung/ Sondern sey Gottes gnedige wirckung allein* (Eisleben: Gaubisch, 1564), the edited text is found in C&C 5:775–787; and memoranda including "Vom freien Willen vnnd von den Worten des Herrn im abentmal," Wr, ETLFB 41:229a–249a;

point, Amsdorf began to charge Strigel with being an adiaphorist. Though Strigel had opposed the Leipzig "Interim," Amsdorf saw an affinity between Strigel's betrayal of Luther's theology in his views on the freedom of the will and the betrayal of those who supported the Leipzig "Interim."[91] Most of Amsdorf's written objections remained unpublished, since Johann Friedrich the Middler had imposed strict censorship on theological writings by members of the clergy in 1562. Amsdorf did publish one critique of Strigel in this period, but it was printed by Urban Gaubisch in Eisleben, in Mansfeld county, in 1564.[92]

At this advanced stage in Amsdorf's life, his relationship with Johann Friedrich the Middler had changed significantly. The duke no longer had a use for Amsdorf as a spokesman for the position and policies of his dukedom. Daniel Gehrt notes that this change was not due so much to a change in the duke's own theological convictions but instead arose from the necessity for the duke to bring peace to his church and lands and deflect pressures from other governments.[93]

In contrast, Amsdorf's stance, like his convictions, continued to be as strong as ever. Amsdorf's objections to Strigel's formulations rested on his presupposition that after the fall, sinners have retained the functions of the intellect and will, but these functions are depraved, corrupt, and captive to Satan. Original sin had so corrupted and ruined the will that the sinner cannot assist in his conversion in any way.[94] Any credit given to the human will before or apart from God's grace denies the sovereignty of God, to whom alone belongs all glory. Amsdorf was certain that Strigel's concept of the *modus agendi* threatened this basic thesis of Amsdorf's soteriology. Though Amsdorf's analysis of Strigel's position betrays that Amsdorf misunderstood Strigel's intention, it does reveal the bishop's own concerns. He disagreed with Strigel's differentiation between God's way of dealing with human creatures on the one hand and with blocks of wood or stone on the other. Amsdorf asserted that God has but one mode of acting toward all creatures: he governs them all with his will and Word. God controls the affairs of all people, and his providential control extends to conversion. He converts those whom he has chosen as vessels of mercy from the mass of humanity.[95]

AS, 128–144; "Contra Synergistas," Wr, ETLFB 39:113a–124b (apparently a rough draft of the foregoing); and the memoranda listed on page 161 (note 88).

91 Gehrt, *Konfessionspolitik*, 244–245.

92 *Wider die Syngergia Victorini*; cf. Gehrt, *Konfessionspolitik*, 232–233, 252.

93 Gehrt, *Konfessionspolitik*, 556.

94 *Wider die Synergia*, A4a; "Vom freien Willen," "Wr, ETLFB 41:233b, 240b; "Ursachen," Wr, ETLFB 39:142b–143a; "Contra Synergistas," Wr, ETLFB 39:117a–118b, 120a.

95 *Wider die Synergia*, A4a; "Vom freien Willen," Wr, ETLFB 41:233b, 240b; "Ursachen," Wr, ETLFB 39:143b; "Das der Mensch," Wr, ETLFB 39:193a, 194b, 197b.

Amsdorf rejected the accusation that he and his comrades were ignoring the human mental processes in conversion. Amsdorf conceded that people make decisions with a free will in relation to other creatures and can do as they wish within certain bounds set by the corruption of original sin. In relationship to God, however, the sinner is like a lump of clay or a pillar of salt—spiritually blind and dead.[96] Instead of a *modus agendi*, an aptitude or capacity used by the person being converted, Amsdorf believed that a person only has a *modus patiendi*, a capacity to receive but not to act. The Holy Spirit's action through Word and Sacrament is received through this *modus patiendi*, but the sinner remains completely passive—like a child in the womb at birth—and contributes nothing to his own rebirth. God justifies the impious whom he has chosen while they are still hostile to him, hating Christ and the Word, and resisting and repudiating the Gospel. The elect are not forced or violently pressed into faith through conversion; rather, they are reborn, re-created. Even after their rebirth, believers have no true *modus agendi* of their own, for their psychological functions only reflect the action of Christ in and through them (Galatians 2:20). Those whom God has not chosen cannot come to faith, Amsdorf asserted. Yet their condemnation is not God's arbitrary action, for they desire to go their own sinful way.[97]

The "Superdeclaration" had defined the *modus agendi* of conversion as roughly equivalent to the ministry of the proclamation of the Word. Amsdorf agreed that preaching and hearing the Word are necessary steps in the process by which God converts sinners. But it is only correct to call the ministry of proclamation and its use God's *modus agendi*, not the *modus agendi* of human beings. The ministry of proclamation is the external means by which God converts humans. Thus, human actions in conversion are the result, not the cause, of justification.[98] He rejected his foes' charges that he was denigrating the preaching of the Word, and that he was teaching that God has two contradictory wills, and that he was teaching that God is the author of sin. Amsdorf believed those charges arose from the malice and error of the adiaphorists, just as they believed his charges against them originated from bad faith.

As was typical in Amsdorf's critiques, again in his critiques of Strigel and the freedom of the will, Amsdorf associated himself with Luther and Scripture and

96 "Das der Mensch," Wr, ETLFB 39:193a–b; "Vom freien Willen," Wr, ETLFB 41:23a–231b, 236b–238b; *Wider die Synergia*, A3a–b, B3b.

97 *Wider die Synergia*, A4b, B2a; *Summarien Bericht*, M1a–M3b; "Das der Mensch," Wr, ETLFB 39:196a; "Ursachen," Wr, ETLFB 39:145a; cf. Amsdorf's letter to Monner of June 17, 1561, Wf, Guelf. 64.42 Extr. 2°:121a, and a letter to his nephew, Wr, ETLFB 41:175b.

98 *Summarien Bericht*, M1a; *Wider die Synergia*, B2a; "Wider Visitatoren," Wr, ETLFB 39:177a; "Das der Mensch," Wr, ETLFB 39:194a; "Antwort auff vier spru[e]ch," Wr, ETLFB 39:225b.

associated his opponents with one another. Amsdorf reverted to a refrain he had used from time to time throughout his career: as had happened throughout the history of the Church, dainty lady Reason and her beautiful sister Philosophy had enchanted the adiaphorists and directed them to do battle against those faithful to Scripture. Reason rejects the Word's foolishness (1 Corinthians 1:23); therefore, it rejects the biblical view of the relationship between God and his human creatures as that of a potter and his clay. The adiaphorists were deserting Luther's doctrine as expressed in his *On Bound Choice*, Amsdorf charged. Amsdorf specifically mentioned Luther's assertion that from God's standpoint, all things happen necessarily, and Luther's comment that "God creates good and evil." Amsdorf observed that the latter is a biblical quotation (Isaiah 45:7). Those who disagreed with Luther on this matter were ranged with all the forces of popes and sophists, according to Amsdorf. Amsdorf regarded the controversy over the *modus agendi* as an extension of Major's "pelagianism." He judged the adiaphorists with the same standards as he had judged his papal enemies in Magdeburg, and he saw in both groups' teachings a place for a human role in salvation. That is why he condemned Strigel and his associates.[99] Amsdorf failed to notice and consider Luther's own cautions about using his *On Bound Choice*[100]—a caution which Strigel may have heard as a student and taken to heart. Amsdorf also failed to notice that his own rejection of universal atonement was the result of allowing reason to master the biblical text as well.

It was possible to interpret Strigel's "Declaration" in a way that was much closer to Amsdorf's theology than Amsdorf recognized. However, numerous personal factors beyond his theological convictions shaped Amsdorf's response to Strigel's view. The bishop was undoubtedly stung by the fact that Strigel, whom he had long regarded as a true friend in the fight against the adiaphorists, proved himself to be a loyal disciple of Melanchthon, especially in relation to Melanchthon's view of contingency, which Amsdorf had criticized a quarter century earlier. Amsdorf ultimately named Melanchthon as the author of Strigel's error, though his motivation for this attribution is not entirely clear; he charged that Melanchthon's philosophy would destroy Luther's Scriptural teaching if it could. It seems Amsdorf's sense of having been betrayed by those he considered friends ran deep. Amsdorf also reacted against the haughtiness and condescension he felt those on the other side who were considered academic

99 "Vom freien Willen," Wr, ETLFB 41:235a–b, 238a–239a; "Das Visitatores Declaration," Wr, ETLFB 39:177a; "Das der Mensch," Wr, ETLFB 39:189b, 197b–198b; *Wider die Synergia*, A2b–A3a.

100 Kolb, *Bound Choice*, 26–28.

theologians were expressing. He blamed all of this division and dispute in ducal Saxony on Strigel.[101]

Although Amsdorf used many of the same principles and Scripture passages in responding to Strigel that he had used in responding to Pfeffinger, he treated his disputes with each of them differently. His use of the metaphor of the potter and clay no longer elicited a doctrine of double predestination, as he had previously taught. The dispute between Amsdorf and Pfeffinger had remained a theoretical discussion between rival theologians who were already suspicious of one another because of the adiaphoristic controversy. However, the dispute between Amsdorf and Strigel cut much deeper. They had been friends. And the complications of the jealousy and competition between Strigel and Flacius, the entanglements with the prince extending his control over the church, and the consequences of Strigel's views being imposed as the ducal Saxon public doctrine made the disagreement between Strigel and Amsdorf much more bitter.

Both Pfeffinger and Strigel provoked Amsdorf with concerns and conceptualizations they had learned from Melanchthon. The poisoned atmosphere that had developed in Saxony through a decade of dispute, with feelings of betrayal and accusations of bad faith and heresy on both sides, tainted and twisted the exchanges between colleagues who had once been friends. The tensions inherent in Luther's and Melanchthon's insistence on simultaneous full divine and full human responsibility could not easily be parsed. These tensions remain when the theological expressions of Luther and Melanchthon are put into practice through the proper distinction of Law and Gospel. But that proper distinction does not allow for easy solutions, and it demands attention to specific human situations and attitudes.

When studying the debates and controversies in the years following Luther's death, it is evident that no group in any of these disputes clearly sorted out their presuppositions and governing concerns. Opponents frequently expressed more clearly the dangers that threatened the integrity of the proclamation of the Gospel of Christ in the other group's teaching than they explained the source of their own concerns. And despite the earnest nature of their attempt to preserve the Gospel, the political and personal factors from which none of us can escape significantly shaped their public positions. Through it all, they were struggling to establish the defining pillars of the Wittenberg proclamation of the Gospel.

101 *Wider die Synergia*, B4a; "Das Victorini Declaration," Wr, ETLFB 39:217b.

Conclusion

CONSTANT IN CONFESSION

Amsdorf had but a year to live when he published his final critique of Strigel's position. He remained to the end God's knight and warrior, a champion of Luther's Reformation, as he had always striven to be. In the final three years of his life, he had continued to use his pen to attack "papists," "ravers," adiaphorists, and even fellow Gnesio-Lutherans.

In 1563, he intervened in a quarrel that ranged his old friends in Magdeburg—both in the ministerium and on the city council—against the city's new Gnesio-Lutheran clerical leadership, especially Johannes Wigand and Tilemann Hesshus. The issues at stake concerned the governance of church discipline, resembling the issues raised by the institution of the Saxon consistory in 1561. But Amsdorf could not approve of the conduct of some of Wigand's and Hesshus's party toward the laypeople and some of the longtime clergy members in the town, some of whom had been serving even when Amsdorf was superintendent.

The situation arose when Tilemann Hesshus, who had become superintendent of the Magdeburg church after Wigand left for Jena, wanted to install his own people in pastoral positions. There were also new political developments in the region. The political authorities of the towns and principalities of Lower Saxony meeting in Lüneburg had issued a mandate in August 1561 that demanded the preaching of pure doctrine but forbade harsh critique of theological opponents in preaching and print. As formal overlord of Magdeburg, the Evangelical archbishop of Magdeburg, Sigismund of Hohenzollern, imposed these restrictions on the city. Magdeburg's city council was seeking to end its banishment by the imperial government, and this policy served that purpose. However, Hesshus joined Flacius, Gallus, Joachim Mörlin, and others in condemning the Lüneburg Mandate; and Hesshus also attempted to strengthen his position as superintendent by placing Wigand and Judex in pastorates in Magdeburg. He encountered opposition from both clergy and civic leadership for these actions.[1]

1 These events are carefully traced in Hartmut Kühne, "Nikolaus von Amsdorf im Streit zwischen dem Magdeburger Rat und lutherischen Theologen um die Amtsenthebung des Tilemann Heshusius," in Dingel, *Amsdorf*, 281–299.

Amsdorf's initial private attitude toward these events favored his Gnesio-Lutheran compatriots in Hesshus's camp. Amsdorf reported to Bartholomaeus Rosinus that the developments in Magdeburg made him "sad unto death."[2] Within a month, however, his former colleague Sebastian Werner, who had joined him as a teacher in Magdeburg's secondary school in 1524 and who had become the senior clergyman in Magdeburg by 1562, presented Amsdorf with a contrary view of Hesshus's behavior and that of his comrades.[3] Amsdorf was also in contact with Nikolaus Gallus, whose brother-in-law, Heinrich Merckel, had served as administrative secretary for the Magdeburg council for many years. The information from these sources convinced Amsdorf that the Hesshus group were "ravers" (*Schwärmer*), who had behaved inappropriately and conducted their duties in unseemly fashion, so that "the council should have tolerated and endured them in no way," as Amsdorf commented to Rosinus in a letter on April 29, 1563.[4] The council, under fierce attack from Hesshus and his colleagues, ordered that Amsdorf's letter and a similar letter of support from Gallus be read from the pulpit of every church in the city. Whether it was his intention or not, Amsdorf's participation in yet another bitter battle among former friends again moved from the private to the public sphere. Amsdorf continued to correspond with members of the remaining clergy and city council, and he published his position in *Admonition to the Council and the Citizenry of Magdeburg*, printed in late summer 1563.[5] In August, Rosinus sought to restrain his elderly friend from public involvement;[6] but Amsdorf's former devotees, Hesshus, Wigand, and Judex, quickly responded, defending themselves against Amsdorf's criticism. An attack from the elderly bishop could not be taken lightly. Matthaeus Judex called Amsdorf "the devil's mask" for opposing the practices of church discipline that he and Tilemann Hesshus had employed.[7] Hesshus accused Amsdorf of false teaching and propagating "the ideas of the flesh."[8] Johannes Wigand, who

2 The letter to Rosinus, dated November 30, 1562, is found in Wr, ETLFB 42:71a, but it must be the letter cited by Judex, as recorded by Kühne, "Amsdorf," 299.

3 Correspondence between Amsdorf and allies of Hesshus, Judex, and Wigand is found in Wr, ETLFB 42:37a–58b, 75a–79a, and in Wf, Guelf. Helmst. 74:305–316.

4 Edited in Kühne, "Amsdorf," 304–306.

5 Amsdorf first publicly criticized Hesshus and Wigand in his *Eine Vermanung An der Rath vnd die Gemein Bu[e]rgerschafft zu Magdeburgk* (Magdeburg, 1563), edited in C&C 4:185–198. On the controversy, see Kühne, "Amsdorf," 299–304, and, in less detail, Martin Kruse, *Speners Kritik an dem landesherrlichen Kirchenregiment und ihre Vorgeschichte* (Witten: Luther Verlag, 1971), 63–70.

6 Kühne, "Amsdorf," 301.

7 Judex, *Einfeltiger vnterricht fu[e]r die Christen in Magdeburgk was von des herrn Amssdorffij vormeintem Vrteil nach Gottes Wort vnd dem heiligen Catechismo zu halten sey* (s.l., 1563).

8 *Gründliche widerlegung des falschen vnnd selbst angemasten vermeinten vrtheils Herrn Niclassen von Ambsdorff in der Magdeburgischen sache* (s.l., 1564); Amsdorf replied in his *Wie Christlich vnd treulich Hesshusius in seinem Buch wieder mich mit der heiligen Schrifft vnnd mir handelt* (Magdeburg, 1564), and *Das Johannes Wigandus vnbillich*

had moved to Wismar when Magdeburg authorities sent him into another exile, expressed his pain that Amsdorf had attacked those whom he had formerly highly regarded "because of his wonderful confession against papists, Interimists, adiaphorists, synergists, and similar people."[9]

This encounter ended with a brief treatise from Wigand trying to resurrect the topic of good works and the Law as it had been discussed at the Eisenach synod. Wigand insisted that the deeds of the Law could indeed win salvation if the Law was kept perfectly. Amsdorf could have cited Luther against this position, but by early 1564, he was no longer prepared to enter the ring in defense of his mentor. A few years earlier, the chief issue in ducal Saxony had been the integrity of the church in relationship to the secular government. At that time, Amsdorf had protested mightily against the prince's interference in ecclesiastical affairs in ducal Saxony; but Amsdorf's old friendships in Magdeburg in this case overcame his allegiance to the younger, like-minded theologians. His sharply worded critiques of Wigand's and Hesshus's procedures in dealing with the city council condemned these two former allies for acting contrary to the Scriptures. They responded with a sharp rejection of his position. However, Amsdorf's name and his argument do not appear in the flurry of treatises exchanged between municipal officials and the exiles, whose case was carried on by Hesshus. The city council did not cite him in its defense,[10] and Hesshus did not mention his criticism either.[11]

As surprising as Amsdorf's conduct in this controversy may seem at first, his comments on how his attitude toward the two sides in Magdeburg was reversed shed light on how he viewed his own earlier conduct of a polemic in this case. In his *Admonition*, he found that Hesshus had acted "without the Spirit or faith," speaking only "external utterances with his mouth" but with "rage, fury, and a mighty impatience," without love and gentleness, to attain what he wanted.[12] Amsdorf later commented, "It is not enough to proclaim the Gospel and battle against corruptions of it, but a person has to preach the Gospel with humility and deal with sinners gently, not with such raging and gashing."[13] Longtime

---

meine vermanung an die von Magdenburgk straffet vnd mich schildt, lestern, vnd Liegen heist (Magdeburg, 1564), edited in C&C 4:219–226. Wigand responded to Amsdorf with *Vom Ampt Des Gesetzes kurtzer vnd Freundtlicher Bericht auff Amßdorffs Sturmschrift* (Frankfurt/M: Peter Braubach, 1564), edited in C&C 4:233–245.

9 Wigand, *Ein Brief Doctoris Johannis Wigandi an Herrn Nicolaum Amssdorff* (1564), edited in C&C 4:207–213.

10 E.g., in *Apologia. Entschu[e]ldigung vnd warhafftige vorantwortunge etzlicher Pfarherrn vnd Prediger der Christlichen Kirchen in der Alten Stadt Magdeburgk wieder die Vnchristliche vnd vngegru[e]ndete schmahe vnd Ehren ruhige schrifft/ so vnter dem Namen D. Thilemanni Hesshusij Vesaliensis wieder Magdebuurgk ausgangen* (s.l., s.d.).

11 E.g., in *Antwort Doct. Tilemanni Heßhusij auff der Lu[e]genprediger von Magdeburg vermeinte vnnd vngegru[e]ndte Apologia* (s.l., 1564).

12 *Vermanung An der Rath*, A4b.

13 *Wie Christlich vnd treulich*, F3a–b.

friendships had been shaken by false teaching, but theological affinities also required decent behavior in the bishop's opinion.

In these final years of his life, Amsdorf also composed a critique of Melanchthon's doctrine of the Lord's Supper that he did not publish. It linked his old friend's view of the presence of Christ's body and blood in the sacramental elements with the views of Zwingli and Calvin.[14] Amsdorf publicly renewed his attack on papal practices and wrote a consolation for Evangelicals in Bavaria who were suffering the impact of Counter-Reformation repression.[15] He continued to warn the Germans of the judgment he was certain was impending for their apostate nation because it had not heeded Luther's call to the Gospel.[16] Constancy in confession and standing firm against those who threatened his faith remained Amsdorf's way of life. Yet his perpetual concern for the faith and piety of the common people also led him to call for families to return to the practice of cultivating the faith of children and servants through the weekly study of the pericopes and review of the sermon, within the framework of the distinction of Law and Gospel.[17]

Increasingly infirm, the old bishop had long yearned for death.[18] He prepared his own epitaph, in which he looked forward to "seeing God the Lord with my own eyes and being his comrade forever."[19] The coffin beside his bed, which had served as a reminder of his mortality and a prayer bench as well, received his body on May 14, 1565, the Monday after Jubilate, "Rejoice" Sunday. God's knight, Christ's exile, the champion of Luther's Reformation, Nikolaus von Amsdorf had

---

14 "Vom freien Willen vnd von den Worten des Herrn im abentmal," Wr, ETLFB 39:230a–249b; AS, 128–144.

15 *Zwo Trost vnnd vermanung Schrifft ahn die verjagten Christen auss dem Bayerlandt, Item ein Rathschlag Joannis Brentij* (1564). Amsdorf's "Ein Trost und vermanung an die verjagten Christen auss dem Bayerlandt" is found in A2a–C1b. The second item in this tract was composed by Johannes Brenz. The suggestion that Amsdorf did not compose the first (see Karl Schottenloher, *Das Regensburger Buchgewerbe im 15. und 16. Jahrundert* [Mainz: Gutenberg Gesellschaft, 1920], 49) is not true since a manuscript of the first item, "Ein Trost vnd vermanung an die veriagten Christen aus Straubingen," is found in Wr, ETLFB 41:269a–278a. On the papacy and papal practices, Amsdorf published at this time *Eine Vermanung vnd Gebet wider den Bapst vnd seinen Anhang* (Jena, 1562) and *Horas Canonicas, Klo[e]stern, vnd Stifften singen Vnd gebotene Adiaphora halten ist eben so wol Abgo[e]tterey Als die schentlichste Opffermesse* (Jena, 1562), which also took aim at the adiaphorists.

16 *Eine Predigt aus dem Comment des heiligen vnd trewen Dieners Christi Lutheri vber das fu[e]nfft Capitel Hosee gezogen von rechtschaffener vnd falscher Busse* (Jena, 1562) and *Eine Predigt aus den Schrifften lutheri vber die Propheten gezogen, Das Deudscheland wie Israel Judea vnd Jerusalem wird zusto[e]rt vnd verwu[e]stet werden vmb gleicher Su[e] nde willen* (Jena, 1562).

17 "Das got gebotten hat das die eldern ihren kindern vnd hausgesinde die predigt (so sie in der kirchn gehort) daheim im hause widerholen vnd ercleren sollen," Wr, ETLFB 41:219a–228a. Cf. Robert Kolb, "Parents Should Explain the Sermon, Nikolaus von Amsdorf on the Role of the Christian Parent," *The Lutheran Quarterly* o. s. 25 (1973): 231–240, and the more complete discussion by Hans-Peter Hasse, "Der Hausvater als Katechet. Beobachtungen zu einem Druckmanuskript Nikolaus von Amsdorfs aus dem Jahr 1562 in seinem handschriftlichen Nachlass," in Dingel, *Amsdorf*, 91–102.

18 As he stated in his *Ein gut newe Jar den grossen herrn in dieser Welt geschanckt* (Jena, 1554), A4a.

19 Philipp Wackernagel, *Das deutsche Kirchenlied von der aeltesten Zeit bis zu Anfang des XVII. Jahrhunderts* 3 (Leipzig: Teubner, 1870), 1262, gives the text of the epitaph and credits Amsdorf with its composition.

fought a good fight. The epitaph on the stone memorial of his burial site, in the chancel of the church of Saint George in Eisenach, expressed his faith in words echoing Job 19:25–27: "I know that my redeemer lives."[20]

Amsdorf's theology was shaped by his reaction against the human-centered soteriology he had learned from his scholastic instructors who had led him along the *via antiqua* of Duns Scotus and others. Though his writings betray little evidence that scholastic concepts lingered in his thoughts, the skill at disputation that he learned through his scholastic training was a tool Amsdorf used throughout his life to defend Luther's message.

Luther's understanding of God's mercy in Christ, more than any other factor, formed and shaped Amsdorf's thinking. However, the bishop only reflected Luther as the moon reflects the sun. Amsdorf's printed works did not reproduce his mentor's liveliness of proclamation. Moreover, certain elements of Luther's thought became fuzzy or were lost when they passed through Amsdorf's prism. For example, no passage in any of Amsdorf's treatises contradicts Luther's understanding of the proper distinction of Law and Gospel. However, Amsdorf never treated this distinction explicitly, nor did he ever develop it as a tool for discussing issues that for Luther were deeply involved in the Law-Gospel dynamic. Amsdorf's penchant for reducing Luther's message to neat, easily communicable categories sometimes drained the reformer's ideas of their original dynamism. Amsdorf's goal was slightly different as he tried to use these easily communicable points to defend the foundations of his friend's thought. The most significant example of this is Amsdorf's view of election. Amsdorf's printed works do not manifest the sense of familiarity with the God-man, Jesus Christ, that makes Luther's writings so alive and responsive to the situations of daily life. Though it must be allowed that Amsdorf's sermons could have exhibited quite a different side of his understanding of salvation in Christ and though he always tried to respond to the pastoral needs of his parishioners, the simplistic approach of his public polemic shows such a different approach than Luther's pastoral sensitivity to bruised souls. Amsdorf's published writings and the corpus that remains of his unpublished manuscripts simply do not address those in need of consolation in the same mode that Luther did.

Nonetheless, the common people were always Amsdorf's prime concern, and his perception that they were vulnerable to the wiles of Satan shaped his

20 Christian F. Paullini, *Historia Isenacensis* (Frankfurt/M: Bauer, 1698), 199. Paullini further reports that the new professors of theology at the University of Jena—Johann Stössel and Nikolaus Selnecker—requested a copy of the sermon preached at Amsdorf's burial by the pastor in Eisenach, Johannes Aldendorf (Paullini, *Historia*, 200.) Aldendorf had served in Eisenach since 1563. He was studying in Wittenberg at the time of Luther's death. In 1573, he was dismissed from his office in Eisenach for being a "*Flacianer*."

printed testimony and his contributions to the theological debates after Luther's death. Amsdorf considered that his parishioners needed elementary answers for their religious questions. Especially as they first learned what Luther's faith was supposed to mean to them, they required simple, neatly structured formulas, easy to understand and digest, so that they could integrate this new faith into their daily thinking. In the streets of Magdeburg in 1525, the restructuring of popular religious life demanded clear, clean cuts that simplified the rich complexities and subtleties of Luther's proclamation of the Gospel. On the siege walls of Magdeburg in 1550, when the bishop again felt his faith confronted with the possibility of extermination, he believed that rigid adherence to incisive, simple formulas would ensure that Luther's message and movement continued. Amsdorf believed that such formulas would keep Luther's followers—peasants, townspeople, or theologians—faithful and constant in their confession.

In his efforts over some four decades to call Luther's followers to faithfulness, Amsdorf first foreshadowed and then helped develop the attitudes and stance of the Gnesio-Lutheran movement, a group of younger Wittenberg graduates concerned about faithfulness to Luther's message in the second half of the sixteenth century. The movement arose within Saxon Lutheranism after Amsdorf had been retired from his official position as bishop of Naumburg-Zeitz. The group developed in response to the events following the defeat of the Smalcald League's forces in 1547 at Mühlberg. The group's leaders responded to what they perceived as threats to Luther's legacy from both ecclesiastical and secular leaders—above all, from leaders who claimed to be adherents of the Wittenberg reform movement. The retired bishop assisted these young "Gnesio-Lutherans" for the rest of his life in their battles against such threats.

In at least four important ways, the bishop's attitudes prefigured and anticipated those of the younger group of Wittenberg students in the Gnesio-Lutheran party a quarter century before the Smalcald War. First, Amsdorf had defended the exclusive role of grace and faith in Christ in Luther's soteriology many years before the Majoristic and synergistic controversies broke out. When he fired the opening volleys in each of those disputes, Amsdorf was taking aim at what he believed were the same opinions that he had faced earlier, and he used the same ammunition that he had employed in the 1520s and 1530s against both Roman and other opponents. This earlier position, when repeated in the 1550s against Major and Menius, and against Pfeffinger and Strigel, received instant sympathy and support from the Magdeburg circle and colleagues. Most of its members had studied together in Wittenberg in the later 1530s and early 1540s. Second, Amsdorf had long attacked medieval ceremony and papally-dominated modes of ecclesiastical life. At Regensburg, his attack had stood in sharp relief to Melanchthon's concerning Evangelical relationships to Rome. The need for a sharp demarcation from the Roman communion in ceremonial and ecclesiastical-political relationships rallied the followers of Flacius and Gallus during their resistance to the ungodly commands of their overlord the emperor in defense of the Gospel. Third, in Magdeburg Amsdorf joined his Gnesio-Lutheran comrades in articulating a stance against secular sovereigns' interference in the life of the church. That stance included Amsdorf's approval of armed resistance to the emperor. Fourth, Amsdorf had modeled forthright, bold confession of the faith in the public arena throughout his career; he found no occasion for any kind of compromising or reconciling stance in relation to those who taught falsely. In at least these four ways, Amsdorf anticipated the mentality and spirit that the Gnesio-Lutheran movement embodied during the struggle to determine the shape of Luther's Reformation.[21]

From Leipzig in 1519 to Eisenach in 1565, Nikolaus von Amsdorf was convinced that he was caught up in an eschatological battle. The warfare was raging between, on the one hand, the persecuted remnant of those loyal to Christ and his Word and, on the other hand, those who exalted human powers according to their own reason, claiming to be God's people while denying or diminishing his grace. Amsdorf's ecclesiology led him to attack any compromise with the forces he believed were vitiating or rejecting Luther's understanding of the Gospel. His radically theocentric faith caused him to reject not only human-centered soteriological expressions but also anthropological approaches to theology. Amsdorf's radical prophetic stance rallied those who agreed with him—the Gnesio-Lutherans—and helped set the tone for their movement. Thus, Amsdorf helped lay out and plow the field in which others planted and cultivated the Lutheran theology called "Lutheran Orthodoxy" in modern designations. Proceeding from the Formula of Concord, this theology that Amsdorf helped preserve sprouted and grew to dominate the spiritual and intellectual life of north-central Europe for nearly a century and a half—a legacy that lasted long beyond Luther's and Amsdorf's own lifetimes.

---

21 These four points are developed in more detail in Robert Kolb, "Dynamics of Party Conflict in the Saxon Late Reformation, Gnesio-Lutherans vs. Philippists," *The Journal of Modern History* 49 (1977): D1289–1305; reprinted in *Luther's Heirs Define His Legacy, Studies on Lutheran Confessionalization* (Aldershot: Variorum, 1996), and in *Calvinismus in den Auseinandersetzungen des frühen konfessionellen Zeitalters*, eds. Herman J. Selderhuis, Martin Leiner, and Volker Leppin (Göttingen: Vandenhoeck & Ruprecht, 2013), 151–167.

Bibliography

Manuscripts

COBURG, Bayrisches Staatsarchiv.
    1554 X Jena, in LA I 28 b 2 aa, Nr. 8, lvs. 18–19.

GÖTTINGEN, Niedersächsische Staats- und Universitätsbibliothek.
    Codex MS. Jurid 492, lvs. 31b–33a.

DRESDEN, Sächsische Landesbibliothek.
    Msc. Dresden A180, pp. 752–770.

MUNICH, Bayrische Staats- und Universitätsbibliothek.
    Co. Germanicus 1318, lvs. 159, 222–223, 231–232.

WEIMAR, in 1971, the "Nationale Forschungs- und Gedenkstätten der klassischen deutschen Literatur, Goethe-Schiller Archiv" (of the former Thuringian Landesbibliothek, now the Thuringian Hauptstaatsarchiv Weimar), gathered with two other volumes of Amsdorf manuscripts in "Nachlass Nikolaus von Amsdorf."

WOLFENBÜTTEL, Herzog August Bibliothek.
    Codex Guelferbytanus:
        Helmst. = Die Helmstedter Handschriften.
        Aug. = Die Augusteischen Handschriften.
        Extr. = Die Extravagantes Handschriften.

Published Works

With the titles of sixteenth-century published works are given the numbers assigned by the authoritative index to such works entitled *Verzeichnis der in deutschem Sprachbereich erschienenen Drucke des XVI. Jahrhunderts*, edited by the Bayerische Staatsbibliothek in Verbindung mit der Herzog August Bibliothek in Wolfenbüttel (Stuttgart: Hiersemann, 1983–2000), under the abbreviation "VD16."

Amsdorf's Works

The following works are listed in chronological order. Arabic numerals denote works that Amsdorf composed or in which he wrote a preface or another part of the text. Alphabetical letters denote works that Amsdorf subscribed to but did not compose.

1. *Eyne christliche fur betrachtung So man wil bethen das heylige vater unser. Getzogen auss den predigtenn Doctoris Martini Luther zu wittemburg Von dem wirdigen Nicolao vonn Amssdorff Licenciaten in deutsch gebracht*. Leipzig: Wolffgang Stöckel, 1519, and in eight subsequent editions. WA 9:223–225.

2. *Die haubtartickel durch welche gemeyne Christenheyt bysshere verfuret worden ist*. Wittenberg, 1522, and in two subsequent editions. VD16:S8230. Written by Lazarus Spengler, edited by Amsdorf, who also wrote the preface and conclusion.

3. *Grund vnd vrsach auss der Cronicke/ Warumb Johannes Huss vnd Jeronimus von Prag verbrant seyn*. Magdeburg: Heinrich Öttinger, 1525. VD16:A2367.

4. *Vermanung Nicolai von Amssdorff an die von Magdeburg/ wider den rotten vnnd secten gaist D. Ciclops*. s.l., 1525. VD16:A2400–2402.

5. *Auff Ciclops antwort replica*. Wittenberg: Nickel Schirlentz, 1525. VD16:A2326.

6. *Widder die lugen prediger des hohen Thumbs zu Magdeburg*. Wittenberg: Nickel Schirlentz, 1525. VD16:A2408.

7. *Grundt vnd orsake worup Marquardus Schuldorp hefft syner suster dochtor thor ehe genamen*. Leipzig: Valentin Schumann, 1526. VD16:A2368.

8. *Ein vormanung an die von Magdeburg/ das sie sich fur falschen Propheten zu huten wissen*. Augsburg: Simprecht Ruff, 1525; Magdeburg: Hans Bart, 1527. VD16:2401.

9. *Dem Erwerdigen vnd Erbarn herrn Senior vnd dem gantzen Thum capitel zu Magdeburg meinen lieben feinden vnd verfolgern*. Magdeburg: Hans Bart, 1528. VD16:A2350.

10. *Was Melchior Hoffman nicht ein wort auff Büchlein geantwortet hat*. s.l., 1528.

11. *Das Melchior Hoffman ein falscher Prophet/ vnd sein leer vom Ju[e]ngsten tag vnrecht/ falsch vnd widder Gott ist*. s.l., 1528. VD16:A2346.

12. *Den Thumbpredigern zu Magdeburg*. Magdeburg: Heinrich Öttinger, 1528. VD16:A2351.

13. *Das der Pauler monich zu Dessa Johan Mensing ym glauben vnd vber den wercken ist vnsinnig/ tol vnd tho[e]richt worden. . . .* Magdeburg: Heinrich Öttinger, 1528. VD16:A2335.

14. *Vnterricht warumb die thumprediger zu Magdeburg nicht disputirn wollen/ vnd doch von offentlich auff der Cantzel geeischet vnd gefordert haben*. Magdeburg: Hans Bart, 1528. VD16:A2395–2396.

15. *Auff erfordern der thumprediger zu Magdeburg erbeut sich zu disputirn auff den kunfftigen reichstag zu Regenspurg*. s.l., 1528?. VD16:A2328.

16. *Das die werck nicht rechtfertigen/ sondern der glaub allein/ Niclas Amsdorff, Widder die Thumprediger zu Magdeburg*. Magdeburg: Heinrich Öttinger, 1528. AS, 1–28. VD16:A2337.

17. *Propositiones D. Mart. Luth. ab initio negocij Euangelici*. Wittenberg, 1530. Theses by Amsdorf on N3a–N4a. VD16:L5746–5748.

18. *Ein scho[e]ner Sermon/ von dem wort/ zeichen/ vnd Sacrament*. Wittenberg: Georg Rhau, 1531. VD16:A2385–2391.

19. *Vrsach warumb die beide predicanten/ Er Johann Grawert vnd er Heinrich Knyge aus Goslar vertrieben sind*. Magdeburg, 1531. VD16:ZV540.

20. *Das Johan Hussen lied vom Sacrament recht Christlich vnd aus dem Euangelio genomen sey/ an alle fromme Christen zu Braunswig*. Magdeburg: Michael Lotter, 1533.

21. *Cogitationes Nicolae Amsdorfii, De Concilio Nvnqvam Fvtvrosi Per Papam Liceat*. Magdeburg: Michael Lotter, 1533. VD16:A2330.

22. *Has Propositiones Defendet Nicolavs Amsdorfivs Magdebvrgae quando uolerint aduersarij*. Magdeburg: Michael Lotter, 1533. VD16:A2373.

23. *Dispvtatio Magdebvrgensis, per Nicolavm Amsdorfivm*. Magdeburg: Michael Lotther, 1533.

24. *Epistolae Domini Nikolai Amsdorfii Et D. Martini Lvtheri, De Erasmo Roterodamo*. Wittenberg: Johannes Lufft, 1533. VD16:A2356–2357.

25. *Consilivm Et Ratio Epistolae De Erasmo Ad Lvthervm Nicolai. Amsdorfii*. Magdeburg: Michael Lotter, 1533. VD16:A2334.

26. *Ein kurtzer auszog/ aus der Cronica Naucleri/ wie vntreulich vnd verreterlich die Bebste zu Rom mit den Romischen Keysern gehandelt haben.* Magdeburg: Michael Lotter, 1534, and two subsequent editions. VD16:N172.

27. *Sendebrieff einer Erbaren frowen/ von wegen ihres gefangenen Pfarherrn. An den Bischop tho Havelberg.* s.l., 1534. Preface by Amsdorf.

28. *Eyn Gesprech zwischen eym Lutherischen vnd Papisten/ das der Römische hoff des Teuffels braut vnd das rechte Antichristlische reich sey/ vnd nicht die kirche Christi.* Magdeburg: Hans Walther, 1535. VD16:A2366.

29. *Eine kleine vnterricht auff die Co[e]lnische zedel mit yhren dreien schiffen.* Magdeburg, 1535. VD16:A2375.

30. *Warhafftige Historia vnd geschicht/ wie der Bapst ist der o[e]berste gewurden/ jnn der Christenheit. Aus bewerten Cronicken.* Magdeburg: Hans Walther, 1535. VD16:A2407.

31. *Vorkündigung des volkommen Ablas der Ro[e]mischen Bullen/ So Bapst Paulus der dritt itzt im XXXV: jar hath lassen aussgehen.* Magdeburg: Hans Walther, 1535. VD16:A2398.

32. *Contra Zwinglianos & Anabaptistas themata.* s.l., 1535. VD16:ZV531.

33. *Widder die Widder teuffer vnd Sacramentirer/ Etliche spru[e]che oder schlussrede.* Erfurt: Wolff Heinick, and Magdeburg: Hans Walther, 1535. VD16:A2410–2411.

34. *Sepvltvra Lvtheri. Ecce quomodo moritur iustus, &c. nemo est qui considerat.* s.l., 1538.

35. *Propositiones D. Mart. Luth. ab initio negocij Euangelici/ ab autore Tractatae/ usque in hunc diem.* Wittenberg: Johannes Lufft, 1538. VD16:A2354–2355.

    Lf. N1a: D. Nicolai Amsdorfii Disputationes sequuntur aliquot.

    Lf. N5a: D. Nicolavs Amsdorfivs S. Ecclesiae Magdeburgensis Pastor, sequential themata disputauit Feria quinta post Martini MDXXV. Ad hanc disputationem omnes Papistae uenire possunt, modo argumentis, & non clamoribus rem againt.

    N8a: Contra Zvvinglianos, & Anabaptistas themata Nicolai Amsdorfij.

    O6a: Cogitationes Nicolai Amsdorfij. De concilio nunquam future, so per Papam liceat. M.D. XXXIII.

36. *Das Bapst/ bischoff/ vnd Cardinal/ die rechten Ketzer seint aus einer alten Prophetzey durch sie selbst gemacht vnd von jhm jerlich gesungen vnd gelesen.* s.l., ca. 1540. VD16:A2349.

37. *Ein Getichte darin angezeigt wird/ wie from Herztog Heinrich von Braunschweig/ Vnd wie bo[e]se die Lütherischen sein.* Wittenberg: Kreutzen, 1541. VD16:A2363–2365.

38. *Vom Concilio/ darvon den Papisten nu gar nahe XXX jar getrewmet hat/ vnd aber itzt in irem schlaffe trewmen will zu Trident. 1541. Bedencken Nico. V. Amsdorffs, verdeutscht durch Justus Jonas.* Halle: Fischmut, 1542. VD16:A2405.

39. *Bvllla des grossen Ablass welchen der Bapst Paulus der Dritte zu diesem Zuge vnd Ausreuttunge der Lutherischen Ketzereyen gegeben hat. Mit einner Vorrhede des Ehrwirdigen jnn Gott Herrn Niclaus Ammssdorff Bischoff zur Naumburgk etc.* Erfurt: Wolfgang Stürmer, 1546. VD16:K423.

40. *Ein Christlich gebet darin der Churfurst zu Sachssen etc. Seinne vnschuldt: jtziges Kriegs: vor Gott vnd aller Welt offentlich bekent.* Magdeburg: Christian Rödinger, 1546, and four subsequent editions. VD16:ZV8733–8737.

41. *Warhafftige Copey einer Schrifft/ so die Ehrwirdigen Herrn Predicanten zu Leiptzig/ an Herzog Moritzen zu Sachsen gethan etc. Desgleichen eine andere Copeyschrift/ des hochwirdigen Herrn Nicolai Amßdorff/*

von Gott bestetigten Bischoff zur Neumburg/ an den Bischoff zu Merßeburg etc. Anno M.D. xlvij. Magdeburg: Christian Rödinger, 1547. VD16:A2376–2377.

A. *Bedencken auff das Interim*. Magdeburg: Michael Lotter, 1548, with two other editions 1549. VD16:P4740.

Lf. C3a: Amsdorf listed at the head of those who subscribed to this statement.

42. *Antwort/ Glaub vnd Bekentnis auff das schöne vnd liebliche INTERIM*. Magdeburg: Michael Lotter, 1548. AS, 29–51; C&C 1:204–236. VD16:A2325.

43. *Antwort auff der Wittenberger La[e]sterung: Quasi Magdeburgenses praedando velint defendere Evangelium*. Magdeburg, 1549.

44. *Antwort auff Doct: Pommers scheltwort/ so er auff der Cantzel aussgeschu[e]tt hat/ am Sontag nach Vdalrici M.D.XLIX*. Magdeburg: Christian Rödinger, 1549, one other printing. VD16:A2323–2324.

45. *Auff die ku[e]nstliche Spo[e]ttische vnd Bitterhonische ORATION So D. Ziegler zu Leiptzig am Oster Montag widder die bestendigen Lutherischen recitirt hat . . . Beurische vnd einfeltige antwort. . . .* Magdeburg: Michael Lotter, 1549. VD16:A2327.

46. *Das die zu Wittenberg im andern teil der bucher Doctoris Martini im buch das diese wort Christ (Das ist men Leib etc.) noch fest stehen mehr denn ein blat vier gantzer Paragraphos vorsetzlich aussgelassen haben wie folget*. Magdeburg, 1549. VD16:L4281.

47. *Ein kurtz vnd klar beweisung aus der heiligen Schrifft Das der Bapst zu Rom der ware Antichrist sey*. s.l., 1550.

B. *Antwort M. Nicolai Galli vnd M. Fla. Jllyrici/ auff den brief etlicher Prediger in Meissen/ von der frage/ Ob sie lieber weichen/ den den Corrock anzihen sollen*. Magdeburg: Christian Rödigner, 1550. Amsdorf's subscription appears on B4a. VD16:G252.

C. *Bekentnis Vnterricht vnd vermanung/ der Pfarrhern vnd Prediger der Christlichen Kirchen zu Magdeburgk. Anno 1550. Den 13. Aprilis*. Magdeburg, 1550. VD16:A2333. Issued simultaneously in Latin, *Confessio et Apologia pastorum & reliquorum ministrorum Ecclesiae Magdeburgensis, Anno 1550, Idibus Aprilis*. Magdeburg: Michael Lotter, 1550. VD16:A2331–2332. Both German and Latin texts edited in C&C 2:442–629. Amsdorf is listed at the head of those who subscribed to this Confession (German: Q3a, Latin: K3a).

48. *Das Doctor Martinus kein Adiaphorist gewesen ist/ vnd Das D. Pfeffinger vnd das buch on namen jhm/ gewalt vnd vnrecht thut*. Magdeburg: Christian Rödinger, 1550. VD16:A2338.

49. *Das nie no[e]ter ist wider den Ro[e]mischen Antichrist zu schreiben/ vnnd predigen/ jtzundt zu dieser zeit do die Adiaphoristen mit gewalt in jhrenn schriften dringen/ das man sich vnter den Bapst begeben/ vnd jhn fu[e]r ein Bischoff vnd hirten der seelen widderumb erkennen vnnd annemen sol*. Magdeburg: Michael Lotther, 1551. VD16:A2347.

50. *Das itzund die rechte zeit sey/ Christum vnd sein Wort zu bekennen/ vnd auff keine andere zu warten sey. Etliche Spru[e]che/ das man den Adiaphoristen nicht trawen noch gleuben sol*. Magdeburg: Christian Rödinger, 1551. VD16:A2343.

51. *Eine erinnerung an die Deudschen/ das sie einfeltigen jhre Su[e]nde/ so sie diese Fu[e]nff jar her gethan haben/ erkennen/ vnd bekennen sollen/ sich bekeren vnd bessern/ Auff das sie selig/ vnd mit dem hauffen nicht verdampt werden*. Magdeburg: Christian Rödinger, 1551. AS, 51–61. VD16:A2358.

52. *Ein Trost an die zu Magdeburg Vnd an alle fromme Christen*. Magdeburg: Christian Rödinger, 1551. VD16:A2392.

53. *Vom Bapst vnd seiner Kirchen/ das sie des Teufels/ vnd nicht Christi vnsers lieben Herrn Kirche sey*. Magdeburg: Michael Lotter or Christian Rödinger, 1551. VD16:A2406.

54. *Qvod Italia sit barbara terra. Qvod Italii svnt barbari popvli. Qvod Papa et cardinales svnt plvs barbari qvam Scythe et Tartari*. Magdeburg: Michael Lotter. VD16:ZV533.

55. *Ein kurtzer Brief an alle Christen/ sonderlich an die gelerten*. Magdeburg: Michael Lotter, 1551. VD16:A2378.

56. *Das Doctor Pomer vnd Doctor Maior mit iren Adiaphoristen eregernis vnnd zurtrennung angericht/ Vnnd den Kirchen Christi/ vnu[e]berwintlichen schaden gethan haben. Derhalben sie vnd nicht wir zu Magdeburg/ von Teuffel erwegt seint/ wie sie vns schmehen vnd lestern*. Magdeburg: Michael Lotter, 1551. Edited in C&C 2:752–777. VD16:A2340.

57. *Deren zu Magdeburgk/ so widder die Adiaphora geschrieben haben/ jhres vorigen schreibens beschlus/ auff der Adiaphoristen beschu[e]ldigung vnnd lesterung/ die zeit jhrer belagerung/ vnd itzt zum teil neulich vnter diesen friedshandlungen wider sie ausgangen. . . .* Magdeburg: Michael Lotter, 1551. VD16:A2352–2353.

58. *Etliche Spru[e]che aus Doctoris Martini Lutheri schriften/ Darinne er/ als ein Adiaphorist sich mit dem Bapst hat vergleichen wollen*. Magdeburg, 1551. VD16:A2359–2360.

59. *Ein kurtzer vnterricht auff D. Georgen Majors Antwort/ das er nit vnschu[e]ldig sey/ wie er sich tragice rhu[e]met. Das gute werck zur seligkeit nit von no[e]ten sind. Das gut werck zu eim Christlichen leben hie auff erden no[e]tig sind*. "Basel," [Magdeburg: Michael Lotter,] 1552. Edited in C&C 3:46–73. VD16:A2379.

60. *Auff Osianders Bekentnis ein Vnterricht vnd zeugnis/ Das die Gerechtigkeit der menschheit Christi/ darinnen sie entpfangen vnd geboren ist/ allen Gleubigen Su[e]ndern geschankt vnd zugerechent wird/ vnd fu[e]r jhr Person hie auff Erden nimmermehr Gerecht vnd Heilig werden*. Magdeburg: Christian Rödinger, 1552. VD16:A2329.

D. *Censvrae der Fürstlichen Sechsischen Theologen zu Weymar vnd Koburg. Auf die Bekendtnis des Andreae Osiandri Von der Rechtfertigung des Glaubens*. Erfurt, 1552. VD16:ZV10866.

Subscription to the several parts included in this treatise by Amsdorf on lvs. F4b, Ff2b, and n4b.

61. *Vnterschreibung des Herrn Niclas Amsdorffs der Sechsischen Kirchen Censurn vnd meinung/ wider Doctor Georg Maiors Antichristische lere von guten wercken als zur seligkeit no[e]tig. . . .* Magdeburg, 1553. VD16:A2397.

62. *Der Prophet Joel durch Doct. Mart. L. in Lateinischer sprach gelesen vnd ausgelegt. Vnd newlich verdeudscht etc. Mit einer Vorrede herrn Niclas von Amsdorff*. Jena, 1553.

63. *Ein gut newe Jar/ den grossen Herrn in dieser Welt geschanckt*. Jena: Christian Rödinger, 1554. VD16:A2369–2372.

64. *Wie sichs mit des Durchleuchtigsten Hochgebornen Fürsten vnd Herrn Herrn Johans Friderich/ des Eldern/ Christlichem abschied zugetragen hat. Sampt einer Leichpredigt/ vber dem Begrebnis zu Weimar/ Montag nach Letare gethan/ Anno 1554*. Jena: Rödinger, 1554. VD16:A2413.

65. *Etliche Trostschrifften vnd Predigten des Ehrwirdig. Herrn Doct. Mart. Luth. Fu[e]r [e]die so in Todes vnd ander Not vnd Anfechtung sind Erstlich anno 1545. zusamen gebracht vnd in Druck gegeben durch D. Caspar Crituziger. Itzt aber von newen zugericht vnd mit vielen scho[e]nen herrlichen Trost vnd andern Schrifften gemehret durch Georgium Rorarium. Allen Gottseligen nu[e]tzlich vnd tro[e]stlich zu lesen. Die Titel der Schrifften sind am folgenden blat in der Vorrede des Herrn Niclas von Amsdorff in gemein kurtzlich angezeigt*. Jena: Christian Rödinger, 1554. VD16:L3481.

66. *Fu[e]nff fu[e]rnemliche vnd gewisse Zeichen aus go[e]ttlicher heiliger Schrifft/ so kurtz vor dem Ju[e]ngsten tag geschehen sollen*. Jena: Christian Rödinger, 1554. VD16:A2361–2362.

67. *Vnterricht vnd Vermanung auffs newe Jar so ich vor zweien jaren den grossen Herrn dieser Welt geschanckt habe*. Jena: Christian Rödinger, 1555. VD16:A2393.

68. *Das in der Schrifft ausdru[e]cklich verku[e]ndigt ist/ Das die Ro[e]mische Kirche vom Christlichen glauben abfallen/ Christum vnd sein Wort verleugnen vnd verdammen sol*. Jena, 1555. AS, 62–78. VD16:A2341.

69. *Brevis defensio viri Deo Martini Lvtheri, in modvm somnij opposite somniatori Adiaphroistico, Autore Ioanne Stoltzio*. Regensburg: Johannes Kohl, 1555. VD16:S9260.

    Lf. 2a–b: Letter from Amsdorf to Stolz, September 19, 1554.

70. *Der Erste Teil aller Bu[e]cher vnd Schrifften des thewren seligen Mans Doct: Mart: Lutheri vom XVII jar an bis auff das XXII V D M I AE*. Jena: Christian Rödinger, 1555. VD16:L3323.

    Lf. +3b: Preface by Amsdorf.

71. *Tomvs primvs omnivm Reuerendi Patris D. M. L. quae vir Die ab Anno XVII. Vsque ad Anni vicesimi aliquam partem, scripsit & edidit, quorum Catalogum in fine Tomi inuenies*. Jena: Christian Rödinger, 1556. VD16:L3422.

    Lf. *3b: Preface by Amsdorf.

72. *Das achtzehend vnd neunzehend Capitel vnd ein Stuck aus dem zwentzigsten S. Johannis von dem Leiden Sterben vnd Aufferstehung vnsers Herrn Jhesu Christi, Gepredigt vnd ausgelegt durch Doc. Mart. Luth. Anno M.D.XXVIII. vnd XXIX*. Jena, 1557. WA 28:765–767. VD16:L3637.

    Preface: A2a. Preface by Amsdorf.

73. *Das Justus Menius sein Vocation vnd Kirche heimlich verlassen/ vnd von der reinen Lere des Euangelij abgefallen sey*. s.l., ca. 1557. VD16:A2345.

74. *Offentliche Bekentnis der reinen lere des Euangelij/ Vnd Confutatio der jtzigen Schwermer*. Jena: Christian Rödinger, 1558. Edited in C&C 5:55–74. VD16:A2381–2382.

75. *Jhenische Hauspostill . . . von D. Martin Luther*. Jena: Tobias Steinman, 1558.

    Lf.)(3b: Preface by Amsdorf.

76. *Das D. Pfeffinger seine missethat bo[e]slich vnd felschlich leugnet/ vnd gewaltiglich vberzeugt wird/ das er die Kirchen Christi zusto[e]rt vnd zuru[e]ttet/ vnd die Schrifft verfelschet vnd verkert hab*. Magdeburg: Ambrosius Kirchner, 1559. Edited in C&C 5:181–209. VD16:A2339.

77. *Das die Propositio <Gute werck sind zur Seligkeit schedlich> ein rechte ware Christliche Propositio sey/ durch die heiligen Paulum vnd Lutherum gelert vnd geprediget*. Magdeburg: Ambrosius Kirchner, 1559. Edited in C&C 3:468–487. VD16:A2336.

E. *Supplicatorii libelli qvorvndam Christi ministororvm de synodo propter controversias gravissimas congreganda. . . .* Oberursel: Nicolaus Heinrich, 1561. Translated as *Demu[e]tige vnd notwendige Supplication Schrifften etlicher Theologen vnd Diener Jesu Christi eines Christlichen Synodi halben geschrieben an die Stende vnd Lerer so der Augspurgischen -Confession anhengig sind*. s.l., 1561. VD16:S10215.

    Latin, p. 96, German, p. 196: Amsdorf's name heads the list of fifty-two subscribers.

78. *Horas Canonicas Jn Klo[e]stern vnd Stifften singen/ Vnd gebotenen Adiaphora halten/ ist eben so wol Abgo[e]tterey/ Als die schentlichste Opffermesse*. Jena: Thomas Rebart, 1562. VD16:A2374.

79. *Eine Predigt aus dem Comment/ des heiligen vnd trewen Dieners Christi Lutheri/ vber das fu[e]nfft Capitel Hosee gezogen/ von rechtschaffener vnd falscher Busse*. Jena: Donat Richtzenhan, 1562. VD16:A2383.

80. *Ein Predigt aus den Schrifften Lutheri vber die Propheten gezogen. Das Deudscheland/ wie Israel/ Judea/*

vnd Jerusalem/ wird zusto[e]rt vnd verwu[e]stet werden/ vmb gleicher Su[e]nde willen. Jena: Thomas Rebart, 1562. VD16:A2384.

81. *Eine Vermanung vnd Gebet/ wider den Bapst vnd seinen Anhang*. Jena: Donat Richtzenhan, 1562. VD16:A2403–2404.

82. *Eine Vermanung An der Rath vnd die Gemein Bu[e]rgerschafft zu Magdeburgk*. Magdeburg: Joachim Walden, 1563. VD16:A2399.

83. *Erzelung, Wie der Hochwichtig vnnd langwirige Religionstreit/ Victorini in Thu[e]ringen/ endlich geschlichtet/ durch die Mitler beschriben . . . Jetzo vonn newem mit fleis Corrigirt vnnd an vilen orthen gemehrt vnd gebessert*. Regensburg: Heinrich Geisler, 1563. VD16:F1383.

    The second edition of this treatise followed the first edition earlier in 1563. It contained two items by Amsdorf:

    G2b: Des Herrn Nicolai Ambsdorffij vrteil vber die Schrifft D. Petri Brem Fu[e]rstlichen rhat zu Sachssen von der Strigelianischen Declaration.

    G3a: Sendbrieff. Herrn Nicolai Ambsdorffij von der vnschuld vnd reiner Lere M. Fl. Ill.

84. *Warhafftiger vnnd Gru[e]ntlicher Summarien Bericht/ Etlicher Predicanten/ Wie vnd Worumb sie in LXII. Vnd LXIII. Jahre/ in Thu[e]ringen seind jres Ampts entsetzt/ vnd zum theil verjagt worden. Dorinnen auch von M. Sto[e]ssels Schlussreden/ den 10. Augusti/ des 1563. Jares zu Jena disputirt/ etwas gesagt wirdt*. . . . s.l., 1564. VD16:W734.

    Lf. M1a: Contra vltimam partem decimae quintae Propositionis, et aliquot sequentes disputationis Stosselij Propositiones. Nicolai Ambstrofij.

85. *Wider die Synergia Victorini. Nemlich Das der Mensch in seiner Bekerung/ kein Synergiam noch modum agendi, habe noch haben kann/ das ist/ allerding nichts mit wircke in seiner Bekerung/ Sondern sey Gottes gnedige wirkcung allein*. Eisleben: Urban Gaubisch, 1564. Edited in C&C 5:775–787. VD16:A2409.

86. *Wie Christlich vnd treulich Hesshusius in seinem Buch wieder mich/ mit der heiligen Schrifft vnnd mir handelt*. Magdeburg, 1564. VD16:A2412.

87. *Das Johannes Wigandus vnbillich meine vermanung an die von Magdenburgk straffet/ vnd mich schildt/ lectern/ vnd Liegen heist*. Magdeburg: Joachim Walde, 1564. VD16:A2344.

88. *Zwo Trost vnnd vermanung Schrifft/ ahn die verjagten Christen/ auss dem Bayerlandt, Item ein Rathschlag Joannis Brentij*. . . . Eisleben: Andreas Petri,1564. VD16:A2414–2415.

89. *Testament vnd Letzter Wille. Weiland deß Ehrwirdigen Edlen vnnd hochgelerten Herrn: Niclas von Ambsdorff/ der H. Schrifft Licentiaten. Darinne er seinen Schatz allen frommen Christen die es begern/ bescheidet*. Edited by Christoph Irenaeus. s.l., 1591.

Primary Sources by Others

Andreae, Jakob. *Kurtzer vnnd einfa[e]ltiger Bericht/ von des Herren Nachtmahl/ vnnd wie sich ein einfa[e]ltiger Christen in die langwirige zwyspalt/ so sich darüber erhebt/ schicken sol*. Augsburg: Hans Gegler, 1557. VD16:2651–2657.

Bucer, Martin. *Axiomata apologetica . . . de sacro eucharistiae mysterio et circa hoc Ecclesiarum Concordia, quibus respondet Thematis. N. Amßdorfij, Argentoratenses falso criminantibus*. Augsburg: Philipp Ulhart, 1535.

Bucer, Martin. *Martin Bucers Deutsche Schriften, Band 18. Nachträge 1541–1551 sowie Ergänzungen und Korrekturen*. Eds. Sephen E. Buckwalter and Thomas Wilhelmi. Gütersloh: Gütersloher Verlagshaus, 2015. 671–692; edited text: 679–692.

Cochlaeus, Johann. *Articuli CCCCC, Martini Luther, Ex sermonibus eius Sex & Triginta*. Cologne, 1525.

Cochlaeus, Johann. *Ein no[e]tig und Christlich Bedencken/ auff des Luthers artickeln/ die man gemeynem concilio fu[e]rtragen sol*. Leipzig, 1538. Edited by Hans Volz in *Drei Schriften gegen Luthers Schmalkaldische Artikel von Cochlaeus, Witzel und Hoffmeister*. Münster: Aschendorff, 1932. VD16:4347.

Cyclop, Wolf. *Von dem Aller hochwirdigsten Nachtmahl Jesu Christi/ Eynes durch Doctor Wolf Cyclop etc. Vorgenommen bu[e]chleins vorrede. . . .* Magdeburg, 1525. VD16:C6506.

Cyclop, Wolf. *Doctor Wolff Cyclops Antwort auff Nickel Amßdorffs Replica*. s.l., 1526. VD16:C6501.

Flacius, Matthias. *Die alte vnd newe Lehr Justi Menij/ jederman zur Warnung vnd jtzt zu einem verdrab*. s.l., 1557. Edited in C&C 3:390–406. VD16:M4537.

Flacius, Matthias. *Apologia M. Fl. Jllyrici auff zwo vnchristliche Schrifften Justi Menij/ Darinnen von den grewlichen Verfelschungen der Adiaphoristerey vnd Maioristerey allerley nu[e]tzlichs angezeigt wird*. Jena: Christian Rödinger, 1558. VD16:F1270–1271.

Flacius, Matthias. *Bericht M. Fla. Jllyrici/ Von etlichen Artikeln der Christlichen Lehr/ vnd von seinem Leben/ vnd enlich auch von den Adiaphorischen Handlungen/ wider die falschen Geticht der Adiaphoristen*. Jena: Thomas Rebart, 1559. VD16:1280.

Flacius, Matthias. *Christliche Bekentnus M. Matth. Flacij Illyrici Von der Erbsunde/ wider das Pelagianische vnd Sophistische Accidens. . . .* s.l., 1571. VD16:F1464.

Flacius, Matthias. *de voce & re Fidei, quodque sola iustificemur . . . Liber*. Basel: Johannes Operinus, 1563. VD16:F1527.

Flacius, Matthias. *Ein kurtz Scartecklein Ill. Vber das lange Comment Maioris. Aus dem buch Maioris widder H. Amsdorff Anno 1552 ausgangen*. Magdeburg: Christian Rödinger, 1553.

Flacius, Matthias. *Eine kurtze Antwort Illyr. Auff das lange Comment D. Ge. von guten wercken*. Magdeburg: Christian Rödinger, 1553. VD16:F1430, ZV5894.

Flacius, Matthias. *Von der einigkeit derer/ so fu[e]r vnd wider die Adiaphora in vergangenen Jaren gestritten haben/ Christlicher einfeltiger bericht. . . .* s.l., 1556. VD16:F1536.

Flacius, Matthias. *Wider den Euangelisten des heiligen Chorrocks/ D. Geitz Maior*. "Basel," 1552. Edited in C&C 3:74–95. VD16:F1558.

Flacius, Matthias, and Nikolaus Gallus. *Antwort M. Nicolai Galli vnd M. Fla. Jllyrici/ auff den brief etlicher Prediger in Meissen/ von der frage/ Ob sie lieber weichen/ den den Corrock anzihen sollen*. Magdeburg: Christian Rödigner, 1550. Amsdorf's subscription appears on B4a. VD16:G252.

Flacius, Matthias, and Nikolaus Gallus, eds. *Der Theologen bedenken odder (wie es durch die ihren inn offentlichem Druck genannet wird) Beschluss des Landtages zu Leipztig . . . welches bedenken odder Beschluss wir, so da wider geschrieben, das Leiptzigische Interim genennet haben*. Magdeburg: Melchior Lotther, 1550. VD16:S926.

Flacius, Matthias, and Simon Musaeus, eds., *Dispvtatio de originali peccato et libero arbitrio, inter Matthiam Flacivm Illyricvm & Victorinum Strigelium*. s.l., 1563. Edited in C&C 5:539–551. VD16:F1353–1354, F1563.

Gallus, Nikolaus. *Auf des Herrn D. Majors verantwortung und Declaration der Leiptzigischen Proposition/ wie gute werck zur seligkeit no[e]tig sind/ zum zeugnis seiner vnschult/ das er mit der Leipztigischen handlung nichts zu thun habe. Antwort*. "Basel," 1552. Edited in C&C 3:96–128. VD16:G255.

Gallus, Nikolaus. *Auff die newe subtile verfelschung der Euangelij Christi/ in Doctor Maiors Comment vber seine Antichristische Proposition/ damit er leret/ Das/ vnd wie gute werck/ zur seligkeit no[e]tig sein sollen. Erklerung vnd antwort Nicolai Galli*. Magdeburg: Michael Lotter, 1553. VD16:G256.

Gallus, Nikolaus. *Quaestio de libero arbitrio. Qvatenvs illa qvibvsqudam nunc disceptatur in Ecclesijs Augustanae Confessionis. . . .* Regensburg: Heinrich Geisler, 1559. VD16:G272.

Formula Reformationis per Caesarem Maiestatem Statibus Ecclesiasticis in Comitijs Augustanis ad deliberandum proposita. . . . Augsburg, 1548. VD16:D975.

Haussen, Heinrich. *In natalem Ioannis Baptistae elegia dedicata Reverendo Viro D. Nicolao Amsdorfio*. Wittenberg: Heirs of Georg Rhau, 1554. VD16:H6200.

Hesshus, Tilemann. *Analysis declarationis Victorini*. Magdeburg, 1562.

Hesshus, Tilemann. *Antwort Doct. Tilemanni Heßhusij auff der Lu[e]genprediger von Magdeburg vermeinte vnnd vngegru[e]ndte Apologia*. s.l., 1564.

Hesshus, Tilemann. *Gründliche widerlegung des falschen vnnd selbst angemasten vermeinten vrtheils/ Herrn Niclassen von Ambsdorff/ in der Magdeburgischen sache*. s.l., 1564. VD16:H3066.

Hoffman, Melchior. *Das Niclas Amsdorff der Magdeburger Pastor ein lugenhafftiger falscher nasen geist sey/ offentlich bewiesen durch Melchior Hoffman*, facsimile in *Schriften des Vereins für Schleswig-Holsteiner Kirchengeschichte* 4 (Sonderheft, 1928).

Hoffman, Melchior. *Dat Nicolaus Amsdorff der Meydeborger Pastor/ nicht weth/ wat he setten/ schriuen edder schwetzen schal*. . . . s.l., 1528.

Judex, Matthaeus. *De typographiae Inventione, et de praelorum legitima inspectione, libellus brevis et utilis*. Copenhagen: Johannes Zimmermann, 1566.

Judex, Matthaeus. *Der Ewigen/ Allmechtigen G[o]ttlichenn Mayest. Mandat/ vnd ernstlicher befelch/ wes sich ein yeder Christ/ nach seinem beruff/ vnnd stande/ gegen dem offenbarten Antichrist/ das gantze Babstumb/ halten solle/ widerhoelt vnd erklert*. s.l., 1561. VD16:R2246.

Judex, Matthaeus. *Einfeltiger vnterricht fu[e]r die Christen in Magdeburgk/ was von des herrn Amßdorffij vormeintem Vrteil nach Gottes WORT vnd dem heiligen Catechismo zu halten sey*. . . . s.l., 1563. VD16:2239–2240.

Judex, Matthaeus. *Von des Herrn Nicolai Amßdorfs feil vrtheil/ Vnd widderru[e]ff des selben/ in der Magdeburgischen sachen von Ausfu[e]hrung der Predicanten*. Frankfurt/M: Peter Braubach, 1564.

Lauterwein, Christian. *Wieder Niclaus von Ambsdorffen vngegru[e]ndte schrifften/ darinne er gute wergk anzeucht/ Als seindt sie zur Seligkeit schedlich/ vnd die Horas Canonicas vngestu[e]mer weyse verwirfft*. Bautzen?: Wolrab?, 1562?. VD16:L794.

Lübeck, Hamburg, Lüneburg, and Magdeburg Ministeria. *Sententia Ministrorvm Christi in Ecclesia Lubecensi, Hamburgensi, Luneburgensi & Magdeburgensi, de corruptelis doctrinae iustificationis, quibus D. Georg. Maior adserit*. Magdeburg, 1553. Reprinted in Conrad Schluesselburg, *Haereticorum Catalogus* 7:561–658. Frankfurt/M: Saurius, 1597. VD16:S5882–5884.

Luther, Martin. *Artickel der Euangelischen Lere/ so da hetten sollen auffs Concilium vberantort warden/ wo es sein wu[e]rde . . . Gestellet auff dem Tage zu Schmalkalden. Anno. 1537*. . . . Edited by Johann Stolz and Johannes Aurifaber. s.l., 1552.

Magdeburg city council. *Apologia. Entschu[e]ldigung vnd warhafftige vorantwortunge etzlicher Pfarherrn vnd Prediger der Christlichen Kirchen in der Alten Stadt Magdeburgk wieder die Vnchristliche vnd vngegru[e]ndete schmahe vnd Ehren ruhige schrifft/ so vnter dem Namen D. Thilemanni Hesshusij Vesaliensis wieder Magdebuurgk ausgangen*. s.l., s.d.

Major, Georg. *Auff des Ehrenwirdigen Herren Niclas von Ambsdorff schrifft/ so jtzundt neulich Mense Nouembri Anno 1551, wider Georgen Maior o[e]ffentlich in Druck ausgegangen. Antwort Georg: Major*. Wittenberg: Georg Rhau's heirs, 1552, edited in C&C 3:18–45. VD16:M1996.

Major, Georg. *Enarratio epistolae Pavli, scriptae ad Philippenses*. Wittenberg: Hans Lufft, 1554. VD16:M2025.

Major, Georg. *Bekentnis D. Georgij Maioris von dem Artickel der Iustification/ das ist/ von der Lere/ das der Mensch allein durch Glauben/ on alle verdienst/ vmb des Herrn Christi willen / vergebung der su[e]nden habe vnd fur Gott gerecht/ vnd Erbe ewiger seligkeit sey. Vnd von guten wercken/ welche des warhafftigen Glauben als fru[e]chte der gerechtigkeit/ folgen sollen*. Wittenberg: Hans Lufft, 1558. VD16:M2013.

Major, Georg. *Confessio De articvlo Ivstificationis*. Wittenberg: Hans Lufft, 1558. Edited in C&C 3:440–467. VD16:ZV10595.

Major, Georg. *De origine et avtoritate uerbi Dei & quae Pontificum, Patrum, & Conciliorum sit autoritas, admonitio hoc tempore, quo de Concilio congregando agitur, ualde necessaria*. . . . Wittenberg: Hans Lufft, 1550. VD16:M2121–2123.

Major, Georg. *Prima pars homeliarvm in epistolas dominicales*. Wittenberg: Hans Lufft, 1562. VD16:M2040.

Major, Georg. *Prima pars homeliarvm in evangelia dominicalia et dies festos*. Wittenberg, 1562. VD16:M2045.

Major, Georg. *Ein Sermon von S. Pauli vnd aller der Gottfu[e]rchtigen menschen bekerung zu Gott*. . . . Leipzig: Wolfgang Günther, 1553. Edited in C&C 3:130–279. VD16:2186.

Major, Georg. *Ewiger: Go[e]ttlicher Allmechtiger Mayestat Declaration Wider Kaiser Carl Künig zu Hispanien etc. Vnd Bapst Paulum den dritten*. . . . Augsburg: Valentin Otmar, 1546. VD16:M2058.

Major, Georg. *Repetitio Widerholung vnd endtliche Erklerung der Bekentnu[e]s D. Georgij Maioris/ Von dem Artickel der Iustification . . . vnd von Guten Werken*. Dresden: Matthes Stöckel, 1567. VD16:M2160–2162.

Major, Georg. *Vorrede D. Georgij Maioris/ in die Ausslegunge der Sontags vnd Festen Euangelion*. . . . Wittenberg: Veit Creutzer, 1562. VD16:M2058.

Mansfeld Ministerium. *Acta oder handlungen des Lo[e]blichen Synodi/ in der Stad zu Eisleben/ in der Graff vnd Herschafft Mansfelt/ den xiij. Febru. Des Jars/ 1554. versamlet/ wider etliche falsche Leren/ darinnen verdammet*. Eisleben: Jacob Berwalt, 1554. Edited in C&C 3:354–389. VD16:A151.

Mansfeld Ministerium. *Bedencken/ das diese Proposition oder Lere/ nicht nütz/ not/ noch war sey/ vnnd one ergernis in der Kirchen nicht möge geleret werden. Das gute werck zur seligkeit nötig sind. Vnd vnmuglich sey/ one gute werck selig werden. Gestellet durch die Prediger zu Mansfelt Vnnd vnterschrieben von andern Predigern derselben Herrschafft*. Magdeburg: Michael Lotther, 1553. Edited in C&C 3:280–314; 5:645–656. VD16:B1456.

Mansfeld Ministerium. *Sententia ministrorum verbi divini in comitatu Mansfeldensi de formula declarationis Vict. Strigelij in quaestione de libero hominis arbitrio*. s.l., 1562. VD16:S5884.

Melanchthon, Philip. Preface to *Der Dritte Teil der Bu[e]cher des Ehrwirdigen Herrn Doctor Mart. Lutheri*. . . . Wittenberg: Hans Lufft, 1550. VD16:L3312.

Menius, Justus. *Bericht Der bittern Warheit Ivsti Menii Auff die Vnerfindlichen aufflagen M. Flacij Illyrici/ vnd des Herrn Niclas von Amsdorff*. Wittenberg: Georg Rhau, 1558. VD16:M4563.

Menius, Justus. *Entschüldigung Justi Menij/ Auff die vnwarhafftige verleumbdung darinnen jm auffgeleget wird/ als solt er von der reinen Lere des Evangelij abgefallen sein*. . . . Gotha, 1555. VD16:M4565.

Menius, Justus. *Kurtzer Beschaid Justi Menij: Das seine Lare/ wie er für der zeit gefurt/ vnd noch fu[e]ret/ nicht mit jr selbs streitig noch widerwertig/ sondern allenthalben einerley/ vnd der warheit des Euangelij gemes sey*. Wittenberg: heirs of Georg Rhau, 1557. Edited in C&C 3:408–438. VD16:M4573.

Menius, Justus. *Verantwortung Justi Menij Auff Matth. Flacij Illyrici gifftige vnd vnwarhafftige verleumbdung vnd lesterung*. Wittenberg: heirs of Georg Rhau, 1557. VD16:M4583.

Menius, Justus. *Von der Bereittung zum seligen Sterben*. . . . Erfurt: Gervasius Stürmer, 1556. VD16:M4590, M4597.

Mensing, Johann. *Bescheidt Ob der Glaube alleyn: on alle gute wercke dem menschen genug sey zur seligkeyt etc*. . . . Leipzig: Jacob Thanner, 1528. VD16:M4646.

Mörlin, Joachim, and Martin Chemnitz. *Repetitio corporis doctrinae ecclesiasticae Oder Widerholung der Summa vnd Inhalt der rechten/ allgemeinen Christlichen/ Kirchen Lehre wie dieselbige aus Gottes Wort/ in der Augspurgischen Confession/ Apologia/ vnd Schmalkaldischen Artickeln begriffen/ Vnd von Fu[e]rstlicher Durchleuchtigkeit zu Preussen etc. Auch allen derselbigen Getrewen Landtstenden vnd Vnterthanen/ Geistlichen vnd Weltlichen/ im Hertzogthumb Preussen/ Einhellig vnd bestendiglichen/ gewilliget vnd angenomen/ Ku[e]rtzlich zusammen verfasset.* Eisleben: Andreas Petri, 1567. VD16:P4794.

Pfeffinger, Johann. *Antwort: D, Johann Pfeffingers/ Pastoris der Kirchen zu Leiptzig: Auff die Offentliche Bekentnis der reinen Lare des Euangelij/ vnd Confutation der jtzigen Schwermerey/ Niclasen von Ambsdorff.* Wittenberg: Georg Rhau, 1558. Edited in C&C 5:153–173. VD16:P2322.

Pfeffinger, Johann. *Demonstratio Manifesti Mendacii, Sycophanticus germanice editus titulo Nicolai ad Amsdorf, Necessaria propter Veritatis assertionem & auersionem Scandali, & tuendam existimationem sincereae doctrinae.* Wittenberg, 1558. VD16:ZV12421.

Pfeffinger, Johann. *Grüntlicher vnd Warhafftiger Bericht der vorigen vnd jetzigen/ fu[e]r vnd nach dem Kriege ergangen Handlungen/ von den Adiaphoris oder Mitteldingen. . . .* Leipzig: Valentin Bapst, 1550. Edited in C&C 2:642–730. VD16:P2326.

Pfeffinger, Johann. *In hoc Libello continentvr vtiles dispvtationes de praecipuis capitibus doctrinae Christianae.* Frankfurt/M: Peter Braubach, 1558. VD16:P2356.

Pfeffinger, Johann. *Nochmals gru[e]ndlicher/ klarer/ warhafftiger Bericht vnd Bekentnis/ der bittern lautern Warheit/ reiner Lere/ vnstrefflichen Handlungen/ vnd vnuermeidliche notwendige Verantwortunge Johanis Peffingers Doctoris. Wider den Lu[e]gengeist/ vnd Lesterschrifften/ newlich in Druck/ vnter dem Namen Matthiae Flacij Jllyrici ausgangen. . . .* Wittenberg: Lorentz Schwenk, 1559. Edited in C&C 5:221–265. VD16:P2328.

Saxon (ducal) government. *Des Durchleuchtigen Hochgebornen Fu[e]rsten vnd Herren/ Herren Johans Friderichen des Mittlern/ Herzogen zu Sachssen . . . in Gottes wort/ Prophetischer vnd Apostolischer Schrifft/ gegru[e]ndete wort Confutationes/ Widerlegungen vnd verdammung etlicher einheit her/ zu wider demselben Gottes wort/ vnd heiliger Schrifft/ auch der Augspurgischen Confession Apologien/ vnd den Schmalkaldischen Artickeln/ Aber zu fu[e]rderung vnd wider anrichtung des Antichristischen Bapstums eingeschlichen/ vnd eingerissenen Corruptelen/ Secten vnd Irrthumen. . . .* Jena: Thomas Rebart, 1559; on opposite pages from Saxon (ducal) government, *Illvstrissimi Principis Ac Domini . . .*, and edited in C&C 5:308–501. VD16:S1099.

Saxon (ducal) government. *Illvstrissimi Principis Ac Domini, Domini Iohannis Friderici Secvndi, Dvcis Saxoniae . . . solida & ex verbo Dei sumpta Confutatio & condemnatio praecipuarum Corruptelarum, Sectarum & errorum, hoc tempore ad instaurationem & propagationem Regni Antichristi Rom. Pontificis aliarumque fanaticarum opinionum . . . contra ueram sacrae Scripturae, Confessionis Augustanae & Schmalkaldicorum Articulorum Religionem. . . .* Jena: Thomas Rebart, 1559; on opposite pages from Saxon (ducal) government, *Des Durchleuchtigen Hochgebornen . . .*, and edited in C&C 5:308–501. VD16:S1100–1101.

Saxon (ducal) government. *Ordenung vnd summarischer Process des Fürstlichen Sechsischen Consistorij, Auffgerichtet in dem jar 1561.* Jena, 1561. VD16:S1105.

Saxon (ducal) pastors. *Warhafftiger vnnd Gru[e]ntlicher Summarien Bericht/ Etlicher Predicanten/ Wie vnd Worumb sie in LXII. Vnd LXIII. Jahre/ in Thu[e]ringen seind jres Ampts entsetzt/ vnd zum theil verjagt worden. Dorinnen auch von M. Sto[e]ssels Schlussreden/ den 10. Augusti/ des 1563. Jares zu Jena disputirt/ etwas gesagt wirdt.* s.l., 1564. VD16:W734.

Schluesselburg, Conrad. *Haereticorum Catologus.* Frankfurt/M: Saurius, 1597–1599. VD16:S3038.

Sleidan, Johann. *Commentariorum de Statu Religionis & Reipublicae, Carolo Quinto Caesare, Libri XXVI.* Strassburg: 1555; Strassburg: Theodosius Rihel, 1559. VD16:S6668–6717.

Spangenberg, Cyriakus. *Adelspiegel. Historischer Ausfu[e]rlicher Bericht/Was Adel mache*... 2. Smalcald: Schmück, 1594. VD16:S7473.

Stolz, Johann. *M. Ioannis Stolzii Concionatoris Aulici Ducum Saxoniae Refutatio propositionum Pfeffingeri de Libero arbitrio, cum Praefatione M. Ioannis Aurifabri. Matth: Fla: Illyrici de eadem controuersia.* Jena: Thomas Rebart, 1558. Edited in C&C 5:79–84. VD16:S9267.

Weidensee, Eberhard and Johann Fritzhans. *Wie Doctor Cubito/ Bonifacius/ vnd der sontags prediger yhm Thum zu Magdeburg/ Gottis wort lestern* . . . *Dyalogus*. Magdeburg: Heinrich Öttinger, 1526. VD16:W1470.

Wigand, Johannes. *Ein Brief Doctoris Johannis Wigandi an Herrn Nicolaum Amßdorff*. s.l., 1564. Edited in C&C 4:207–213. VD16:W2724–2726.

Wigand, Johannes. *Vom Ampt Des Gesetzes kurtzer vnd Freundtlicher Bericht auff Amßdorffs Sturmschrift*. Frankfurt/M: Peter Braubach, 1564. Edited in C&C 4:233–245.

Wittenberg scholastici. *Scholasticorum Academiae Witebergensis* . . . *Epistolae Duae, Tertia, et Quarta*. Wittenberg, 1558. VD16:S3805.

Wittenberg scholastici. *Ad Toties cum Fastidio et Nausea Repetitas Virulentissimas et falsissimas criminationes Flacij responsio* . . . *a Scholasticis Academiae Witebergensis*. Wittenberg, 1559. VD16:M2421.

Wittenberg scholastici. *Ex Actis Synodicis Et Aliis Diligenter Et Fideliter Collecta Expositio Eorvm, Qvas Theologi Academiae VVitebergensis & harum Regionum alij* . . . *de libro Augustano, qui nominator Interim*. Wittenberg, 1559. VD16:W3725–3726.

Witzel, Georg. *Antwort auff Martinn Luthers letzt bekennete Artickel vnsere gantze religion und das concili belangend*. Cologne: Johann Quentel, 1538. Edited by Hans Volz in *Drei Schriften gegen Luthers Schmalkaldische Artikel von Cochlaeus, Witzel und Hoffmeister*. Münster: Aschendorff, 1932. VD16:W3853.

Editions of Primary Sources

Abhandlungen Alexander von Oettingen zum siebzigsten Geburtstag gewidmet. Munich: Beck, 1898.

Bindseil, H. E., ed. *Philippi Melanchthonis Epistolae*. Halle: Schwetschke, 1874.

"Der Bischof Nikolaus zu Naumburg kündigt dem Zeizischen Kapitel die vorzunehmende Kirchenvisitation an. 1545," *Archiv der sächsischen Geschichte* 2 (1785): 339–340.

"Eine bisher ungedruckte satyrische Schrift aus dem 16. Jahrhundert (Nic. Von Amsdorfs Gespräch eines Raben mit einer Taube)," *Zeitschrift für die gesammte lutherische Theologie und Kirche* 25 (1864): 78–86.

Bretschneider, C. G. and H. E. Bindweil, eds. *Corpus Reformatorum. Philippi Melanthonis Opera quae supersunt omnia*. Halle and Braunschweig: Schwetschke, 1834–1860.

Die Chroniken der Deutschen Städte, . . . *Magdeburg* volume 2. Leipzig: Hirzel, 1899.

Dingel, Irene, ed. *Die Bekenntnisschriften der Evangelisch-Lutherischen Kirche*. Göttingen: Vandenhoeck & Ruprecht, 2014.

Dingel, Irene, ed. *Die Bekenntnisschriften der Evangelisch-Lutherischen Kirche. Quellen und Materialien Band 2: Die Konkordienformel*. Göttingen: Vandenhoeck & Ruprecht, 2014.

Dingel, Irene, ed. *Controversia et Confessio. Theologische Kontroversen 1548–1577/80. Kritische Auswahledition*. 9 vols. Göttingen: Vandenhoeck & Ruprecht, 2008– .

Druffel, August von, ed. *Briefe und Akten zur Geschichte des sechszehnten Jahrhunderts*, volume 2. Munich: Rieger, 1875.

Ehwald, Rudolf. "Beschreibung der Handschriften und Inkunabulen der Herzogl. Gymnasialbibliothek zu Gotha nebst vier Briefe von Eobanus Hessus, Melanchthon, und Niclas von Amsdorff," in *Programm des Gymnasiums Ernestinum zu Gotha* (Gotha: Engelhard-Reyher, 1893), 18–20.

Eichhorn, Carl. "Amsdorfiana aus dem Codex chartaceus Nr. 43 der Dorpater Universitätsbibliothek," *Zeitschrift für Kirchengeschichte* 22 (1901): 605–645.

Förstemann, Karl Eduard. *Denkmäle, dem D. Martin Luther von der Hochachtung und Liebe seiner Zeitgenossen errichtet*. Nordhausen: Förstemann, 1846.

Förstemann, Karl Eduard. *Neues Urkundenbuch zur Geschichte der evangelischen Kirchen-Reformation*. Hamburg: Perthes, 1842.

Friedensburg, Walter. "Ein Brief Georg Majors an Nikolaus von Amsdorff, 1563," *Archiv für Reformationsgeschichte* 21 (1924): 254–255.

Herrmann, Johannes, and Günther Wartenberg, eds. *Politische Korrespondenz des Herzogs und Kurfürsten Moritz von Sachsen*, volume 4. Berlin: Akademie Verlag, 1992.

Hortleder, Fredrich. *Der Römischen Keyser . . . Handlungen vnd Rathschläge . . . Von Rechtmässigkeit, Anfang, Fort- vnd endlichen Ausgang dess Deutschen Krieges Keyser Carls des Fünfften*, volume 2. Frankfurt/M: Hoffmann, 1618.

Jäger, Hagen, ed. *Nikolaus von Amsdorff. Ausgewählte Schriften der Jahren 1550 bis 1562 aus der ehemaligen Eisenacher Ministerialbibliothek*. Leipzig: Evangelische Verlagsanstalt, 2017.

Kapp, Johann Erhard. *Kleine Nachlese . . . nützlicher Urkunden*, volume 2. Leipzig: Braun, 1727.

Kawerau, Gustav, ed. *Der Briefwechsel des Justus Jonas*. Reprint, Hildesheim: Olms, 1964.

Kawerau, Gustav. "Zwei Briefe aus den Tagen des Todes Luthers," *Theologische Studien und Kritiken* 70 (1907): 468–471.

Kolb, Robert, and James A. Nestingen, eds. *Sources and Contexts of the Book of Concord*. Minneapolis: Fortress, 2001.

Lerche, Otto, ed. *Nikolaus von Amsdorff, Ausgewählte Schriften*. Gütersloh: Bertelsmann, 1938.

Luther, Martin. *D. Martin Luthers Werke*. Weimar: Böhlau, 1883–1993.

Luther, Martin. *Luther's Works*. Saint Louis/Philadelphia: Concordia/Fortress, 1958–1986.

Mentz, Georg, ed. *Die Wittenberger Artikel von 1536. (Artickel der christlichen lahr, von welchen die legatten aus Engelland mit dem herrn doctor Martino gehandelt anno 1536)*. Darmstadt: Wissenschaftliche Buchgesellschaft, 1968.

Die Männer der Reformation. Hildburghausen: Bibliographische Institut, 1859.

Mehlhausen, Joachim, ed. *Das Augsburger Interim von 1548, deutsch und lateinisch*. Neukirchen-Vluyn: Neukirchener Verlag, 1970.

Moritz, elector of Saxony. *Politische Korrespondenz des Herzogs und Kurfürsten Moritz von Sachsen*. Edited by Johannes Herrmann and Günther Wartenberg, volume 4. Berlin: Akademie Verlag, 1992.

Müller, Gerhard, and Gottfried Seebaß, eds. *Andreas Osiander d. Ä. Gesamtausgabe*, volumes 8–10. Gütersloh: Mohn, 1990, 1994, 1997.

Neudecker, Christian Gotthold. *Neue Beiträge zur Geschichte der Reformation*, volume 1. Leipzig: Fleischer, 1841.

Rembe, Heinrich. *Der Briefwechsel des M. Cyriacus Spangenberg*, volume 1. Dresden: Naumann, 1887.

Richter, Aemilius Ludwig, ed. *Die Evangelischen Kirchenordnung des 16. Jahrhunderts*. Reprint, Nieuwkoop: De Graaf, 1967.

Scheible, Heinz et al., eds. *Das Widerstandsrecht als Problem der deutschen Protestanten, 1523–1546*. Gütersloh: Mohn, 1969.

Schiess, Traugott, ed. *Briefwechsel der Brüder Ambrosius und Thomas Blaurer, 1509–1567*. Freiburg im Breisgau: Fehsenfeld, 1908–1912.

Schubart, Christof. *Die Berichte über Luthers Tod und Begräbnis*. Weimar: Böhlau, 1917.

Schmidt, Gustav L. "Bekenntniss Johann Friedrichs des Grossmüthigen über das Interim," *Zeitschrift für die historische Theoologie* 38 (1868): 431–444.

Schmidt, Gustav L. "Drei Briefe Amsdorfs über das Interim, Aus dem Sächs. Ernest. Gesamtarchiv zu Weimar mitgeteilt," *Zeitschrift für die historische Theologie* 38 (1868): 469–471.

Schumacher, Andreas. *Gelehrter Männer Briefe an die Könige in Dannemark, vom Jahr 1522 bis 1663*, volume 2. Copenhagen: Pelt, 1758.

Schwarz, J. C. E. "Johann Friedrich's des Grossmüthigen Correspondenz mit Brück und Amsdorf vor dem Augsburger Reichstage 1547," *Zeitschrift des Vereins für Thüringische Geschichte und Altertumskunde* 1 (1854): 408–414.

Sehling, Emil, ed. *Die evangelischen Kirchenordnungen des 16. Jahrhunderts*, volume 1, 2. Leipzig: Reisland, 1902.

Sillem, C. H. W., ed. *Briefsammlung des Hamburgischen Superintendenten Joachim Westphal*. Hamburg: Gräfe & Sillem, 1903.

Soden, F. von and J. K. F. Knaake, eds. *Christoph Scheurl's Briefbuch*, volume 2. Potsdam: Gropius, 1872.

Voigt, Johannes, ed. *Briefwechsel der berühmtesten Gelehrten des Zeitalters der Reformation mit Herzog Albrecht von Preussen*. Königsberg: Bornträger, 1841.

Volz, Hans, ed. *Drei Schriften gegen Luthers Schmalkaldische Artikel von Cochlaeus, Witzel und Hoffmeister*. Münster: Aschendorff, 1932.

Wackernagel, Philipp. *Das deutsche Kirchenlied von der aeltesten Zeit bis zu Anfang des XVII. Jahrhunderts*, volume 3. Leipzig: Teubner, 1870.

Walz, Otto. "Epistolae Reformatoren," *Zeitschrift für Kirchengeschichte* 2 (1878): 117–188.

Secondary Literature

Andersen, Ragnar. *Concordia Ecclesiae. An Inquiry into Tension and Coherence in Philipp Melanchthon's Theology and Efforts for Ecclesiastical Unity, Especially in 1527–1530*. Zurich: LIT-Verlag, n.d. [2016].

Arand, Charles P. "The Apology as a Backdrop for the Interim of 1548." In *Politik und Bekenntnis. Die Reaktion auf das Interim von 1548*, edited by Irene Dingel and Günther Wartenberg, 211–227. Leipzig: Evangelische Verlagsanstalt, 2006.

Arand, Charles P., Robert Kolb, and James A. Nestingen. *The Lutheran Confessions, History and Theology of the Book of Concord*. Minneapolis: Fortress, 2012.

Asendorf, Ulrich. *Eschatologie bei Luther*. Göttingen: Vandenhoeck & Ruprecht, 1967.

Barnes, Robin. *Prophecy and Gnosis, Apocalypticism in the Wake of the Lutheran Reformation*. Stanford: Stanford University Press, 1988.

Barton, Peter F. *Um Luthers Erbe. Studien und Text zur Spätreformation, Tilemann Heshusius (1527–1559)*. Witten: Luther-Verlag, 1972.

Beck, August. *Johann Friedrich der Mittlere*. Weimar: Böhlau, 1858.

Bauer, Joachim, and Stefan Michel, eds. *Der "Unterricht der Visitatoren" und die Durchsetzung der Reformation in Kursachsen*. Leipzig: Evangelische Verlagsanstalt, 2017.

Berndorff, Lothar. "Nikolaus von Amsdorf als Argument. Zum Gebrauch protestantischer Schiedsautorität in Publizistik und Kirchenpolitik am Beispiel des Mansfelder Klerus." In *Nikolaus von Amsdorf (1483–1565) zwischen Reformation und Politik*, edited by Irene Dingel, 217–236. Leipzig: Evangelische Verlagsanstalt, 2008.

Berwinkel, Roxane. *Weltliche Macht und geistlicher Anspruch. Die Hansestadt Stralsund im Konflikt um das Augsburger Interim*. Berlin: Akademie Verlag, 2008.

Beutel, Georg. *Über den Ursprung des Augsburger Interims*. Dresden: Paessler, 1888.

Beyer, Michael. "Hintergründe der Lehre vom 'freien Willen' und der 'christlichen Freiheit' im 'Unterricht der Visitatoren.'" In *Der "Unterricht der Visitatoren" und die Durchsetzung der Reformation in Kursachsen*, edited by Joachim Bauer and Stefan Michel, 241–254. Leipzig: Evangelische Verlagsanstalt, 2017.

Biundo, Georg. "Aquila und das Interim," *Theologische Literaturzeitung* 74 (1949): 587–592.

Bollbuck, Harald. *Wahrheitszeugnis, Gottes Auftrag und Zeitkritik: die Kirchengeschichte der Magdeburger Zenturien und ihre Arbeitstechniken*. Wiesbaden: Harrassowitz, 2014.

Bräuer, Siegfried, "Nikolaus von Amsdorfs Schrift zum Tod Johann Friedrichs d. Ä." In *Nikolaus von Amsdorf (1483–1565) zwischen Reformation und Politik*, edited by Irene Dingel, 117–133. Leipzig: Evangelische Verlagsanstalt, 2008.

Brathe, Paul. "Das Geschlecht des Nikolaus von Amsdorf, "*Archiv für Sippenforschung und alle Verwandten Gebiete* 21 (1944): 113–115.

Brinkel, Karl. "Nikolaus von Amsdorf, als verjagter Bischof im Thüringer Land." In *Des Herren Name Steht Uns Bei, Luthers Freunde und Schüler in Thüringen*, edited by Karl Brinkel and Herbert von Hintzenstern, 1:78–92. Berlin: Evangelische Verlagsanstalt, 1961.

Brinkel, Karl. "Zu Johann Walters Stellung als Hofkapellmeister in Dresden," *Jahrbuch für Liturgik und Hymnologie* 5 (1960): 135–143.

Brosseder, Claudia. *Im Bann der Sterne: Caspar Peucer, Philipp Melanchthon, and andere Wittenberger Astrologen*. Berlin: Akademie-Verlag, 2004.

Brunner, Peter. *Nikolaus von Amsdorf als Bischof von Naumburg*. Gütersloh: Mohn, 1961.

Büttgen, Philippe, Ruedi Imbach, Ulrich Johannes Schneider, and Hermann J. Selderhuis, eds., *Vera Doctrina: zur Begriffsgeschichte der Lehre von Augustin bis Descartes*. Wiesbaden: Harrassowitz, 2009.

Bundschuh, Benno von. *Das Wormser Religionsgespräch von 1557, unter besonderer Berücksichtigung der kaiserlichen Religionspolitik*. Münster: Aschendorf, 1988.

Burnett, Amy Nelson. *Karlstadt and the Origins of the Eucharistic Controversy: A Study in the Circulation of Ideas*. Oxford/New York: Oxford University Press, 2011.

Cargill Thompson, W. D. J. *The Political Thought of Martin Luther*, edited by Philip Broadhead. Sussex: Harvester, 1984.

Chalybaeus, Albert. *Die Durchführung des Leipziger Interims*. Chemnitz: Oehme, 1905.

Christman, Robert J. *Doctrinal Controversy and Lay Religiosity in Late Reformation Germany: The Case of Mansfeld*. Leiden: Brill, 2012.

Delius, Hans-Ulrich. "Der Briefwechsel des Nikolaus von Amsdorf als Bischof von Naumburg-Zeitz (1542–1546)," Habiliationsschrift, University of Leipzig, 1968. Summarized in *Theologische Literaturzeitung* 96 (1971): 153–155.

Dettloff, Werner. *Die Entwicklung der Akzeptations- und Verdienstlehre von Duns Scotus bis Luther, mit besonderer Berücksichtigung der Franziskanertheologen*. Münster: Aschendorf, 1963.

Dettloff, Werner. *Die Lehre von der Acceptatio Divina bei Johannes Duns Scotus mit besonderer Berücksichtigung der Rechtfertiungslehre*. Werl/Westfalen: Colde, 1954.

Dingel, Irene. *Concordia controversa, Die öffentlichen Diskussionen um das lutherische Konkordienwerk am Ende des 16. Jahrhunderts*. Gütersloh: Gütersloher Verlagshaus, 1996.

Dingel, Irene. "Culture of Conflict in the Controversies Leading to the Formula of Concord (1548–1580)." In *Lutheran Ecclesiastical Culture, 1550–1675*, edited by Robert Kolb, 18–34. Leiden: Brill, 2008.

Dingel, Irene. "Flacius als Schüler Luthers und Melanchthons." In *Vestigia pietatis, Studien zur Geschichte der Frömmigkeit in Thüringen und Sachsen. Festschrift für Ernst Koch*, edited by Gerhard Graf, Hans-Peter Hasse, and Markus Hein, 77–93. *Herbergen der Christenheit: Sonderband 4*. Leipzig: Evangelische Verlagsanstalt, 2000.

Dingel, Irene. "Die Kultivierung des Exulantentums im Luthertum am Beispiel des Nikolaus von Amsdorf." In *Nikolaus von Amsdorf (1483–1565) zwischen Reformation und Politik*, edited by Irene Dingel, 153–175. Leipzig: Evangelische Verlagsanstalt, 2008.

Dingel, Irene. "Luther's Authority in the Late Reformation and Lutheran Orthodoxy." In *The Oxford Handbook to Martin Luther's Theology*, edited by Robert Kolb, Irene Dingel, and L'ubomír Batka, 525–539. Oxford: Oxford University Press, 2014.

Dingel, Irene. "Melanchthon's Efforts for Unity between the Fronts: the Frankfurt Recess." In Irene Dingel, Robert Kolb, Nicole Kuropka, and Timothy J. Wengert, *Philip Melanchthon. Theologian in Classroom, Confession, and Controversy*, 123–140. Göttingen: Vandenhoeck & Ruprecht, 2012.

Dingel, Irene. "Melanchthon's Paraphrases of the Augsburg Confession, 1534 and 1536, in the Service of the Smalcald League." In Irene Dingel, Robert Kolb, Nicole Kuropka, and Timothy J. Wengert, *Philip Melanchthon. Theologian in Classroom, Confession, and Controversy*, 103–122. Göttingen: Vandenhoeck & Ruprecht, 2012.

Dingel, Irene, ed. *Nikolaus von Amsdorf (1483–1565) zwischen Reformation und Politik*. Leipzig: Evangelische Verlagsanstalt, 2008.

Dingel, Irene. "Philipp Melanchthon, Freunde und Feinde," *Theologische Literaturzeitung* 135 (2010): 788–790.

Dingel, Irene. "Pruning the Vines, Plowing Up the Vineyard: The Sixteenth-Century Culture of Controversy between Disputation and Polemic." In *The Reformation as Christianization. Essays on Scott Hendrix's Christianization Thesis*, edited by Anna Marie Johnson and John A. Maxfield, 397–408. Tübingen: Mohr/Siebeck, 2012.

Dingel, Irene. "'Der rechten lehr zuwider.' Die Beurteilung des Interims in ausgewählten theologischen Reaktionen." In *Das Interim 1548/50. Herrschaftskrise und Glaubenskonflikt*, edited by Luise Schorn-Schütte, 292–311. Gütersloh: Gütersloher Verlag, 2005.

Dingel, Irene. "Die Rolle Georg Majors auf dem Regensburger Religionsgespräch von 1546." In *Georg Major (1502–1574): Ein Theologe der Wittenberger Reformation*, edited by Irene Dingel and Günther Wartenberg, 189–206. Leipzig: Evangelische Verlagsanstalt, 2005.

Dingel, Irene. "Streitkultur und Kontroversschrifttum im späten 16. Jahrhundert. Versuch einer methodischen Standortbestimmung." In *Kommunikation und Transfer im Christentum der Frühen Neuzeit*, edited by Irene Dingel and Wolf Friedrich Schäufele, 95–111. Mainz: von Zabern, 2007.

Dingel, Irene. "Strukturen der Lutherrezeption am Beispiel einer Lutherzitatensammlung von Joachim Westphal." In *Kommunikationsstrukturen im europäischen Luthertum der Frühen Neuzeit*, edited by Wolfgang Sommer, 32–50. Gütersloh: Gütersloher Verlagshaus, 2005.

Dingel, Irene. "Von der Wittenberger Reformation zum Luthertum. Konfessionelle

Transformationen." In *Luther: Katholizität & Reform. Wurzeln – Wege – Wirkungen*, edited by Wolfgang Thönissen, Josef Freitag, and Augustinus Sander, 239–260. Paderborn: Bonifatius; Leipzig: Evangelische Verlagsanstalt, 2016.

Dingel, Irene. "Zwischen Disputation und Polemik. 'Streitkultur' in den nachinterimistischen Kontroversen." In *Streitkultur und Öffentlichkeit im Konfessionellen Zeitalter*, edited by Henning P. Jürgens and Thomas Weller, 17–29. Göttingen: Vandenhoeck & Ruprecht, 2013.

Dingel, Irene, and Günther Wartenberg, eds. *Politik und Bekenntnis. Die Reaktion auf das Interim von 1548*. Leipzig: Evangelische Verlagsanstalt, 2006.

Edwards, Mark U., Jr. *Luther and the False Brethren*. Stanford: Stanford University Press, 1975.

Edwards, Mark U., Jr. *Luther's Last Battles. Politics and Polemics, 1531-46*. Ithaca: Cornell University Press, 1983.

Fabian, Stefanie. "*Ein feste Burg* wider den Kaiser – Alltag und Leben im belagerten Magdeburg." In *Magdeburg und die Reformation. Teil 1. Eine Stadt folgt Martin Luther*, edited by Maren Ballerstedt, Gabriele Köster, and Cornelia Poenicke, 403–423. Halle: Mitteldeutscher Verlag, 2016.

Fischer, Paul Charles. *Nikolaus D'Amsdorf, écrits et influence d'un controversiste Luterien du seizieme Siècle*. Strassburg: Silbermann, 1863.

Fligge, Jörg Rainer. "Herzog Albrecht von Preussen und der Osiandrismus, (1522–1568)." Dissertation, University of Bonn, 1972.

Friedeburg, Robert von. "Bausteine widerstandsrechtlicher Argumente in der frühen Neuzeit (1523–1668): Konfessionen, lassische Verfassungsvorbilder, Naturrecht, direkter Befehl Gottes, historische Rechte der Gemeinwesen." In *Konfessionalität und Jurisprudenz in der frühen Neuzeit*, edited by Christoph Strohm and Heinrich de Wall, 115–166. Berlin: Duncker & Humblot, 2009.

Friedeburg, Robert von. "Die lutherische Orthodoxie und die Debatte um das Widerstandsrecht." In *Religion Macht Politik. Hofgeistlichkeit im Europa der Frühen Neuzeit (1500–1800)*, edited by Matthias Meinhardt, Ulrike Gleixner, Martin H. Jung, and Siegrid Westphal, 307–322. Wiesbaden: Harrassowitz, 2014.

Friedeburg, Robert von. *Self-Defence and Religious Strife in Early Modern Europe. England and Germany, 1530–1680*. Aldershot: Ashgate, 2002.

Gehrt, Daniel. "Der 'Erzbischof' von Thüringen? Nikolaus von Amsdorf und die Genese der ernestinischen Landeskirche nach dem Schmalkaldischen Krieg." In *Nikolaus von Amsdorf (1483–1565) zwischen Reformation und Politik*, edited by Irene Dingel, 217–236. Leipzig: Evangelische Verlagsanstalt, 2008.

Gehrt, Daniel. *Ernestinische Konfessionspolitik: Bekenntnisbildung, Herrschaftskonsolidierung und dynastische Identitätsstiftung vom Augsburger Interim 1548 bis zur Konkordienformel 1577*. Leipzig: Evangelische Verlagsanstalt, 2011.

Gehrt, Daniel. "Strategien zur Konsensbildung im innerlutherischen Streit um die Willensfreiheit. Edition der Declaratio Victorini und der ernestinischen Visitationsinstruction von 1562," *Zeitschrift für Thüringische Geschichte* 63 (2009): 143–190.

Gensichen, Hans-Werner. *We Condemn. How Luther and 16th Century Lutheranism Condemned False Doctrine*. Translated by Herbert J. A. Bouman. Saint Louis: Concordia, 1967.

Gilson, Étienne. *Jean Duns Scot, Introduction à ses Positions Fondamentales*. Paris: Vrin, 1952.

Gleiß, Friedhelm. *Die Weimarer Disputation von 1560. Theologische Konsenssuche und Konfessionspolitik Johan Friedrichs des Mittleren*. Leipzig: Evangelische Verlagsanstalt, 2018.

Greschat, Martin. *Melanchthon neben Luther. Studien zur Gestalt der Rechtfertigungslehre zwischen 1528 und 1537*. Witten: Luther Verlag, 1965.

Green, Lowell C. "The Three Causes of Conversion in Philipp Melanchthon, Martin Chemnitz, David Chytraeus, and the Formula of Concord," *Lutherjahrbuch* 47 (1980): 89–114.

Grimm, Harold J. *Lazarus Spengler, a Lay Leader of the Reformation*. Columbus: Ohio State University Press, 1978.

Hartmann, Julius. *Erhard Schnepf, der Reformator in Schwaben, Nassau, Hessen und Thüringen*. Tübingen: Osiander, 1870.

Hase, Hans Christoph von. *Die Gestalt der Kirche Luthers, Der Casus Confessionis im Kampf des Matthias Flacius gegen das Interim von 1548*. Göttingen: Vandenhoeck & Ruprecht, 1940.

Hasse, Hans-Peter. "Der Hausvater als Katechet. Beobachtungen zu einem Druckmanuskript Nikolaus von Amsdorfs aus dem Jahr 1562 in seinem handschriftlichen Nachlass." In *Nikolaus von Amsdorf (1483–1565) zwischen Reformation und Politik*, edited by Irene Dingel, 91–102. Leipzig: Evangelische Verlagsanstalt, 2008.

Haussleiter, Johann. *Die Universität Wittenberg vor dem Eintritt Luthers nach der Schilderung des Mag. Andreas Meinhardi vom Jahre 1507*. Leipzig: Deichert, 1903.

Hendrix, Scott H. *Luther and the Papacy. Stages in a Reformation Conflict*. Philadelphia: Fortress, 1981.

Heppe, Heinrich. *Geschichte des deutschen Protestantismus in den Jahren 1555–1581*, volume 2. Marburg: Elwert, 1852.

Hequet, Suzanne. *The 1541 Colloquy at Regensburg: In Pursuit of Church Unity*. Saarbrücken: VDM Verlag Mueller, 2009.

Heerdegen, Arno. *Geschichte der allgemeinen Kirchenvisitation in den ernestinschen Landen im Jahre 1554/1555*. Jena: Fischer, 1914.

Herrmann, Johannes. "Augsburg—Leipzig—Passau. (Das Leipziger Interim nach Akten des Landeshauptarchivs Dresden, 1547–1552)." Dissertation, University of Leipzig, 1962.

Herrmann, Rudolf. "Die Generalvisitation in den ernestinischen Landen zur Zeit der Lehrstreitigkeiten des 16. Jahrhunderts (1554/55, 1562, 1569/70, 1573)," *Zeitschrift des Vereins für thüringische Geschichte und Altersthumskunde* 22 (30) (1915): 77–91, 94–109.

Hirsch, Emanuel. *Die Theologie des Andreas Osiander und ihre geschichtlichen Voraussetzungen*. Göttingen: Vandenhoeck & Ruprecht, 1919.

Hölscher, Uvo. *Die Geschichte der Reformation in Goslar*. Hannover/Leipzig: Hahn, 1902.

Höss, Irmgard. *Georg Spalatin, 1484–1545. Ein Leben in der Zeit des Humanismus und der Reformation*. Weimar: Böhlau, 1989.

Horst, Alvin H. "The Theology of Justus Menius," Th.D. dissertation, Concordia Seminary, Saint Louis, 1973.

Hülsse, Friedrich. "Beiträge zur Geschichte der Buchdruckerkunst in Magdeburg," *Geschichts-Blätter für Stadt und Land Magdeburg* 17 (1880): 53–68, 150–181, 211–242, 358–397.

Hülsse, Friedrich. *Die Stadt Magdeburg im Kampfe für den Protestantismus während der Jahre 1547–1551*. Halle: Verein für Reformationsgeschichte, 1892.

Hund, Johannes. "Amsdorfs Testament in seinen theologischen und historischen Zusammenhängen." In *Nikolaus von Amsdorf (1483–1565) zwischen Reformation und Politik*, edited by Irene Dingel, 325–344. Leipzig: Evangelische Verlagsanstalt, 2008.

Hund, Johannes. "Autorität und Identität. Die Bedeutung Luthers in den nachinterimistischen Streitkreisen im Bereich der Wittenberger Reformation." In *Georg Rörer (1492–1557). Der Chronist der Wittenberger Reformation*, edited by Stefan Michel and Christian Speer, 287–311. Leipzig: Evangelische Verlagsanstalt, 2012.

Ilgner, Friedrich Christoph. "Nikolaus von Amsdorf 'wider den rotten vnnd secten gaist.'" In

Nikolaus von Amsdorf (1483–1565) zwischen Reformation und Politik, edited by Irene Dingel, 251–279. Leipzig: Evangelische Verlagsanstalt, 2008.

Ilić, Luka. *Theologian of Sin and Grace. The Process of Radicalization in the Theology of Matthias Flacius Illyricus*. VIEG 225. Göttingen: Vandenhoeck & Ruprecht, 2014.

Issleib, S. "Moritz von Sachsen, 1547–1548," *Neues Archiv für sächsische Geschichte und Altertumskunde* 13 (1892): 197–219.

Jannasch, Wilhelm. *Reformationsgeschichte Lübecks vom Petersablass bis zum Augsburger Reichstag 1515–1530*. Lübeck: Schmidt-Römhild, 1958.

Jauernig, Reinhold. "Die Konkurrenz der Jenaer mit der Wittenberger Ausgabe von Martin Luthers Werke," *Lutherjahrbuch* 26 (1959): 75–94.

Jauernig, Reinhold. "Zur Jenaer Lutherausgabe," *Theologische Literaturzeitung* 67 (1952): 747–762.

Jauernig, Reinhold. "Zur Jenaer Lutherausgabe," *Wissenschaftliche Zeitschrift der Friedrich-Schiller-Universität Jena/Thüringen, Gesellschafts- und sprachwissenschaftliche Reihe* 4 (1954–1955): 267–277.

Jenson, Gordon A. *Wittenberg Concord. Creating Space for Dialogue*. Minneapolis: Fortress, 2018.

Jung, Hildegard. *Kurfürst Moritz von Sachsen, Aufgabe und Hingabe*. Hagen: Jung, 1966.

Kaufmann, Thomas. *Das Ende der Reformation. Magdeburgs "Herrgotts Kanzlei" (1548–1551/2)*. Tübingen: Mohr/Siebeck, 2003.

Kawerau, Gustav. "Synergismus, Synergistischer Streit." In *Realencyklopädie für protestantische Theologie und Kirche*, 3rd edition, volume 19, edited by Albert Hauck, 219–235. Leipzig: Hinrichs, 1899.

Kawerau, Gustav. "Die Flugschrift Septultura Lutheri 1538," *Theologische Studien und Kritiken* 72 (1899): 281–293.

Kawerau, Waldemar. "Erasmus Alberus in Magdeburg," *Geschichts-Blätter für Stadt und Land Magdeburg* 28 (1893): 19–29.

Kingdon, Robert M. "The First Expression of Theodore Beza's Political Ideas," *Archiv für Reformationsgeschichte* 46 (1955): 88–100.

Kipf, J. Klaus. "Cyclopius." In *Deutscher Humanismus 1480–1520. Verfasserlexikon*, volume 1, edited by Franz Josef Worstbrock, 537–546. Berlin: de Gruyter, 2008.

Kipf, J. Klaus. "Wolfgang Cyclopius und die Einführung der Reformation in Magdeburg 1524–1526. Dargestellt anhand des Flugschriftenstreits mit Nikolaus von Amsdorf." In *Magdeburg und die Reformation. Teil 1. Eine Stadt folgt Martin Luther*, edited by Maren Ballerstedt, Gabriele Köster, and Cornelia Poenicke, 129–155. Halle: Mitteldeutscher Verlag, 2016.

Kjellgaard-Pedersen, Steffan. *Gesetz, Evangelium und Busse: Theologiegeschichtliche Studien zum Verhältnis zwischen dem jungen Johann Agricola (Eisleben) und Martin Luther*. Leiden: Brill, 1983.

Koch, Ernst. "Der Ausbruch des adiaphoristischen Streits und seine Folgewirkungen." In *Politik und Bekenntnis. Die Reaktion auf das Interim von 1548*, edited by Irene Dingel and Günther Wartenberg, 179–190. Leipzig: Evangelische Verlagsanstalt, 2006.

Koch, Ernst. "Die Bedeutung von Gesetz und Evangelium nach dem 'Unterricht der Visitatoren.'" In *Der "Unterricht der Visitatoren" und die Durchsetzung der Reformation in Kursachsen*, edited by Joachim Bauer and Stefan Michel, 195–211. Leipzig: Evangelische Verlagsanstalt, 2017.

Koch, Ernst. "Johann Agricola neben Luther: Schülerschaft und theologische Eigenart." In *Lutheriana*, edited by Gerhard Hammer and Karl-Heinz zur Mühlen, 131–150. Cologne: Böhlau, 1984.

Koch, Ernst. "Viktorin Strigel (1524–1569). Von Jena nach Heidelberg." In *Melanchthon in seinen Schülern*, edited by Heinz Scheible, 391–404. Wiesbaden: Harrassowitz, 1997.

Köpf, Ulrich. "Nikolaus von Amsdorf an der Universität Wittenberg." In *Nikolaus von Amsdorf (1483–1565) zwischen Reformation und Politik*, edited by Irene Dingel, 35–55. Leipzig: Evangelische Verlagsanstalt, 2008.

Kohnle, Armin. "Die Folgen des Interims am Beispiel Württembergs." In *Politik und Bekenntnis. Die Reaktion auf das Interim von 1548*, edited by Irene Dingel and Günther Wartenberg, 83–96. Leipzig: Evangelische Verlagsanstalt, 2006.

Kohnle, Armin. "Nikolaus von Amsdorf und das Interim." In *Nikolaus von Amsdorf (1483–1565) zwischen Reformation und Politik*, edited by Irene Dingel, 135–151. Leipzig: Evangelische Verlagsanstalt, 2008.

Kolb, Robert. *Andreae and the Formula of Concord, Six Sermons on the Way to Lutheran Unity*. Saint Louis: Concordia Publishing House, 1977.

Kolb, Robert. "'Bekentnis der reinen lere des Euangelij Vnd Confutatio der jtzigen Schwermer,' Nikolaus von Amsdorf und die Entfaltung einer neuen Bekenntnisform." In *Nikolaus von Amsdorf (1483–1565) zwischen Reformation und Politik*, edited by Irene Dingel, 307–324. Leipzig: Evangelische Verlagsanstalt, 2008.

Kolb, Robert. *Bound Choice, Election, and Wittenberg Theological Method: From Martin Luther to the Formula of Concord*. Grand Rapids: Eerdmans, 2005.

Kolb, Robert. "The Braunschweig Resolution: The *Corpus Doctrinae Prutenicum* of Joachim Mörlin and Martin Chemnitz as an Interpretation of Wittenberg Theology." In *Confessionalization in Europe, 1555–1700, Essays in Honor and Memory of Bodo Nischan*, edited by John M. Headley, Hans J. Hillerbrand, and Anthony J. Papalas, 67–89. Aldershot, Hampshire: Ashgate, 2004.

Kolb, Robert. "Controversia perpetua. Die Fortsetzung des adiaphoristischen Streits nach dem Augsburger Religionsfrieden." In *Politik und Bekenntnis. Die Reaktion auf das Interim von 1548*, edited by Irene Dingel and Günther Wartenberg, 191–209. Leipzig: Evangelische Verlagsanstalt, 2006.

Kolb, Robert. "Dynamics of Party Conflict in the Saxon Late Reformation, Gnesio-Lutherans vs. Philippists," *The Journal of Modern History* 49 (1977): D1289–1305; reprinted in *Luther's Heirs Define His Legacy, Studies on Lutheran Confessionalization*, item I (Aldershot: Variorum, 1996); and in *Calvinismus in den Auseinandersetzungen des frühen konfessionellen Zeitalters*, edited by Herman J. Selderhuis, Martin Leiner, and Volker Leppin, 151–167 (Göttingen: Vandenhoeck & Ruprecht, 2013).

Kolb, Robert. "Georg Major as Controversialist: Polemics in the Late Reformation," *Church History* 45 (1976): 455–468.

Kolb, Robert. "Georg Major as Preacher." In *Georg Major (1502–1574), ein Theologe der Wittenberger Reformation*, edited by Irene Dingel and Günther Wartenberg, 93–121. Leipzig: Evangelische Verlagsanstalt, 2005.

Kolb, Robert. "Good Works are Detrimental to Salvation, Amsdorf's Use of Luther's Words in Controversy," *Renaissance and Reformation/Renaissance et Réforme* 4 (O.S. XVI) (1980): 136–151.

Kolb, Robert. "Jakob Andreae's Preaching in the Public Arena (Augsburg 1559)," *Lutheran Quarterly* 29 (2015): 10–32.

Kolb, Robert. "The Legal Case for Martyrdom, Basilius Monner on Johann Friedrich the Elder and the Smalcald War." In *Reformation und Recht. Festgabe für Gottfried/Seebaß zum 65. Geburtstag*, edited by Irene Dingel, Volker Leppin, and Christoph Strohm, 145–160. Gütersloh: Kaiser/Gütersloher Verlagshaus, 2002.

Kolb, Robert. *Luther's Heirs Define His Legacy, Studies on Lutheran Confessionalization*. Aldershot, Hampshire: Variorum, 1996.

Kolb, Robert. "Luther's *On Bound Choice* from Publication to the Formula of Concord," *Logia* 27 (2018): 23–32.

Kolb, Robert. *Martin Luther and the Enduring Word of God. The Wittenberg School and Its Scripture-Centered Proclamation*. Grand Rapids: Baker Academic, 2016.

Kolb, Robert. *Martin Luther as Prophet, Teacher, and Hero. Images of the Reformer, 1520–1620*. Grand Rapids: Baker Books, 1999.

Kolb, Robert. "Matthaeus Judex's Condemnation of Princely Censorship of Theologians' Publications," *Church History* 50 (1981): 401–414.

Kolb, Robert. "Melanchthon's Doctrinal Last Will and Testament: The *Responsiones ad articulos Bavaricae inquisitionis* as His Final Confession of Faith." In Irene Dingel, Robert Kolb, Nicole Kuropka, and Timothy J. Wengert, *Philip Melanchthon. Theologian in Classroom, Confession, and Controversy*, 141–160. Göttingen: Vandenhoeck & Ruprecht, 2012.

Kolb, Robert. "Melanchthon's Influence on the Exegesis of his Students: The Case of Romans 9." In *Philip Melanchthon (1497–1560) and the Commentary*, edited by M. Patrick Graham and Timothy J. Wengert, 198–217. Sheffield: Sheffield Academic Press, 1997.

Kolb, Robert. "Nikolaus Gallus' Critique of Philip Melanchthon's Teaching on the Freedom of the Will," *Archiv für Reformationsgeschichte* 91 (2000): 87–110.

Kolb, Robert. *Nikolaus von Amsdorf (1483–1565), Popular Polemics in the Preservation of Luther's Legacy*. Bibliotheca Humanistica & Reformatorica 24. Nieuwkoop: De Graaf, 1978.

Kolb, Robert. "Nikolaus von Amsdorf on Vessels of Wrath and Vessels of Mercy: a Lutheran's Doctrine of Double Predestination," *Harvard Theological Review* 69 (1976): 325–343.

Kolb, Robert. "Parents Should Explain the Sermon, Nikolaus von Amsdorf on the Role of the Christian Parent," *The Lutheran Quarterly* o. s. 25 (1973): 231–240.

Kolb, Robert. "Philipp's Foes but Followers Nonetheless: Late Humanism among the Gnesio-Lutherans." In *The Harvest of Humanism in Central Europe, Essays in Honor of Lewis W. Spitz*, edited by Manfred P. Fleischer, 159–177. Saint Louis: Concordia, 1992.

Kolb, Robert. "Die theologische Pilgerschaft von Viktorin Strigel Vom 'gnesiolutherischen' Hoftheologe zum 'calvinistischen' Professor." In *Calvinismus in den Auseinandersetzungen des frühen konfessionellen Zeitalters*, edited by Herman J. Selderhuis, Martin Leiner, and Volker Leppin, 79–96. Göttingen: Vandenhoeck & Ruprecht, 2013.

Kropatscheck, Hans. "Das Problem theologischer Anthropologie auf dem Weimarer Gespräch von 1560 zwischen Matthias Flacius Illyricus und Viktorin Strigel." Licentiate dissertation, University of Göttingen, 1943.

Kruse, Martin. *Speners Kritik an dem landesherrlichen Kirchenregiment und ihre Vorgeschichte*. Witten: Luther Verlag, 1971.

Kühne, Hartmut. "Nikolaus von Amsdorf im Streit zwischen dem Magdeburger Rat und lutherischen Theologen um die Amtsenthebung des Tilemann Heshusius." In *Nikolaus von Amsdorf (1483–1565) zwischen Reformation und Politik*, edited by Irene Dingel, 281–306. Leipzig: Evangelische Verlagsanstalt, 2008.

Kümper, Hiram. "Das Glaubensverhör der Jüdin Rahel im Juni 1554 durch Nikolaus von Amsdorf als 'Modus et forma judaei convertendi'," *Archiv für Reformationsgeschichte* 99 (2008): 120–138.

Lau, Franz. "Georg III. von Anhalt (1507–1554), erster evangelischer 'Bischof' von Merseburg. Seine Theologie und seine Bedeutung für die Geschichte der Reformation in Deutschland,"

Wissenschaftliche Zeitschrift der Karl Marx Universität Leipzig. Gesellschafts- und Sprachwissenschaftliche Reihe 3 (1953/1954): 139–152.

Lau, Franz, and Ernst Bizer, *A History of the Reformation in Germany to 1555*. Translated by Brian A. Hardy. London: Black, 1969.

Leppin, Volker. *Antichrist und Jüngster Tag. Das Profil apokalyptischer Flugschriftenpublizistik im deutschen Luthertum 1548–1618*. Gütersloh: Gütersloher Verlagshaus, 1999.

Leppin, Volker. "Nikolaus von Amsdorf und Johann Friedrich d. Ä." In *Nikolaus von Amsdorf (1483–1565) zwischen Reformation und Politik*, edited by Irene Dingel, 103–115. Leipzig: Evangelische Verlagsanstalt, 2008.

Leppin, Volker. "Die Normierung der Frömmigkeit im 'Unterricht der Visitatoren,'" in *Der "Unterricht der Visitatoren" und die Durchsetzung der Reformation in Kursachsen*, edited by Joachim Bauer and Stefan Michel, 167–194. Leipzig: Evangelische Verlagsanstalt, 2017.

Leppin, Volker. "' . . . und das Ichs nicht fur gotlich sondern fur eine lauter teufels lehr halte und achte,' Die theologische Verarbeitung des Interims durch Johann Friedrich den Älteren." In *Politik und Bekenntnis. Die Reaktion auf das Interim von 1548*, edited by Irene Dingel and Günther Wartenburg, 111–123. Leipzig: Evangelische Verlagsanstalt, 2006.

Lerche, Otto. *Amsdorff und Melanchthon. Eine kirchengeschichtliche Studie*. Berlin: Lerche, 1937.

Loewenich, Walther von. "Das Interim von 1548." In Walther von Loewenich, *Von Augustin zu Luther*, 391–406. Witten: Luther Verlag, 1959.

Lohrmann, Martin. *Bugenhagen's Jonah: Biblical Interpretation as Public Theology*. Minneapolis: Lutheran University Press, 2012.

Lück, Heiner. "Univeristät und Stadt Wittenberg zur Zeit des Nikolaus von Amsdorf. Ein Rekonstruktionsversuch möglicher Wahrnehmungen (1502–1524)." In *Nikolaus von Amsdorf (1483–1565) zwischen Reformation und Politik*, edited by Irene Dingel, 15–34. Leipzig: Evangelische Verlagsanstalt, 2008.

Mahlmann, Theodor. "*Doctrina* im Verständnis nachreformatorischer lutherischer Theologen." In *Vera Doctrina: zur Begriffsgeschichte der Lehre von Augustin bis Descartes*, edited by Philippe Büttgen, Ruedi Imbach, Ulrich Johannes Schneider, and Hermann J. Selderhuis, 199–264. Wiesbaden: Harrassowitz, 2009.

Mehlhausen, Joachim. "Der Streit um die Adiaphora." In *Bekenntnis und Einheit der Kirche. Studien zum Konkordienbuch*, edited by Martin Brecht and Reinhard Schwarz, 105–128. Stuttgart: Calwer Verlag, 1980.

Mentz, Georg. *Johann Friedrich der Grossmütige 1503–1554*, volume 2. Jena: Fischer, 1908.

Mirkovic, Mijo. *Matija Vlačić Ilirik*. Zagreb: Jugoslavenska akademijs znanosti i umjetnosti, 1960.

Muller, Richard A. *Calvin and the Decree: Christology and Predestination in Reformed Theology from Calvin to Perkins*. Durham: Labyrinth, 1986.

Myconius, Friedrich. *Historia Reformationis, vom Jahr Christi 1517, bis 1542. . . .* Edited by Ernst Salomon Cyprian. Leipzig: Georg Weidmann, 1718.

Nahrendorf, Carsten. *Humanismus in Magdeburg: das Altstädtische Gymnasium von seiner Gründung bis zur Zerstörung der Stadt (1524–1631)*. Berlin: de Gruyter, 2015.

Oberman, Heiko A. "Some Notes on the Theology of Nominalism with Attention to its Relation to the Renaissance," *Harvard Theological Review* 53 (1960): 47–76.

Olson, Oliver K. *Matthias Flacius and the Survival of Luther's Reform*. Wiesbaden: Harrassowitz, 2002.

Olson, Oliver K. "Politics, Liturgics, and *Integritas Sacramenti*." In *Discord, Dialog, and Concord. Studies in the Lutheran Reformation's Formula of Concord*, edited by Lewis W. Spitz and Wenzel Lohff, 74–85. Philadelphia: Fortress, 1977.

Oyer, John S. *Lutheran Reformers against Anabaptists: Luther, Melanchthon, and Menius and the Anabaptists of Central Germany*. The Hague: Nijhoff, 1964.

Pannenberg, Wolfhart. *Die Prädestinationslehre des Duns Skotus im Zusammenhang der scholastischen Lehrentwicklung*. Göttingen: Vandenhoeck & Ruprecht, 1954.

Paullini, Christian F. *Historia Isenacensis*. Frankfurt/M: Bauer, 1698.

Peters, Christian. "Der Macht des Kaisers widerstehen. Die süddeutschen Theologen und das Augsburger Interim." In *Politik und Bekenntnis. Die Reaktion auf das Interim von 1548*, edited by Irene Dingel and Günther Wartenburg, 65–81. Leipzig: Evangelische Verlagsanstalt, 2006.

Peterson, Luther D. "The Philippist Theologians and the Interims of 1548: Soteriological, Ecclesiastical, and Liturgical Compromises and Controversies within German Lutheranism." Ph.D. dissertation, University of Wisconsin-Madison, 1974.

Planck, Gottlieb Jacob. *Geschichte der Entstehung . . . der Konkordienformel*, 4 volumes. Leipzig: Crusius, 1796–1800.

Pommerien, Albert. *Viktorin Strigels Lehre von dem Peccatum originis*. Hannover: Stephanusstift, 1917.

Postel, Rainer. "Die Hansestädte und das Interim" In *Das Interim 1548/50. Herrschaftskrise und Glaubenskonflikt*, edited by Luise Schorn-Schütte, 91–104. Gütersloh: Gütersloher Verlag, 2005.

Preger, Wilhelm. *Matthias Flacius Illyricus*, 2 volumes. Erlangen: Bläsing, 1859, 1861.

Pressel, Theodor. *Nicolaus von Amsdorf*. Elberfeld: Friedrichs, 1862.

Preuss, Hans. *Die Vorstellungen vom Antichrist im späteren Mittelalter, bei Luther, und in der konfessionellen Polemik*. Leipzig: Hinrich, 1906.

Rabe, Horst. *Reichsbund und Interim. Die Verfassungs- und Religionspolitik Karls V. und der Reichstag von Augsburg 1547/1548*. Cologne/Vienna: Böhlau, 1971.

Rehtmeyer, Philipp Julius. *Historiae ecclesiasticae inclytae urbis Brunsvigae Pars III. Oder: Der beru[e] hmten Stadt Braunschweig Kirchen-Historie Dritter Theil*. . . . Braunschweig: Johann Georg Zillinger, 1710.

Reichert, Ernst-Otto. *Amsdorf und Das Interim*, edited by Hans-Otto Schneider. Leipzig: Evangelische Verlagsanstalt, 2011.

Reichert, Ernst-Otto. "In Tanta Ecclesiarum Mestitia . . . Eine Antwort Nikolaus von Amsdorffs an Philipp Melanchthon," *Zeitschrift für Kirchengeschichte* 78 (1967): 253–270.

Rein, Nathan. *The Chancery of God. Protestant Print, Polemic and Propaganda against the Empire, Magdeburg 1546–1551*. Aldershot: Ashgate, 2008.

Reske, Christoph. *Die Buchdrucker des 16. und 17. Jahrhunderts im deutschen Sprachgebiet*. Wiesbaden: Harrassowitz, 2015.

Richter, Matthias. *Gesetz und Heil. Eine Untersuchung zur Vorgeschichte und zum Verlauf des sogenannten Zweiten Antinomistischen Streits*. Göttingen: Vandenhoeck & Ruprecht, 1996.

Ritschl, Otto. *Dogmengeschichte des Protestantismus* 2. Leipzig: Hinrich, 1912.

Rockwell, William W. *Die Doppelehe des Landgrafen Philipp von Hessen*. Marburg: Elwert, 1904.

Rogge, Joachim. *Johann Agricolas Lutherverständnis unter besonderer Berücksichtigung des Antinomismus*. Berlin: Evangelische Verlagsanstalt, 1960.

Roth, E. "Mörlin und seine Rechtfertigungslehre," *Jahrbuch der Gesellschaft für niedersächsischen Kirchengeschichte* 50 (1952): 59–81.

Salig, Christian August. *Vollständige Historie der Augspurgischen Confession*, 3 volumes. Halle: Renger, 1730–1733.

Schäufele, Wolf-Friedrich. "Kirche Christi und Teufelskirche. Verfall und Kontinuität der Kirche bei Nikolaus von Amsdorf." In *Nikolaus von Amsdorf (1483–1565) zwischen Reformation und Politik*, edited by Irene Dingel, 57–90. Leipzig: Evangelische Verlagsanstalt, 2008.

Schilling, Johannes. "Auditor, Scriba, Autor und Editor. Luthers Werke in Rörers Händen." In *Georg Rörer (1492–1557). Der Chronist der Wittenberger Reformation*, edited by Stefan Michel and Christian Speer, 171–179. Leipzig: Evangelische Verlagsanstalt, 2012.

Schmidt, Georg. "Freiheit, Pluralität und Frieden. Überlegungen zur deutschen Reformationsgeschichte." In *Faszinierende Frühneuzeit. Reich, Frieden, Kultur und Kommunikation, 1500–1800. Festschrift für Johannes Burkhardt zum 65. Geburtstag*, edited by Wolfgang E. J. Weber and Regina Dauser, 75–94. Berlin: Akademie Verlag, 2008.

Schmidt, Gustav L. *Justus Menius, der Reformator Thüringens*, volume 2. Gotha: Perthes, 1867.

Schneider, Hans-Otto. "Amsdorf als Statthalter Luthers in Magdeburg." In *Magdeburg und die Reformation, Teil 1, Eine Stadt folgt Martin Luther*, edited by Maren Ballerstedt, Gabriele Köster, and Cornelia Poenicke, 113–127. Halle: Mitteldeutscher Verlag, 2016.

Schorn-Schütte, Luise. *Das Interim 1548/50, Herrschaftskrise und Glaubenskonflikt*. Gütersloh: Gütersloher Verlag, 2005.

Schottenloher, Karl. *Das Regensburger Buchgewerbe im 15. und 16. Jahrundert*. Mainz: Gutenberg Gesellschaft, 1920.

Schultz, Robert C. "Original Sin: Accident or Substance: The Paradoxical Significance of FC I, 53–62 in Historical Context." In *Discord, Dialogue and Concord. Studies in the Lutheran Reformation's Formula of Concord*, edited by Lewis W. Spitz and Wenzel Lohff, 38–57. Philadelphia: Fortress, 1977.

Schwarz, J. C. E. "Amsdorf, Nikolaus von." In *Realencyklopädie für protestantische Theologie und Kirche*, 3rd edition, volume 1, edited by Albert Hauck, 464–467. Leipzig: Hinrichs, 1896.

Schwarz, J. C. E. *Das Erste Jahrzehnd der Universität Jena*. Jena: Fromann, 1858.

Seebaß, Gottfried. *Bibliographica Osiandrica*. Nieuwkoop: De Graaf, 1971.

Seebaß, Gottfried. *Das reformatorische Werk des Andreas Osiander*. Nuremberg: Verein für Bayerische Kirchengeschichte, 1967.

Seeberg, Reinhold. *Die Theologie des Johannes Duns Scotus, eine dogmengeschichtliche Untersuchung*. Reprint, Aalen: Scientia, 1971.

Sehling, Emil. *Die Kirchengesetzgebung unter Moritz von Sachsen 1544–1549 und von Georg von Anhalt*. Leipzig: Deichert, 1899.

Seifert, Friedrich. "Johannes Pfeffinger, der erste lutherische Pastor zu St. Nicolai und Superintendent in Leipzig," *Beiträge zur Sächsischen Kirchengeschichte* 4 (1888): 33–162.

Silcock, Jeffrey G. "Luther and the Third Use of the Law," Th.D. dissertation, Concordia Seminary, Saint Louis, 1993.

Slenczka, Bjorn. *Das Schisma der Augsburger Konfessionsverwandten von 1557: Protestantische Konfessionspolitik und Theologie im Zusammenhang des zweiten Wormser Religionsgesprächs*. Tübingen: Mohr/Siebeck, 2010.

Sparn, Walter. "'Lex iam adest.' Luthers Rede vom Gesetz in den Antinomerdisputationen." In *Martin Luther—Biographie und Theologie*, edited by Dietrich Korsch and Volker Leppin, 211–249. Tübingen: Mohr/Siebeck, 2010.

Sparn, Walter. "Substanz oder Subjekt? Die Kontroverse um die anthropologischen Allgemeinbegriffe im Artikel von der Erbsünde (Artikel I)." In *Widerspruch, Dialog und Einigung. Studien zur Konkordienformel der Lutherischen Reformation*, edited by Wenzel Lohff and Lewis W. Spitz, 107–135. Stuttgart: Calwer Verlag, 1977.

Sparn, Walter. "Begründung und Verwirklichung, Zur anthropologischen Thematik der lutherischen Bekenntnisse." In *Bekenntnis und Einheit der Kirche. Studien zum Konkordienbuch*, edited by Martin Brecht and Reinhard Schwarz, 129–153. Stuttgart: Calwer Verlag, 1980.

Spitz, Lewis W., Jr., "Man on This Isthmus." In *Luther for an Ecumenical Age*, edited by C. S. Meyer, 23–66. Saint Louis: Concordia, 1967.

Stille, Hans. *Nikolaus von Amsdorf. Sein Leben bis zu seiner Einweisung als Bischof in Naumburg (1483–1542)*. Zeulenroda: Sporn, 1937.

Stupperich, Martin. *Osiander in Preussen 1549–1552*. Berlin: de Gruyter, 1973.

Stupperich, Robert. "Melanchthons Gedanken zur Kirchenpolitik des Herzogs Moritz von Sachsen (nach bisher unveröffentlichten Papiern aus den Jahren 1546/53)." In *Reformatio und Confessio. Festschrift für D. Wilhelm Maurer*, edited by F. W. Kantzenbach and Gerhard Müller, 84–92. Berlin: Lutherisches Verlagshaus, 1965.

Thieme, Karl. "Die Schädlichkeit der guten Werke bei Luther," *Theologisches Literaturblatt* 29 (1908): 41–42.

Tschackert, Paul. *Die Entstehung der lutherischen und der reformierten Kirchenlehre*. Göttingen: Vandenhoeck & Ruprecht, 1910.

Vogt, Otto. "Melanchthon's und Bugenhagen's Stellung zum Interim und die Rechtfertigung des Letzteren in seinem Jonascomment," *Jahrbücher für protestantische Theologie* 3 (1887): 5–8.

Waldeck, Oskar. "Die Publizistik des Schmalkladischen Krieges," *Archiv für Reformationsgeschichte* 7 (1909–1910): 44–133.

Wartenberg, Günther. "Das Augsburger Interim und die Leipziger Landtagsvorlage zum Interim." In *Politik und Bekenntnis. Die Reaktion auf das Interim von 1548*, edited by Irene Dingel and Günther Wartenberg, 15–32. Leipzig: Evangelische Verlagsanstalt, 2006.

Wartenberg, Günther. "Moritz von Sachsen." In *Theologische Realenzyklopädie*, volume 23, edited by Gerhard Müller, 302–311. Berlin: de Gruyter, 1994.

Wartenberg, Günther. "Philipp Melanchthon und die sächsisch-albertinische Interimspolitik," *Lutherjahrbuch* 55 (1988): 60–82.

Wartenberg, Roxanne. "Städtische Theologen und das Interim, Johannes Äpinus in Hamburg." In *Politik und Bekenntnis. Die Reaktion auf das Interim von 1548*, edited by Irene Dingel and Günther Wartenberg, 97–102. Leipzig: Evangelische Verlagsanstalt, 2006.

Weller, Hieronymus. *Opera Omnia* 3. Leipzig: Stock, 1702.

Wenck, W. "Kurfürst Moritz und die Ernestiner in den Jahren 1551 und 1552," *Forschungen zur Deutschen Geschichte* 12 (1872): 1–54.

Wengert, Timothy J. "Caspar Cruciger (1504–1548): The Case of the Disappearing Reformer," *Sixteenth Century Journal* 20 (1989): 417–441.

Wengert, Timothy J. "The Day Melanchthon Got Mad: A Study in Lutheran Ecclesiology," *Lutheran Quarterly* 6 (1991): 419–433.

Wengert, Timothy J. *Defending Faith. Lutheran Responses to Andreas Osiander's Doctrine of Justification, 1551–1559*. Tübingen: Mohr/Siebeck, 2012.

Wengert, Timothy J. "Georg Major (1502–1574). Defender of Wittenberg's Faith and Melanchthonian Exegete." In *Melanchthon in seinen Schülern*, edited by Heinz Scheible, 129–156. Wiesbaden: Harrassowitz, 1997.

Wengert, Timothy J. *Law and Gospel, Philip Melanchthon's Debate with John Agricola of Eisleben over Poenitentia*. Grand Rapids: Baker, 1997.

Wengert, Timothy J. "Melanchthon and Luther / Luther and Melanchthon," *Lutherjahrbuch* 66 (1990): 55–88.

Wengert, Timothy J. "'Not by Nature *Philoneikos*,' Philip Melanchthon's Initial Reactions to the Augsburg Interim." In *Politik und Bekenntnis. Die Reaktion auf das Interim von 1548*, edited by Irene Dingel and Günther Wartenburg, 33–49. Leipzig: Evangelische Verlagsanstalt, 2006.

Wengert, Timothy J. "Philip Melanchthon and the Origins of the 'Three Causes' (1533–1535): An Examination of the Roots of the Controversy over the Freedom of the Will." In Irene Dingel, Robert Kolb, Nicole Kuropka, and Timothy J. Wengert, *Philip Melanchthon. Theologian in Classroom, Confession, and Controversy*, 183–208. Göttingen: Vandenhoeck & Ruprecht, 2012.

Wengert, Timothy J. "'We Will Feast Together in Heaven Forever': The Epistolary Friendship of John Calvin and Philip Melanchthon." In *Melanchthon in Europe, His Work and Influence beyond Wittenberg*, edited by Karin Maag, 26–33. Grand Rapids: Baker, 1999.

Whitford, David. *Tyranny and Resistance: the Magdeburg Confession and the Lutheran Tradition*. Saint Louis: Concordia, 2001.

Winter, Christian. "Nikolaus von Amsdorf und Moritz von Sachsen." In *Nikolaus von Amsdorf (1483–1565) zwischen Reformation und Politik*, edited by Irene Dingel, 177–195. Leipzig: Evangelische Verlagsanstalt, 2008.

Wolf, Gustav. "Das Augsburger Interim," *Deutsche Zeitschrift für Geschichtswissenschaft* NF 2 (1897–1898): 39–88.

Wolf, Gustav. *Zur Geschichte der deutschen Protestanten 1555–1559*. Berlin: Seehagen, 1888.

Wolgast, Eike. "Der Streit um die Werke Luthers im 16. Jahrhundert," *Archiv für Reformationsgeschichte* 59 (1968): 75–94.

Wolgast, Eike. "Die Wittenberger Luther-Ausgabe. Zur Überlieferungsgeschichte der Werke Luthers im 16. Jahrhundert," *Archiv für Geschichte des Buchwesens*, 11, 1–2 (1970): 122–137.

Wolgast, Eike. *Die Wittenberger Theologie und die Politik der evangelischen Stände*. Gütersloh: Mohn, 1977.

Index